EVERYMAN, I will go with thee,

and be thy guide,

In thy most need to go by thy side

BENVENUTO CELLINI

Born at Florence on 3rd November
1500. He became famous as a goldsmith and sculptor and was patron-
ized by Pope Clement VII and
various courts. He died in Florence
on 13th February 1571.

The Life of
Benvenuto Cellini

WRITTEN BY HIMSELF

TRANSLATED BY
ANNE MACDONELL

INTRODUCTION BY
WILLIAM GAUNT

DENT: LONDON
EVERYMAN'S LIBRARY
DUTTON: NEW YORK

NO. 51

SBN: 460 00051 9

INTRODUCTION

THIS famous work, completed in manuscript in the year 1562, but not printed until the eighteenth century, has since then never ceased to fascinate the world, and has been acclaimed, with good reason, one of the best and most interesting autobiographies ever written.

It is fascinating from more than one viewpoint. As a story, full of exciting episodes and physical adventure, giving vivid glimpses of society at various levels, it is like a first-rate picaresque novel ('better,' Horace Walpole thought, 'than any novel')—a sort of *Gil Blas* of real life.

As a commentary on a splendid period of art—the Renaissance at the stage it had reached in the sixteenth century—it is of equal interest and even more value. This Florentine goldsmith and sculptor sets us on familiar terms with the pontiffs and princes for whom he worked. He is instructive as well as entertaining about his craft, and conveys all that delight in works of beauty that animated and linked together artist and patron in his time.

Benvenuto Cellini's autobiography, above all, uniquely fulfils the prime requirement of revealing its author: and it is a very remarkable man who comes to life in its pages. He is an artist-craftsman, passionately devoted to art, the worshipper of the great men of his time, the 'divine' Michelangelo, the 'marvellous' Titian (the adjectives are Cellini's). He loathed the sculptor Torrigiano because he had broken Michelangelo's nose. He is also, strangely enough, a 'bravo': intensely proud of himself and his skill in fashioning beautiful objects of metal, he is no less proud of his prowess with poniard, sword, and gun. He tells us not only how he made a statue in bronze or a salt-cellar in enamel and gold, but also (with considerable relish) how he killed several men. He informs us also of amours which were, to say the least of it, lacking in refinement and gallantry: and of his contact with shady creatures who expose him to what he calls 'devilish scandals.' The only moral sense he displays is an unfailing conviction that right is always on his side. When accused of misdemeanour or crime, he complains bitterly of conspiracy against him, and in his own eyes his deeds of violence were acts of justice.

We have to take him as he was, a remarkable man in an age different from ours. It is not incumbent on us either to excuse or condemn the faults he reveals as frankly as his merits. As the author of the present translation, Miss Macdonell, has wisely remarked, 'the apologist of Cellini is as absurdly out of place as the vindictive moralist.' We cannot even regard him as a Jekyll and Hyde, a personality split as between gentle artist and ferocious desperado. There was a unity, a functional completeness about him, the same energy and passion was in all he did: and so regarded he is not only an astonishing character but an historical type.

'The Genius of the Renaissance, incarnate in a single personality, leans out and speaks to us.' In this striking phrase, John Addington Symonds, who studied and translated Cellini with so much care, invites us to consider him as a 'Renaissance man,' a type to which he conforms in more ways than one. He had the then prevalent feeling of belonging to a superhuman category by virtue of his art, a wish to be 'truly terrible,' to adopt the phrase which his contemporary Vasari applied to him in an approving sense. To be 'terrible' was to be all compact of energy and power, to live and create works of art with the same intense fervour, which recognized no bounds. The strange connection that sometimes resulted between art and violence can be studied in a succession of Italian artists, a notable instance, a little after Cellini's time, being the brilliant painter Caravaggio.

In a less formidable aspect, he was typical in his feeling of sympathy with, and nearness to, the art and the spirit of classical antiquity. When he describes how he eagerly acquired and copied the ancient gems brought to him by Lombard peasants who had found them in the vineyards, he illuminates all the influence of classical art on Renaissance Italy.

At the same time Cellini comes late in the Renaissance, when it was losing its original impetus and changing form. Though such giants as Michelangelo and Titian were his contemporaries, yet a phase of mannerism and imitation had already begun, and to this, so far as he was an artist in addition to being a craftsman, Cellini belonged. He lacked the spirit of intellectual inquiry that had earlier inspired the artists of the Renaissance, he had not their complete mastery of the human figure. Where he excelled was in skilfully devising intricate ornamentation, in the 'arabesques'—the interlaced leaves and masks with which he covered a vessel of silver or gold for sideboard or dining-table. The famous Salt (now at Vienna)—which he describes so vividly in the *Life*—is entirely admirable in workmanship but the figure group that surmounts it may be thought not altogether easy in balance and composition. The 'Nymph of Fontainebleau,' now in the Louvre, has the mannered weakness and exaggeration of the later Renaissance style, as transplanted in France. He produced one outstanding work of sculpture in the statue of Perseus with the head of Medusa (at Florence); but, fine as it is, it attempts the same effect as Donatello's 'Judith' without quite achieving the same grandeur.

Cellini clearly does not represent the 'genius of the Renaissance' in the same sense as Leonardo da Vinci. It is scarcely vindictive moralizing to say that his violence was an inferior expression of the fiery energy that a Michelangelo devoted to works of art alone. Judged by the standards of Italian greatness, Cellini as an artist is a minor figure. Yet whatever qualifications of this kind are made, they need not interfere with the enjoyment and appreciation of his masterpiece in words.

The autobiography is wonderfully free and conversational in style. Probably the fact that Cellini dictated most of it accounts for its absence of literary artifice. One may picture him, a thickly bearded man of fifty-eight, when he starts his life-story (much as Vasari portrayed him in a fresco), glaring in anger at the memory of enmity or chuckling over some remembered triumph while a boy apprentice writes his words down. Students of the manuscript have thought they found a shakiness in the youthful hand at certain of the more horrific passages.

When he finishes he has ranged over sixty-two years. He tells of his early days in Florence where he was born in 1500. The startling actuality of his descriptions appears in his childhood memory of picking up a scorpion: '. . . when I clenched it in my little fist, the tail stuck out from one end and from the other its two claws.' 'Look, Grandad,' he said, 'at my dear little crab.' The efforts of his father, who made organs, spinets, and

lutes, to turn him into a musician are related with a character-
istic humour. The young Benvenuto despised the 'damnable
playing on the flute.' He found employment with a goldsmith
at the age of fifteen, and when eventually he left Florence after
a brawl, his manual skill as well as his performance on a cornet
commended him to the Pope. He was kept busy in Rome
making pieces of jewellery, the jugs for the table in which bones
and other debris of a meal were thrown, medals to be worn in
the hat (as was then fashionable), copies of antique gems; and
also in minting the state coinage. His Roman days were full of
tumult. He was twenty-seven when the Constable de Bourbon, who had taken service with the Emperor, entered Rome
and laid siege to the Castle of S. Angelo. Cellini is expansive
on the heroic part he played in its defence and boasts of firing
the shots that killed de Bourbon and wounded the Prince of
Orange.

He is stricken by the plague and cures himself by a charac-
teristic defiance of the doctor's instructions. He dabbles in
necromancy and the scene when the attempt is made to conjure
up spirits in the Colosseum by night is a superb Walpurgis
mixture of comedy and terror. His assassinations of the arquebusier who had killed his brother and of the rival goldsmith
Pompeo lead to his imprisonment. Further charges were made:
that he had abstracted part of the Papal treasure entrusted to
him during the hostilities and that he had produced false coins:
though he protests, and was apparently able to demonstrate,
his innocence. His account of his captivity in S. Angelo under
the mad castellan (who thought he was a bat), his escape by
means of an improvised rope, his recapture, his confinement in
a cell 'full of tarantulas and venomous worms,' is a chapter of
adventure equal to any in fact or fiction.

Released, he is welcomed to France in 1537 by Francis I,
whose policy it was to encourage the settlement in his country
of Italian artists and craftsmen. He pleased the king with a
number of works, including the famous Salt—a foot high,
worked with a chisel in solid gold; and the reclining nymph
intended for the doorway of the palace at Fontainebleau. But
the king's favourite, Mme d'Etampes, was jealous of him. He
did not get on with the French (detesting both them and the
English). He was involved in the unpleasant court case in
which his model, Caterina, figures. For one reason or another
he returned to Florence and there undertakes the production

(described at length) of his masterpiece, the 'Perseus.' A brief outline of course conveys nothing of the incomparable vividness of the reported conversations, the verbal portraiture, the humour (conscious and otherwise), his gift for making a scene visible to the mind's eye. Thus in his account of travel through the Alpine passes, albeit with a minimum of landscape description, he gives the reader all the sensation of being among precipices, torrents, tottering bridges. He can make even a technical process an exciting adventure; as when he tells how, in the casting of the 'Perseus,' the household pewter is thrown into the furnace at the moment of crisis, to make the molten metal flow.

Throughout he is the hero, alike when he stabs an enemy in the neck or by some prodigy of skill causes his patron to exclaim, 'The man is a wonder.' It is impossible not to be captivated by the character he has created out of himself, fantastically boastful, apparently void of reticence, unlimited in self-satisfaction, a demon of energy, hugely enjoying himself, intensely alive.

Even Cellini does not tell us quite everything. He does not speak of two imprisonments of his middle age or the reasons for them. He does not tell us that he took the first tonsure quite late in his career: why he contemplated entering, and why withdrew from, the Church. Perhaps these matters would have confused or introduced either flaws or inconsistencies into his self-portrait that he would not admit. He was no Rousseau writing his *Confessions*—'confession' belonged to another age or a different type of being. Melancholy, a tortured morality, painful introspection, were alien to the man he wished to appear and seems to have been. Happily extrovert, he gives us a key to the spirit of the *Life* in the observation he makes in it, 'I am going on my way rejoicing.'

WILLIAM GAUNT.

1956.

NOTE ON EDITIONS AND TRANSLATIONS

THE original manuscript of *La Vita di Benvenuto Cellini scritta da lui medesimo* was begun in 1558 and was long owned and jealously guarded by the Cavalcanti family. It was first printed from a defective copy in 1728, and first translated into English in 1771 by Thomas Nugent, who dedicated his version to Sir Joshua Reynolds. Thomas Roscoe improved upon Nugent with his version printed in 1822.

The Cavalcanti original went through several strange adventures, disappearing from more than one library. It was found in a bookshop in 1805 by Luigi Poirot, who bequeathed it to the Biblioteca Medicea-Laurenziana. A new edition was produced in 1830 by Giuseppe Molini, word for word from the original manuscript.

The English translation by J. A. Symonds (1888) marked a great advance on the previous versions. 'Only one,' says Miss Macdonell, 'who has grappled with the same task can adequately know his unsparing conscientiousness, his patient, unremitting zeal for accuracy.' There was still room, however, for another interpretation of the racy idiom of the original, which at times Symonds rather disguised by his own scholarly quality of style. Miss Macdonell's spirited English version from the authentic Italian text, first published in the Temple Autobiographies in 1903, is that appearing in the present edition. Another English translation is that of R. H. H. Cust (1910). Goethe, it may be noted, translated the work into German.

Other Works by Cellini are *Due Trattati* (1568); *I discorsi e i ricordi intorno all' arte* (1587); *Rime* (ed. A. Mabellini, 1891). *See* R. H. H. Cust: *Benvenuto Cellini*, 1912; E. Allodon: *Benvenuto Cellini*, 1930; H. Klapsia: *Benvenuto Cellini*, 1943.

CONTENTS

LETTER OF BENVENUTO CELLINI TO BENEDETTO VARCHI

(To whom he had sent some part of the MS. of his Memoirs)

Your lordship tells me that the simple discourse of my Life contents you more in its first shape than were it polished and retouched by others—for then the truth of what I have written would show less clear; and I have taken great care to say nothing of things for which I should have had to fumble in my memory. Indeed, I have told naught save the truth, omitting many wonderful happenings which others in my place would have made very prominent; for I had so many great things to tell that not to make too thick a volume I have left out many of the smaller. I now send my own servant, to whom you can give my wallet and the book. I think you cannot have been able to read the whole, but I do not wish to weary you with a wretched trifle like this. I have had from you what I wanted, and am much satisfied therewith. So with all my heart I thank you. Now I beg you not to trouble to read farther, but to send it back to me, all save the sonnet, which I am fain should have some polishing from that marvellous file of yours. Ere long I shall come to visit you, and I am ever at your service so far as my knowledge and my power extend.

Keep well, I beg of you; and hold me still in your good favour.

FLORENCE, *22nd May*, 1559.

If your lordship would keep in mind to do some little service to my young friar, I should be much beholden to you. Awaiting your lordship's commands,

BENVENUTO CELLINI.

PREFATORY SONNET AND DECLARATION
BY CELLINI

Here my life's struggling story I make plain
  To thank the God of Nature, who has still
  Tended the soul He gave me. By His will,
Diverse and high my deeds—and I remain.
My cruel fate hath warr'd with me in vain:
  Life, glory, worth, and all unmeasur'd skill,
  Beauty and grace, themselves in me fulfil,
That many I surpass, and to the best attain.
  But man's frail thoughts fly 'fore the wind like sand.
Now know I all the waste, and sorely blame
  The precious time I have in trifles spent.
  Yet, since remorse is vain, I'll be content.
Welcome I mount, as Welcome down I came
  Into the flower of this good Tuscan land.

*I had begun to write this Life of myself with my own hand, as
may be seen in certain mended pages [of the MS.]. But I reflected
that I was losing too much time, and that this was but excessive
vanity. So falling in with a son of Michele di Goro of Pieve a
Groppine, a lad of about fourteen years old, and weakly, I set him
to write for me. Thus while I worked I dictated to him my Life.
And as I took no little pleasure in the thing, I worked all the more
diligently and was the more productive. So I left the burden of the
writing to the boy : and I hope to go forward with the task as far
as my recollections will serve me.*

THE LIFE OF BENVENUTO

SON OF MAESTRO GIOVANNI CELLINI OF FLORENCE

WRITTEN BY HIMSELF IN THAT CITY

BOOK I

i. All men, whatever be their condition, who have done anything of merit, or which verily has a semblance of merit, if so be they are men of truth and good repute, should write the tale of their life with their own hand. Yet it were best they should not set out on so fine an enterprise till they have passed their fortieth year. And now this very thing occurs to me, when I am fifty-eight years old and more, here in Florence, where I was born. Many are the adversities I can look back on such as fall to the lot of man; yet am I freer from the same than I have ever been till now. In truth it seems to me I have greater content of mind and health of body than at any time in the past. Some pleasant happenings I recall, and, again, some unspeakable misfortunes, which, when I remember, strike terror into me and wonder that I have, indeed, come to this age of fifty-eight, from which, by God's grace, I am now going on my way rejoicing.

ii. Doubtless, such men as have laboured and gained some repute have given to the world thereby a knowledge of themselves; and it should be enough for them to have proved they were men and to be known for such. Yet we must live as we find others do; and so it is but natural some little vain-glory should creep into a thing of this kind; and this may show itself

3

in divers ways, the first thing when a man lets the world know he comes of a very long and virtuous line.

My name is Benvenuto Cellini, and I am the son of Maestro Giovanni, son of Andrea, son of Cristofano Cellini. My mother was Madonna Elisabetta, daughter of Stefano Granacci; and both my parents were citizens of Florence. In the chronicles drawn up by our Florentines of ancient days, men worthy of faith, according to the report of Giovanni Villani, it stands written that the city of Florence must have been built after the pattern of the fair city of Rome. And some traces of the Colosseum and of the Baths are still to be seen near Santa Croce. The Capitol was where the Old Market is to-day. The Rotonda, built for the temple of Mars, still stands; now it belongs to our Saint John. That so it was can be very plainly seen, and none can deny it; but these buildings are much smaller than those of Rome. They say it was Julius Cæsar had them built, in conjunction with certain noble Romans, who, when Fiesole had been laid siege to and taken, built a city in this place, each of them undertaking to erect one of these famous monuments. Among Julius Cæsar's chief captains was a valorous man, by name Fiorino of Cellino, a hamlet about two miles from Monte Fiascone. Now this Fiorino having taken up his abode under Fiesole, where Florence now is, in order that he might be near the river Arno for the convenience of the army, all the soldiers and other persons who had intercourse with the said captain, were wont to say, "Let us go to Fiorenze,"—first, because this captain's name was Fiorino, and likewise because, from the nature of the soil, flowers grew abundantly on the spot where he had taken up his quarters. So at the foundation of the place, this name seeming to Julius Cæsar a very fair one, and offered naturally, and since flowers are of good augury, he gave the name of Florence to the city. Moreover, he wished to give pleasure to his valorous captain, all the more that he had raised him from a very lowly place, and that he had been the making of such an able man. Learned contrivers and investigators of the origin of words would have the name to mean, on the flowing Arno; but this it seems impossible to accept, for Rome is on the flowing Tiber, Ferrara on the flowing Po, Lyons on the flowing Saone, Paris on the flowing Seine, yet are their names different and come at by another road.

Thus much we find; and so do we believe ourselves descended from a man of worth. Besides, we Cellinis are to be found in Ravenna, the most ancient city of Italy, and men of noble birth are not wanting there. In Pisa, too, there are some, and I have come upon them in many places of Christendom; moreover, in this State the name is not extinct among men following the profession of arms. For not long ago, a young man called Luca Cellini, nay, a beardless boy he was, fought with a practised soldier and a most valiant man, Francesco da Vicorati by name, who was a noted duellist. Yet Luca, by his own might, sword in hand, overcame him and killed him with such bravery and skill that everybody was astonished, having looked for just the contrary. So that I glory in my descent from men of valour.

And now whatever honours I may have won for my house in the ordinary course of life as it is lived to-day, and by my art—though I make no great account of these—I shall tell of the same in due season. But much prouder am I of having been born in a humble station, and of having laid an honourable foundation for my house, than if I had been of great lineage, and by my vices had blackened and defaced it. So now I begin my story by telling how it pleased God I should be born.

iii. My forefathers dwelt in the Val d'Ambra, where they had great possessions. Having retired there on account of the raging factions, they lived like little lords; and all of them were doughty men of arms. In that time a younger son of the house, Cristofano by name, had a great quarrel with certain neighbours and friends. The heads of both houses intervened, and so great a fire was seen to be kindled as imperilled the very existence of the two families. The elders pondered the matter, and it was agreed my own people should send away Cristofano, while the other side removed the youth who had been the cause of the quarrel. They sent their man to Siena; our family dispatched Cristofano to Florence, where they bought for him a little house in the Via Chiara, near by the convent of Sant' Orsola, and likewise some excellent property at Ponte a Rifredi. Cristofano took to himself a wife in Florence, and begat sons and daughters. When all the daughters were settled in life, the sons after their father's death divided the rest of the inheritance. The house in the Via Chiara, with some other few things, fell to one of the said sons, Andrea by name. He in his turn took a wife, and had four sons, the eldest of whom was called Girolamo; the second Bartolommeo; the third Giovanni—afterwards my father; and the fourth Francesco.

This Andrea Cellini had a good understanding of the fashion of architecture of those days; adopted it as his profession, and lived by it. Giovanni, who was my father, took more interest in it than did any of the others. And because Vitruvius says, amongst other things, that he who would be an adept at this art must needs know something of music and of good design, Giovanni became an able draughtsman, and then began to study music, learning, along with the science of that art, to play excellently on the viola and the flute. Being a man of studious habits, he seldom went out of the house. Next door to them lived one Stefano Granacci, who had several daughters, all of them very beautiful. Now as it pleased God, Giovanni saw one of these girls whose name was Elisabetta, and so much did she please him that he asked her for his wife. And because both the fathers were well acquainted with each other, from being such near neighbours, it was easy to bring about the marriage, and each thought the arrangement a good one for himself. First the two old fellows settled the match, and then they set about discussing the dowry, which gave rise to a little friendly dispute between them. For Andrea said to Stefano: "My son Giovanni is the bravest young man in Florence, nay in all Italy; and if I had cared to find a wife for him before now, I might have had the best dower which is ever given in Florence among folk of our condition." And Stefano answered: "You are a thousand times right; but here am I saddled with five girls and as many boys. I have made my calculations, and this is as much as I can afford." Here Giovanni, who, unseen by them, had been listening for a while, came out suddenly and said: "My father, it is the girl I have longed for and loved, not their money. Bad luck to such as would get rich on his wife's dowry. Indeed, since you have been bragging of my great cleverness, shall I not be able to keep my wife and satisfy her needs even with a less sum of money than you have set your heart on? Now I would have you understand that the lady is mine. As for the dowry, I leave it to you." Hereat Andrea Cellini, who was of rather an irritable temper, was somewhat displeased. But in a few days Giovanni brought home his lady, and never asked for any other portion. For eighteen years they rejoiced in their youth and their blessed love, yet longing greatly for children; after which time Elisabetta miscarried of two male children by reason of the doctor's blundering. Later she was again with child, and bore a girl, to whom they gave the name of Cosa, after my father's mother. Two years passed and she was once more with child; and whereas the strong cravings to which pregnant women are slaves, were precisely like those she had on the former occasion, they all made up their minds she was about to bear another daughter, and the name of Reparata was agreed on, after my mother's mother. Now it happened that the child was born on the night after All Saints' Day of the year 1500, at half-past four exactly. The midwife, who knew that a woman-child was expected, so soon as she had washed the creature and swaddled it in finest white linen, crept up softly to Giovanni, my father, and said, "I bring you a good gift which you were not looking for." My father, who had been pacing up and down the floor, said, like the true philosopher he was, "What God sends is ever dear to me." Then he took off the swaddling clothes and beheld the unexpected male child. Clasping his old hands together, and raising his eyes to God, he said, "Lord, I thank Thee with all my heart. This is very precious unto me. I bid him welcome." Everybody who was there asked him in their joy what name he had given the child, and Giovanni gave no other answer than to say, "He is Welcome [Benvenuto]." And so was it determined. This name was given me in Holy Baptism; and with it I am living still by the grace of God.

iv. My grandfather, Andrea Cellini, was still alive when I was about three years old and he was more than a hundred. One day a cistern pipe was being moved, when out of it came a great scorpion. Unseen by the others, it slipped from the cistern to the ground and crept away under a bench. I saw it and ran and laid hold of it. So large was it that when I clenched it in my little fist the tail stuck out from one end and from the other its two claws. In high delight, I ran, they tell me, to my grandfather, saying, "Look, grandad, at my dear little crab." When he saw it was a scorpion, he all but fell dead of fright and anxiety for me. With many caresses he begged me to give it to him; but I only clutched it the tighter, weeping and declaring I would not give it up to anybody. My father, who was also in the house, came running at the sound of my cries. Dazed with terror, he could for the moment think of no way of preventing the venomous animal from killing me. But suddenly his eyes fell on a pair of shears, and so, coaxing me the while, he cut off the tail and the claws. Then when the great danger was over, he took the happening for a good omen.

One day when I was about five years old, my father was sitting in a ground-floor room of ours in which washing had been going on, and where a large fire of oak logs had been left. Giovanni, his viola on his arm, was playing and singing by himself near the fire—for it was very cold. Looking into the fire he chanced to see in the middle of the most ardent flames a little creature like a lizard disporting itself in the midst of the intensest heat. Suddenly aware of what it was, he called my sister and me and pointed it out to us children. Then he gave me a sound box on the ears, which made me cry bitterly, on which he soothed me with kind words, saying, "My dear little fellow, I did not hurt you for any harm you had done, but only that you might remember that the lizard in the fire there is a salamander, which never has been seen for a certainty by any one before." Then he kissed me and gave me some farthings.

v. My father began to teach me to play the flute and to sing music; and though I was of very tender years when little children are wont to be pleased with a whistle and such-like playthings, I had a particular dislike to it, so that only from obedience did I ever play or sing. In those days my father made wonderful organs with wooden pipes, and spinets the best and finest that had ever been seen, as well as violas, lutes, and harps, all of them beautifully and excellently fashioned. He was an engineer, too, and showed a wonderful talent in inventing instruments for lowering bridges, for fulling, and other machines. Likewise was he the first to work well in ivory. But when he had fallen in love with her who became my mother—and perhaps the little flute played some part in that, for he gave more time to it than he should—he was asked by the fifers of the Signory to play with them. This he did for a time for his own pleasure, and then they worked on him till he became one of their company. But Lorenzo de' Medici and Piero his son, who were very fond of him, presently began to see that he was giving himself up entirely to fifing, thus neglecting his fine inventive talent and his delightful art. So they took his place away from him. At this my father felt very sore, for he thought a great wrong had been done him. But he betook himself without delay to his art once more, and made a mirror, about a cubit in diameter, of bone and ivory, with figures and foliage exquisitely wrought and of beautiful design. The mirror was in the shape of a wheel; in the middle was the glass, and round about were seven circles, in which were carved, of combined ivory and black bone, the seven Virtues; and the whole mirror, and therefore, likewise, of course, the Virtues, were poised so that as the wheel turned, all the figures turned too; but as weights were attached to their feet they kept upright. And since he had some knowledge of the Latin language, he put a Latin verse round the mirror, namely:

Rota sum : semper, quoquo me verto, stat Virtus.
(Turn Fortune's wheel whithersoe'er it may,
    Still Virtue stands erect.)

In a little while his post of fifer was given back to him. (Although some of these things took place before I was born, still, remembering what I heard of them, I have been unwilling to leave them untold.) In those days the musicians of this company all belonged to most honourable crafts, some of them being even members of the greater guilds of silk and wool. For this reason my father did not disdain to follow the profession of music, and the greatest desire which he had in all the world for me was that I should become a fine player. As for me, the greatest worry of my life was his constantly saying to me that, if I had but the will—such great aptitude for it did he see in me—I might be the foremost man in all the world.

vi. As I have said, my father was a loyal and much-attached servant of the house of the Medici; and Piero, when he was exiled, confided many things of the utmost consequence to him. Afterwards, when the magnificent Piero Soderini succeeded, and was aware of the wonderful talents of my father—who was still at his musical post—he began to employ him in very important work as an engineer; and, indeed, while Soderini remained in Florence he showed him every favour possible. At that time I was of tender age, and my father had me carried to the palace and made me play upon the flute, my treble accompanying the musicians of the palace, before the Signory, while a beadle held me on his shoulder. On such occasions the gonfalonier, namely, Soderini, loved to make me prattle; he used to give me sweetmeats, and he would say to my father, "Maestro Giovanni, along with music you should teach him your other delightful arts." To which my father answered, "I would rather he followed no other save music and its composition; for in this profession I hope to make him the greatest man in the world, so but God spare him unto me." Whereupon one of the old Signors replied, "Ah, Maestro Giovanni, do as the gonfalonier tells you. Why should the boy never be anything better than a good player?"

And so time went on till the Medici came back again. No sooner were they back than the Cardinal, who was afterwards Pope Leo, began to make much of my father. While they had been away from Florence the balls had been blotted from the scutcheon on their palace, and a great red cross painted in instead—the same being the arms and insignia of the Commune. But at once on their return the red cross was erased, and the Medici red balls on a field of gold were put back in the shield, and all arranged to perfection. My father, who had a quiet

vein of poetry in him, and something, too, of the divine gift of
prophecy, wrote the following four lines under the coat-of-arms
as soon as it was uncovered:

> Under the meek and holy cross of late
> These arms, our pride, have deeply buried lain.
> They show a glorious, joyful face again;
> For Peter's sacred mantle they await.

The epigram was read by all Florence. A few days later Pope
Julius II. died. The Cardinal de' Medici repaired to Rome, and
against every one's expectation was made Pope, the liberal and
magnanimous Leo X. My father forwarded to him his prophetic
quatrain, and the Pope sent him word it would be to his advantage to come to Rome. But my father was unwilling; and so
instead of reward, his place in the palace was taken from him
by Jacopo Salviati, when the latter became gonfalonier. This
is how it came to pass that I was put to the goldsmith's craft;
and part of the time I learned that art, and the rest—but much
against my will—I spent in music.

vii. When my father worried me to become a musician,
I answered begging him to let me draw so many hours a day,
promising him that all the rest of the time I would give myself
up to playing, just to please him. "Then you have no pleasure
in music?" he asked. Whereupon I said "No"; for it seemed
to me an art far below the one on which my own mind was set.
Then in despair the good man placed me in the shop of the
Cavaliere Bandinello's father, who was called Michel Agnolo, a
goldsmith of Pinzi di Monti, very strong in his craft. He had
no advantages of birth, being the son of a coal-chandler. No
blame is this to Bandinello, who was the founder of his house.
If only he had founded it honourably! However that be, I have
nothing to say of him now. I had only been there a few days
when my father took me away from Michel Agnolo, being so
made that he could not live without seeing me constantly. So,
ill content, I gave myself up to music till I was fifteen. If only
I cared to describe all my adventures up to that age, and the
mortal dangers that I ran, I should astonish whoever should
read of them; but that my story be not too long, and since
I have much other to tell, I shall leave them aside.

Now when I was fifteen I placed myself against my father's
wish in a goldsmith's shop with a man called Antonio di Sandro,
known to most as Marcone the goldsmith. An excellent craftsman was he, and a right honest man, high-minded and liberal
in all his dealings. My father did not wish him to pay me wages

as he did his other lads, so that, as I had chosen this art for my own pleasure, I might be free to draw as much as ever I liked. This I did very willingly, and my good master took endless pleasure in my work. He had an only and natural son to whom he was wont to give orders so that I might be spared. My desire to excel in this art was great, or rather, I might say, my love for it; but, indeed, both were strong in me; so that in a few months my work came up to that of the good, nay, to that of the best young practicians of the art, and I began to reap the fruit of my labours. Nevertheless I did not fail to give my father pleasure now and then by playing on the flute or on the cornet; and every time I played, I drew tears and deep sighs from him as he sat listening. And so I would often dutifully please him in this way, as if it had been a joy to me as well.

viii. At that time I had a brother two years younger than myself, a very daring, proud-spirited lad, who later became one of the great soldiers in the school of the marvellous Giovannino de' Medici, father of Duke Cosimo. This child was then about fourteen, and I was two years older. One Sunday, about two hours before nightfall, between the San Gallo and the Pinti gates, he fell out with a young man of twenty or so. They fought with swords, and so valorously did he close with his opponent that he dealt him a serious wound, and was for following the thing up. Among the crowd that stood about were many of the young man's kinsfolk, who seeing the affair go ill for him, took out their slings. One of the stones struck my poor young brother's head, and he fell suddenly to the ground, where he lay senseless and as if dead. Now I, who happened to be there without friends and unarmed, had been crying to my brother to make off, that he had done enough, just at the very moment when, as chance willed it, he was struck down. Running to him speedily, I took his sword and planted myself between him and the other threatening swords and the shower of stones. Nor did I leave him till from the San Gallo gate came up some valiant fighting men and saved me from the wild rage of the crowd. And much they marvelled to find such bravery in so young a lad. Then I carried my unconscious brother home, where with much difficulty he came to his senses. When he was better, the Eight—who had already arrested our adversaries and sentenced them to several years' banishment—ordered us also to a six months' exile at a distance of ten miles from Florence. "Come with me," said I to my brother. And so we parted from our poor father, who instead of providing us with money, of which he had none, gave us his blessing. I set off to Siena to find a certain good friend of mine, Maestro Francesco Castoro by name. Once before this, when I had run away from my father, I had sought out this good man, and had stayed with him some days, working at my goldsmith's craft till my father sent for me. When I reached him this time he recognised me, and set me to work. Besides that he gave me lodgings for such time as I should be in Siena, and thither I repaired with my brother, and stuck to my work for many months. My brother had made a beginning in Latin letters, but he was too young to have yet tasted the savour of learning, and so he wasted his days in idleness.

ix. After a time the Cardinal de' Medici, who became Pope Clement, called us back to Florence at my father's prayers. But a certain pupil of my father's, moved thereto by his natural baseness, advised the Cardinal to send me to Bologna to learn music from a famous master there, who was called Antonio, truly a notable man in the musical profession. The Cardinal told my father that, if he sent me thither, he would give me letters of introduction that would help me. Accordingly my father, who nearly died of joy at such a proposition, sent me off; and I, eager to see the world, went with a good will. Reaching Bologna, I set to work under a man called Maestro Ercole del Piffero, and began to make some little money. Every day I went for a music lesson, and in a few short weeks made no little progress in that accursed art. But I made a great deal more out of my goldsmith's craft; for having received no help from the Cardinal, I placed myself in the house of a Bolognese minia-turist, called Scipione Cavalletti, who lived in the street of Our Lady of Baraccan; and there I took to designing and working for a Jew called Grazia Dio, with whom I made a fairly good living.

Six months later I went back to Florence; whereat Pierino, the fifer who had been my father's pupil, was very much vexed. Yet, to please my father, I went to see Pierino at his house, and played the cornet and the flute with one of his brothers, Girolamo by name, several years younger than Pierino, a very honest, good young fellow, just the opposite of his brother. On one such day my father came to Piero's house to hear us play, and, full of his pleasure in my skill, he cried, "I'll make you a wonderful performer yet, and I defy any one to prevent me!" To this Piero replied—and it was the truth he spoke— "Your Benvenuto will reap far more gain and honour if he sticks to his goldsmithing than to this fifing business." So angry was my father at these words—for he saw I was of the same mind as Piero—that he cried out with great heat, "Well I knew it was you who stood in the way of this great desire of mine; and you it was who had me dismissed from my post at the palace, paying me with that gross ingratitude which is the usual reward of great benefits. I got you appointed there, and you've had me sent packing. It was I taught you whatever you know of music, and you hinder my son from doing my will. But keep in mind these prophetic words: Not years, nor months, I say, shall pass, but a few weeks, ere this shameful ingratitude prove your ruin." Then Pierino answered and said, "Maestro Giovanni, most men grow mad as they get old. So is it with you. And this is no surprise to me, since I have watched you freely squander all your property, heedless of your children's needs. Wherefore I mean to do just the contrary: to leave so much to my sons that they may be able to come to the help of yours." Thereto my father replied, "No rotten tree brings forth good fruit, but just the opposite. Moreover, I say to you, you are a worthless man; and your sons will be mad and poor, and a day will come when they will beg alms of my virtuous and prosperous children." And so we left the house, he and Pierino muttering angry words at each other. I had taken my dear father's part; and as we came out together I said to him I would fain revenge the insults which that ribald fellow had cast at him—provided he let me betake myself to the art of design. "O my dear son," said my father, "I too have been a good draughtsman; but as a relief from the extraordinary labours that entails, and for love of me, who am your father, who begat you, reared you, and gave you the beginnings of such distinguished talents, will you not promise me, as repose after your labours, now and then to take up that flute and that enchanting cornet and give yourself up to the pleasure of your own music?" Yes, I said; right willingly would I do so for love of him. Then my dear father said that it was by the display of such talents I should best revenge him for the insults of his enemies.

Not quite a month had passed when Pierino, who was having a vault built in his house in the Via dello Studio, was one day with some companions in his basement room over the vault. There he began speaking of his former master, my father, and repeating the words which he had said to him respecting his coming ruin. No sooner had he uttered them than the floor of the room where he was fell in—mayhap the vault was badly built; nay, rather was it not by the mere power of God, who does not pay on Saturday?—and the stones and bricks falling with him, both his legs were fractured. Meanwhile those who were with him remained on the edge of the vault and took no harm, but stood there stupefied and astounded—all the more on account of what he had been telling them a moment ago as a jest. When my father heard the news, he girt on his sword and went to see him; and in the presence of the injured man's father, who was called Niccolaio of Volterra, a trumpeter of the Signory, addressed him thus: "Piero, my dear pupil, I am indeed sorry for your misfortune; but if you recollect, it is only a little time since I warned you of it; and all I said then respecting your children and mine will come to pass." Shortly afterwards the ungrateful Piero died of this accident. He left a wife of low character and one son, who some years later came to beg alms of me in Rome. I gave him something, both because it is in my nature to give alms to the poor, and because I called to mind with tears the happy condition in which his father had lived when mine had prophesied that Pierino's sons should one day beg from his own worthy children. But now enough has been said about this. Only, none should make mock of the predictions of an honest man when he has been unjustly abused; for it is not he that speaks; it is verily the voice of God.

x. So I gave myself up to goldsmith's work, and by that means I was of help to my dear father. His other son, my brother Cecchino, had, as I said before, made a beginning in the study of Latin letters. It was my father's wish that I, the elder, should be a great musician and performer, and that his younger son should become a great and learned lawyer. But he could not force us from our natural bents, which bound me to the art of design, and my brother, who was finely proportioned and full of grace, to the profession of arms. When he was still a young lad, he came home once from his first lesson in the school of the marvellous Signor Giovannino de' Medici. I was not in when he arrived. In want of seemly clothes to wear, he sought out our sisters, and they, unknown to my father, gave him a doublet and cloak of mine, both of them fine and new. (For, besides helping my father and my good honest sisters, I had been able to buy myself these fine clothes out of my savings.) When I discovered I had been cheated and robbed of my clothes, and could not find my brother, from whom I would have taken them away, I asked my father why he let me be so wronged, seeing that I laboured so hard and with such good-

will to help him. To this he replied that I was his good son,
but that he had got back again the one he had thought lost.
Moreover, it was but right, and, indeed, according to the word
of God Himself, that he who had possessions should give unto
him who had none. Therefore, he begged me for his sake to bear
this injury, and God would give me increase of good things.
Then I, being an inexperienced youth, answered my afflicted
father with heat; and taking with me the poor remains of my
clothes and money, I made off towards one of the gates of the
city. But not knowing which one led towards Rome, I found
myself at Lucca; and from Lucca I went on to Pisa.

When I reached Pisa—I was about sixteen at the time—
I stopped near the middle bridge, just where the Fish Stone is,
and in front of a goldsmith's workshop. While I was watching
attentively what the master was doing, he came out and asked
me who I was, and what was my calling. I replied that I worked
a little in his own business. The good man then invited me into
his shop, and gave me work to do on the spot, saying, "You
have a look about you which makes me think you are an honest
fellow." Then he set gold and silver and jewels before me. And
at the end of the first day he took me home to his house, where
he lived in honourable condition with his beautiful wife and
children. Calling to mind the grief which my good father might
be suffering on my account, I wrote to him that I was in the
house of an honest man, whose name was Ulivieri della Chiostra,
under whom I was doing very fine and important work. I bade
him keep his mind easy, for I hoped to learn much, and by my
attainments to win ere long what would bring him profit and
honour. My dear father answered my letter at once, saying,
"My son, such is the love I bear you, that were it not for our
honour, which above all things I respect, I should have set out
without delay to come to you; for of a truth I seem to be without the light of my eyes when I do not see you every day as
has been my wont. I shall stay here, therefore, for the right
conduct of my home affairs, and you meanwhile will give yourself to the perfection of your art. Only, I wish you to keep in
mind these two or three simple words, and observe them, and
never forget them—

> In whatever house you'd stay,
> Keep your hands from theft alway."

xi. Now it happened that this letter fell into the hands of
my master Ulivieri; and, unbeknown to me, he read it. Afterwards he confessed having done so, saying, "And now, my

Benvenuto, I was not deceived in your pleasant face. This much I learn from a letter from your father, which has fallen into my hands. So now think of yourself as in your own home, and with your own father."

While I was in Pisa I used to go and see the Campo Santo; and there I found many fine antique marble sarcophagi. Also in other places in Pisa I found beautiful antiques, which I studied zealously every day when I could be spared from the labours of the workshop. And when my master paid me visits in the little room he had given me, and came to know that I spent all my time so virtuously, he took as great a liking for me as if he had been my father. In the year I was with him I made a great advance, working in silver and gold, and at most important and beautiful things; and this gave me the keenest desire to get on still further. My father, in the meantime, kept writing to me most piteously to return to him; and in every letter he reminded me not to lose the music which had cost him so much trouble to teach me. Whereupon all desire to return to him left me, so much did I loathe that damnable playing on the flute; and it seemed to me I was in Paradise the whole year I stayed in Pisa, where I never played at all. But when the year was up, Ulivieri, my master, had occasion to go to Florence to sell some gold and silver filings which he had. And as the unwholesome air had given me a little fever, I returned, before I had shaken it off, in my master's company to Florence. There my father gave him the heartiest welcome, but, unknown to me, begged him piteously not to take me back. I was ill for about two months; and my father had me treated and cared for most affectionately. But ever he would say it seemed to him a thousand years till I should be well enough to play a little to him on the flute. Now while he spoke to me of this, holding his hand on my pulse the while—for he had some knowledge of medicine and of Latin letters—he perceived such a great alteration in its beating the very moment he began speaking on the subject, that often he would go away from me terrified and weeping. Wherefore, one day, seeing his great unhappiness, though the fever was still upon me, I begged one of my sisters to bring me a flute, since it was the least fatiguing instrument of all, and did me no hurt. Then I played with so fine a touch of hand and lips that my father, coming in suddenly, blessed me a thousand times, and said he thought I had made great progress while I had been away. And he begged me to go on, and not to let so fine a talent run to waste.

xii. As soon as I was well again I returned to my friend Marcone, the honest goldsmith, who gave me such good wages I was able to help my father and the rest of my family. About this time there arrived in Florence a sculptor called Piero Torrigiani. He had come from England, where he had lived for many years. Now he was a great friend of my master and paid him a visit every day; and having seen my designs and my work, he said to me, "I have come to Florence to pick up as many young men as I can, for I have a great work in hand for my king, and I want the help of my own Florentines. Now your method of working and designing pertains more to sculpture than to the goldsmith's art; so while you are helping me with a great work in bronze I have undertaken, I will make you both a skilful artist and a wealthy man." This Torrigiani was singularly handsome, with a bold bearing, and the air rather of a great soldier than of a sculptor, especially having regard to his commanding gestures and his fine sounding voice; while his frown was enough to scare the bravest. And every day he would tell us of his ruffling it with those beasts of Englishmen. Now in talking of his adventures, he fell to speaking of Michel Agnolo Buonarroti, led to this by a drawing I had made from a cartoon of that most divine master. This cartoon was the first work in which Michel Agnolo displayed his great genius to the full; and he made it in competition with another, namely Leonardo da Vinci. Both were for the Council Chamber of the Palace of the Signory. The subject was the taking of Pisa by the Florentines; and the admirable Leonardo da Vinci had chosen to delineate a skirmish of horse-soldiers, with a capture of standards, all as divinely drawn as you can imagine. Michel Agnolo Buonarroti in his represented a company of infantry bathing in the Arno, for it was summer time; and he showed them just as there had sounded a call to arms, and the naked soldiers were running to the fight. So finely were the actions portrayed that neither amongst the ancients nor the moderns has ever been seen a work that reached so high a point of excellence. And so likewise, as I have said, the great Leonardo's was of marvellous beauty. One of these cartoons was placed in the Medici Palace and one in the Pope's Hall; and while they could be seen there, they were the school of all the world. Although the divine Michel Agnolo afterwards decorated the great chapel of Pope Julius, he never came near that height again; never again did his genius attain to the power of those early studies.

xiii. And now to return to Piero Torrigiani, who, holding my drawing in his hand, spoke thus: "Buonarroti and I, when we were lads, used to go to the Church of the Carmine to study in the chapel of Masaccio. Now Buonarroti had a habit of teasing all the rest of us who were drawing there; and one day in particular he was annoying me, and I was more vexed than usual; so I stretched out my hand and dealt him such a blow on the nose that I felt the bone and the cartilage yield under my fist as if they had been made of crisp wafer. And so he'll go with my mark upon him to his dying day." These words roused such loathing in me—for I had ever before my eyes the works of the divine Michel Agnolo—that not only did I refuse to go with him to England, but I could not bear the sight of the man. While I was in Florence I took as my pattern the fine style of Michel Agnolo, and from that I have never wavered.

In those days I was bound in close friendship with a charming young man of my own age, and was much in his company. He also was a goldsmith. His name was Francesco, and he was the son of Filippo, son of Fra Filippo, the most excellent painter. Our companionship bred so great an affection in us that we were never apart night or day. Then, too, his house was still full of fine studies from the hand of his distinguished father. Several books of these were there, taken from the splendid antiquities of Rome, and when I set eyes on them I also became enamoured of them. So for about two years we were the closest friends.

At this time I made a low-relief in silver as big as a little child's hand. It was meant for the buckle of a man's belt, for they were then worn of that size. Carved on it was a cluster of leaves after the antique, with heads of cherubs and other charming masks. This work I made in the shop of one Francesco Salimbene. When it was shown about among the members of the goldsmith's guild, they boasted of me as the best young artist in the trade. Now there was a certain Giovanbatista, commonly known as Tasso, a wood-carver, a young man of my own age; and one day he said to me that if I cared to go to Rome, he would willingly come with me. This talk we had together was just after dinner, and being angry with my father —music was as ever the cause—I said to Tasso, "Oh, but you're a man of words, not of deeds." Whereupon Tasso answered, "I, too, am on bad terms with my mother; and if only I had the wherewithal to take me to Rome, I'd never go back to turn the key on that wretched little shop of mine." To this I said that if he was only staying for that, I had on me as much as would take us both to Rome. So, talking all the time, we found ourselves at the gate of San Piero Gattolini before we knew where we were. Whereupon I said, "Tasso, my friend, it is God's doing our reaching this gate unawares. But now that I am here I feel as if I had gone half-way." And so it was agreed; and as we went upon our road we said, "Oh, what will our old folks say to-night?" Then we made a pact together not to think more about them till we had got to Rome. So, tying our aprons behind, we set off for Siena, with hardly a word to each other by the way. Having reached there, Tasso said his feet hurt him, and that he would rather not come farther; and he asked me to lend him money to return. To which I answered, "There would not be enough left for me to go on with, so you should have thought well before you left Florence; but if it be because of your feet you stop behind, we shall find a return-horse bound for Rome, and then you'll have no excuse." So I hired a horse; but as he gave me no answer, I betook myself towards the Roman gate. Seeing that I had made up my mind, he limped along as well as he could, slowly and far behind me, and grumbling all the time. As soon as I had reached the gate I felt pity for my companion; so I waited for him and set him on the crupper, saying, "What would our friends say of us to-morrow if, having left them to go to Rome, we had not the spirit to get past Siena?" Then my good Tasso confessed I spoke the truth; and as he was a cheerful fellow, he began to laugh and sing; and so, singing and laughing all the time, we made our way to Rome. I was just nineteen years old then, and so was the century.

As soon as we reached Rome I placed myself in a workshop under a master called Firenzuola. His own name was Giovanni, but he came from Firenzuola in Lombardy, and he was a noted maker of plate, working generally at things on a large scale. When I let him have a glance at the design of the clasp I had made in Florence with Salimbene, he was greatly pleased, and turning to one of his apprentices, a Florentine, Giannotto Giannotti by name, who had been with him several years, he said, "Here is one of the Florentines who know, and you are one of their incapable fools." At that moment I recognised Giannotto, and hastened to say a word to him; for before he went to Rome we used often to draw together, and we had been on most intimate terms. But he was so mortified by the words his master had thrown at him that he declared he did not recognise me, nor know who I was. Indignant at his saying such a thing, I burst out, "O Giannotto, once mine own familiar friend! Have we not often been together in such and such places? Have we not drawn together, and eaten, drunk, and slept in your villa? Yet I do not care whether you speak for me or not to this good man your master; for I hope that, without any help from you, my own hands will bear witness as to whom I am."

xiv. When I had ended, Firenzuola, who was a most impulsive and fiery man, turned to Giannotto and said to him, "O you vile rascal! Aren't you ashamed to behave like that to one who has been so close a comrade?" And with the same impetuosity he wheeled round to me and spoke—"Come into the shop, and do as you have said: let your hands bear witness to the man you are." Then he set me to work on a very beautiful silver piece for a cardinal. This was a little box copied from the porphyry sarcophagus which stands at the door of the Rotonda. Not content merely to copy the design, I enriched it with some charming masks done all out of my head; so that my master went about showing it through all the trade, and boasting of the skilled work that came out of his shop. It was about the size of half a cubit, and was meant for a salt-cellar for the table. This brought me the first of my earnings in Rome. Part of the money I sent to help my dear father; the rest served to keep me while I went round studying the antiquities, till, my money coming to an end, I had to go back and work in the shop. My friend Batista del Tasso had not been long in Rome when he returned to Florence. I took new works in hand; but the desire came upon me, as soon as I should have finished them, to change my master, being cajoled thereto by a certain Milan man called Maestro Pagolo Arsago. But Firenzuola, my first master, had hot words with this same Arsago, flinging insults at him in my presence; whereupon I took up the cudgels for the latter, telling Firenzuola I was born free, and that free I would live; that of Arsago he had no reason to complain, and still less of me, for some crowns were owing to me for my wages; that as a free craftsman I should go wherever it pleased me, and doing so I wronged no one. Then my new master took up the word, saying he had never asked me to come, and that I should be doing a pleasure if I were to return to Firenzuola. To this I retorted that I could not see I was doing him any wrong whatsoever, and that having finished the works I had begun, I wanted to be my own man and no one else's; and whoever wanted me might come and seek me. To which Firenzuola answered, "I'll not come and seek your services. And don't show your face here again on any account." When I reminded him of my money he laughed at me; whereupon I said that well as I had worked at the making of those things he had seen, I should handle the sword no less well in the recovery of my rights. Now as we were disputing in this fashion, an old man chanced to come up to us, Messer Antonio da San Marino by name. He was the foremost of the goldsmiths of Rome, and had been Firenzuola's master. Hearing my case, which I stated plainly for their comprehension, he immediately took my part, and ordered Firenzuola to pay me. The quarrel grew fierce, for indeed Firenzuola shone more as a swordsman than as a goldsmith. Still justice made its way, though I helped its victory by my firm determination, so that I was paid at last. Some time after, the said Firenzuola and I became friends again; and at his request I was godfather to a child of his.

xv. Continuing to work with Messer Pagolo Arsago, I earned good wages, and I always sent the bigger share to my good father. At the end of two years, moved by his prayers, I went back to Florence, and set myself once more to work with Francesco Salimbene. With him I earned a very fair amount, and gave my mind to learning more of my art. I renewed my acquaintance with Francesco di Filippo; and though I was much given to pleasure, drawn thereto by that accursed music, I always kept certain hours of the day and night free for study. About this time I made a silver heart-key—for so were such things called in those days—which was a belt three fingers broad, to be worn by a bride. It was worked in half-relief, with some little figures in the round; and I made it for a man called Raffaello Lapaccini. Although I was very badly paid for it, the honour I gained came to more than the price it might fairly have brought me. By this time I had worked with many different persons in Florence, and had made the acquaintance of some honest men among the goldsmiths. Such an one was Marcone, my first master. But I knew others who had the name of honest men, yet who did their utmost against me in my work, and cheated me whenever they could. Perceiving this I kept aloof from them, holding them as scoundrelly thieves. But one of the goldsmiths, called Giovan Battista Sogliani, kindly obliged me with a part of his shop, which was at the corner of the New Market, hard by the Landi's Bank. There I completed many fine pieces, and, making good earnings, was able to be of real service to my family. But my success roused the envy of some of those villains I had once had to do with, namely, Salvadore and Michele Guasconti, who owned three large goldsmith's shops, and did a deal of business. When, therefore, I saw that they bore me ill will, I laid my complaint before an honest man, saying they might be well content to have robbed me, as they had done under the cloak of pretended kindness. This coming to their ears, they boasted they would make me finely repent of my words; but I, not knowing the colour of fear, minded their threats hardly at all.

xvi. It happened one day I was leaning up against the shop of one of them. He called out to me, and began to speak in a half-scolding, half-bullying tone. I answered that if they had done their duty towards me I should have spoken of them as men of worth and honour are spoken of; since they had done the contrary, they should blame themselves and not me. While I stood there talking, one of the family, their cousin, called Gherardo Guasconti—perhaps at their instigation—waited till there came by a beast of burden with a load of bricks; and when the beast was just opposite, shoved it on me with such force that I was much hurt. Turning suddenly and seeing that he was laughing, I dealt him such a blow with my fist on his temple that he fell in a dead faint. Then facing his cousin, I said, "That's what thieves and cowards of your sort get." They made as if to attack me, for they were numerous enough, and I whose blood was boiling, put my hand on a little knife I had, and roared, "If one of you dares come out of the shop, the other can run for the priest: there will be nothing left for the doctor to do!" Such terror did these words strike into them that not one of them moved to their cousin's aid. I had no sooner gone than the father and sons ran to the Eight, and told how I had attacked them with a sword in their shop, an unheard-of thing in Florence. So the Eight Signors had me summoned; and I appeared before them. They reproved me severely—perhaps because they saw me in a cloak, while the others wore their citizen's mantle and hood; but also because my enemies had gone to those signors' houses to speak to them privately, and I, being inexperienced, had spoken to nobody, trusting solely in my own good cause. I pleaded that when Gherardo had grossly insulted me, I had been greatly moved to anger, yet did but give him a box on the ear; and thus it did not seem to me I deserved so sharp a rebuke,

Hardly had Prinzivalle della Stufa, who was of the Eight, heard me utter the word "box on the ear," than he said, "It was a blow you gave him: you did not box his ears." Then the bell was rung, and we were all sent out. In my defence Prinzivalle said to the company, "Consider, my lords, the simplicity of this poor fellow, who accuses himself of having boxed the other's ears, thinking it a less offence than a blow; for the penalty of the former in the New Market is five and twenty crowns, and that of a blow little or nothing at all. He is a very clever young man, and generously maintains his own poor family by his work. Would to God that our city had many of his kind, instead of lacking them as it does!"

xvii. Among the Eight were some Puritan fellows, with the tails of their hoods twisted up; and they, moved by the appeals and the lying tales of my enemies, and also because they were of Fra Girolamo's faction, would willingly have sent me to prison, and condemned me without mercy. But good Prinzivalle prevented that. So they let me off with a fine of four bushels of flour to be given in alms to the Murate Convent. As soon as we were called in, he ordered me not to speak a word under pain of their displeasure, and to obey the sentence they had passed. Then administering to me a sharp rebuke, they sent us to the Chancellor, I grumbling all the time, "It was a box on the ear, not a blow," so that we left the Eight laughing heartily. The Chancellor, on the part of the magistrates, ordered us both to find security; but only I was condemned to pay the four bushels of flour. I felt outraged; nevertheless, I sent for one of my cousins, who was called Maestro Annibale the surgeon, the father of Messer Librodoro Librodori, begging him to stand security for me. But he would not come. At this I was furious, and in my rage I swelled like an asp, and resolved on a desperate thing. Here may verily be seen how the stars do not so much influence as compel our ways. When I thought under what obligations Annibale lay to our house, my anger grew to such a degree that I let my evil passion have its way—and then, too, by nature I am somewhat choleric. Thus I waited till the company of the Eight had gone to dinner; and then, left to myself, and seeing that none of them had their eye on me, I went out of the palace in a fever of rage, and ran home to my shop. There I picked up a stiletto, and rushed to my enemies' house, which was above their shop. I found them at table; and young Gherardo, who had been the beginning of the quarrel, threw himself upon me at my entrance. Thereupon I stabbed him in the breast, right through his doublet and vest to his shirt, but did not touch his flesh, nor do him any injury whatsoever. Only, seeing the dagger disappear, and hearing the tearing of his clothes, I thought I had wounded him sorely; and, as he fell from sheer terror to the ground, I shouted, "O traitors, this is the day appointed unto me to murder you all!" The father, mother, and sisters, thinking that it was the Day of Judgment, threw themselves at once on their knees, calling for mercy with all their lungs. Seeing they made no resistance, and looking at the man stretched out on the floor like a corpse, I felt it would be too vile a thing to lay hands on them. But, still furious, I rushed to the stairs and, having reached the street, I found all the rest of the household assembled there, more than a dozen in all. One had an iron shovel, another carried a big iron pipe, others hammers, anvils, and sticks. Like a mad bull I rushed into their midst, knocked down four or five of them, and fell with them, but dealing dagger-thrusts all the time, now here, now there. Those who kept their feet pressed in on me as hard as they could, having at me with both hands with their hammers, their anvils, and their cudgels. But as God in His mercy sometimes intervenes, it so pleased Him that they did not do me, nor did I do them, the very least harm in the world. Only my cap was left on the field, and that my enemies bore off, each of them digging at it with his weapon—though they had fought shy of it before. Then they looked among their company for the dead and wounded; and, lo, every man of them was safe and sound!

xviii. I was on the road to Santa Maria Novella when I suddenly hit up against Frate Alesso Strozzi, whom I did not know. Yet I begged this good brother, for the love of God, to save my life, for I had committed a great crime. The honest friar told me to fear nothing; that though I had done all the evil in the world, in his little cell I should be altogether safe. Nearly an hour passed, and the Eight, who had been called together for an extraordinary sitting, sent out one of the most terrible proclamations against me that ever was heard, and threatened the severest penalties against whoever should shelter me or know of my whereabouts, without regard to the place, or to the quality of him who should give me refuge. My poor afflicted father ran to the Eight, threw himself on his knees before them, and begged mercy for his unhappy young son. Then stood up one of those fanatics, and tossing the crest of his twisted hood, spoke these insulting words to the poor old man, "Get up," he said, "and out with you! For to-morrow morning we shall send him out of town by the lances." Then my father answered haughtily, "What God has ordained, that shall you do, and nothing more"; whereupon the man answered that of a certainty God had so ordained. And my father replied, "I comfort myself with the thought that you have no knowledge of what shall happen." Leaving them, he came in search of me, along with a youth of my own age, Piero, the son of Giovanni Landi. We loved each other better than if we had been brothers. This young man carried under his mantle a magnificent sword and a splendid coat of mail. Having found me, my brave father told me how things were, and what the Eight had said to him. Then he kissed me on the forehead and on the two eyes, and blessed me from his heart, saying, "The strength of God be your aid!" Bringing me the sword and armour, he helped me with his own hands to put them on. And said he, "O my good son, armed with these you live or die." Pier Landi, who was with us, could not stop weeping. He gave me ten golden crowns; and I asked him to pluck out some hairs from my chin, the first traces of my beard. Then Frate Alesso dressed me like a friar, and sent a lay brother along with me as guide. Leaving the convent, I went out of the city by the Prato gate and along the walls till I came to the Piazza of San Gallo; and having climbed the Montui hill, I found in one of the first houses a man called Grassuccio, brother to Messer Benedetto da Monte Varchi. Off I threw my frock, and was a man again. Then my companion and I mounted the two horses waiting for us, and went away through the night to Siena. There Grassuccio left me, returned to Florence, saluted my father, and told him I had reached safety. My father rejoiced greatly thereat; and he could hardly wait till he found that one of the Eight who had girded at him. Finding him at last, he said, "Do you see, Antonio, that it was God who knew what should befall my son, and not you?" "Wait till we catch him again," said the other; and my father rejoined, "In the meanwhile I will give my mind to thanking God who has saved him now."

xix. At Siena I waited for the courier to Rome, and went along with him. When we had passed the Paglia, we met the messenger who carried the news of the election of the new Pope, Clement VII. Once at Rome, I set to work in Maestro Santi the goldsmith's shop. Although Santi was dead, one of his sons kept on the place; but he did not work himself, and all the business was carried on by a young man, called Luca Agnolo of Jesi, a peasant, who had come as quite a little lad to work with Maestro Santi. This Luca Agnolo was short of stature, but well proportioned. He worked more skilfully than any man

I had ever seen till then, with the greatest ease, too, and with infinite fancy, but only on large pieces, on fine vases, basins, and such-like things. Setting to work in this shop, I took in hand some candlesticks for a Spaniard, the Bishop of Salamanca. These candlesticks were as richly worked as such things can be. Now, there was a pupil of Raffaello da Urbino, called Gianfrancesco, nicknamed Il Fattore. He was a great friend of this bishop, and got me into his good graces, too, so that I obtained a great many commissions from the dignitary, and made a very good living. In those days I used to go and draw, now in the chapel of Michel Agnolo, and now in the house of Agostino Chigi, the Sienese, where there were a great many beautiful paintings from the hand of the most excellent Raffaello of Urbino. There I went on holidays, for Gismondo, brother of Messer Agostino Chigi, lived in the palace; and they were very proud when young men of my standing were seen studying in their houses. The wife of Messer Gismondo had often seen me there—a most noble lady was she, and of wonderful beauty— and so one day she approached me, and, looking at my drawings, asked me if I were a sculptor or a painter. I answered the lady that I was a goldsmith. Whereupon she said that I drew too well for a goldsmith; and she ordered one of her maids to fetch a lily of wonderful diamonds set in gold. Showing it to me, she begged me to price it. I estimated the value to be eight hundred crowns, and she told me that I had valued it very exactly. Then she asked me if I had a mind to contrive a fine new setting for it. "Right willingly," said I; and there and then drew a little sketch of the design. And my skill was the greater for my pleasure in dealing with this lovely and most pleasant lady. When I had finished the design, in came another noble Roman lady, who was also very beautiful. She had been upstairs, and now, coming down, she asked Madonna Porzia what she was doing, who answered, smiling, "I am amusing myself in watching this worthy young man at his drawing, for he is both honest and comely." By this time I had summoned up some boldness, yet was it still mixed with a trifle of shy modesty, and I blushed as I said, "Whatever I am, Madonna, I shall ever be most ready for your service." The lady also reddened a little as she added, "You know well that I desire your service," and handing me the lily, told me to take it away. Moreover, she gave me twenty gold crowns which she had in her pocket, saying, "Set the jewel for me according to the design you have made, and return to me the old gold of its present setting." Then the other Roman lady said, "If I were in that young man's shoes, I'd soon make off with it." Whereupon Madonna Porzia rejoined that virtues rarely exist alongside vices, and that if I were to do such a thing I should much belie my honest face. Then, turning away, she took the Roman gentlewoman's hand and said, with a pleasant smile, "Adieu, Benvenuto!" I stopped for some time busy on the drawing I had in hand, which was a copy of a figure of Jupiter by Raffaello of Urbino. As soon as I had finished I set off for home, and began to make a little model of wax, to show how the thing would look in the end. This I took to Madonna Porzia. The Roman lady who had been there before was again present, and both, greatly pleased with my labours, showed me such favour that, gathering some boldness, I promised them the work should be twice as good as the model. Then I set about the thing, and in twelve days I had finished the lily-shaped jewel, adorning it with little masks, cherubs, animals, all of them charmingly enamelled, so that the diamonds which made the lily looked ever so much better than before.

xx. Now while I was working at this piece, that clever Lucagnolo, of whom I have spoken above, showed his strong disapproval of me; and many a time did he tell me that I would earn much more profit and honour by helping him to make great silver vases, as I had done in the beginning. To this I replied that I should be capable of making these whenever I had a mind; but as for the kind of thing I was doing, it did not come in one's way every day; that it was no less honourable than what he proposed, and a great deal more profitable. At this Lucagnolo laughed, saying, "Let's wait and see, Benvenuto. By the time you have finished your work I shall endeavour to have finished the vase I began at the same time as you did the jewel; and experience will prove to you what profit I draw from my work, and what can be made from yours." It was a great pleasure, I replied, to engage in such a contest with so able a man as he, and in the end it would be seen which of us was mistaken. And so both of us, smiling somewhat disdainfully at each other, set our faces proudly to our tasks, and so eager were we for their completion, that at the end of ten days we had each finished our own with great skill and elegance. Lucagnolo's was a very large vase designed for the table of Pope Clement, into which at dinner-time were thrown bones and the rinds of fruits. It was made rather for display than necessity. The vase was adorned with two fine handles, with masks both big and little, and clumps of beautiful foliage, and

all worked with such perfect grace and art that I declared it
to be the finest thing of the kind I had ever seen. Whereupon
Lucagnolo, thinking he had convinced me of my mistake, said,
"Your own work seems just as beautiful to me; but soon we
shall see the difference between them." So, taking up his vase,
he carried it to the Pope, who was entirely satisfied with it,
and ordered him to be paid at once according to the standard of
payment for works on that scale. Meanwhile I took my jewel
to the lady, Madonna Porzia, who was altogether astonished,
and said I had far surpassed the promise I had made her. Then
she went on to say I might ask whatever I liked for my pains,
for to her mind my deserts were such that, were she to give me
a castle, she would hardly think me paid. But since that she
could not give me, she continued with a smile, I must ask
something within her means. To this I replied that I could
imagine no better reward than to have satisfied her ladyship.
Then I, too, smiling, made her a reverence and took my leave,
saying I desired no other recompense. Thereat Madonna Porzia
turned to the Roman lady, and said, "See you, those virtues
we believed to be in him keep good company, and have no
dealings with vice." And both of them were astonished. Then
said Madonna Porzia, "Benvenuto, my friend, have you never
heard the saying that when the poor man gives to the rich the
Devil laughs?" Whereupon I answered, "Well, he has a deal of
trouble, and for once I'd like to see him merry"; but she rejoined, as I was going away, that on this occasion she had no
desire to do him any such good turn. When I got back to my
shop, Lucagnolo had the money for his vase in a little packet,
and when I came in he said, "Now, as a test, put your earnings
for the jewel side by side with mine from the vase." But I asked
him to keep his money intact till next day. Then, inasmuch as
my work was, of its kind, no less fine than his, I hoped to
convince him so would be its reward.

xxi. Next day Madonna Porzia sent her steward to my shop.
He called me outside, and put into my hand a paper cornet
full of money from his mistress, with a message that she did
not wish the Devil to have all the fun; and explaining that what
she had sent was not the full payment which my labours deserved
—with many other courtesies of speech befitting such a lady.
Lucagnolo, to whom it seemed a thousand years till he might
compare his packet with mine, that very instant dashed into
the shop, where a dozen workmen and neighbours were gathered,
all eager to see the upshot of the contest. Taking up his packet

with a scornful laugh, and saying, "Ou! ou!" over and over again, he poured the money noisily out on the counter. There were five-and-twenty giulio crowns, and he thought to himself that my payment might come to four or five crowns *di moneta*. Hardly able to endure his cries, the mocking glances and the laughing of the bystanders, I gave a peep into my parcel, and saw that there was nothing in it but gold. So going to one end of the counter, keeping my eyes cast down the while, as quietly as possible I raised my packet high with both my hands, and made the money run out as if from a mill-hopper. Mine was twice as much as his; so that all the bystanders, who had been fixing somewhat disdainful eyes on me, now turned on him with cries of, "Lucagnolo, Benvenuto's coins are gold, and twice as many as yours, and they make a much better show!" I thought that from envy and shame the poor fellow would have fallen dead there and then. And though a third part of my money would come to him, for I was but his workman—and such is the custom that the workman receives two-thirds and the rest goes to the master of the shop—yet wild envy was stronger in him than avarice, though it should have been just the opposite, seeing that Lucagnolo was the son of a peasant of Jesi. Now he cursed his own art and those who had taught it to him, saying that from this time forward he would work no more at these big things, but would give himself entirely to silly toys like mine, since they were so well paid. I, not a whit less angry, remarked that every bird sang its own song, and that his speech reeked of the low shanty he was born in. I stoutly maintained that I could succeed admirably in turning out such clumsy rubbish as his, while he would never attain to skill in my dainty toys. Then I left him in a rage, promising to prove my words ere long. The bystanders blamed him loudly, looking on him as the boor he was, and holding me for the man I had shown myself to be.

xxii. Next day I went to thank Madonna Porzia. But I told her ladyship she had done just the contrary of what she had said; for I had wished to make the Devil merry, and she had made him once more deny God. And so we laughed together pleasantly; and she gave me other fine and important pieces of work to do for her.

In the meanwhile, through a pupil of Raffaello of Urbino the painter, I got a commission from the Bishop of Salamanca to make a great water-pot, of the kind called *acquereccia*, which serve as sideboard ornaments. The bishop wished to have two made of the same size, and commissioned Lucagnolo to make one, and me the other; and for the moulding of the vases we got a design from the painter Gianfrancesco, whom I have just mentioned.

So I took the vase in hand with all the energy possible; and a Milan man, called Maestro Giovanpiero della Tasca, was good enough to give me a corner of his shop to work in. There I made my preparations, calculated the money I should need for some affairs I had in hand, and all the rest I sent to succour my good father. When he was on his way to cash it in Florence, he chanced on that fanatic who had been of the Eight when I had got into that little trouble, the very man who had insulted him by saying I was, of a certainty, going to be sent into the country with the lances. Now this fanatic had worthless sons, and so my father said to him, "Any man may get into trouble, especially a hot-tempered one, if he feel himself to be in the right, as my son did. But look at the rest of his life, and see how virtuously I have brought him up. I pray God in your behalf that your sons behave neither better nor worse to you than mine do to me. For God has enabled me to train them well; and when my own strength could not avail, He Himself saved them for me out of your violent hands, and that when you least expected it." And so leaving him, my father went and wrote all this to me, begging me for the love of God to play sometimes on my flute, and not waste the fine art which he had been at such pains to teach me. The letter was full of the most loving and fatherly words imaginable; so that it moved me to pious tears, and filled me with the desire that, before he died, I might satisfy him fully on the count of music. So does God grant us all the lawful desires which we ask of Him in faith.

xxiii. While I was hard at work on Salamanca's fine vase I had as my sole help a little lad, whom, at the earnest prayers of friends, and half against my own will, I had taken as apprentice. This child, who was about fourteen years old, was called Paolino, and he was the son of a Roman citizen, who lived on his rents. He was the best bred, the most honest, and the handsomest boy I have ever seen in my life; and for his modest ways and habits, his wonderful beauty, and the great affection he bore me, I loved him with all the love the heart of man can hold. This tenderness drew me once more to music, that I might sit and watch his lovely face, naturally so modest and so melancholy, lighten at the sound. For when I took up my cornet, there dawned there a smile so charming and so beautiful that

I in nowise wonder at those fables which the Greeks wrote of
the divine gods. Indeed, had Paolino lived in those days, perhaps
he would have set them fabling still more extravagantly. Now
Paolino had a sister called Faustina; and I think that the other
Faustina, of whom there is such a talk in the ancient books,
never was so fair. Sometimes he brought me home to their
vineyard, and, so far as I could judge, that worthy man, his
father, would have willingly had me for his son-in-law. All this
made me play a great deal more than I had been doing. It
happened at that time that a certain Giangiacomo, a fifer from
Cesena, who was in the Pope's household, and a most admirable
musician, sent word to me by Lorenzo, the trumpeter from
Lucca—who to-day is in the service of our Duke—asking if
I would help them for the Pope's Ferragosto by playing the
soprano part on my cornet in certain lovely movements they
had chosen for that day. Although I had the greatest desire
to finish the fine vase I had begun, yet, since music has a marvellous power, and also that I might give some satisfaction to
my old father, I consented to play in their company. So for
eight days before the Ferragosto, and every day for two hours,
we rehearsed together. Then on the appointed day in August
we went to the Belvedere, and while Pope Clement dined we
played our well-rehearsed movements in such a fashion that the
Pope declared he had never heard music more sweetly played,
or more harmoniously. Calling Giangiacomo to him, he asked
him where and how he had managed to procure so good a
soprano cornet, and inquired most minutely who I was. Giangiacomo told him my name with all exactness, to which the
Pope rejoined, "So he is the son of Maestro Giovanni?" And
he was told that it was so. Then the Pope said he wished to
have me in his service among the other musicians. But Giangiacomo replied, "Most holy father, I have no hope of procuring
him for you; for his profession, to which he gives the whole of
his time, is the goldsmith's art, wherein he works with wonderful skill, drawing from it much more profit than he would from
music." Then said the Pope, "I want him all the more for his
having a talent over and above the one I looked for. Settle on
him the same salary you others have, and tell him from me to
enter my service, and that I will give him quite enough daily
employment in his other profession." Then he handed him a
hundred gold crowns of the Camera in a handkerchief, saying,
"Divide them so that he may have his share." Giangiacomo left
the Pope and came and told me exactly all that his Holiness

had said to him. Then he divided the money among the eight of us; and as he gave me my share said, "I am going to inscribe you in the number of our company." To which I answered, "Leave it for to-day; and to-morrow I shall give you the answer." When I left them, I went on my way wondering if I should accept the proposal, knowing how harmful it would be, were I distracted from the great studies of my art. The night following, my father appeared to me in a dream, and with most loving tears, begged me for the love of God and of himself, to consent. In my dream I seemed to answer him that I would have nothing to do with it. Then suddenly I saw him in horrible guise, so that I was terrified, and he said, "If you refuse, your father's curse shall rest upon you. If you consent, you shall ever be blessed of me." Waking up, in sheer fright I ran and had my name put down; and then I wrote to my old father, who, out of his excessive joy, fell into a sickness which brought him to the verge of death. But before long he wrote to me that he, too, had had almost the same dream as myself.

xxiv. Now I had satisfied the modest wish of my dear father, methought all my affairs should advance to an honoured and glorious fulfilment. So I set myself with the greatest energy to finish the vase which I had begun for Salamanca. This bishop was a wonderful man, very rich, but most difficult to satisfy. Every day he sent to see what I had done; and every time his messenger did not find me, Salamanca fell into the greatest fury, swearing that he would take away the work from me and give it to another to finish. And that damnable music was at the root of all the mischief. Still, with the greatest application I kept at the thing by day and by night; and when it reached a point where it might be shown, I took it to the bishop. But this only whetted his desire to see it finished, and I repented having let him get a sight of it. At the end of three months I had completed the thing, having worked on it all the loveliest little animals and leaves and figures you can imagine. Without delay I sent it by the hands of my boy Paolino to that clever man Lucagnolo, of whom I have spoken above. And Paolino, with his infinite grace and beauty, spake thus: "Messer Lucagnolo, Benvenuto, mindful of his promises, sends you this as a sample of his work in your own gross manner, hoping that you have some of his own silly toys to show him in return." When he had made an end, Lucagnolo took the vase in his hands, and looking at it long, he said to Paolino, "My pretty boy, tell your master that he is a very clever man, and that I beg him to be my friend; and let's forget the past." And very gladly did the modest and charming boy bring back the message. When the vase was taken home, Salamanca wished it to be valued. At this valuation Lucagnolo was present, and he estimated it very high, praising it far above my own opinion of it. Then taking it in his hands, Salamanca, in true Spanish fashion, said, "I swear to God that I will put off paying him just as long as he has made me wait for it." Hearing this I was very ill pleased, and cried a murrain upon Spain and whoever wished it well.

Among its other fine ornaments, the vase had a handle all of a piece, and most elaborately contrived, which, by means of a spring, would stand right above the mouth. One day Monsignor, from sheer vanity, was showing the vase to some Spanish gentlemen; and when his back was turned, one of them touched the handle very carelessly, and the delicate spring, which was not made to stand such clumsiness, broke in his hand. Seeing the damage he had done, he begged the butler who had charge of it to take it at once to the master who had made it, that it might be repaired without delay, promising any price that might be asked, if only it could be mended at once. Having got the vase back into my hands, I gave the desired promise, and repaired the thing. It had been brought to me before dinner, and two hours before sundown the messenger came back all of a sweat from having run the whole way, Monsignor having asked for it again to show to some other gentlemen. Indeed, the butler did not let me utter a word with his "Quick, quick! Let's have the vase." Whereupon I determined to take my own time, and not to let it out of my hands. So I said I was in no hurry to give it up. Then the servant got into a terrible fury, and made as if to pull out his sword with one hand, and with the other to force his way into the shop. But this at once I put a stop to with my own weapon, crying fiercely to him the while, "I shall not give it you. Go and tell Monsignor your master that I want the money for my work before it goes out of this shop." The man, seeing nothing was to be gained by bullying, began to beseech me as if he were appealing to the Cross, promising that if only I would give it to him he would see after the payment. But these words turned me not at all from my purpose, and I only repeated what I had said. At last, despairing of the business, he swore he would come with a great band of Spaniards and cut me in pieces. Then off he went running; while I, who thought there might be something in this threat of their assassinating me, determined bravely to defend my life. So I loaded an excellent little fowling-piece which I used for sport, saying to myself, "Who robs me of my goods and my labours may take my life as well." While I was arguing the matter with myself, up came a band of Spaniards headed by their majordomo, who with Spanish insolence ordered them to go in, take away the vase, and give me a good drubbing. Hearing this, I pointed my loaded gun at them, and shouted, "Infidels! Traitors! Do you dare thus attack houses and shops in a great city like Rome? As many of you thieves as come near this door I will shoot dead with this gun!" And taking aim at their leader, and making as if to draw the trigger, I cried, "And you, you thief, who are egging them on, you shall be the first to fall." Whereupon he stuck his spurs into his jennet and made off as hard as he could. All the neighbours rushed out at the noise; and some Roman gentlemen who were passing, cried, "Knock these infidels down! We're on your side." These words were said in such good earnest that the Spaniards took to flight; and they were forced to tell the whole affair to Monsignor. He, being a very haughty man, rated all those servants and officers of his soundly for having gone to such an extreme, and also for not having seen the thing through once they had begun it. Just then the painter who had had to do with the affair came in; and Monsignor bade him go and tell me that, if I did not bring the vase at once, there would not be much left of me after he had finished; but that if I returned it he would pay me promptly. This did not frighten me in the least, and I let him know I should go straight and tell the Pope. However, his wrath and my fear both somewhat passed off; and certain great Roman noblemen gave me their word that the bishop would not injure me. And having the assurance, too, of being paid for my work, I provided myself with a great dagger, put on my coat of mail, and arrived at Monsignor's house. All his household were assembled when I entered, Paolino after me, carrying the silver vase. It was like nothing more or less than passing through the Zodiac—for one was like a lion, another like a scorpion, and another like a crab —till at last we reached the presence of that scoundrelly prelate, who spluttered out all the priestly Spanish rubbish you can imagine. But I never raised my head to look at him, nor answered ever a word, at which his anger seemed to grow. Then telling them to bring me writing materials, he ordered me to write with my own hand that I was well satisfied with his payment of me. At that I raised my head and said right willingly would I do so, when I had seen the colour of his money. The bishop fumed with rage, and insults and abuse rained thick. But in the end I got my money, wrote the acknowledgment, and, pleased and happy, went my way.

xxv. Later, Pope Clement—who had seen the vase before this, though it was not shown him as my work—heard of the affair. He was much pleased with me, and sang my praises loud, saying publicly that he wished me all success. So Monsignor Salamanca was very sorry for having bullied me as he had done; and that we might be friends again, he sent me word by the same painter that he would fain give me a great deal of important work to do. To this I replied that I was quite willing; but should like to be paid in advance. This, too, came to the ears of Pope Clement, and made him laugh heartily. Cardinal Cibo was with him at the time, and the Pope told him the whole story of my dispute with the bishop. Then turning to one of his ministers, he bade him to give me constant employment for the palace. Cardinal Cibo sent for me, and after some pleasant talk, he ordered a vase from me larger than Salamanca's. So did Cardinal Cornaro and many others of the College, especially Ridolfi and Salviati. I had commissions from all of them, so that my earnings were very good. Madonna Porzia, of whom I have already spoken, advised me to open a shop of my own; and this I did. Indeed, I never stopped working for that noble and most worthy gentlewoman, who paid me handsomely, and to whom I probably owed my chance of showing the world I was good for something. I became very friendly with Signor Gabriele Ceserino, Gonfalonier of Rome; and for him I did a great deal of work, amongst other notable things a large gold medal to wear in a hat. The engraved design on it was Leda with her swan. Being much pleased with my work, he said he would like to have it valued so that I might be fairly paid. But the medal had been made with great skill, and the valuers in the trade put a much higher price on it than he had thought it would cost. And so I kept the medal in my own hands, and got nothing at all for my pains. This affair of the medal turned out very like that of Salamanca's vase; but that these matters may not take up space which belongs to more important things, I shall pass them over briefly.

xxvi. Even though I break off a little from the story of my professional career, I must—since I am writing my life—tell shortly something of other matters, though not in minute detail. Well, one St. John's morning I was dining with some of my compatriots of diverse professions—painters, sculptors, and goldsmiths. Among the notable men were Rosso the painter, and Gianfrancesco, a pupil of Raffaello of Urbino. There were others, too. I had assembled them at our meeting-place very informally, and we were all laughing and jesting as men will do when they get together to rejoice on such a great festival. Now there happened to pass the house a feather-brained youth, who was a soldier belonging to the company of Signor Rienzo da Ceri. Hearing our noise he made mock of us, and cast insults on our Florentine nation. Since I was the host of all those distinguished men, it seemed right to take the insults to myself. So quietly, without any one seeing me, I went out and accosted the fellow. He had one of his loose women with him, and he was going on with his ribald jesting to make her laugh. Going up to him, I asked him if it was he had been bold enough to speak ill of the Florentines; and he flashed back, "Yes, I'm the man." Hearing which, I up with my hand and struck him in the face, saying, "Well, and I'm the other man." In a trice each of us had out his sword; but our fight had no sooner begun than people came between us, though most of them took my part rather than his, convinced by what they heard and saw that I was in the right. Next day a challenge from him was brought to me, which I received very gladly, saying this was a thing I could put through much more speedily than anything pertaining to my own business. So without delay I went off to take counsel with a veteran called Bevilacqua, who had the name of being the first swordsman in Italy—for in his time he had fought more than twenty duels, and come out of them all with honour. This worthy man was a great friend of mine. I was known to him as a goldsmith, and, besides, he had been mediator between me and others in certain serious quarrels. So now with right good will he said, "Benvenuto, my friend, if Mars had challenged you, I'm sure you'd come out of the business with honour; for in all the years I have known you, I have never seen you enter a quarrel without right on your side." So he undertook my affair. Then we went armed to the appointed place; but no blood was shed. My enemy sought for peace, and I came out of the thing with great credit. I shall go into no more particulars, for though they would be very interesting of their kind, I shall rather keep my words to speak of my art, which is the thing that has drawn me on to all this scribbling. And about that I have only too much to say.

Although, moved by an honest ambition, I was desirous to do some other work which should be as good as, or even surpass, that of the able man Lucagnolo, yet I never forsook my own delightful jeweller's art; so that between one thing and another a great deal of profit and honour accrued to me, and in both arts I worked constantly, copying no man's designs. In those days there lived in Rome a very clever Perugian, Lautizio by name, who worked only in one branch of art, where he was unique in all the world. Now in Rome every cardinal has a seal, on which is stamped his title. These seals are about the size of a twelve-year-old child's hand; and, as I have just said, the cardinal's title is cut on them along with diverse figure ornaments. For a good seal of the kind a hundred crowns, or even more, would be paid. Now I felt spurred to an honourable rivalry with this man also, though his art was far removed from the goldsmith's business—which, indeed, was the reason why Lautizio knew no other craft save seal-making. So I set myself to practise this one, and although I found it very difficult, yet I never tired of the labour it imposed on me, and gave all my energies to profit and to progress. There was another most excellent and clever man in Rome, who hailed from Milan, Messer Caradosso by name. He worked only at medals chiselled on thin plates and such-like things; paxes, for instance, in half-relief, and various Christs of the length of your palm, made of the thinnest gold plates, and so skilfully worked that I looked on him as the best master in this line I had ever seen, and envied him more than any one else. Then again there were masters who worked at medals cut in steel, which are patterns and absolute guides to whoever would perfect himself in the art of coin-making. And all those diverse crafts I set myself to learn with the greatest eagerness. Then think of the charming art of enamelling, which I never saw better done by any one than by a Florentine called Amerigo, whom I did not know, but whose marvellous works I was well acquainted with. Nowhere have I seen any one who came near him in genius. And to this kind of work I betook myself with energy, though it is exceedingly difficult, having regard to the fire to which the finished works must be subjected, and which often utterly ruins them. But though I found it no easy matter, yet such pleasure did I take in it that its great difficulties were a rest to me. And this sprang from a special gift lent me by the God of Nature, a temperament so healthy and well-proportioned that I could confidently carry out whatever I had made up my mind to do. These arts

I have been speaking of are entirely different from one another, so that a man skilled in one of them rarely attains to equal success in any other, whereas I strove with my whole strength after them equally; and in its own place I shall show that I succeeded.

xxvii. At this time, when I was a young man of twenty-three or thereabouts, so terrible a pestilence broke out that in Rome every day many thousands died of it. Being somewhat afraid, I began to take recreation of a kind to my liking, drawn thereto for a reason which I shall relate. I was in the habit of going on fête days to the ancient monuments, and there making copies, now modelling in wax, and now drawing. As these old places are all in ruins, a great number of pigeons have taken to breed there, and I took it into my head I should like to have a shot at them. So thus, to avoid contact with other people, for I was afraid of the plague, I put my gun on the shoulders of my Paolino, and he and I by ourselves set off for the ruins; and, as it came about, many a time I returned laden with fine fat pigeons. I never liked loading my gun with more than one ball, so that it was by real marksman's skill I brought down so many. My gun I had made myself, and inside and outside it shone like a mirror. With my own hand, too, I made the finest powder, discovering wonderful secrets, which to this day are unknown to any one else. I will not enlarge on the matter, but just give one hint to astonish skilled sportsmen. It is this—that with a charge a fifth of the weight of my ball, it carried two hundred paces point-blank. Now although the great pleasure which I got from sport might seem to have distracted me from my art and my studies—and it really did so—yet in another sense it gave me much more than it took away, for every time I went out shooting, my health was much the better for it, the air putting fresh vigour into me. I am naturally of a melancholy temper, but while I was amusing myself in this way I grew light-hearted, and so I worked the better and with more skill than when I had no distraction from my studies and the exercise of my art. Thus in the end my gun was more of a gain than a loss to me.

Besides, while I was engaged in this amusement, I made the acquaintance of some collectors, who followed in the steps of those Lombard peasants who used to come and dig the vineyards in the due season. In turning up the soil they would find antique medals, agates, chrysoprases, cornelians, cameos, and even precious stones like emeralds, sapphires, diamonds, and rubies. The collectors sometimes got such things from the peasants for trifling sums; and so now and then—indeed frequently—I bought them from the curiosity-hunters for as many golden crowns as they had given giulios. Apart from the considerable gain I drew from the business, tenfold and more, my collection made me welcome amongst not a few of the Roman cardinals. But I shall only mention the most notable and rarest of these treasures. Among many other things there came into my hands a dolphin's head about the size of a big voting-bean. Now though the head was very beautifully fashioned, the material much surpassed the art; for this emerald was of so lovely a colour that he who bought it from me for a score or so of crowns, had it set for a ring and got hundreds for it. Then there was another thing, namely, a head made out of the finest topaz that ever was seen; and here the art was as good as the material. It was about the size of a big hazel-nut, and the carving of the head of Minerva was as exquisite as you can imagine. And then there was still another—a cameo on which was cut Hercules binding the three-headed Cerberus. This was of such extraordinary beauty and artistic skill that our great Michel Agnolo himself said he had never seen so marvellous a thing. Among a great many bronze medals I got hold of one with a head of Jupiter on it. It was larger than any I had ever seen, and the head was fashioned to perfection. On its beautiful reverse were some little figures just as well modelled. I could talk a long time about this, but I will say no more, lest I grow too lengthy.

xxviii. As I have already told, the plague had broken out in Rome. Although I am now about to turn back a little in my story, I shall not be deviating from my plan. There came to Rome a very great surgeon called Maestro Giacomo da Carpi. This clever man, in the course of his other professional duties, took certain desperate cases of the French evil. Now in Rome priests are particularly liable to this disease, especially the richest of them. Well, when this distinguished man became known, he declared he would cure the malady in the most marvellous fashion by means of fumigations. But before beginning a cure he first bargained for his fees, and it was by hundreds and not by tens of crowns that these were reckoned. Now this clever man had a great understanding of the art of design. One day, passing my shop by chance, he saw a collection of drawings I had lying about, among which were some of fantastic little vases I had designed for my own pleasure, entirely different from any that had ever been seen before. Maestro Giacomo wished me to make some for him in silver, and this I did with all the good will in the world, for it fell in with my fancy. Although the distinguished man paid me very well for them, the honour it brought me was a hundred times more; for the best men in the goldsmith's trade said they had never seen anything more beautiful or better executed. No sooner had I finished than he showed them to the Pope; and next day he took his departure. He was very learned, and could speak admirably on the subject of medicine. The Pope wished him to remain in his service; but Carpi said he would not be in the service of any one in the world, and whoever wanted him might come and seek him. A very shrewd person he was, too, and he did wisely in leaving Rome; for not many months after, all those whom he had treated were a hundred times worse than before; and he would have been killed had he stopped. He showed my little vases to many noblemen, amongst others to his Excellency the Duke of Ferrara, telling him how he had got them from a great lord in Rome, to whom he had said, if he would be cured of his malady, he must give him the two vases. The lord had replied that they were antiques, and offered him anything else of a portable size, if he but left him those. Carpi's tale was that he pretended he would not treat him, and then he got his way. This I was told by Messer Alberto Bendedio in Ferrara, who very pompously showed me some terra-cotta copies of them. Whereat I laughed, and as I said nothing, Messer Alberto Bendedio, who was a proud man, flew into a rage and said, "You laugh, eh? But I tell you that for a thousand years back not a man has come into the world who could do as much as copy them." Then I, so as not to do harm to their reputation, kept my mouth shut, but stood looking at them in dumb wonder. Several noblemen in Rome—some of them my friends—said of these works that they had a marvellously antique look; and, emboldened by this appreciation, I confessed I was their maker. They refused to believe it; therefore, in order to retain their credit, I was forced to prove my claim by making the designs for them over again; for my word was not enough, seeing that Maestro Giacomo had shrewdly carried off the old drawings. But I did not come badly out of this little affair.

xxix. Still the plague raged on for many months, but I had kept it at a distance. Many of my comrades had died, yet I remained safe and free from infection. Now it happened one night that one of my intimate acquaintances brought a Bolognese prostitute called Faustina home to supper. She was a very beautiful woman, though she was about thirty years old; and she had with her a little maid of thirteen or fourteen. Now as Faustina was my friend's property, I would not have had any dealings with her for all the gold in the world; and although she said she was much in love with me, I never swerved from my loyalty to my friend. But after they were in bed, I ran off with the little maid, who was as fresh as fresh; and it would have been a bad job for her if her mistress had known. So I spent a much pleasanter night than if I had had the mistress Faustina. Next day when dinner time came near, I was tired and hungry as after a walk of many miles. Then I was seized with a violent headache; swellings rose in my left arm, and I discovered a carbuncle just by my left wrist-bone. Every one in the house was terrified; my friend, the big cow, and the little calf all fled away, and I was left alone with my poor little shop-boy, who refused to leave me. I felt suffocated, and I looked on myself as a dead man. Just then the father of my apprentice passed by, who was Cardinal Jacobacci's household physician. The boy ran out to meet him, crying, "Come, father, and see Benvenuto, who is in bed, and not very well." Not thinking what my illness might be, he came in at once, felt my pulse, and then too clearly saw what he would fain have been blind to. Turning quickly on his son, he cried, "O you faithless boy, you have ruined me! How can I ever again go into the Cardinal's presence?" To which the boy replied, "My master, father, is worth more than all the cardinals in Rome." Then turning to me, the doctor said, "Now that I am here I will treat you. Only of one thing I warn you, that if you have been with a woman, there is no help for you." To this I answered, "I was with one last night." "With what sort of creature?" asked the doctor, "and how long?" "The whole night," I replied, "and with a very young girl." Then seeing he had spoken rashly, he made haste to add, "Since the sores are still fresh and not putrid, and since there has been no delay about the remedy, do not be over-anxious, for I certainly hope to cure you." When he had treated me and gone away, there came in one of my dearest friends, called Giovanni Rigogli, who grieved over my illness, and at my solitary condition. "Depend upon it, Benvenuto, my friend," he said, "I shall never leave you till I see you cured." Then I told him not to come near me, for I was doomed. Only I begged him to be good enough to take a quantity of crown pieces that were in a little box near my bed, and, as soon as God should have taken me from the world, to send them to my poor father. He was to write to him cheerfully how I, too, had succumbed to the common fate of that terrible season. But my dear friend swore he would not be parted from me for anything; and whatever should come to pass, were it good or ill, he knew quite well what it behoved him to do for his friend. So we went on by the help of God; and, thanks to the marvellous remedies which were applied, a great improvement set in, and I came happily out of that terrible illness. While still the wound was open, but stuffed with lint and bandaged, I used to ride about on a little wild horse I had. It had hair four fingers long, was just the size of a young bear—and, indeed, looked very much like one. On it I rode away to find the painter Rosso, who was living outside Rome, towards Città Vecchia, at a place called Cervetera, on the estate of the Count of Anguillara. I found my friend, who was delighted to see me. Whereupon I said to him, "I am come to do to you what you did to me many months ago." At that he burst out laughing, and embracing and kissing me, told me to be quiet for the Count's sake. Thus happily I stopped there about a month, eating and drinking of the best, and made much of by the Count. Every day I went off by myself to the sea-shore, and there dismounting, used to gather curious and beautiful pebbles, shell-fish, and shells. The last day I went there I was attacked by a number of masked men, who had disembarked from a Moorish galley. When they thought they had got me into a corner, whence it did not seem possible for me to escape from their hands, I sprang upon my pony, making up my mind that in the perilous pass I had come to, it was now a choice of being shot or drowned. But, as God willed, my little horse, which was the one I have spoken of above, took an extraordinary leap, and I made off, giving thanks to Heaven. I told the Count all about it, and he went armed in their pursuit; but their galley was already out at sea. Next day I went back to Rome in good health and spirits.

xxx. By this time the plague had almost passed away, and all who survived lived a merry life and made much of each other. From this there sprang up a society of painters, sculptors, and goldsmiths, the best in Rome; and the founder of it was a sculptor, Michel Agnolo. This Michel Agnolo came from Siena. He was a very clever man, one who could bear comparison with any in his profession; but above everything else the pleasantest and most affectionate fellow in the world. He was the eldest in years, but having regard to bodily strength, the youngest of us all. We used to meet at least twice every week without fail. I must not forget to say that to this company belonged Giulio Romano, the painter, and Gianfrancesco, both distinguished pupils of the great Raffaello of Urbino. When we had been meeting over and over again, our great master of the ceremonies suggested that the Sunday following we should all come to supper at his house, and that every one should be obliged to bring with him his "crow"—such was the name Michel Agnolo gave to these ladies. If any man failed to bring one, he should be fined a supper to the whole club. Whoever of us had no traffic with such women of the town, had to provide himself with one, at whatever expense and trouble, that he might not be shamed among all the great artists at the supper. Now I had thought I was very well provided for in a pretty girl called Pantasilea, who was very much in love with me; but I was forced to concede her to one of my best friends called Bachiacca, who had been, and still was, very amorous of her. This gave rise to a slight lover's quarrel, for when she saw that I gave her up to Bachiacca without a word, she thought I held her of very little account. Out of this there grew a very big affair in the course of time, when she wished to revenge herself for the slight I had put upon her; but that I shall recount in its own place. Now as the hour drew near when we were to present ourselves to the worthy assembly, each man with his "crow," I found myself with nobody. I thought it would be ridiculous to fail for so silly a reason, yet I could not make up my mind to take some foul drab under my wing into such a distinguished company. Then I bethought me of a pleasant jest which might add to our amusement. So having made up my mind on the point, I called a young lad of sixteen who lived near me, the son of a Spanish coppersmith. This youth was giving himself to Latin letters, and was very studious. His name was Diego. He was handsome, and had a marvellously beautiful complexion, while the moulding of his head was even more beautiful than that of an antique Antinous; and many a time had I drawn him, and had got much reputation where I had used him as a model. The boy was acquainted with no one, so that he was not known. He dressed in a careless, slovenly fashion, the one thing he loved being his precious studies. Calling him into my house, I begged him to let me deck him out in the women's garments I had got ready. He made no objection, and put on the things at once. By dressing his hair in elegant fashion I much enhanced the beauty of his face, and I put rings in his ears. These rings were split; and only clipped the ears, which had, nevertheless, the look of being pierced. After that I put round his neck a golden necklace, set with beautiful and rich jewels; and I adorned his pretty hands with rings. Then I led him gently by the ear in front of my large mirror; and when the boy saw himself, he called out lustily, "Gracious Heaven! is this Diego?" Whereupon I answered, "Yes, it is Diego, of whom I have never yet asked a favour. Now all I ask of him is that he oblige me in an honest thing—to wit, that in these garments he come to supper with the distinguished company of artists of whom many a time I have spoken to him." The lad, who was modest, honest, and intelligent, lost his confidence of a moment ago, looked on the ground, and remained so some time without speaking a word. Then all at once he lifted his eyes, and said, "With Benvenuto I am ready to go. So now let us set off."

Wrapping up his head in a great kerchief, which in Rome they call a summer cloth, we came to the appointed place, where already everybody else was assembled; and they all gave us greeting. When I took the kerchief from my pretty one's head, Michel Agnolo, who, as I said before, was the drollest and pleasantest man in the world, seized Giulio with one hand and Giovanfrancesco with the other—he was sitting between them—and with all his strength forced them to bow down; while kneeling on the ground himself he begged for mercy, and called to all the company, saying, "Look, look, of such are the angels of Paradise—for though they are called angels (*Angeli*), yet are there some in women's form (*Angiole*)." Then he cried aloud—

> "Angel of goodness, angel fair,
> Save and bless me! Hear my prayer!"

At this my charming creature laughed, and with "her" right hand gave him a papal benediction, saying many pretty things besides. Then rising to his feet, Michel Agnolo said, "We kiss the Pope's feet, but we kiss the angels' cheeks"; and when he suited the action to the word, the youth flushed, and so did his beauty grow the more.

When this had been gone through, the whole room was found to be full of sonnets, which we had all made and sent to Michel Agnolo. The youth began to read them aloud, and as he did so, his wonderful beauty grew beyond telling. Then followed a great deal of talk, which I will not set down here, for it is beside my purpose. Only one jest I must not omit, which was uttered by the great painter Giulio. Looking shrewdly round the room, but letting his eyes rest longer on the ladies than on us, he turned to Michel Agnolo and said, "Michel Agnolo, dear friend, your nickname of 'crow' is very suitable to-day, indeed, they seem even less lovely than crows by the side of one of the loveliest peacocks imaginable."

The viands being prepared, and we about to sit down, Giulio begged us to let him appoint our places at table. This being granted, he took the ladies by the hand, and led each in turn to the inner side of the board, and placed my companion in the middle. Then he arranged all the men on the outside, with me in the centre; for he said I deserved every honour. As a background to the ladies, there was a trellis covered with natural jasmine blossoms at their fairest, so becoming to them all, but especially to mine, that words must fail to tell it. And so we all gave ourselves up to the enjoyment of that rich supper, where every good thing was most abundantly provided. After we had supped, singers accompanied by instruments entertained us with wonderful music, and since they sang and played out of books, my lovely creature requested to sing a part too. Then when "she" performed her rôle almost better than the others, the astonishment was so great that Giulio and Michel Agnolo no longer spoke of her jestingly, as at first, but their words were grave, serious, and full of real admiration.

After the music, a certain Aurelio Ascolano, a marvellous improvisatore, began to speak the praises of the ladies in divine and beautiful fashion, yet while his rhythmic words flowed out, the two ladies who sat by my fair one never stopped chattering. One of them told the story of her own misfortune; and the other asked my charmer how it had happened with her, and who were her friends, and how long she had been at Rome, and much else of the kind. Of course, if I had nothing better to do than to describe all the amusing little incidents that occurred, I could tell of many which arose out of Pantasilea's infatuation for me. But such things being not in my plan, I pass them over briefly. Now the conversation of those horrid women began to annoy my "girl"—to whom, by the way, we had given the name of Pomona; and Pomona, in her effort to escape from their foolish talk, turned now to one side and now to the other. Then the woman whom Giulio had brought asked her if she felt ill. She said yes, and that she believed she was a month or so gone with child, and that she was suffering great pain. The two who sat one on each side of her were at once full of compassion, and, putting their hands on her, found she was a boy. Quickly withdrawing their hands, they got up from the table, flinging words at her as might have befitted a handsome youth. Then cries broke out on all sides, and in the midst of the laughter and the astonishment, Michel Agnolo asked leave of all to impose on me a penance of his own fashioning. This granted, he hoisted me up, amid the loud cries of the guests, calling out, "Viva il signore! Viva il signore!" And this, said he, was the penance I merited, for having played them so fine a trick. Thus ended that very merry supper and that pleasant day; and we all went home.

xxxi. If I were to describe minutely the kind and the number of works which I made for all sorts of people, my story would be too long. All I need say is, that I strove with every effort and diligence to attain skill in all the various arts of which I have already spoken. At this time I was practising the whole of them side by side. I have not yet found an opportunity of telling of the most important things I was engaged on, but I shall wait for a more fitting place, which will soon come. Michel Agnolo, the Sienese sculptor, was now at work on the tomb of the dead Pope Adrian. The painter Giulio Romano left us for the service of the Marquis of Mantua. The other comrades were scattered, one here, one there, on business of their own; so that the company of artists I have spoken of was almost entirely dispersed.

About this time there came into my hands some little Turkish daggers. Their handles as well as their blades were of steel; and even the sheaths were of the same material. On them were chased, with iron gravers, groups of delightful foliage in the Turkish manner, and the spaces were filled in with gilt. I was seized with a great desire to prove myself in a kind of art so different from the others I had tried; and finding that I succeeded admirably, I made several things of the kind. Mine were far finer and more lasting than the Turkish ones, for several reasons. In the first place, with my graver I cut much deeper and with a wider scoop than is ever seen in Turkish work. Then, again, the Turkish designs are only the leaves of the Egyptian bean, mingled with sun-flowers; and though these have a certain grace of their own, one gets tired of them sooner than of our arabesques. Of course, in Italy we design foliage in many different fashions. The Lombards have a charming way of arranging ivy and bryony in their patterns with the loveliest turns and twists, which give delight to the eye. Then the

Tuscans and the Romans make even a better choice, counter-feiting the leaves of the acanthus, called bear's foot, with its stems and flowers winding variously about; and amongst the foliage may be fittingly set divers little figures of birds or animals, which display the designer's fancy. Some of their patterns they find in nature, among wild flowers—those called snap-dragons, for instance, and these are not the only ones which clever artists work in along with their other pretty fantasies. Such things are called by the ignorant "grotesques." They have got this name in modern times from having been found by antiquaries in certain underground caves in Rome, these caves having been in ancient times chambers, bath-houses, studies, halls, and such like. The antiquaries finding them in those cavernous places—for while the ground has been raised in the course of time, these chambers have remained below, and in Rome are called grottos—hence has sprung the term "grotesques." But this is not their right name. The ancients delighted in drawing creatures, for the different parts of which they took hints from goats and cows and horses, and they called these curious mixtures by the name of monsters; so do our craftsmen compose from their medley of leaves another sort of monster. Therefore, monsters, not grotesques, is their real name. And when I designed foliage after this fashion, my work was much finer than the Turkish.

Now about this time I came across some vases, or little antique urns, filled with ashes. Among the ashes I found iron rings worked in gold by the ancients, in each of which was set a little shell. I inquired of scholars, who said these rings were worn by such as did greatly desire to remain with minds un-moved in the midst of any extraordinary occurrence, whether it brought them good or evil. At the request of some gentle-men, who were great friends of mine, I therefore set about making some of those little rings. But I made mine of fine tempered steel, and when they were delicately chased and inlaid with gold, they were very beautiful objects; and for making one of them I sometimes got more than forty crowns.

In those days little gold medals were much in fashion, and noblemen and men of rank had some emblem of their own devising engraved on these, and they wore them in their caps. I made a great many, and it was no easy task. Now Caradosso, the very clever artist of whom I have already spoken, did this kind of work; and as his designs contained more than one figure, he would not sell them for less than a hundred gold crowns apiece. So I was preferred to him by certain gentlemen, yet not so much on account of his high prices as because he was a slow worker. For these customers I made, amongst other things, a medal in competition with this great artist. There were four figures in it, over which I took a great deal of trouble. Now as it fell out, when these nobles and gentlemen put mine alongside that of the famous Caradosso, they declared it to be much better made and more beautiful, and said I might ask whatever I liked for my trouble—for as I had given them full satisfaction, they wished to do no less for me. Whereupon I said the best reward of my labours, and the one I most desired, was to have equalled the work of so accomplished a man, and that if their honours were of this opinion I held myself to be handsomely paid. And thus I took my leave. Without delay they sent after me so liberal a present that I was content; and so strong a desire to do well grew within me that it was the starting-point of what will be heard of by and by.

xxxii. Now must I diverge a little from the story of my profession, having a mind to tell of certain unfortunate occurrences which have happened in my toilsome life. I have already spoken of that company of artists and of the amusing incidents brought about by my connection with the lady Pantasilea, who bore me that false and burdensome love. She was terribly angry with me for that jest of mine—I mean when Diego the Spaniard came to the supper-party I have spoken of—and she had sworn to have her revenge. Now, as I am going to relate, an opportunity for the same in due course arose, which put my life in the greatest danger. Here I must tell that a young man called Luigi Pulci came to Rome about this time. He was the son of the Pulci who was beheaded for incest with his daughter. Now this young man had a marvellous poetic talent, with a knowledge of good Latin letters, and he wrote well. In person he was extraordinarily handsome and graceful; he had left the service of I do not know which bishop, and was stricken with the French evil. When he was a boy in Florence, it was the custom on summer nights to assemble in certain places out of doors; and on such occasions he would sing with the best of the *improvisatori*. His voice was so beautiful that the divine Michel Agnolo Buonarroti, prince of sculptors and painters, would go and hear him with the greatest eagerness and pleasure whenever he knew where he could be found. And a certain man called Piloto, a very clever goldsmith, and myself used to go along with him. It was so I had got acquainted with Luigi

Pulci. That had been years ago, and now in a wretched condition he came to Rome, found me out, and begged me to help him for the love of God. Moved by compassion, partly on account of his great talents, partly for love of my native place, and also because by nature I am tender-hearted, I took him into my house, and had him treated by a physician. As he was still young, he soon recovered. But while he was seeking his health he studied continually, and I helped him to procure as many books as I could. So Luigi, aware of the great benefits he was receiving from me, thanked me over and over again, by words and by tears, saying that if God ever put the chance in his way, he would recompense me for all I had done for him. I answered that I had done not what I should have wished, but what I could; and that it was the duty of human creatures to help one another. Only, I reminded him that the kindness I had done to him he should return to whosoever might need his help as much as he had needed mine; likewise, that he should treat me as a friend, for I was indeed his.

Very soon this young man began to haunt the Court of Rome, where he soon found a place for himself; and ere long he entered into an arrangement with a bishop of eighty years of age, who was called Gurgensis. This bishop had a nephew called Messer Giovanni, a Venetian gentleman. Now Messer Giovanni seemed to be much enamoured of Luigi Pulci's talents, and these were a pretext for his making the young man as much at home in the household as he was himself. Luigi having spoken of me, and of his great obligations to me, Messer Giovanni wished to make my acquaintance. So one evening when I was giving a little supper to Pantasilea, just as we were going to sit down to table, Messer Giovanni came in along with Luigi Pulci, and after some formalities, stayed to eat with us. As soon as the brazen-faced whore set eyes on the fair youth, she had her designs on him. Seeing this, as soon as our pleasant supper was over, I called Luigi aside and told him that for the sake of the kindness he owned I had done him, he must never seek the company of that prostitute. His reply was, "Alas, my friend Benvenuto, do you take me then for a madman?" "Not for a madman, but for a young man," I answered; "and I swear to you by God that I have no thought of her at all, but I should be very sorry if through her you broke your neck." Whereupon he swore and called God to witness that if ever he spoke to her he might break his neck upon the spot. The poor young fellow must have sworn this oath to God with all his heart, for he did, indeed, break his neck, as shall soon be told. Messer Giovanni, it could be seen, loved him in an unnatural fashion. Every day we saw the youth with new suits of velvet and silk, and perceived he was all given up to evil ways and was neglecting his wonderful talents. He pretended not to see me, nor to know me; for I had reproached him with giving himself over as a prey to hideous vices, which would be the death of him one day, as I had said.

xxxiii. Now his friend Messer Giovanni bought a very fine black horse for him, for which he paid a hundred and fifty crowns. The horse was admirably trained, and Luigi went caracolling round on it, paying his attentions to the prostitute Pantasilea. I was aware of what was going on, but gave no heed, saying to myself that a man must do what he must; and I bent all my mind to my studies. Now it happened that one Sunday evening we were invited to supper with Michel Agnolo, the Sienese sculptor; and it was summer-time. To this supper came Bachiacca, of whom I have already spoken, and he brought with him Pantasilea, his first love. At table she was seated between me and Bachiacca. But just in the middle of supper she got up, saying she wished to retire, for she was in pain, but that she would soon return. In the meanwhile we went on pleasantly talking and supping, and she stopped away a long time. Now it happened that being on the alert, I felt sure I heard something like muffled laughter in the street. I had the knife in my hand which I had been using at table. The window was so near that by stretching a little I could see Luigi Pulci outside with Pantasilea, and I heard Luigi saying, "Oh, if that devil of a Benvenuto could only see, it would be the worse for us!" And she answered, "No fear. Listen to the noise they are making. They are thinking of anything rather than us." At this point I—who knew perfectly who they were—threw myself down from the window, and seized Luigi by the cloak. With the knife in my hand I had certainly slain him, had he not spurred the white horse he was riding and left his cloak in my hands, to escape with his life. Pantasilea ran for refuge to a neighbouring church. The rest, who had been sitting at table, now sprang up, and all came down to me, begging me not to disturb myself or them for so worthless a trollop. To which I answered that for her I cared not a rap, but it was that rascally youth, who flaunted his contempt for me, I was bent on punishing. So I refused to yield to the persuasions of those artist friends of mine, and with my sword in my hand I went away by myself towards Prati, for the house where we had been supping was near to the Castello gate, which led there. As I was making my way along slowly in this direction the sun went down ere long, and as I re-entered Rome it was already night and murky, but the gates were not yet locked.

About two hours after sundown I came on the house of Pantasilea, intending, if so be that Luigi Pulci was there, to make myself very unpleasant to them both. But when my eyes and ears gave evidence there was nobody in the house save a little slut of a servant-maid called Canida, I went off to stow away my cloak and the scabbard of my sword. Then I returned to the house, which was on the Tiber, behind the Banchi. Opposite the house was the garden of an inn-keeper called Romolo. The garden was shut in by a thick thorn hedge, in which I stood in hiding, waiting till the lady should come home with Luigi. When I had been there some time I was joined by my friend Bachiacca, who had perhaps guessed I might be found there, or, it may be, had been directed thither. Whispering to me "Gossip!"—for so we called each other in jest—"I entreat you for the love of God"—and he was almost weeping as he spoke—"I beseech you, dear gossip, do no hurt to that poor little thing, for she is not a whit to blame." To which I replied, "If you do not get out of this at once when I tell you, I'll hit you on the head with my sword!" My poor gossip got such a turn that he was taken ill and was forced to go and relieve himself. It was a starry night and of wonderful radiance. Suddenly I heard the hoofs of many horses, and from this side and that they came up. It was Luigi and Pantasilea, accompanied by a certain Messer Benvegnato from Perugia, Chamberlain of Pope Clement. In their train came four doughty Perugian captains with other gallant young soldiers. In all there were more than a dozen men-at-arms. When I perceived this, and bethought myself I did not know how to escape, I made up my mind to stick in the hedge. But the sharp thorns hurt me, and, goaded like a bull, I determined to jump out and make off, when at that very moment Luigi, who had his arm round Pantasilea's neck, said, "Once more I must kiss you just to spite that traitor Benvenuto." Then, pricked by the thorns and stung by the young man's words, I sprang out, raised my sword, and shouted, "You be all dead men!" My sword fell heavy on Luigi's shoulder, but his satyr-like friends had lined his doublet with coats of mail and such-like things. Yet I had struck fiercely, and the sword, swerving, came down on Pantasilea's nose and mouth. Both Luigi and she fell to the ground, and Bachiacca, still unbraced, screamed and ran away. Hotly I turned to the others with my sword, and the gallant men, hearing a great commotion in the inn, thought an army of a hundred strong was coming up. They had bravely put their hands to their swords, but a couple of horses, which had got frightened, threw them into disorder. Two of the best riders were thrown, and the rest took to flight. When I saw things were turning out well for me, with hasty step, but with honour, I withdrew from the field, not wishing to tempt fortune more than was necessary. In this extraordinary confusion some of the soldiers and captains were wounded with their own swords, and Messer Benvegnato, the Pope's Chamberlain, was bruised and trampled by his mule. One of his servants, too, who had drawn his sword, fell at the same time as his master, and wounded him sorely in the hand. In his pain Benvegnato swore worse than the rest, crying out in his Perugian accent, "By God, I'll see that Benvegnato gives Benvenuto a lesson!" And he ordered one of his captains—perhaps a braver fellow than the others, but a youth, and so with less sense—to go in search of me. This young fellow came to seek me out in the place to which I had retired, namely, the house of a great Neapolitan noble, who, knowing something of my attainments in my profession and the soldier-like disposition of my mind and body —which was the thing he felt most interest in—had taken a great fancy to me. Now, seeing my good reception and feeling myself quite at home, I gave such an answer to the captain that I think he much repented having come to brave me. After some days, the wounds of Luigi and his prostitute and the rest being nearly healed, this great Neapolitan gentleman was approached by Messer Benvegnato—whose anger had all passed away—that he might induce me to make peace with young Luigi and the brave soldiers, who had no ill-will against me, and, indeed, wished to make my acquaintance. Accordingly my host promised them all that he would bring me to whatever meeting-place they wished, and that he would willingly use his influence with me to make up the quarrel. But he insisted that there should be no throwing about of words on either side, for it would be too undignified. It was enough merely to go through the forms of drinking together and embracing; and he would be the spokesman, and would do all he could to serve them. And so it fell out. One Thursday evening this gentleman took me to the house of Messer Benvegnato, where were gathered all the soldiers who had been routed in the scuffle. They were sitting at table. My friend had in his train more than thirty gallant men, all well armed, which Benvegnato did not expect. When we entered the hall, my host first, and I after him, he said, "God save you, gentlemen! Benvenuto, who is to me as my own brother, is come with me here to do right willingly whatever you propose." Messer Benvegnato, at the sight of so many persons filing into the hall, replied, "We seek peace and nothing else." He promised, therefore, that I should have no annoyance from the governor of Rome and his minions. Then we made peace, and afterwards I went back to my shop, where I never could be for an hour without that Neapolitan coming to see me or sending for me.

In the meanwhile Luigi Pulci had recovered, and every day he was to be seen riding about on his well-trained black horse. One day, though it was raining, he was showing off his horsemanship just near Pantasilea's gate, when he slipped and fell, with the animal on the top of him, and fractured his right thigh. He died a few days after in Pantasilea's house; and in this way was fulfilled the vow he had sworn so earnestly to God. Thus it is seen that God keeps count of the good and the bad, and to each man gives his deserts.

xxxiv. At this moment the whole world was in arms. Pope Clement had sent to Giovanni de' Medici to ask for troops. But when they came to Rome, they were so unruly that it was not safe to be in public shops. This was the reason why I retired to a pretty little house behind the Banks, where I worked for all the friends I had made. My works, however, about this time were not of great importance, so I do not mean to speak of them. Just then I took great delight in music and similar pastimes.

Pope Clement, by the advice of Messer Jacopo Salviati, disbanded the five companies sent him by my lord Giovanni, who had died in Lombardy. Therefore, Bourbon, knowing that Rome was unprotected, forced on his army with all speed to our gates. Then all Rome rushed to arms. Now I was a great friend of Alessandro, son of Piero del Bene. Indeed, when the Colonnesi had attacked Rome, he had asked me to guard his house. So now, on this more important occasion, he begged me to enlist fifty men as a guard for his palace, and I was to be at the head of them, as in the Colonnesi affair. So I collected fifty right gallant young fellows, and we took possession of his house, and were well paid and well entertained. When Bourbon's army appeared before the walls of Rome, Alessandro del Bene wished

C 5¹

to go and see them, and begged me to accompany him. So with one of the best of my men we set out; and on the way a young man called Cecchino della Casa joined us. When were reached the walls near the Campo Santo, we caught sight of that wonderful army, now doing its very utmost to force an entrance. Just where we were posted on the walls many young fellows were lying dead, killed by the enemy's fire. The fight was at its hottest here, and the smoke as thick as you can imagine. Turning to Alessandro, I said, "Let us get home as quick as we can, for here it is hopeless. Look! they come up, and our men flee." Then Alessandro, desperately frightened, replied, "Would to God we had never come!" And with that he turned in the maddest terror to escape. But I checked him, saying, "Since you have brought me here, I must play the man"; and aiming my arquebuse where I saw the enemy was thickest, I fired at one I saw raised above the others. The cloud prevented me seeing whether he was on horseback or on foot. Turning hastily to Alessandro and Cecchino, I ordered them to discharge their guns, and showed them how to escape a return shot from the enemy outside. When we had each fired twice, I crept stealthily up to the wall, and saw an extraordinary tumult among the enemy, for one of our shots had knocked down Bourbon. And, so far as I could hear afterwards, he it was whom I had seen raised above the others. Leaving this place, we went through the Campo Santo, and entered by St. Peter's. Then we came out just at the Church of Sant' Agnolo, and reached the great gate of the castle with much difficulty; for Rienzo da Ceri and Orazio Baglioni were attacking and slaughtering all those who had left their places on the walls. Reaching this gate, we found some of the enemy had entered Rome, and they were at our heels. As the castellan wished to let the portcullis fall, he had to clear the way somewhat, and so we four got inside. No sooner had I entered than the captain, Pallone de' Medici, took possession of me as a member of the castle household, and thus forced me to leave Alessandro, which I did much against my will. While I was going up to the donjon, Pope Clement had entered by the corridors. He had been unwilling to leave the palace of St. Peter before this, never imagining that the enemy would make their way into the city. Now, having got inside in the way I have described, I took up my post near some big guns, which were under the charge of a bombardier called Giuliano the Florentine. This Giuliano, hanging over the battlements of the castle, saw his poor house being sacked and his wife and

children outraged; so, lest he should massacre his own kith and
kin, he did not dare discharge his guns, but threw his fuse upon
the ground, and wailed aloud, and tore his face. And other
bombardiers were doing the same. Therefore I seized one of
the fuses, and, with the help of some who were calmer in their
minds, pointed some swivels and falconets where I saw a chance,
slaughtering therewith a great many of the enemy. But for this,
those that came into Rome that morning, marching straight
to the castle, might have made an easy entry, for the artillery
were doing nothing to stop them. I kept up the fire, for which
several cardinals and noblemen blessed me, giving me the
greatest encouragement. Of course, in my impetuous mood I
was trying to do the impossible; enough that it was through me
the castle was saved that morning, and that the other bombardiers came back to their duty. So I toiled on through all
that day. When evening had come, while the army was entering
Rome by the Trastevere, Pope Clement appointed a great
Roman nobleman, Messer Antonio Santa Croce by name, head
of all the gunners. This great lord came up to me at once, made
much of me, and stationed me with five splendid pieces of
artillery in the most exposed part of the castle, which is called
the Angel. This place goes all round the keep, and looks over
both Prati and Rome. Then he gave me a company of men to
help me in the management of the guns, handed me an instalment of my pay, consigned me bread and a little wine, and
entreated me to go on as I had begun. There have been times
when I have been more inclined to the profession of arms than
to the one of my choice, and with such goodwill did I give
myself to it now, that I did better in it than in my own art.
When night came on and the enemy were in Rome, we who
were in the castle—but especially myself, who have always
delighted in new experiences—stayed looking on at the extraordinary scene and the conflagration, which only those who were
with us could have any clear idea of. Yet I will not set myself
to describe the event, but will go on with the tale of my own
life which I have begun, and of such things as appertain to it.

xxxv. Continuing, as I did, my artillery practice for the whole
month when we were besieged in the castle, I had a great many
wonderful adventures the while, all worthy of being recounted.
But as I do not wish to be too lengthy, nor to diverge over-
much from the tale of my profession, I shall leave the greater
part of them untold, only mentioning those I am forced to,
which will be few in number, but the most remarkable. And

here is the first. Messer Santa Croce ordered me down from the Angel that I might fire on certain houses near the castle, where some of our enemies had been seen to enter. While I was firing, one of their cannons marked me; but as it struck a corner of a battlement and took away some of the stone, it did not do me much harm. The mass of stone, however, struck me in the chest, and, all breathless, I lay prone on the ground as one dead. Yet I could hear all that the bystanders were saying. Among them was Messer Antonio Santa Croce lamenting loud, "Alas! for we have lost our best helper." Hearing the noise, a certain companion of mine ran up. He was Gianfrancesco the fifer, but he had greater talents for medicine than for music. Bursting into tears at the sight of me, he ran for a flask of excellent Greek wine. Then he made a tile red-hot, sprinkled on it a good handful of wormwood, and then poured the Greek wine over it. When the wormwood was well soaked, he put it at once on my chest, where the mark of the blow was plainly to be seen. And such was the virtue of the thing that my wandering senses came back to me at once. But when I would fain have spoken I could not, for some foolish soldiers had filled my mouth with earth. To give me the sacrament had been their thought, but it was liker excommunication; and I could scarce regain my senses, for the earth was more harmful than the blow I had received. But that danger passed, I turned once again to the fury of the guns, keeping up the firing with the force and energy of my whole being.

Now Pope Clement had sent for help to the Duke of Urbino, who was with the Venetian army. By his ambassador he sent a message to his Excellency, to wit, that while the castle of an evening showed three fires upon its topmost point, and fired thrice a triple discharge from its guns, it should be for a sign it had not surrendered. It was I who had charge of lighting the beacons and firing the guns, and by day I directed our fire wherever it could do mischief. So for these reasons the Pope's opinion of me grew still higher, for he saw I performed my business with all the foresight it demanded. The Duke never came to our help. But I'm not here to explain that, and I'll say no more.

xxxvi. While I was up here at my devilish business, several of the cardinals who were in the castle came to see me, in especial the Cardinal Ravenna, and the Cardinal de' Gaddi. Many a time I told them not to expose themselves, for those red caps of theirs were marks for the enemy. Indeed, from neighbouring palaces, such as the Torre de' Bini, both they and I ran the greatest danger; so that at last I had them locked up, and gained only their ill-will thereby. Then, too, I often had visits from Orazio Baglioni, who was very friendly with me. One day when we were talking together he noticed something going on in a certain tavern outside the Porta di Castello, at a place called Baccanello. This tavern had for its sign a sun painted red, which hung between two windows. The windows were shut, but Signor Orazio guessed that between them, on the inner side of the wall, some soldiers were sitting drinking. So he said to me, "If you could hit the wall, a cubit's length from that sun, with your smaller cannon I think you would do a good stroke of business. For from the noise I hear I judge them to be men of great importance." To which I answered that I could easily hit the sun through its centre, but a barrel of stones was standing near the mouth of the gun, and it might be knocked down by the firing and the shock. But he replied, "Don't waste time, Benvenuto, for, in the first place, it is not possible that, being where it is, the blast from the gun should knock it down; and, secondly, even if the Pope were down there, there would be less harm done than you think. So, fire away!" Then without another thought I hit the middle of the sun, just as I had said I should do. But, as I had foreseen, the barrel toppled, fell exactly between Cardinal Farnese and Messer Jacopo Salviati, and would to a certainty have flattened them both, had not the Cardinal at that moment been railing at Messer Jacopo for causing the sack of Rome, and so, stepping aside to call each other names, they escaped being crushed by my barrel. Hearing the loud noise which this made in the court below, good Signor Orazio hastened down; and I, stretching over at the point where the barrel had fallen, heard some people say they would like to make an end of that bombardier. Whereupon I placed two falconets in front of the staircase, and resolved to fire on the first man who should come up. Now certain servants of Cardinal Farnese must have been sent to do me a mischief. So I faced the staircase with the lighted fuse in my hand, and cried to some of those on the stairs whose faces I knew, "Oh, you idle beggars, if you don't get out of this, if but one of you dare came up these steps, I have two falconets ready to blow you to atoms! So go and tell the Cardinal and his friends that I only did my superior's bidding; and what was done, and what is being done, is in defence of their priests, and not to do harm to them." Off they went, and then came Signor Orazio Baglioni running. Him, too, I ordered to stand back, else I'd be the death of him, I said; for I knew very well who he was. He hesitated a bit, and I could see he feared me somewhat, and then rejoined, "Benvenuto, I am your friend." To which I responded, "Come up, my lord, if so be you come alone." Now this signor, who was a very haughty man, stopped short for a moment, and then burst out angrily, "I've a good mind not to come a step farther, and to do just the contrary of what I had intended for you." To this I answered, that just as I had been stationed there for the defence of others, I should be quite as well able to take care of myself. Then he said that he was coming up alone. When he had mounted I saw his look had changed to me more than there seemed cause for. So I put my hand on my sword and stood there grimly facing him, whereupon he began to laugh; the pallor of rage passed away, and he said to me pleasantly, "Benvenuto, my friend, I could not love you better than I do, and when God pleases I will prove it to you. Would to God you had killed those two rascals! One of them is at the bottom of the mischief, as we know, and the other may yet be the cause of worse." Then he told me that, if I were asked, I must not tell he was with me when I fired the gun. And as for the rest, I was to have no fear. The confusion was tremendous, and we did not hear the end of it for a long time. But I will not discourse longer on the matter; enough that I had very nearly revenged my father on Messer Jacopo Salviati, who, as he used to lament, had done him a thousand wrongs. At any rate, though unintentionally, I had given him a great scare. Of Farnese I will say no more at present. But it shall be told in its own place how much better it would have been for me had I killed him.

xxxvii. Thus I went on looking after my guns, every day being marked by some notable feats of mine, so that I acquired boundless credit and favour in the eyes of the Pope. Never a day passed but I killed some of the besiegers. Once when the Pope was walking round the keep, he saw a Spanish colonel in the Prati, whom by certain signs he recognised; for the man had once been in his service. While he watched he talked about him. I, who was alone in the Angel, and knew nothing of what was going on, nevertheless saw a man occupied about the trenches. He had a little javelin in his hand, and his dress was all of rose colour. Bethinking myself what I could do against him, I took one of the gerfalcons which I had there, a piece bigger and longer than a sacro, and very like a small culverin.

First I emptied it, and then loaded it with a good quantity of fine powder mixed with coarse. Then I aimed well at the red man, raising the muzzle tremendously, for he was far away, and guns of this sort cannot be expected to carry with precision at that range. When I fired, I aimed exactly at the red man's middle. He had slung his sword in front in arrogant Spanish fashion, and my ball hitting his blade, the man fell cut in two. The Pope, who was looking for nothing of the kind, was greatly pleased and astonished, for it seemed impossible to him a gun should have so long a range; nor could he understand how the man should have been cut in half. Sending for me, he asked me to explain. So I told him what ingenuity I had used; but as for cutting the man in two, it was a thing neither of us could get at the bottom of. Then, kneeling down, I begged him to remove from me the curse of this homicide and of others I had committed in that castle in the service of the Church. Whereupon the Pope, raising his hands, made the sign of the cross broadly over my face, gave me his blessing and his pardon for all the homicides I had committed, or ever should commit, in the service of the Church Apostolic. So I left him, and once on the tower again I went on firing without stop, and hardly ever was shot of mine in vain. My drawing, my fine studies, and my skill in music were all drowned in the roar of those guns; and were I to tell minutely all the fine things which I did in that infernally cruel business, I should strike the world with wonder. But not to be too lengthy, I shall pass them all over, save just a few of the most notable which I am forced to tell. So here, I kept thinking day and night how best I could do my part in the defence of the Church. Now I knew that when the enemy changed guard, they passed through the big gate of Santo Spirito, which was within a moderate range. So I began to fire in that direction. But as I had to fire obliquely, I did not do all the mischief I should have liked, though every day my slaughter was considerable. Then the enemy, seeing their passage hindered, one night piled up more than thirty barrels on the crest of a roof, thus blocking up my view. Considering the matter rather more carefully than I had done before, I turned all my five pieces of artillery right on the barrels, and waited till two hours before sunset, when the guard would be changed. Now, thinking themselves secure, they came along more slowly and in denser mass than had been their wont; so, when I fired, I not only knocked down the barrels in my way, but killed more than thirty men in that one blast. This

I repeated twice again, and threw the soldiers into great disorder; and the incident, joined to the fact that they had stuffed themselves with loot from the great sack, and were longing to enjoy the fruits of their labours, was the cause of their threatening to revolt and to desert. They were restrained, however, by their valorous captain, Gian di Urbino. To their great inconvenience, they were forced henceforth to take another passage when changing guard, a roundabout way of three miles, instead of only half a mile as before. This business being successfully carried through, all the gentlemen in the castle showered favours on me. Inasmuch as it had important consequences, I have wished to relate this event and have done with it; for such things do not belong to the tale of my own art, which is the reason of my writing. If I cared to adorn my story with such things, too much would remain to tell. There is, however, just one more adventure I must relate, and this seems the place to do so.

xxxviii. I am now making a great leap forward when I tell how Pope Clement, desiring to save the tiaras and all the mass of jewels belonging to the Apostolic Camera, ordered me to come before him. Then he shut himself up in a room with only Cavalierino and me. This Cavalierino had been a stableman in the service of Filippo Strozzi, and was a Frenchman of the lowest birth. But being an excellent servant, Pope Clement had showered riches on him, and trusted him as he trusted himself. Now when the Pope, Cavalierino, and I were shut up in this room, the tiaras and all the jewels of the Apostolic Camera were placed before me, and his Holiness ordered me to take them out of their gold settings. This I did, and then rolled each up in a little bit of paper, and we sewed them into the linings of the clothes which the Pope and Cavalierino wore. Then they handed all the gold over to me, telling me to melt it as secretly as I could. So I went up to the Angel, where my own room was, which I could lock, and where I might be free from disturbance. There I made myself a little furnace of brick, and put into the bottom of it a fair-sized ash-pot shaped like a plate. Then I threw the gold on the top of the coals, and little by little it melted and fell down into the pot. Yet all the while this furnace was working, I was watching for chances of doing hurt to our enemies; and as they were about a stone's-throw from us in the trenches below, I fired some rubbish at them from the piles of old ammunition belonging to the castle. Taking a swivel and a falconet, both rather damaged at the muzzle,

I loaded them with this useless stuff, and when I fired, it went down with headlong fury, and did much unlooked-for damage in the trenches. So I kept on merrily at this work while I was melting the gold. Then a little before vespers I saw some one coming along the edge of the trench riding on a mule. The mule was going very quickly, and the rider was speaking to those in the trenches. Before he came opposite me I had been prudent enough to get ready my guns, and thus I fired just at the right moment. One stone hit him in the face. The rest struck the mule, which fell dead. Then arose a great tumult in the trench, and I fired my other piece, and dealt destruction. It was the Prince of Orange I had wounded, and now he was borne through the trenches to a tavern in the neighbourhood; and thither ran in great haste all the great men in the army. Pope Clement, hearing what I had done, sent for me at once. He asked me how it happened, and I told him all. Moreover, I said the fallen man must be a person of the utmost importance, since, so far as could be seen, all the chiefs of the army had run at once to the tavern where they had carried him. Then the Pope, who was a quick-brained man, sent for Messer Antonio Santa Croce, the head of the gunners, as I have said, and bade him order all his bombardiers to direct their guns, which were very numerous, on that house, the firing of an arquebuse to be the signal. Thus the chiefs being slaughtered, he hoped the army, already demoralised, would all fall to pieces. Perhaps, he said, God had heard the prayers they had sent up continually, and in this way was going to free them from these impious rascals. So we got our guns ready, in obedience to the command of Santa Croce, and were waiting for the signal, when Cardinal Orsino heard of the thing, and began to revile the Pope. On no account should such a thing be done, said he; for they were on the point of concluding peace; and if the chiefs were slain, the army, left to itself, would take the castle, and utter ruin would be the result. So they refused to allow the order to be carried out. The poor Pope, in despair, seeing himself fatally menaced from within and without, said he would leave the plans to them. Thus the order to us was countermanded; but I, who could not hold myself in, when I realised they were coming to prevent us firing, discharged one of my small cannons, and the ball struck a pillar in the courtyard of the house where I had seen so many people gathered. This shot dealt such destruction to the enemy, that they were almost for abandoning the house. Cardinal Orsino would have had me hanged or shot without mercy; but the Pope hotly defended me. As for the angry words that passed on the occasion, though I know what they were, I have no intention of telling them. For the writing of history is not my business. I shall only attend to my own affairs.

xxxix. As soon as I had melted the gold, I took it to the Pope, who thanked me much for what I had done, and ordered Cavalierino to pay me twenty-five crowns, excusing himself that he had no more to give me. A few days after peace was made, I set off with Signor Orazio Baglioni and a company of three hundred men towards Perugia; and there Orazio would have consigned to me the company; but I did not wish for it then, and told him I was going to see my father first, and redeem the ban which was on me still in Florence. Then he told me he was made Captain of the Florentines; and here, too, was Ser Pier Maria di Lotto, the Florentine envoy, to whom Orazio heartily recommended me as his man.

And so I came to Florence with several other companions. There the plague was raging furiously. On my arrival I found my dear father, who had been thinking I had died in the sack, or that I should return to him naked and despoiled. But it was just the contrary, as he discovered. Here I was, alive, with my pockets full of money, with a servant and a good mount. So great was the joy with which I saw my father that, when he embraced and kissed me, I certainly thought I should have died on the spot. I told him the whole infernal history of the sack, and filled his hands with crowns, which I had gained in my military service, and we embraced each other over and over again. Then off he went to the Eight to redeem the ban on me. Now, as chance would have it, there still belonged to the Council one of those who had passed the sentence on me; indeed, the very man who had harshly told my father that he would send me into the country with the lances. So now my father had his revenge in some significant words, which were backed by his knowledge of the favour shown me by Orazio Baglioni.

Things were at this point when I told my father how Signor Orazio had made me captain; and that I must be thinking of gathering my company. At these words the poor old man was terribly disturbed; and he begged me, for the love of God, to undertake no such enterprise, though he was certain I was fit for it, and even for a greater. Then he added that his other son, my brother, was a mighty man of war, and my duty was to give myself up to that wonderful art at which, for so many years, I had laboured so earnestly. Though I promised to obey him, he was too shrewd not to know that if Signor Orazio came I could not but continue my military career. I had given my promise, and there were other reasons as well. So, bethinking himself of the best means of getting me out of Florence, he said to me, "Oh, my dear son, here the plague is terrible; and I am always imagining you coming home with it on you. Now, I remember when I was a young man, that I went away to Mantua, where I was made much of, and there I stayed several years. Therefore, I beg, nay, I command you, by your love for me, to leave this and go thither—and let it be rather to-day than to-morrow."

xl. Now, it has always been my delight to see the world; and as I had never been at Mantua, I went off willingly. The greater part of the money I had brought home I left with my dear father, promising to help him always wherever I should be. I left my elder sister to take care of the poor old man. She was called Cosa, and as she had never wished to marry, she had been received as a nun in Santa Orsola; but she had not yet gone to live there, that she might take care of our old father, and be a guide to our younger sister, who had married a sculptor called Bartolommeo. So, with my father's blessing, I departed, and rode off on my good horse to Mantua.

I should have too many things to tell, were I to write down all the details of that little journey. The world lying under a cloud of pestilence and war, it was with the utmost difficulty I reached my destination. But once there, I immediately began to seek for work; and got employment from a certain Maestro Niccolò of Milan, who was goldsmith to the Duke of Mantua. About two days after I was in full work, I went to pay a visit to Messer Giulio Romano, the distinguished painter, and my great friend. He received me with the utmost affection; but he took it ill of me that I had not got down at his house. He was living like a great lord, and was engaged on work for the Duke outside the gate of Mantua, at a place called the Palazzo del Tè—a marvellous undertaking, on a great scale, as may probably be seen to this day. With all haste, Messer Giulio spoke of me to the Duke in the highest terms; and I was commissioned to model a reliquary for the Blood of Christ, which the Mantuans possess, brought thither, they say, by Longinus. Then, turning to Messer Giulio, he told him to make me a design for the reliquary. Whereupon Messer Giulio answered, "My lord,

Benvenuto is a man who has no need of the designs of others and with this your Excellency will heartily agree when you see his model."

Taking the work in hand, I designed the reliquary so that the ampolla should fit well into it. Then I made a little model in wax of the lid—a Christ sitting with His left hand raised and supporting His great Cross, on which He leaned, while with His right He seemed to be opening the wound in His side. When the model was finished, the Duke was so pleased that he heaped favours on me, and gave me to understand he would keep me on in his service on such terms as would be profitable to me. Meanwhile I had paid my respects to the Cardinal his brother, who begged the Duke to be good enough to let me make the Pontifical seal of his most excellent reverence. This work I began, but while I was about it I took ill of the quartan fever; and whenever the fit was on me I lost my senses and cursed Mantua and its lord and whoever stayed there of his own accord. These words were reported to my patron by his Milanese goldsmith, who saw quite well that the Duke was going to give me employment. When my lord heard those sick words of mine he flew into a rage; and I was out of temper with Mantua, and so one of us was just as angry as the other. I finished the seal, which, together with some other little things for the Duke, ordered in the name of the Cardinal, was four months' work. I was well paid for it by the latter, who begged me to return to Rome, that wonderful city where we had become acquainted with each other.

Setting off, therefore, with a good supply of Mantuan crowns, I came to Governolo, the place where the most valiant Signor Giovanni had been slain. Here I had another little bout of fever, which did not, however, hinder my journey, for I quickly threw it off and had no more of it. When I got to Florence I thought to find my dear father. But when I knocked at the door there appeared at the window an old angry hunchbacked woman, who drove me off with insults, telling me my face would be the death of her. Addressing the hunchback, I said, "Tell me, you cross, misshapen hag, is there no better-looking face in the house than yours?" "No," she answered. "The Devil take you!" And I shouted back, "May two hours see the end of it then!" Hearing this altercation, a neighbour woman came out and told me that my father and the whole household had died of the plague. As I had been thinking this might be the case, my grief was the less. Then she added that only my younger

sister Liperata had survived, and that she had been taken in
by a pious woman called Monna Andrea de' Bellacci.

Then I left to go to the inn, but on the way there I met a
dear friend of mine, Giovanni Rigogli, and got down at his house.
Afterwards we went off to the piazza, where I heard that my
brother was alive. Off I set to seek him at the house of a friend
of his called Bertino Aldobrandi. There I found him, and our
greetings and caresses were endless; and reason was there for
some extravagance of joy, seeing he had heard news of my
death and I of his. Then, breaking out into a long fit of laughter,
he took me by the hand, saying, "Come, brother, I shall take
you to a place you never would think of. For I must tell you
I have given our sister Liperata again in marriage, and for a
certainty she thinks you dead." On our way to her home we
entertained each other with all the great things that had happened to us. When we arrived at her house, she was so overpowered by the unlooked-for event that she fell into my arms
as if dead; and if my brother had not been there, her excitement
and her dumbness must have made her husband think I was
some one other than her brother, as at first he was inclined to.
But Cecchino told him all, and helped to revive her from her
swoon. Then with some tears for the father, sister, husband,
and little son she had lost, she began to prepare supper; and
for the rest of that festive evening nothing more was said of
the dead—we spoke of weddings rather. And thus merrily and
most pleasantly our supper went by.

xli. Moved by the prayers of my brother and sister, I stopped
on in Florence, though my own desire would have led me back
to Rome. And, besides, that dear friend of mine, Piero di
Giovanni Landi, of whose help to me in my troubles I have
already spoken, also advised me to remain where I was for
some time. Just then the Medici were exiled from Florence—
that is, Signor Ippolito, who was afterwards Cardinal, and
Signor Alessandro, afterwards Duke. So Piero said I should
stay for a little time to see what was going to happen. I began,
therefore, to work in the Mercato Nuovo, where I did a large
business in setting jewels, and made a good living.

About this time there came to Florence a Sienese called
Girolamo Marretti, who had lived a long time in Turkey, and
was a very intelligent man. One day he came to my shop and
commissioned me to make a gold medal for wearing in a hat,
the design to be a Hercules wrenching the lion's mouth open.
So I set about the thing, and while I was working at it Michel

Agnolo Buonarroti came several times to see it. Now I had taken a great deal of pains with it, and the attitude of the figure was so fine, and the spirit of the animal so admirably expressed, that it had nothing in common with the work of such artists as had designed the same kind of thing before. Then, also, my method of working was entirely new to the divine Michel Agnolo. And so he praised my work; and this was such an incitement to me to do well as I cannot describe. But I had nothing else in hand save jewel-setting; and though my best earnings came from this, yet I was not contented, for I wished to do something higher than merely setting stones. Now I fell in with a certain young man of lofty spirit called Federigo Ginori. He had lived many years in Naples, where his handsome figure and his fine presence gained him such fame that he had been the lover of a princess. Well, this man, wishing to have a medal made—Atlas with the world on his shoulders to be the subject—he asked the great Michel Agnolo to make a sketch of a design. He answered Federigo thus: "Go and seek out a young goldsmith called Benvenuto. He will serve you very well; and you may be sure he will have no need of a design from me. But that you may not think I seek to shirk such a trifle, I'll make a sketch with pleasure. Meanwhile speak to Benvenuto, and let him make a little model as well. Then the better design of the two can be carried out." So Federigo Ginori came to see me, and said what he wanted, adding how much the wonderful Michel Agnolo had praised me, and how he had advised my making a little model in wax, while he— the marvellous man—had promised to make a drawing. Such encouragement was contained in the words of the great genius that I set to the work at once with the utmost energy. When he had finished it, a certain painter, a great friend of Michel Agnolo, called Giuliano Bugiardini, brought me the sketch of the Atlas. At the same time I showed Giuliano my little wax model, which was quite different from Michel Agnolo's design. And so Federigo, and Bugiardini as well, said I should carry out the thing according to my model. I began it, therefore; and when the most excellent Michel Agnolo saw it, he praised it more than I can tell. It was, as I have said, a figure engraved on a thin plate of gold; the heaven on its back was a crystal ball, upon which was cut the zodiac on a field of lapis-lazuli. The whole thing was indescribably beautiful. Under it ran the motto, *Summa tulisse juvat*. Federigo being satisfied, paid me most liberally. Now about that time Aluigi Alamanni was in

Florence. He was a great friend of Federigo Ginori, who often brought him to my shop; and by his recommendation we became close friends.

xlii. Pope Clement had now declared war on the city of Florence, which made preparations for its defence. In every quarter the militia was organised, and I was under orders to serve too. For this I made sumptuous preparations. I was intimate with the best nobility of Florence, who showed a right good will in undertaking the defence of the city; and in every quarter of the town were delivered the speeches usual at such times. The young men met together more than was their wont, and nothing else was ever talked about. One day, towards noon, a number of persons were gathered in my shop,—men full grown, and youths, the chief in the city—when a letter from Rome was brought to me. It came from a man called Maestro Jacopino della Barca. His real name was Jacopo dello Sciorina, but in Rome he was known as della Barca, because he owned a ferry-boat which crossed the Tiber between Ponte Sisto and Ponte Santo Agnolo. This Maestro Jacopo was a person of great talent, and of amusing and delightful conversation. Once he had been a designer for the Florence cloth-weavers. He was on very friendly terms with Pope Clement, who took great pleasure in his talk. So one day when they were speaking together, the question arose of the sack, and the part which the Castle played in the defence of the city. Then the Pope, recalling me, paid me all the compliments you can think of; and added that if he only knew where I was, he would very much like to have me back again. Maestro Jacopo told him I was in Florence; whereupon his Holiness ordered him to write to me to return. The letter was to the effect that I should come back to the service of Clement, and that it would be to my advantage so to do. The young fellows who were with me wanted to know what the letter was all about; but this I hid from them as best I could; and afterwards wrote to Maestro Jacopo, begging him on no account to write to me again, for good or ill. But his determination only grew the stronger; and he wrote to me once more, and in so exaggerated a style, that it would have gone ill with me had it been seen. The letter said the Pope desired me to go to Rome without delay, as he wanted me to undertake a thing of the greatest importance; and that if I wished to do my duty, I should leave everything else behind me immediately, and not linger to war against a Pope in company with those mad fanatics.

When I read the letter, I was so afraid that I went in search of my dear friend Pier Landi. At the sight of me he asked me at once what had happened that I seemed so worried. I said to my friend that I could not bring myself to tell him what was vexing me. Only, I begged him to take the keys I gave him, and return the jewels and the gold to such and such people, whose names he would find written down in my little book; also to take away my household things and keep some account of all—with his usual kindness; and in a few days I should let him know where I was. This shrewd young man, perhaps correctly guessing how things were, said to me, "My brother, be off with you at once. Then write to me; and as for your things, don't give them another thought." This I did. He was the most faithful, the wisest, worthiest, discreetest, most loving-hearted friend whom I have ever known. Quitting Florence, I went to Rome, and from there I wrote.

xliii. As soon as I reached Rome, I sought out some of my old friends, by whom I was welcomed with great affection. I set myself to work, which brought me in some money, but which is not worth describing. Now there was a certain goldsmith in the city, an old fellow called Raffaello del Moro. His reputation in the trade was high, and he was a very good sort of man besides. He begged me to do him the favour of working in his shop, for he had some important works on hand, out of which excellent profits could be made. And I willingly closed with his offer.

More than ten days passed and I had not yet gone to see Maestro Jacopino della Barca. But when he met me by chance he gave me the heartiest greeting, and asked me how long it was since I had come. About a fortnight, I told him. This he took very ill, saying I made very little account of a Pope who, with much insistence, had made him write three times for me; and I, who had been still more vexed, answered him never a word, swallowing my wrath. He was a man of most fluent speech, and now he burst into a torrent of words. When at last I saw him worn out, I only said he might take me to the Pope whenever he liked. "Any time then," he answered; and I was always ready, I replied. So off he set towards the palace, I with him, and the day was Maundy Thursday. When we reached the Pope's apartments, we were at once admitted, he being known, and I expected. The Pope was in bed, a little indisposed; and Messer Jacopo Salviati and the Archbishop of Capua were with him. His Holiness was extraordinarily delighted at the sight of me; and when I had kissed his feet with all the humility possible, I came nearer, and gave him to know I would fain talk with him of some weighty matters. Immediately he made a sign with his hand, and Messer Jacopo and the Archbishop retired a long way off. Without delay I began, "Most holy Father, ever since the sack I have not been able to confess or communicate, for they refuse me absolution. And this is why. When I melted the gold, and had all the trouble of taking the jewels out of their setting, your Holiness ordered Cavalierino to pay me some little money for my pains. But I never got anything. Indeed, he showered abuse on me instead. So going up to the place where I had melted the gold, I washed the ashes, and found about a pound and a half of gold in little grains as fine as millet-seed. And as I had not money enough to take me home in decency, I bethought me to use this, and to return it when I had a chance. Now here I am at the feet of your Holiness, who is the true confessor. Of your favour, grant me leave to go and confess and receive the communion, that by your grace I may regain the grace of the Lord my God."

Then the Pope, with something like a sigh, recalling perhaps his afflictions, said to me, "Benvenuto, most true it is I am what you say, and, therefore, I can absolve you of any offence you may have committed. Likewise I am willing. So tell me everything quite freely, and with good courage; for had you taken the value of a whole tiara, I am quite willing to pardon you." Then I answered, "I have done no more, most Holy Father, than what I have said; and it did not come up to the value of a hundred and forty ducats, when I changed it at the mint at Perugia. And that sum I took home to comfort my poor old father." The Pope replied, "Your father was as talented, good, and worthy a man as ever was born; and you do not in any way disgrace him. I am much vexed the money was so little; but such as you say it was, I make you a present of it, and pardon you for all. Tell this to your confessor, if you have done nothing else which touches me. Then having confessed and communicated, come again to see me, and your visit shall not be in vain."

As soon as I had left the Pope, Messer Jacopo and the Archbishop drew near again, and his Holiness spoke to them of me more warmly than I can tell, and told them he had confessed and absolved me. Then he ordered the Archbishop of Capua to send for me to ask if I had any need save in the matter we had spoken of; and he told him he was to absolve me, for he had full authority so to do, and to treat me with every kindness possible.

On our way back, Maestro Jacopino was full of curiosity, and asked me what I had been talking about so long and secretly with the Pope. When he had repeated his question more than once, I said I should not tell him, for it concerned things that were no business of his, and he need not ask me again.

I did all that I had arranged with the Pope; and when the two festivals were over, went again to see him. His reception of me was even more kind than before; and he said, "If you had come to Rome a little earlier, I should have had you repair those two tiaras of mine which we destroyed in the Castle. But as they are of little value apart from the jewels, I'll set you on a work of the greatest importance, where you'll have a chance of showing what you can do. It is a button for my cope, which is to be round like a trencher, and almost as big, that is, about the third of a cubit in diameter. On it I wish you to make a God-the-Father in half-relief; and in the middle I want you to set in that fine diamond you know of and some other valuable jewels. A certain Caradosso once began it, but never finished it. Now I wish you to get it done quickly, for I would fain have some enjoyment out of it still. So go away and make me a good design." He showed me all the jewels, and then I was off home like a shot.

xliv. While Florence was being laid siege to, Federigo Ginori, for whom I had made the medal of Atlas, died of consumption; and the medal fell into the hands of Messer Luigi Alamanni, who soon after took it as a present to Francis, King of France, together with some of his own finest writings. It pleased the king beyond measure; and the most ingenious Luigi spoke so favourably to his Majesty of my personal character, as well as of my artistic skill, that the king declared his desire to make my acquaintance.

Just then I was putting my whole energies into the model for the Pope's button, which I made exactly the size the finished work was to be. But many men in the goldsmith's trade resented my being employed on it, for they felt capable of doing the thing themselves. Now there had come to Rome a certain Michelotto, very skilful in engraving on cornelian, a very clever jeweller withal, and a man of years and great reputation. He had undertaken the repair of the Pope's two tiaras. While I was making the model, he was much surprised I did not come to him for advice, he being a very able man, and in great favour with the Pope. In the end, when he saw I did not mean to approach him, he came to me and asked me what I was working at. "On a commission from the Pope," I answered. Then he went on, "The Pope has ordered me to supervise everything that is made for him." To which I replied that I should first ask his Holiness, and then should know what answer to make him. He said I should be sorry if I did this; and going away from me in a rage, he foregathered with all the others of his trade. When they had talked the matter over, they gave it into the hands of Michele, who was clever enough to get more than thirty designs made by able designers of the button which had been ordered. Now he had the ear of the Pope; and making a pact with another jeweller called Pompeo, a Milan man—also a great favourite of his Holiness, and a relation of Messer Traiano, first chamberlain of the household —these two, to wit, Michele and Pompeo, told Pope Clement they had seen my model, and that in their opinion I was not capable of carrying out so important a thing. The Pope replied that he, too, must see it. Then if I were really not capable, he would find some one who was. Whereupon they told him they had some splendid designs ready. That was a very good thing, said he, but added that he would rather not see them till I had finished mine, when he would inspect them all together. In a few days I had completed my model, and I took it one morning to his Holiness. Messer Traiano made me wait, and sent off at once for Michelotto and Pompeo, bidding them bring their designs. As soon as they had come, we were all shown in. Michele and Pompeo made haste to open out their drawings, and the Pope was just as eager to look at them. Designers who are not in the jeweller's trade do not know how stones should be placed, and these had not been taught by practical men. For, of course, a jeweller, when he has to introduce figures among his precious stones, must know how to draw and compose a design; otherwise he can do nothing of any worth. So in all those designs the marvellous diamond had been set right in the middle of God-the-Father's breast. The Pope, who had excellent taste, saw this blunder, and had no opinion of them at all. When he had looked at ten, he threw the rest on the floor, and said to me, who was standing aside, "Now, Benvenuto, let's have a glance at yours, that I may see if you have made the same mistake." I stepped forward, and opened a little round box. A light seemed to kindle in the Pope's eye, and he cried aloud, "If you had been my very own self, you must have done it just like this. These fellows could have found no better way of shaming themselves." And many great lords coming up, the Pope pointed out the difference between my model and the others' designs.

When he had praised it to the skies, and the rest stood terrified and dazed in the presence, he turned to me with, "But one difficulty occurs to me, and it is no slight matter. Benvenuto, my friend, wax is easy to work in. The point is to do it in gold." To this I replied eagerly, "Most holy Father, if I do not do it ten times better than my model here, it is agreed you do not pay me." Hereupon there arose cries from the courtiers standing round; for they said I was promising too much. But one of them, a very great philosopher, spoke up for me, saying, "If I may judge from this young man's countenance and the symmetry of his person, he will do all that he says, and more." And the Pope rejoined, "That's why I, too, have confidence in him." And calling his chamberlain, Messer Traiano, he bade him bring five hundred gold ducats of the Camera. While we were waiting for the money, he again, and more at leisure, examined my ingenious method of employing the diamond with the God-the-Father. I had placed it exactly in the middle, and above it I had represented the Almighty seated in a noble posture, turned away somewhat from the spectator. This was a harmonious arrangement, and did not destroy the effect of the jewel. With His right hand held up, He was giving the benediction. Beneath the diamond I had placed three cherubs, supporting the stone with their uplifted arms. The middle one was in high relief, the other two in half. Round about were others, variously arranged with the rest of the fine jewels. God-the-Father had a floating mantle, from which my little cherubs peeped out; and there were other charming decorations besides, each adding to the exquisite result. I had made the thing in white stucco on black stone. When the money was brought, the Pope gave it to me with his own hand, and in his pleasantest manner begged me to finish the button so that it might be worn in his days; adding that it would be a good thing for me.

xlv. I carried off the money and the model; and it seemed to me an age till I could put my hand to the work. At the end of eight eager and laborious days, the Pope sent his chamberlain, a very great Bolognese nobleman, with a message that I was to go to him and take with me what I had done. On our way this chamberlain, who was the most agreeable person about the Court, told me it was not altogether to see the work that the Pope had sent for me. He meant also to give me another thing to do of the greatest importance, namely, the making of dies for the money of the Roman Mint. I had better be prepared with an answer to his Holiness; and for that reason he had warned me. On being admitted to the Pope, I displayed the thin gold plate, on which was fashioned as yet only the God-the-Father. But this first sketch showed more strength and skill than the wax model, so that the Pope cried in his astonishment, "From this day forward I am willing to believe whatever you tell me." Then he paid me the most extravagant compliments, and added, "I want to give you another commission which I have as much at heart as this one—nay, more—if you are able to undertake it." Then he told me of his great desire to have dies made for his money; asked me if I had ever made any, and if I was bold enough to attempt such a thing. I replied that I was most willing, that I had seen how such things were done, though I had never made them. In the presence was a certain Messer Tommaso of Prato, datary to his Holiness. Now he was very thick with my enemies, and so he said, "Most holy Father, you heap such favours on this young man, who is naturally over-confident, that he would promise to remake the world for you. Already you have given him one big piece of work; now you add a bigger, and one will fight against the other." The Pope turned on him in a rage, telling him to mind his own business. Then he ordered me to make a model of a broad golden doubloon. On one side was to be a Christ, naked, with His hands tied, and the legend *Ecce Homo*; on the reverse a pope and an emperor, both of them propping a cross on the point of falling, with the inscription, *Unus spiritus et una fides erat in eis*. When the Pope had given me the commission for this beautiful coin, in came Bandinello the sculptor, who was not yet made a knight, and with his wonted presumption clothed in ignorance, he said, "When these goldsmiths get such fine work to do, one has to find designs for them." At which I turned on him, saying I had no need of his help in my art, but had good hope, in time, with my designs to trouble him a bit in his own business. The Pope was as delighted as possible with these words, and said to me, "Go now, my Benvenuto, and give all your mind to serving me, and pay no heed to what fools say." So I went away, and with all the speed in the world made two steel dies. Then having stamped a coin, I carried them all to the Pope one Sunday after dinner. When he saw them he was astounded, and his great satisfaction was not merely on account of the fine work, but also for the quickness of my execution. And to add to his pleasure and wonder, I had brought with me all the old coins which had been made in the past by those skilful men who had served Pope Julius and Pope Leo. Seeing he was much more pleased with mine, I drew out of my bosom a petition asking for the office of Stampmaster to the Mint. It was worth six golden crowns a month, without counting the dies, which were paid by the Master of the Mint at a ducat for three. The Pope took my petition, and giving it into the hands of the datary, told him to see to the business at once. The datary took the paper, but as he was putting it in his pocket, he said, "Most holy Father, your Holiness should not go at such a furious pace. These are matters that merit some consideration." Then the Pope answered, "I have heard you. Now give me back the petition." And taking it, he signed it with his own hand, and returned it with the words, "There, the thing is settled. Hasten the matter; such is my will—for Benvenuto's shoes are worth more than the eyes of all those other dull idiots." So having thanked his Holiness, I went off to my work in the highest spirits.

xlvi. I was still working in the shop of Raffaello del Moro, whom I have spoken of. Now the good man had a fair young daughter, for whom he had his eye on me. And I, half aware of this, was quite willing. But while inwardly cherishing the desire, I showed nothing of it to the world. Indeed, so distant was I in my courtesies that he wondered at me. Now this poor child had a disease in her right hand, which had eaten into the bones of the little finger and the next one. Through the heedlessness of her father, she was attended by an ignorant quack, who said her whole right arm would be maimed, even if nothing worse came to pass. When I saw her poor father appalled at the prospect, I told him I did not believe all the ignorant doctor said. He replied that he had no acquaintance with any doctors or surgeons; and begged me, if I knew of one, to call him in. Without delay I sent for a certain Maestro Giacomo of Perugia, a most distinguished surgeon. The poor young girl was in despair, having guessed the verdict of the quack; but when the man of skill had seen her, he said, on the contrary, that no harm would come of the thing, and that she would be perfectly able to use her right hand; and that though the two last fingers might be a little weaker than the others, this would not matter in the least. So he began his treatment; and when, after a few days, he was about to cut out the diseased portions of the bones, the father called me and asked me to look on while this was being done. For his operation Maestro Giacomo used some rough steel instruments. Seeing that with these he made little way, and hurt the girl terribly, I told him to stop and to wait a few minutes for me. So I ran to the shop, and made a little tool of finest steel, curved, thin as a hair, and sharp as a razor. Then I ran back with it to the Maestro, who began to operate so gently that she felt no pain; and in a short time the thing was finished. For this service, and for other reasons, too, the worthy man conceived a greater affection for me than for his two sons. And so it was he set himself in good earnest to the care of his lovely young daughter.

I had a very good friend in Messer Giovanni Gaddi, a clerk of the Camera, who took the greatest delight in the arts, though he had no talent for them himself. Living with him were Messer Giovanni, a very learned Greek; Messer Lodovico da Fano, another man of learning; Messer Antonio Allegretti; and the young Messer Annibal Caro. Belonging to this society, though not of the household, were Messer Bastiano the Venetian, a most eminent painter, and myself; and nearly every day we saw each other at Messer Giovanni's. So it came about that the worthy goldsmith Raffaello, aware of this friendship, said to Messer Giovanni, "My friend, you know me. Now I want to marry my young daughter to Benvenuto; and as I can think of no better go-between than your honour, I beg you to help me, and to settle as it please you what portion of my property shall be her dowry." Hardly had the good fellow finished speaking when the scatter-brained fool broke in, in the most purposeless fashion, with "Speak no more of this, Raffaello, for you are farther from your end than is January from mulberries." So his hopes being dashed, the poor man tried to marry her to some one else; and the mother, the girl herself, indeed the whole family, were angry with me, while I knew nothing of the reason. When I saw I was only getting bad money for all the courtesy with which I had treated them, I made up my mind to open a shop in their neighbourhood. And Messer Giovanni never told me a word of the matter till the girl was married, which took place a few months later.

In the meantime I was striving hard to finish my work, and was serving the Mint the while; for the Pope again gave me an order for a coin of the value of two carlins. His own head was to be stamped on the face; and on the reverse, a Christ upon the waters stretching out His hand to St. Peter, with the legend, *Quare dubitasti ?* This coin gave so much satisfaction that a certain secretary of the Pope, a very able man called Il Sanga, said: "Your Holiness may congratulate yourself on having such coins as the ancients, with all their splendour, never possessed." Whereupon the Pope replied, "And Benvenuto, too, is fortunate in serving an Emperor like me, who know his talents." While I was working at the great gold piece, I showed it often to the Pope, for he entreated me so to do, and every time he saw it he was more astonished.

xlvii. My brother was now also in Rome, in the service of Duke Alessandro, to whom the Pope had lately given the duchy of Penna, and who attached to himself a number of right valiant soldiers, trained in the school of that distinguished captain, Giovanni de' Medici. My brother was of this company, and by the Duke esteemed among the best. Well, after dinner one day, he went to the shop of Baccino della Croce, in the Banks, which was a gathering-place of these braves. There sitting down on a seat, he fell asleep. Just then passed by the Bargello guards, conducting a certain Captain Cisti, a Lombard, to prison. He, too, had been of the school of the great Lord Giovannino, but was not now in the service of the Duke. Captain Cattivanza degli Strozzi happened to be also in Baccino della Croce's shop. Cisti caught sight of him, and said to him in passing, "I was bringing you some crowns I owed you; if you want them, come for them before they lock me up." Now Cattivanza loved to egg others on, though he would not risk much himself; so seeing several young fellows of spirit, more ready to dare than fit to embark on such an adventure, he bade them step up to Captain Cisti and make him give them the money. Should the guard resist, they were to defy it, if they had spirit enough. There were only four of these youths, and all four beardless. One was called Bertino Aldobrandi, another Anguillotto, of Lucca. The names of the others I cannot recall. Now Bertino had been trained by my brother, who felt the warmest affection for him. So, behold the four plucky young fellows coming up with the Bargello guards, who were more than fifty, and armed with pikes, arquebuses, and two-handed swords. Wasting but few words, the four put their hands to their weapons, and so harassed the guards, that had Captain Cattivanza but shown himself, even had he never drawn his sword, they would have put the gang to flight. But he delayed, and Bertino was wounded sorely, and he fell. Then Anguillotto at the same moment was wounded in the right arm, and no longer able to hold his sword, he retired as well as he could. The others did the same, and Bertino Aldobrandi was lifted from the ground in a serious condition.

xlviii. While all this was happening we were at table, for that morning we were dining more than an hour later than usual. Hearing the noise, one of the sons, the elder, Giovanni by name, rose to go and see the fight. I called to him, "For God's sake, don't go! There's always something to lose and nothing to gain in rows of that sort." And his father, too, said, "My son, I beg you not to go." But the youth would listen to none of us, and ran downstairs. Reaching the Banks, where the fight was going on, he saw Bertino being lifted from the ground. Then he turned and ran back. But on the way he met Cecchino, my brother, who asked him what was up. Some of the people standing by signed to Giovanni not to tell; but like the mad fool he was, he blurted out that Bertino Aldobrandi had been murdered by the guard. My poor brother set up such a roar you might have heard it ten miles off. Then he said to Giovanni, "Ah, could you but tell me which of them has been the death of my friend!" Giovanni answered, "Yes; it was a man with a two-handed sword and a blue feather in his cap." On rushed my poor brother, and recognising the murderer by these signs, he threw himself with all his marvellous agility and dash into the midst of the guards; and ere his particular enemy could help himself, he struck him in the belly, ran him through, and felled him to the ground with his sword-hilt. Then he turned on the others with such skill and fire that he alone would have put the whole of them to flight, had he not wheeled round to have at an arquebusier, who, to defend himself, let off his gun and hit the brave unlucky youth just above the right knee. As soon as he had fallen, the scattered guards made off in haste, lest another, like unto this assailant, should come up. Hearing that the tumult still continued, I, too, rose from table, and girt on my sword—for every man carried one in those days. At the Santo Agnolo bridge I saw a large group of men. I pushed on, and being known to some of them, place was made for me; and I saw the last thing in the world I would have seen—yet there I was, all eagerness to look. At first I did not recognise him, for he was dressed in different clothes from those I had seen him in a little while before. So it was he that first knew me, and said, "Dearest brother, do not lament my evil case, for in my profession I was bound to look for this. Only let me be taken away from here at once, for I have but a little while to live." While he was speaking they told me all that had happened, with the brevity the case called for. Then I replied, "Brother, this is the greatest grief, the greatest evil that can ever befall me. But be of good heart, for before you lose sight of him who wrought you this hurt, you shall see yourself revenged by my hands." His words and mine were to this clear effect, but of the briefest.

xlix. The guard was now fifty paces off, for Maffio, their captain, had made a portion of them turn back to take away the body of the corporal whom my brother had killed. So hurrying along, wrapped round closely in my mantle, I came up with Maffio. Of a certainty I was near killing him, for the crowd was thick enough, and I was in the midst of it. Quick as lightning I had drawn my sword half out of its scabbard, when Berlinghier Berlinghieri, a most valorous young man, and a great friend of mine, seized my arms from behind. Four other young fellows were with him, and they cried to Maffio, "Off with you, for this man by himself was on the point of killing you." "Who is he?" asked Maffio. "Brother of the man you see lying there," they answered. Having heard quite enough, the captain retired to the Torre di Nona as fast as possible, and my friend, turning to me, said, "Benvenuto, we kept you back against your will, but we did it for your good. Now let us go and help him who is shortly to die." So we went back to my brother, whom I had carried into a house. The doctors consulted together and treated him, but they could not make up their minds to cut off his leg, else they might perchance have saved him.

As soon as the wound had been seen to, Duke Alessandro appeared, and spoke words of kindly affection; and my brother, who was still clear in his mind, said to him: "My lord, for nothing do I grieve save that your Excellency loses a servant who might be excelled in valour in his profession, but than whom none ever served you with more love and faithfulness." The Duke bade him make up his mind to live; as for the rest, well did he know him for a man of worth and valour. Then turning to the men who were with him, he told them to let the gallant youth want for nothing. After the Duke had gone, Cecchino became delirious from the great flow of blood which could not be staunched; so that all next night he was quite frenzied, save that when they wished to give him the communion, he said, "You would have done well to confess me before. Now it is not possible for me to receive the divine sacrament in this wrecked body of mine. Be satisfied that I receive it with the divinity of the eyes, through which it shall reach my immortal soul, which begs mercy and pardon of God." When he had said these words, the host was raised; but he fell at once into the same delirium as before—nay, his ravings grew still worse, and he uttered the most horrible words imaginable all that night till daybreak. As the sun rose above the horizon, he turned to me and said, "My brother, I will stay no longer here, for these people will drive me to what will make them repent having meddled with me." Then he flung out both legs, and raised the injured one (which we had placed in a very heavy box) as if he were about to mount his horse. Turning his face to me, he said three times, "Adieu! adieu! adieu!" and with the last word that valiant soul passed out.

At the appointed hour, which was evening, at twenty-two of the clock, I had him buried with the greatest honour in the Church of the Florentines; and later I raised to him a beautiful marble monument, on which were cut trophies and banners. I must not forget to say that, when one of his friends asked him which of the arquebusiers shot him, and if he recognised him, he said yes, and he described the man. Although my brother took precautions against my hearing this, yet I had heard it perfectly; and in the proper place I shall tell what came of it.

l. To return to the stone. Certain very distinguished men of letters, who knew my brother, brought me an epigram, which they said the admirable young man had merited. It ran thus: *Francisco Cellino Florentino, qui quod in teneris annis ad Joannem Medicem ducem plures victorias retulit et signifer fuit, facile documentum dedit quantæ fortitudinis et consilii vir futurus erat, ni crudelis fati archibuso transfossus, quinto aetatis lustro jaceret, Benvenutus frater posuit. Obiit die xxvii Maii, MDXXIX.* He was twenty-five years old. Now because among the soldiers he was called Cecchino del Piffero—his real name being Giovanfrancesco Cellini—I wished to have the name by which he was commonly known written under our arms. So I had it cut in fine antique letters, which were all broken save the first and last. I was asked by those men of learning who had made the fine epitaph for me, the reason of the broken letters; and I said because that wonderful machine, his body, was wrecked and dead. And as for the two entire letters, the first was in memory of that great gift from God, his soul, lit up by His divinity, the which was never broken; the last was for the glorious fame of his valorous deeds. This conceit pleased them very much; and since then others have made use of the same device. Near the name I cut on the stone the arms of our house of Cellini, which, however, I did not follow quite exactly. For, as may be seen in Ravenna, that most ancient city, where there are Cellinis of honourable and gentle quality, the arms are a golden lion rampant on a field of azure, clasping a lily gules in its right paw, with a label-in-chief and three little lilies or. These are the real Cellini arms. My father showed me a scutcheon which had only the paw along with the other bearings; but I like better to keep to that of the Ravenna Cellinis. To return to what I carved on my brother's tomb. I put in the lion's paw, but it grasped a hatchet instead of the lily, with the field of the arms quartered; and the hatchet was there only that I might not forget to revenge him.

li. I worked with the utmost energy to finish the gold work for Pope Clement, which he was in a great hurry for. Two or three times a week would he call me, so much did he want to see it, and each time he was better pleased. But frequently he reproved me, almost scolding me for my deep gloom on account of my brother's death; and still seeing me more overcome and wretched than was right, he said, one day, "Oh, Benvenuto, I did not know you were demented. Haven't you learnt before now that for death there is no remedy? You are doing your best to follow him."

I took my leave of the Pope, and went on with my gold work and the dies for the Mint; but now better to me than courting a sweetheart was watching that arquebusier who had killed my brother. This man had once been a light cavalry soldier, and then had enlisted as arquebusier among the Bargello's corporals. Now what added to my wrath was that he boasted of the thing, saying, "If it hadn't been for me, who killed that brave young fellow, in another minute, he, by himself, would have put us all to flight, with great damage, too." At last I saw that my suffering, caused by the constant sight of him, was hindering me from sleeping and from eating, and leading me along an evil road. I stifled the thought of how low and dishonourable the undertaking was, and one evening I resolved once and for all to be done with the trouble. The man lived near a place called Torre Sanguigna, next door to a house where lodged one of the most favourite courtesans of Rome, called Signora Antea. The clock had just struck twenty-four. The arquebusier stood in the doorway after supper, sword in hand. I crept up stealthily, and with a Pistojan dagger dealt him a back stroke, thinking to cut his head right off. But he wheeled round suddenly, and the blow fell on the top of his left shoulder, cleaving the bone. Up he sprang, and dazed by the sore pain, he threw aside his sword, and began to run. I followed after, and came up with him in a step or two. Then raising my dagger above his bent head, I struck him on the nape of the neck, and the weapon went in so deep that I could not for all my efforts draw it out. For just then out of Antea's house came four soldiers clutching their swords, so that I was forced to handle mine to defend myself from them. Leaving my dagger sticking there, I made off, for fear of being recognised, to Duke Alessandro's house, between the Piazza Navona and the Rotunda. As soon as I got there I told the Duke, who gave me to understand that, if I was alone, I had only to keep quiet and all should be well. I was to go on with the Pope's work, since he was so anxious to have it; and for eight days I had better work within doors. The soldiers who had stopped me had now arrived, and were relating the whole affair; they had the dagger in their hands, and told the great trouble they had had to pull it out of the neck-bone and head of the dead man, whose name they did not know. At this up came Giovan Bandini and said to them, "This dagger is mine, and I lent it to Benvenuto, who wanted to revenge his brother." Then the soldiers could not say enough of their regret at having interrupted me, though, indeed, I had got my fill of revenge.

More than eight days passed, and the Pope did not send for me as was his wont; but at last he begged his chamberlain, the Bolognese nobleman of whom I have already spoken, to go and fetch me. With the utmost courtesy, the messenger told me that his Holiness knew everything, that he wished me well in every way, and that I was to go on working and keep quiet. Nevertheless, when I was admitted, he glowered: his eyes alone were enough to scare me. But when he examined my work, his face softened; he heaped praises on me, and said I had done a very great deal in very little time. Then looking me straight in the face, he added, "Now that you have recovered, Benvenuto, give heed to your way of life." And I catching his meaning, said I would do so. Without delay I opened a handsome shop in the Banks, opposite Raffaello's, and there in a few months' time I finished the piece of work I had in hand.

lii. The Pope had sent me all the jewels except the diamond, which in an hour of need he had pledged to some Genoese bankers. So I had all the other stones, but only a model of the diamond. I kept five excellent journeymen; for besides this piece of work I was doing a great deal of other business, so that the shop was crammed with valuable property, jewels, and gold, and silver. Now I kept a hairy dog in the house, a big, handsome creature which had been given me by Duke Alessandro. Though he was really a hunting dog, good for picking up all sorts of birds and other creatures when I was out shooting, yet he was wonderfully useful, too, as a watch dog. Now it happened about this time that (allowing myself the privileges of my age, which was nine and twenty) I had engaged a very beautiful and graceful girl as my servant. I used her as a model in my work, and also enjoyed her favours. So I had my room apart from those of my workmen, and far away from the shop, and joined by an ante-room to the little hole which belonged to the young servant-maid. I used often to be with her; and though I sleep as lightly as any man, yet on such occasions my slumber was very heavy and deep. So it was one night in particular. Now a thief, who had given himself out to be a goldsmith, had been watching me, had cast an eye upon the jewels, and made up his mind to rob me. So this night he ransacked the shop, and found a number of little gold and silver articles. But while he was in the act of breaking open some boxes to find the jewels, the dog rushed at him, and it was all he could do to defend himself with his sword. Then the creature ran hither and thither about the house, and entered the workmen's rooms, which were open, for it was summer time. When, for all his loud barking, they would not awake, he pulled the coverlets off them. And when still they would not hear, he seized one after another by the arm till he forced them to look up. Then barking with all his might, he tried to make them follow him. But at last he saw they would not, for the villains got angry, and began to throw stones and sticks at the dog. This they could see to do, for by my orders they kept a light burning all night. Then in the end they shut their doors, and the creature giving up all hope of help from the rascals, set himself alone to the adventure. Down he ran, only to find the thief had left the shop. But he found him, and struggling with him, tore the cloak from his back; and who knows what else would have happened, if the man had not called on some tailors to help him, begging them for the love of God to defend him from a mad dog. Thinking he spoke the truth, they rushed out and with great trouble drove the beast off.

Day broke, and when the workmen came down to the shop they found it open, everything in confusion, and all the cases broken into. Then they began to call aloud, "Alack-a-day! alack-a-day!" and I, hearing this, and alarmed at the noise, ran out. When I appeared, they cried, "Oh, unhappy men that we are! We have been robbed by someone who has broken all the cases, and taken everything away!" These words wrought so strongly on me that I had not the courage to go to my chest to see if the Pope's jewels were still there. Indeed, such was my terror, that bewildered and almost blinded, I told them instead to open the box and see what was missing. The young men, who were all in their shirts, opened the chest and found all the jewels and with them the gold article I was working on. Then overjoyed, they cried out, "There's no great harm done, for your work and the jewels are all here—though the thief has left us nothing but our shirts; for last night we all undressed in the shop on account of the great heat, and we left our clothes here." My strength then came back to me, and I said to my men, "Thank God all of you; and clothe yourselves anew, and I shall pay for everything when I have heard the whole story more at leisure."

What troubled me most,—what, indeed, bewildered and terrified me, on whom fear is not wont to have much hold, was the thought that people might say I had made up the story of the robber only that I might steal the jewels. For, indeed, Pope Clement had been warned by some of his most intimate friends, such as Francesco del Nero, Zano de' Biliotti, his accountant, the Bishop of Vaison, and others of that sort, who said to him, "Most holy Father, how can you trust jewels of such value to a reckless, fiery young man, who is more immersed in arms than in art, and is not yet thirty years old?" To this the Pope replied by asking if they knew of my having done anything which would give colour to such suspicions. Francesco del Nero, his treasurer, at once replied, "No, most holy Father, because he has never had a chance." Whereupon the Pope answered, "I believe him to be honest through and through, and even did I see him do wrong, I should not believe my eyes." So this was the thing which troubled me most, and which I now suddenly recalled.

When I had made provision for the young men's new clothes, I took my piece of work, setting the jewels as best I could in their places, and went off with them in all haste to the Pope. Francesco del Nero had told him of the noises which had been heard in my shop, and his suspicions had been roused at once. Rushing to the conclusion that some misfortune had occurred, he turned a terrible look on me, and said in a haughty voice, "What have you come here for? What is the matter?" "Here are all your jewels and the gold! Not a thing is missing," I cried. At that his face cleared, and he said, "Then you are welcome." I showed him the gold piece, and while he was looking at it, I told him all about the thief and my anxieties, and what had been my greatest worry. While I was speaking, he turned several times and looked me straight in the face, and as Francesco del Nero was also with him, it seemed as if he half regretted his suspicions. In the end the Pope burst out laughing at all the things I had to tell him, and as he took leave of me said, "Be off, and see that you remain the honest fellow I know you for."

liii. While I was engaged on the Pope's commission, and working steadily for the Mint as well, there began to circulate in Rome certain false coins stamped with my own special dies. They were immediately brought to the Pope, who, when suspicion was cast on me, said to Jacopo Balducci, the Master of the Mint, "Do your very utmost to find the culprit, for we know that Benvenuto is an honest man." But this rascally Mint-master, who was my enemy, rejoined, "Please God, most holy Father, that it be as you say, for we have reason to think the contrary." Whereupon the Pope turned to the governor of Rome, and ordered him to take immediate steps to find the guilty man. While the inquiries were being made, he sent for me; cunningly led up to the question of the coins, and just at the right moment, said, "Benvenuto, would you dare to make false money?" To this I answered that I believed I could do it better than any of the men engaged in the vile trade; for those who betake themselves to that mean business are not such as know how to earn money, nor have they any real talent, whereas I, with my poor wits, earned as much as I needed. For when I made dies for the Mint, every morning before dinner I had earned at least three crowns—such was the usual payment; and indeed that rascal of a Mint-master bore me no goodwill, because he would fain have got them cheaper. Thus what I gained by God's grace and men's favour was quite enough for me; and in making false coins I should not come off so well. The Pope saw clearly what I meant; and whereas before he had ordered them to watch shrewdly lest I should leave Rome, now he said they were to make thorough search for the real culprit, and to leave me out of the business; for he had no wish to vex me, and thus perhaps to lose my services. Those to whom he gave these peremptory orders were clerks of the Camera, who set about the search with due diligence, in accordance with their duty, and found the culprit without delay. He was a stamper of the Mint, called Ceseri Macherone, a citizen of Rome. His accomplice, a metal-founder, also in the service of the Mint, was arrested along with him.

liv. On that same day I happened to be passing through the Piazzo Navona with my fine dog. I had reached the Bargello gate when the creature gave a great bound, and, barking loudly, dashed in at the opening and threw himself on a young man, who had just been arrested on suspicion of robbing a certain Donnino, a Parma goldsmith, once a pupil of Caradosso. My dog was evidently so bent on tearing him savagely to pieces that the police were moved to pity; and the more so as the bold young fellow had plenty to say for himself, and Donnino could not make out a clear case against him. Besides, one of the corporals of the guards, a Genoese, knew the youth's father. So what between the dog and these other circumstances, they were in a mind to let the fellow go his way without hindrance. But as soon as I came up, the dog, afraid of neither swords nor sticks, was throwing itself again on him; and I was told that if I did not take the beast away, they would murder it. I tugged at the creature as hard as I could; but while the young man was pulling up his cloak, some little paper packets fell out of the hood, and Donnino recognised in them some things of his. I, too, caught sight of a little ring I knew well, and cried out, "This is the man who broke into my shop and robbed me. That's why my dog knows him again." I let go the dog, and he flew at the fellow once more. Then the thief pleaded with me, promising to return what he had of mine. So while I held the dog fast, he gave up all the gold and silver and rings he had stolen, and five and twenty crowns besides. Then he begged for mercy, whereat I advised him to recommend himself to God, saying I should do him nor harm nor good. Then I went back to my business. A few days after, Ceseri Macherone, the coiner, was hanged in the Banks, in front of the door of the Mint, and his companion was sent to the galleys. The Genoese robber was hanged in the Campo di Fiore; and my fame as an honest man was higher than ever before.

lv. I had just nearly finished my work when the huge inundation took place which flooded the whole of Rome. The day was waning as I stood watching it. Twenty-two o'clock had just struck, and I saw the water rising very fast. Now the front of my house and shop was towards the Banks; but the back was several cubits higher, and looked towards Monte Giordano. So thinking first of my safety, and then of my honour, I secured all the jewels on my person, and left my gold work in the keeping of my workmen. Then, barefoot, I got down through my back window, and, as well as I could, waded through the water till I found myself at Monte Cavallo, where I found Messer Giovanni Gaddi, clerk of the Camera, and Bastiano Veneziano, the painter. Greeting Messer Giovanni, I gave all the jewels into his custody; for he looked on me as his brother. A few days later, when the fury of the flood had passed, I went back to my shop, and finished my work so happily, by God's help and my own efforts, that it was held to be the finest thing of the kind ever seen in Rome. When I took it to the Pope, he could not sing my praises loud enough. "If I were a rich emperor," said he, "I would give my Benvenuto all the land his eyes could run over. But we in these days are poor bankrupt princes; nevertheless, we shall give him bread sufficient for his little wants." I let him chatter his fill; and then I asked him for a mace-bearer's place which was vacant. On which he said he wanted to give me something far more important than that. But I begged his Holiness to give me this little thing in the meanwhile as a pledge. He burst out laughing, and said he was willing, but he did not want me to serve; and he bade me arrange with the other mace-bearers that I should be exempt. Then he granted the favour which they had already asked of him, namely, leave to make legal claim for their salaries. This was done. And out of the mace-bearer's post I made little less than two hundred crowns a year.

lvi. I continued to work for the Pope, now in little things, now in big; and one day he ordered me to design a splendid chalice for him. For this I made both a drawing and a model in wood and wax. For the knob of the lid I had conceived three little figures of a fair size, in the round—Faith, Hope, and Charity,—and for the stand, three corresponding designs, modelled in low relief, one being the Nativity of Christ, another the Resurrection, the third St. Peter crucified with his head downwards—for so was I ordered to do the thing. While I was at work on this, the Pope was always wanting to see it. But as his Holiness had never remembered to give me anything, and as a post in the Fraternity of the Piombo was vacant, one evening I asked him for it. The good Pope, quite forgetting his wild eulogy of me when I had finished the other pieces of work, said, "The place in the Piombo is worth more than eight hundred crowns, so that if I give it to you, you'll do nothing but sit and scratch yourself in the sun; and then your fine dexterity of hand will all be wasted, and the blame will be mine." Whereupon I broke out that cats of good breed hunt better fat than lean, and honest men use their talents to better purpose when they have enough to live on. "And so let it be known unto your Holiness," I continued, "that those princes who generously maintain such men, give increase to their talents, which are born starveling and diseased; know, likewise, that I did not ask for the place thinking to obtain it. I am lucky enough to have that wretched mace-bearer's post. I only played with the fancy of having this one. And your Holiness will do well, since he does not wish me to have it, to give it to an able and deserving man, and not to some great lazy lubber, who will sit and scratch himself in the sun, to use your Holiness's own words. Take example from Pope Julius of happy memory, who gave such an office to Bramante, the distinguished architect." And hastily doing him reverence, I went off in a rage.

Then there came in to him Bastiano Veneziano, the painter, who said, "Most holy Father, let your Holiness be pleased to give the place to one who is zealous in his art. Now you know my zeal, and I beg that you will deem me worthy of it." Said the Pope, "That devil of a Benvenuto will not brook being spoken to. I was disposed to give it to him, but he shouldn't be so haughty with a Pope. So I am not sure what I shall do." At that moment in came the Bishop of Vaison, who pleaded for Bastiano, saying, "Most holy Father, Benvenuto is young, and a sword by his side befits him better than a friar's frock. Let your Holiness be pleased to give the place to this worthy man Bastiano, and at another time you can give Benvenuto something which perhaps may suit him better than this." Then the Pope turned to Messer Bartolommeo Valori, and said, "When you meet Benvenuto, tell him from me that it is his own fault that Bastiano the painter has got the post in the Piombo. But also let him know that the first good thing vacant shall be his. In the meantime he is to conduct himself well and finish my work." Next evening, two hours after nightfall, I met Messer Bartolommeo Valori at the corner of the Mint. Two torch-bearers were walking in front of him, and he was in a tremendous hurry, having been called to the Pope. But when I saluted him, he stopped and called my name, and with the

greatest courtesy told me all his Holiness's message. I replied
that I should go on with my work with even greater diligence
and zeal than I had shown before, but quite without hope of
reward. Then he reproved me, saying this was not the way to
respond to the overtures of a Pope. To which I answered that,
knowing his promises to be empty, I should be a fool were
I to build my hopes on such words, or to give any other reply.
And so I left him, and went to attend to my business. Now
Messer Bartolommeo must have repeated my hot words, and
perhaps he added to them, so that for more than two months
the Pope never sent for me; and in all that time I would not
have gone to the palace for anything in the world. But his
Holiness was dying to have the work, and so he ordered Messer
Roberto Pucci to look after me a bit. That good fellow came
every day to see me, and had always a kindly word for me,
as I had for him. The day was drawing near when the Pope
was to go to Bologna. Perceiving at last that I would not go
to him of my own accord, he sent me word by Messer Roberto
that I was to bring my work, for he wished to see how I had got
on. This I did, and having proved that the greater part was
done, I begged him to give me five hundred crowns, part in payment of the work, and the rest to procure gold to finish it.
"Get on with it first," said he; "make haste and have done
with it." I repeated that I would complete it, if he provided me
with money; and so I took my leave.

lvii. When the Pope went away to Bologna, he left Cardinal
Salviati his legate in Rome; and he ordered him to harry me
about the work, saying, "Benvenuto is a man who thinks little
of his own talent, and still less of us. Therefore, see that you
keep him at the work, that I may find it complete on my
return." So that brute of a cardinal sent for me at the end
of eight days, telling me to bring the thing; whereupon I went
to him, but without the chalice. When I was before him, he
broke out with, "Where's that rubbish heap of yours? Is it
ready?" To which I replied, "O most reverend monsignor, it
is not ready—nor is it likely to be so. Can one make bricks
without straw?" At these words the Cardinal, who looked more
like an ass than a human being, became uglier than ever, and
cut into my answer with, "I'll send you to the galleys, and you'll
have the chance of finishing it there." I answered the beast
according to his beastliness, and said, "Monsignor, when I have
committed a crime worthy of the galleys, you shall send me
there; but for my present sins I don't fear your galleys. More-

over, I tell you that, just because of your lordship's meddling, I'll not do a stroke more work on the thing. So don't send for me again. This is the last you'll see of me, were you to send the guards to fetch me." The Cardinal afterwards adopted a coaxing tone, trying several times to show me it was my duty to continue the work, and to bring it up for inspection. But I answered his messengers, "Tell Monsignor to send me the straw if he wishes me to finish my bricks"; and never another word did I answer, so that he gave up the business as a bad job.

lviii. When the Pope came back from Bologna, he asked for me at once, for the Cardinal had written the worst report possible of what I was about. In the greatest fury imaginable he sent word to me to come and show him the work; and I did so. Now while the Pope had been absent, I had had such a serious attack of inflammation in the eyes, that I almost died of the pain. That was the reason why I had not gone forward with the work. So much did I suffer that I thought of a certainty I should lose my sight. Indeed, I had been calculating how much would suffice me to live on when I should be blind. Well, on my way to see the Pope I thought of how I could excuse myself for not having been able to get on with the work, and I determined, while his Holiness was examining the thing, to tell him about my case. But I had no chance of doing so, for at my entrance he burst out rudely, "Here with your work! Is it finished?" So I began unwrapping it. Then with still greater fury he cried, "God's truth! you brag of not caring a rap for anybody. I tell you that, if it weren't for the example of the thing, I'd throw you and your work out of the window!" Seeing that he was in a beast of a temper, my one thought was to remove myself from his presence; and while he was still hectoring, I put the thing under my cloak, muttering, "Nothing in the world could force a blind man to finish a piece of work like that"; whereat he roared still louder, "Come here! What are you saying?" I was in two minds whether I should rush headlong downstairs or not; but I decided to stay, and, throwing myself on my knees, I cried out lustily—for he was roaring all the time—"And when I have become blind, am I still forced to work?" Whereupon he answered, "But you saw well enough to find your way here; and I don't believe a word you tell me!" Then when he had begun to speak in a calmer voice, I answered, "Let your Holiness ask his own doctor, and he will learn the truth." "At our leisure we shall find out if things be as you say," he rejoined. Perceiving by this that he was giving some heed to me at last, I went on, "The sole cause of my serious malady, according to my belief, is Cardinal Salviati. For as soon as your Holiness had gone away, he sent for me, and when I had come he called my work a rubbish heap, and said he would make me finish it in the galleys. And so did his insolent words affect me, that in my wild passion I felt my face on fire, and such a tremendous heat seized on my eyes that I could hardly find my way home. Then a few days after, two cataracts appeared, and I saw no light at all. Therefore, after your departure I was able to get no work done." Rising from my knees, I took my leave, and afterwards was told that the Pope said, "Give orders as one may, one cannot give discretion with them. I never told the Cardinal to put such heat into the business; and if it be true that Benvenuto has something the matter with his eyes, which I shall learn from my doctor, one must have some pity on him." Now there was in the presence a great friend of the Pope, a most distinguished person. He asked his Holiness what manner of man I was. "I ask you, most blessed Father, because it seemed to me you were at once more angry than I have ever seen you and more indulgent. That is why I ask you who he is. For if he deserves to be helped, I can let him into a secret which will cure his malady." So the Pope replied, "He is the greatest master in his profession, and one day when you are with me, I shall let you see some wonderful work of his. I'll show you himself at the same time, and if you see you can do him some good, I shall be much pleased." So three days later the Pope sent for me after dinner, and when I arrived this nobleman was with him. His Holiness bade my cope button be fetched, and in the meanwhile I drew out my chalice. The nobleman said he had never seen so wonderful a work; and when the button was brought, his wonder grew still more, and, looking me in the face, he said, "He is young to know so much, and still most apt to learn." Then he asked my name. "Benvenuto is my name," I replied. To which he answered, "Benvenuto shall I now be to you. Take fleur-de-lis—blossoms, stalks, roots, and all—and stew them over a slow fire. With this water bathe your eyes several times a day, and you will certainly be cured of the malady. But first purge yourself, and then go on using the water." The Pope spoke some affectionate words to me, and I went off rather more content than I had been.

lix. It was true I had been ill; but I think I had caught the malady from that pretty young servant girl whom I had in my house at the time I was robbed. The French evil was latent in me for four whole months; then all at once it covered my body. It did not show itself in the usual form, for I was covered with red boils of the size of farthings. The doctors were never willing to call it by the name of the French evil; and yet I told them why I thought it was so. I continued to treat myself in their fashion, and got no better. Then at last I made up my mind to take lignum vitæ, against the wishes of the first doctors in Rome. I took it with the greatest system and abstinence you can imagine, and in a few days I felt very much better, so that at the end of fifty days I was cured, and as sound as a fish in the sea. Then as a restorative after my great exhaustion, as soon as winter came on, I amused myself with shooting. This forced me through the wind and the water, and to stand about in the marshes, so that in a few days I was a hundred times worse than before. Once more I put myself into the hands of the doctors, and they went on treating me; but I grew worse. When the fever attacked me again, I made up my mind to take the guaiac. The doctors would not hear of it, and told me that did I have recourse to it while I still had fever, I should be dead in a week. However, I made up my mind to disobey them, and I kept to the same system as before. When I had drunk the guaiac water for four days, the fever left me quite, and I began to feel wonderfully restored. While I was treating myself thus, I was all the time getting on with the models; and during this period of abstinence I made the finest things and the rarest designs I ever did in my life. At the end of fifty days I was altogether cured, and with the utmost care set myself to fortify my health. After this long fast I was cleansed from my malady as if I had been born again. But though I took pleasure in the restoration of my health, I did not work the less, now at the Pope's chalice and now at the Mint; each of these tasks had its due share of my energies.

lx. Now it fell out that Cardinal Salviati was made legate to Parma; and he bore me a great ill-will, as I have told you already. Well, in Parma a certain Milanese, a goldsmith and false coiner called Tobbia, was arrested and sentenced to be hanged and burned. His case was referred to the legate, who was told he was a man of great talent. So the Cardinal stayed the execution of the sentence, and wrote to Pope Clement, telling him that he now had in his hands the cleverest man in the goldsmith's trade, and that he was condemned to be hanged and burned for coining false money. But the man was simple and good, he said; for he had asked the advice of his confessor

who had, according to Tobbia, given him liberty to do it. And
the Cardinal added, "If you have this great man in Rome,
your Holiness will be taking down Benvenuto's pride; and I am
sure that Tobbia's work will please you much more." And so
the Pope sent for him to Rome. When he had come, his Holiness
called for the two of us, and ordered us to make a design for
the setting of a unicorn's horn, the finest ever seen, which had
cost seventeen thousand ducats of the Camera. The Pope
intended it as a gift for King Francis, and wished to have it
richly set in gold. As soon as we had made our designs, each of
us brought his to the palace. Tobbia's was a kind of candelabra,
with the fine horn taking the place of the candle, while at the
base were four unicorns' heads, so wretched in design that
when I saw it I couldn't help sniggering. The Pope noticed
this, and called out, "Show yours." Now mine was one unicorn's
head of a size corresponding to the horn. I had made the finest
thing of it imaginable, for I had modelled it half on a horse
and half on a stag, and had added a very fine mane and other
kinds of adornments. As soon as mine was seen, of course every
one declared it was the best. But some Milanese people were
present during the contest, and they said, "Your Holiness is
going to send this fine gift to France. But surely you know that
the French are gross persons, who will not recognise the excellence of Benvenuto's work. A thing like this now," they said,
pointing to Tobbia's design, "will please them, and such things
do not take so long to make. Then Benvenuto can give himself
up to finishing your chalice, and thus two things will be done
in the same time. Besides, this poor man whom you have sent
for, will be employed too." The Pope, most anxious to have his
chalice, seized on the advice of the Milan men, and next day
ordered Tobbia to set the unicorn's horn, and sent word to me
by his Master of the Wardrobe that I was to finish the chalice.
To this message I replied that I desired nothing better, that if
it were made of anything else than gold I could easily do so
without his help; but as it was of gold, his Holiness must provide
me with the material, if he wished to have it completed. At these
words this low-born minion of the court cried, "Oh, do not ask
the Pope for gold, or you will put him into such a rage as will
be your undoing." "Will your honour inform me how to make
bread without flour?" I asked. "Well then, without gold this
work will never get done." And the Master of the Wardrobe,
not unaware I was laughing at him, said he would report all
I had said to the Pope. And so he did. The Pope got into a

fierce passion, and said he just wished to see if I was mad enough not to finish it. And so two months passed. Though I had indeed said I would not do a stroke more, I was better than my word, for I went on working with the greatest eagerness. But seeing that I did not bring it to him, his Holiness began to bear me a real grudge, and to say he would make me suffer for my conduct in some way or another. He said so one day in the presence of one of his own jewellers, a Milanese called Pompeo, nearly related to a certain Messer Traiano, Pope Clement's favourite servant. These two put their heads together, and said to Clement, "If your Holiness were to take away his place at the Mint, perhaps you would breed in him a desire to finish the chalice." But the Pope answered, "Then I should incur two evils. I should be badly served at the Mint, which is a thing of great importance to me, and most certainly I should never have the chalice." Nevertheless, these two Milanese —seeing him badly disposed towards me—so swayed him in the end that he did indeed take away the Mint from me, giving it to a young Perugian known by the name of Fagiuolo. Then came Pompeo to tell me how his Holiness had deprived me of my place; and that if I did not finish the chalice, he would take other things away too. To which I answered, "Tell his Holiness that, for the Mint, the loss is his, not mine; and so shall it be with the other things; and if he should desire me to accept it again, I shouldn't think of consenting." And the graceless, ill-conditioned fool thought he could not run back quickly enough to tell him all I had said—and what he had invented besides. Eight days after the Pope sent me another message by the same man, that he no longer desired me to finish the chalice, and that he wanted it back just as it was. I answered Pompeo, "This is not like the Mint, which he had the power to take from me. True, the five hundred crowns which I had, belong to his Holiness, and these I shall return at once. But this work is mine, and I shall do just what I like with it." Off ran Pompeo to tell the Pope these words, and some other stinging ones too, which, not without reason, I had shot at himself.

lxi. After two or three days, one Thursday there came to me two of his Holiness's favourite chamberlains. One of them is alive now, and a bishop. His name was Messer Pier Giovanni, and he was attached to the Pope's Wardrobe. The other was of still higher rank, but his name has gone clean out of my head. When they had come to me they said, "We are sent by the Pope, Benvenuto, to bid you, since mild measures are useless

with you, either give us up the chalice, or go with us to prison."
Then I looked cheerfully in their faces as I answered, "My
lords, if I were to give it up to his Holiness, I should be giving
what belongs to me and not to him; and for the moment I have
no desire to do anything of the kind, for I have worked at this
thing with my best energies, and I do not want it to get into
the hands of some ignorant bungler, who would spoil it with a
light heart." The goldsmith Tobbia was standing by as I said
this, and he had even the face to ask me for the design of the
work. I answered the rascal according to his deserts; but what
I said need not be repeated here. Then when the gentlemen of
the chamber urged me to make my preparations, I told them
I was ready, and took up my cloak. But before I went out of
my shop, I turned most reverently, my cap in my hand, to an
image of Christ, and said, "O our gracious, immortal, just,
and holy Lord! all that Thou doest is according to Thy justice,
which is without equal. Thou knowest that I have come to the
age of thirty, and never till now have I been threatened with
prison. Now that Thou willest I should go to prison, I thank
Thee with all my heart." Then turning to the two chamberlains I said, with one of my menacing looks, "No meaner guards
than you would befit a man like me. So put me between you,
and as your prisoner take me where you will." The two gentlemen burst out laughing, placed themselves one on each side
of me, and, with pleasant discourse by the way, conducted me
to the governor of Rome, who was called Magalotto. When
we had reached him, we found the procurator-fiscal with him,
and they were both waiting me. Then the two lords of the
chamber, still laughing, said to the governor, "We consign to
you this prisoner; have good care of him. It is a great satisfaction to us that we have done your police officers' business,
for Benvenuto has been telling us that, as this is his first arrest,
guards of our rank are no more than his due." Then they left
us and went to the Pope. When they had told him everything
exactly, it looked at first as if he were to burst out in a fury.
But then he forced a laugh, for in the presence were certain
lords and cardinals, friends of mine, in whose favour I stood high.

Meanwhile the governor and the fiscal were now bullying me,
now exhorting me, now giving me advice. It was only reasonable, said they, that one who ordered a piece of work could take
it back when he liked, and as he liked. To which I said that
justice allowed nothing of the sort—no, not even to a Pope.
For surely a Pope was not like those tyrannic little lords who

do every wrong possible to their people, observing neither law nor justice. 'Twas not for a Vicar of Christ to act like that. Whereupon the governor, putting on his Jack-in-office air, said, "Benvenuto, Benvenuto, you are doing your best to make me give you your deserts. You should treat me with respect and courtesy, if you would behave towards me according to my merits." Then again he said, "Send for the work at once, and don't wait a second telling." To this I replied, "My lords, of your grace I would say just a word or two concerning my case." The fiscal, who was far discreeter in the exercise of his office than the governor, turned to the latter and said, "Monsignor, give him leave to speak a hundred words if he pleases. If so be he gives up the chalice, that's all we want." Then I took up the word, "Supposing any man whatsoever had ordered the building of a palace or a house, he might with justice say to the man who was building it, 'I do not wish you to work any more on my house or my palace.' When he had paid him for his labours, he could send him away. Again, supposing some lord who owned a jewel worth a thousand crowns, wished to have it set. If the jeweller did not serve him as he wished, he might say, 'Give me back my jewel, for I do not want your work.' But this case of mine does not come under either of these heads. It is not a matter of a house or a jewel. You can say nothing to me save that I should return the five hundred crowns which I have had. Therefore, my lords, do whatever you can, for you shall have nothing of me except the five hundred crowns. And tell this to the Pope, 'Your threats do not frighten me in the least. I am an honest man, and have no sins to be ashamed of.'" Thereupon the governor and the fiscal rose, telling me that they were going to the Pope and should return with orders, and then I might look out for myself! So I remained guarded, and walked in the meanwhile up and down a large hall. It was nearly three hours before they came back from the Pope. During this time all the best of our Florentine merchants came and entreated me not to quarrel with his Holiness, for it might be the ruin of me. But I replied that I was quite clear in my mind as to what I wanted to do.

lxii. As soon as the governor and the fiscal had returned from the palace, they sent for me, and the former spoke to me in this wise, "Benvenuto, of a truth, it grieves me to come from his Holiness with the orders I have—to wit, that you find the chalice instantly—or look to your own safety." Then I answered I had never believed till that hour a holy Vicar of Christ could

do such injustice; and even now must see it before I could believe
it. "So, therefore, do what is in your power," I added. Once
more the governor replied, "I have still two words to say to
you from the Pope, and then I shall execute the orders given me.
He says you are to bring the chalice here to me, and I am to
see it put in a box and sealed. Then I am to take it to the Pope,
who promises upon his honour not to break the seal. He will
return it to you at once. But he insists on this being done, that
his honour also may be satisfied." I answered, laughing, that
I would give up my work right willingly in the way he suggested,
for I had a mind to find out what a Pope's word was made of.
And so, having sent for the thing and sealed it in the way
agreed on, I gave it to him. Then the governor went back to
the Pope with the sealed chalice, and—according to what he
told me—his Holiness took the case, turned it over several
times, and then asked the governor if he had seen it. He answered yes, and that it had been sealed in this way in his
presence, adding that it had seemed to him a wonderful work.
Whereupon the Pope said, "Tell Benvenuto that Popes have
authority to loose and to bind much greater things than this";
and while he said these words he opened the box with something like anger, taking off the cord and the seal with which it
was fastened. He gazed at it for a long time, and, as I believe,
showed it to Tobbia, the goldsmith, who praised it loudly.
When the Pope asked him if he could make something like it,
he answered yes. His Holiness told him he was to follow the
design exactly, and, turning to the governor, he said, "Find
out if Benvenuto will give it up to us. If he will, I'll pay him
what connoisseurs say it is worth. Or, if he really wishes to
finish it, let him fix a date; and if you see he is actually in earnest,
let him have whatever he needs for the work—in reason." Then
said the governor, "Most Holy Father, I know the violent
nature of the young man. Authorise me to give him a sound
rating in my own fashion." To this the Pope replied that he
might do what he liked, so far as words were concerned, though
he was sure he would make the thing worse; also if he saw he
could do nothing more, he was to tell me to take the five hundred
crowns to Pompeo, his jeweller.

The governor came back, called me into his room, and looking
at me as if I had been in the dock, said, "Popes have authority
to loose and to bind anything in the world, and Heaven at once
proclaims the deed well done. Here is your chalice, opened and
examined by his Holiness." At that I lifted up my voice and

cried, "I thank God that now I can tell what a Pope's word is
made of." Then the governor's words and manner to me became intolerably insolent; but seeing that he gained nothing
by this, and altogether hopeless of the business, he took on a
milder tone and said, "Benvenuto, I am much grieved that you
refuse to see where your advantage lies. But go, take the five
hundred crowns whenever you like to Pompeo." With my
chalice in my hand, away I went, and without delay delivered
up the money. Now the Pope probably thought that I should
not have ready money enough, or that for other reasons I might
not deliver the whole sum so promptly, and he was desirous
of binding me once more to his service. Therefore when he saw
Pompeo coming in to him smiling, with the money in his hand,
he flung insults at him, and was much annoyed that the thing
had turned out like this. So he said, "Go and find Benvenuto
in his shop, and be as civil to him as an ignorant brute like you
can be, and tell him that if he will only finish the work, for a
reliquary to carry the body of the Lord in when I go in procession, I will supply him with all that he needs—provided he
works." So Pompeo came to me, called me out of the shop,
paid me the most fatuous compliments, like the donkey he was,
and gave me the Pope's message. I replied at once that the
greatest treasure I could wish for in all the world was to have
regained the favour of so great a Pope, which had strayed from
me, yet not by my fault, but through my terrible infirmity and
the wickedness of envious men who delight in making mischief.
"But since his Holiness has an abundance of servants," I went
on, "don't let him send you here again, if you value your safety.
So off you go, and mind your own business. I shall never fail,
night or day, by thought or deed, in the service of the Pope;
but keep this well in your mind—when you have delivered
my message, never meddle again in any affairs of mine, or I'll
let you discover your mistake through the chastisement it
deserves." The man went and reported everything to the Pope,
using, however, much more brutal words than I had spoken.
So stayed the thing for a while, and I looked after my shop
and my business.

lxiii. Tobbia, the goldsmith, was finishing the ornamentation
of the unicorn's horn. And, besides, the Pope had told him to
set to work on the chalice, using that design of mine which he
had seen. But when he asked Tobbia to show him what he had
done, he was so ill satisfied with it that he regretted sorely
having broken with me, found fault with his other work as

well, and was inclined to fall out with the men who had brought him to his notice. Several times there came to see me Baccino della Croce, on the part of the Pope, to urge me to make the reliquary. In reply I begged his Holiness to let me rest after the terrible illness I had had, from which I had not altogether recovered. But, I continued, I should prove to his Holiness that every hour when I was fit to work should be spent in his service. I had set myself to do his portrait, and was making a medal for him secretly, the steel dies for which I was fashioning at home. This I could the better do as I had a partner in my shop who had once been my apprentice, Felice by name.

Now about this time I had fallen in love—as a young man will—with a young Sicilian girl who was very beautiful. And as she too gave signs of being very fond of me, her mother, becoming aware of it, grew anxious as to what might happen. And, in fact, I had made up my mind to run away to Florence for a year with this girl, without letting her mother know. But hearing of this, the woman left Rome secretly by night, and went in the direction of Naples. She said she was going to Città Vecchia, but she really went to Ostia. I followed on their traces as far as Città Vecchia, and committed a thousand follies in trying to find her. It would be too long to tell them all exactly; enough to say that I was on the verge of going mad or dying. At the end of two months she wrote to me that she was in Sicily, and very ill pleased to be there. By that time I had been giving myself up to all the pleasures imaginable, and I had taken another love, but only to extinguish this earlier flame.

lxiv. Through certain odd circumstances it came about that I gained the friendship of a Sicilian priest, a man of most lofty mind, and with an excellent knowledge of Latin and Greek. While we were conversing one day together, we chanced to talk of the art of necromancy, concerning which I said, "All my life long I have had the greatest desire to see and hear something of it." Whereupon the priest answered, "Strong and steady must be the mind of him who sets himself to such an enterprise." I replied that strength and steadiness of mind I should have and to spare, if only I had the means of testing these. Then answered the priest, "If you have but the courage for it, I'll give you your fill of the rest." So we agreed to put the thing in hand. One evening the priest began to make his preparations, and told me I was to find a companion or two, but not more. I called on my great friend Vincenzio Romoli, and he brought with him a Pistoja man, who was also given to necromancy. Together we set off for the Coliseum, and there, having dressed himself after the wont of magicians, the priest began to draw circles on the ground, with the finest rites and ceremonies you can imagine. Now he had bidden us bring precious perfumes and fire, and evil-smelling stuff as well. When all was ready, he made an entrance to the circle, and, taking us by the hand, led us one by one within. Then he distributed the duties. The pentacle he gave into the hands of his companion magician; we others were given the care of the fire for the perfumes; and he began his conjuring. This had lasted more than an hour and a half, when there appeared many legions of spirits, so that the Coliseum was full of them. I was attending to the precious incense, and when the priest perceived the great multitudes, he turned to me and said, "Benvenuto, ask of them something." I answered, "Let them transport me to my Sicilian Angelica." That night he got no reply at all, but my eager interest in the thing was satisfaction enough for me. The necromancer told us we must come back another time, when I should have the fulfilment of my desire. But he wished me to bring with me a young boy of perfect purity.

So I brought a shop-boy of mine about twelve years old. Once more I sent for Vincenzio Romoli; and as a certain Agnolino Gaddi was a close friend of both of us, we took him too on the business. When we had again reached the appointed place, the necromancer made the same preparation with even greater care, and led us into the circle, which he had made this time with still more wonderful skill and ceremonies. Then he gave to my friend Vincenzio the care of the perfumes and the fire, with Agnolino Gaddi to help him, put the pentacle into my hand, telling me to turn it in the directions he would indicate, while under the pentacle stood my little shop-boy. This done, the necromancer began to utter the most terrible invocations, and to call by their names many of the princes of the demoniac legions (speaking the while in Hebrew words, also in Greek and Latin), and commanding them, by the strength and power of God increate, living, and eternal; so that in a brief space the whole Coliseum was full of them, and there were a hundred times more than there had been the first night. Meanwhile Vincenzio Romoli, along with Agnolino, was attending to the fire and to the burning of the precious perfumes. Once more I asked, by advice of the magician, to be with Angelica. Then he turned to me and said, "Do you hear what they say? —that in a month's time you will be where she is." And again he entreated me to stand firm, for the legions were a thousand more than he had called; and since they had agreed to what I had asked, we must speak soft to them, and gently bid them go. On the other side, the boy, who was under the pentacle, said, all trembling, that round us were a million of the most warlike men, and that they were threatening us. Moreover, said he, four huge giants had appeared. They were armed, and they made as if they would enter our circle. At this the necro- mancer, who was shaking with fright, tried with all the soft and gentle words he could think of to bid them go. Vincenzio Romoli, looking after the perfumes, was quivering like a reed. But I, who was just as much afraid, forced on myself a braver mien, and inspirited them in wonderful fashion, though, indeed, I nearly died when I saw the magician's fright. The boy, who had put his head between his knees, said, "I'll die in this way, since die we must." Then I said to the child, "These creatures are all lower than us, and what you see is only smoke and shade; so lift your eyes." When he had done so he spoke once more, "The whole Coliseum is on fire, and the fire is upon us"; and, putting his hand to his face, again he said he was dead, and he would not look any more. The necromancer entreated me to stand by him, also to make fumes of assafœtida. So, turning to Vincenzio Romoli, I told him to do this, and looked at Agnolino Gaddi the while, whose eyes were starting from his head with terror, and who was more than half dead. "Agnolo," I said to him, "this is no time to shiver and shake. Up and make yourself useful! Throw the assafœtida quickly on the fire." At the instant when he moved to do this, he yielded so powerfully to the needs of nature that it served better than the assafœtida. The boy lifted his head at this great stench and noise, and, hearing me laugh, his fear was calmed a little, and he told us the spirits were riding off tumultuously. So we re- mained till the chimes of day began to sound. Then again the boy spoke, saying that but few remained, and they were far off. The magician, having gone through the rest of his cere- monies, doffed his robes, gathered up a great load of books he had brought, and we all came out of the circle together, sticking as close as possible to one another—especially the boy, who squeezed himself into the middle of us, and clutched the magician by the vest and me by the cloak. On our way towards our houses in the Banks, he told us that two of the demons he had seen in the Coliseum were going before us, now leaping, now running over the roofs, now along the ground. The wizard told us that in all the times he had entered the circles nothing so great had ever happened to him. And he tried to persuade me to help him in making incantations over a book. Out of this we should draw infinite riches; for we should ask the demons to teach us where to find the treasures, of which the earth was full, and thus should become very rich. As for love and such-like things, he said they were vanity and folly, which profited nothing at all. I answered that if I were learned in Latin I would do so right willingly. But he persuaded me that Latin letters would in no wise serve me; that, had he wished, he could have got many a one learned in Latin; but that he had never found any man of so steadfast a mind, and that I should give heed to his counsel. Talking thus, we reached our homes, and all that night each of us dreamt of devils.

lxv. We used to see each other every other day, and the necromancer was most insistent I should take part in the enterprise. So I asked him how long it would take, and where we should have to go. He replied that less than a month would see the end of it, and that the most fitting place was in the mountains of Norcia, although one of his masters had made his incantations near here, at a place called the Badia di Farfa. But he himself had experienced some difficulties there, which would not be met with in the mountains of Norcia. The Norcian countryfolk, too, were trustworthy, he said, and had some practice in the art; in a strait could even be of great service. This wizard-priest, of a truth, was so persuasive that I was quite willing to join him in the thing; but first, I said, I wished to finish the medals I was making for the Pope. I had told him, and no one else, about these, begging him to keep the secret. Yet I kept on asking him if he thought that at the stated time I should find myself with my Sicilian Angelica; for now the day was drawing very near, it seemed to me strange I heard nothing of her. The wizard replied that most certainly I should find her, for the spirits never failed in their word when they promised in the fashion they had done. But I was to watch open-eyed, and to be on the alert against a misfortune which might come upon me in this regard; also I must steel myself to endure something that would go against the grain, for he saw in it a very great danger. Likewise, he said, it would be well for me to go away with him and make the incantations over the book; for thus my great peril would pass, and I could gain fortune both for myself and for him. I was beginning to care a great deal more about it than he did himself. Nevertheless, I told him that there had come to Rome a certain Maestro Giovanni of Castel Bolognese, a most skilful man in making medals of my kind in steel, and that I desired nothing better in the world than to compete with him, and shine out to the world in such an undertaking. So by my great talents, and not by the sword, did I hope to put my enemies to rout. Yet the necromancer still said, "I entreat you, Benvenuto mine, come with me, and flee a great danger I see threatening you." But I was resolved, in spite of everything, to finish my medal. Now already the end of the month was nearly on us; yet so in love was I with my medal that I never gave a thought to Angelica or anything of the sort. My work was everything to me.

lxvi. One day, about the hour of vespers, I had occasion to go at an unusual hour to my shop in the Banks. I was living in a little house behind the Banks, and seldom went to my shop, leaving all my business to be done by my partner Felice. When I had been there a little time, I remembered I had to go and speak to Alessandro del Bene. So I set out, and in the Banks I met a great friend of mine called Ser Benedetto. He was a notary, and a native of Florence, the son of a blind Sienese beggar who used to say prayers in the streets for alms. Now this Ser Benedetto had lived at Naples for many many years, and afterwards had come to Rome, where he did business for certain Sienese merchants of the Chigi family. My partner had time after time asked him for money due for some rings which had been entrusted to him. That very day Felice had met him in the Banks, as was his wont, while Ser Benedetto was in the company of some of his patrons. They, taking notice of the thing, cried out on Ser Benedetto, saying they would employ some one else who had no barking dogs at his heels. As he went off with them he defended himself as best he could, swearing he had paid the goldsmith, and that he could not help a madman's fury. When the Sienese merchants took these words in bad part, and dismissed him summarily, he came like a shot to my shop, perhaps to have his spite out on Felice. But as it happened, right in the middle of the Banks we ran against each other, and I, who knew nothing of all this, greeted him with my usual politeness. Rude words were my only answer. Then I called to mind all that the necromancer had told me, and, reining myself in as well as I could, as I had been told I must do, I said, "Ser Benedetto, my brother, do not be wroth with me who have done you no harm, and who know nothing of what has happened to you. If you have anything against

Felice, for any sake go and have it out with him; he must know best what to say to you. But as I am quite in the dark, you do wrong to snarl at me in this fashion, especially as you know that I am not a man to put up with insults." To which he answered that I did know all about it; that he was a man who could make me bear the weight of it and more; and that Felice and I were two great scoundrels. Already a great many people had gathered round to watch the quarrel. Stung by his ugly words, I bent down suddenly and picked up a handful of mud —for it had been raining—and, quick as lightning, aimed it at his face. But he ducked, so that he got it in the middle of his head. Now in this mud was a bit of hard rock with sharp corners, and one of these striking him, he fell senseless to the ground, and all the bystanders, seeing the great flow of blood, made up their minds he was indeed dead.

lxvii. While he was lying there, and the people were preparing to carry him away, there passed by Pompeo, the jeweller, of whom you have heard before. The Pope had sent for him about some jewel business. Seeing the man in a bad way, he asked who had struck the blow, and he was answered, "Benvenuto. But the fool has only himself to blame." Well, no sooner was Pompeo in the presence of the Pope than he cried out, "Most Holy Father, Benvenuto has this moment murdered Tobbia. I saw it with my own eyes." Whereupon the Pope in a fury ordered the governor, who was present, to seize me and hang me at once in the place where I had committed the crime, commanding him to leave no stone unturned in his search for me, and never to show his face again until I was hanged.

Now when I saw that unlucky man lying there, my mind ran to my own affairs. I thought of the power of my enemies, and all that might follow from this occurrence. So taking myself off, I withdrew to the house of Messer Giovanni Gaddi, clerk of the Camera, meaning to make speedy preparations for escape. But Messer Giovanni advised me not to be in such a hurry to go off, for it might be the evil was not so great as I thought; and he called Messer Annibal Carol who lived with him, and bade him go and get information on the affair. Meanwhile there appeared a Roman nobleman of the household of the Cardinal de' Medici, and sent by him. Calling Messer Giovanni and me apart, he told us that the Cardinal had repeated to him the words he had heard the Pope say, and that as he had no means of helping me, I must do all I could to escape his first fury, and not trust myself in any house in Rome. As soon as the nobleman had gone, Messer Giovanni, looking in my face, made as if he would weep. "Ah me!" he said. "Ah, woe is me! for I can do nothing at all to help you." But I answered, "God willing, I shall help myself. The only thing I ask is that you lend me one of your horses." A black Turkish horse was already saddled, the handsomest and the best in Rome. So I mounted, with an arquebuse in front of my saddle-bow ready loaded, and thus I was prepared for any attack. At the Sistine bridge I found the whole guard of the Bargello, horse and foot; so making a virtue of necessity, I boldly spurred on my horse at a trot, and, thanks be to God, who dimmed their eyes, I passed over free; then with all speed possible I set off for Palombara, a place belonging to Lord Giovanbatista Savello. From here I sent back the horse, though I kept Messer Giovanni in the dark as to my whereabouts. Signor Giovanbatista housed me with great kindness for two days, and then advised me to depart and go towards Naples till the tempest should blow over; and, giving me a companion, he put me on the Naples road. On the way I met in with a sculptor friend of mine, who was going to San Germano to finish the tomb of Pier de' Medici at Monte Cassino. This man, who was called Solosmeo, brought me news, how, the very evening of my flight, Pope Clement had sent one of his chamberlains to ask after Tobbia; how they had found him at work, and that there was nothing the matter with him, nor did he even know anything of the affair. This being reported to the Pope, he turned to Pompeo and said, "You are a scoundrel, but I warn you that you have roused a serpent that will bite you, and it will be no more than you deserve." Then he ordered the Cardinal de' Medici to keep his eye on me, saying that for nothing in the world would he lose me. And then Solosmeo and I went on our road singing towards Monte Cassino, our plan being to go from there to Naples.

lxviii. As soon as Solosmeo had seen to his business at Monte Cassino we took the road again for Naples. We had come within half a mile of the city when an innkeeper met us and bade us come to his inn, telling us he had been in Florence many years with Carlo Ginori. If only we would put up at his place, he would do us every kindness, because we were Florentines. Several times we told him that we did not wish to go with him, but he now rode on before and now waited behind, repeating over and over again the same thing, that he wanted us to come home with him. This I found wearisome at last; so I asked him if he knew the whereabouts of a certain Sicilian lady called Beatrice, who had a beautiful young daughter called Angelica. They were courtesans. The innkeeper, thinking I was jesting, said, "God confound courtesans and all who have dealings with them!" And giving his horse a dig with his foot, he made as if to leave us for good. It seemed as if I had got fairly rid of the beast at last, though not without some loss to myself, for I called to mind the great love I bore to Angelica. While I was talking of her to Solosmeo, not without some amorous sighing, we saw mine host coming back in a furious hurry, and as soon as he came up to us he said, "Two or three days ago a lady and a young girl returned to a house near my inn. They bore those names, but I do not know if they are from Sicily or some other country." Then I answered, "Such power has the name of Angelica over me that I will certainly come home with you." So we went off with mine host to the city of Naples, and got down at his inn. Then it seemed to me a thousand years before I settled my things, which nevertheless I did with the utmost speed. In a house near the inn I found my Angelica, whose endearments to me were warmer than I can describe. It was then twenty-two of the clock, and I stayed with her till next morning, with an enjoyment the like of which I have never known. But while I was indulging in this pleasure, I remembered that exactly on that day the month was up of which prophecy had been made by the demons in the wizard's circle. So let every man who deals with such beings ponder the incalculable perils through which I passed.

lxix. Now I showed to the goldsmiths in Naples a diamond which happened to be in my purse. And here I should say, that though I was a young man, such repute had I even in those parts, that the heartiest reception was given me. Among the others who showed me kindness was a very good fellow, Messer Domenico Fontana by name. This worthy man left his shop for three whole days while I was in Naples, nor would he be parted from me. He was my guide to many of the splendid antiquities in the city and outside. He took me, besides, to pay my respects to the Viceroy of Naples, who had manifested a strong desire to see me. Presenting myself, I received a most honourable welcome from his Excellency, who, by the way, did not fail to catch sight of the diamond. He bade me show it to him, and said that if I were thinking of parting with it, I mustn't forget him. When I had it back again in my own hands I offered it anew to his Excellency, saying that both the diamond and I were at his service. He replied that he valued the stone highly, but were I to stay with him he would rate that much higher, and would make such arrangements as should quite satisfy me. We exchanged many courteous words; and, coming to the merits of the diamond, his Excellency asked me to state its price right out. Whereupon I said it was just two hundred crowns. He replied that this was reasonable, as it had been mounted by me, the first jewel-setter in the world; but if the setting were done by any one else, it would not show the full brilliance of the stone. I told him, however, it had not been set by me; that the work, indeed, was not well done, and its fine effect was due to its own excellence. If I were to set it again I should improve it enormously. Then applying my thumb nail to the sharp edges of the facets, I drew the stone from the ring, and, rubbing it up a little, I gave it into the Viceroy's hands. Much pleased and astonished, he gave me a bill for the two hundred crowns I had asked.

Going back to my lodging, I found letters from the Cardinal de' Medici, wherein he bade me return to Rome with the utmost diligence, and get down at once at his most reverent lordship's house. When I read the letter to Angelica, she begged me most lovingly, and with tears, to stop in Naples, or else to take her with me. I answered that if she would come along with me, I would give into her keeping the two hundred ducats I had got from the Viceroy. Then her mother, seeing us converse secretly together, came up to us and said, "Benvenuto, if you are going to take my Angelica away to Rome, leave me fifteen ducats to pay for my lying-in, and after that I'll follow you." I told the wicked old woman that I'd give her thirty with a good will, if she would be pleased to give up her Angelica to me. And so the bargain was struck. Angelica begged me to buy her a gown of black velvet, which was very cheap in Naples. I did all they asked me willingly; sent for the velvet, bargained for and paid it; but the old woman, who thought me fatuously in love, demanded a gown of fine cloth for herself, would have had me lay out a great deal on her sons, and begged for more money than I had offered her. At this I turned to her good-naturedly and said, " My dear Beatrice, didn't I offer you enough?" "No," said she. So I replied that what was not enough for her would suffice for me, and having kissed my Angelica, we parted, she with tears, I with a laugh, and in haste I took the road for Rome.

lxx. It was night when I left Naples, with my money concealed on my person, for one may expect to be attacked and murdered in that country. When I reached Selciata, I had to defend myself with the greatest skill and strength of body against some horsemen who were bent on having my life. A few days after, I left Solosmeo at his work on Monte Cassino, and one morning I stopped to dine at an inn in Anagni. When I was nearing the inn, I shot at some birds with my arquebuse, and knocked down several; but a splinter of iron from the lock of my gun tore my right hand. Though there was no great harm done, it seemed at first rather serious, because of the great amount of blood I lost. Entering the inn yard, I put my horse in the stable, and mounted to an upper floor, where I found a company of Neapolitan gentlemen, who were just sitting down to table. With them was a young gentlewoman, the loveliest creature I have ever seen. Now there followed me up the stairs my sturdy young serving-man with a huge halbert in his hand; so that between this weapon and the blood on my person we struck such terror into the poor gentlemen—all the more as the place was a nest of cut-throats—that they got up from the table, trembling the while, and prayed God to come to their aid. On which I answered, laughing, that God had indeed sent them aid, since I was the very man to defend them from whoever should molest them. Then I begged for some help in bandaging my hand, and the lovely lady took out a handkerchief richly worked in gold, and was about to tie up my wound with it. This I would not have; but she tore it in half then and there, and with the utmost gentleness bound up my wound with her own hand. Then were the rest somewhat reassured, and we dined very merrily together. After dinner we mounted our horses and went off in company. But as their fear had not yet all vanished, the gentlemen shrewdly engaged me in conversation with the lady, while they remained somewhat behind. So I rode by her side on my pretty little horse, signing to my servant to keep at a distance. Thus we could talk together in confidence, and it was not about everyday matters, you may be sure. It was thus I made my way to Rome, and it was the pleasantest journey of all my remembrance.

Reaching Rome, I dismounted at the palace of the Cardinal de' Medici. As his most reverend Excellency was at home, I got word with him, and thanked him exceedingly for calling me back. Then I begged his lordship to ensure my not being put in prison, and, if it were possible, against a fine. The Cardinal received me very gladly, and told me I was to fear nothing. Then turning to one of his gentlemen, a Sienese called Pierantonio Pecci, he bade him tell the Bargello from him to keep his hands off me, and asked him how it went with the man whose head I had wounded with a stone. Messer Pierantonio replied that he was very ill, and that he would be worse, for if he knew I had come back to Rome, he would do his best to die just to spite me. At this the Cardinal laughed heartily, and said, "He couldn't do better, if he wished to prove his Sienese birth." Then turning to me, he continued, "For our honour and your own, wait four or five days before appearing in the Banks. After that go where you like, and let fools die if they want to." So off I went to my house, and set myself to finish the medal I had already begun, with Pope Clement's head on one side, and a figure of peace on the reverse. Peace was represented by a slender female figure, clothed in thinnest raiment, and girdled, with a torch in her hand, which was kindling a heap of weapons bound together like a trophy. You could see likewise part of a temple, in which was Fury bound by many chains. Round about was the device *Clauduntur belli portae*. While I was finishing this medal, the man I had struck recovered, and the Pope never stopped asking for me. But meanwhile I refused to go and see the Cardinal de' Medici; for every time I went, his lordship gave me something important to do for him, so that my work on the medal was hindered. But Messer Pier Carnesecchi, a great favourite of his Holiness, undertook to keep his eye on me, and from time to time insinuated how much the Pope desired me to work for him again. I replied that in a few days I would prove to his Holiness that I had never left his service.

lxxi. A few days after, having finished my medal, I stamped it in gold, in silver, and in brass. When I had let Messer Pietro see it, he brought me at once to the Pope. It was after dinner time on a lovely April day, and his Holiness was in the Belvedere. When I came into his presence, I gave the medals with the steel dies into his hands. He took them, and saw at a glance the magnificent art they displayed; then looking Messer Piero in the face, he said, "The ancients were never so well served with medals." While he and the others were examining, now the dies, now the medals, I began to speak modestly as follows: "If a Higher Power had not ruled over my unlucky stars, preventing that violence with which they threatened me, your Holiness had lost, without fault on his side or mine, a faithful and loving servant. And so I hold, most holy Father, that one cannot go wrong in cases where all is staked upon a single throw, if, after the saying of poor simple men, we count seven

before we cut one. The slanderous lying tongue of my worst
enemy so easily stirred your Holiness's wrath, that, in a great
fury, you ordered the governor to hang me there and then.
Yet later, when you had seen the great injustice of such a
punishment—which would have done you a great wrong by
depriving you of such a servant as your Holiness owns me to
be—I verily believe that, in face of God and the world, you would
have felt no little remorse. Thus good and virtuous fathers, and
masters too, should not let fall their arm so rashly on their
sons and servants; for afterwards remorse will be of no use at
all. Now since God has hindered the malign course of the stars,
and saved me for your Holiness, I entreat that next time your
wrath be not so quickly roused against me."

The Pope had stopped looking at the medals, and was listening
to me with great attention; and as in the presence were many
lords of high degree, he reddened somewhat, and looked as if
he were ashamed; but not knowing how to get out of the coil
any other way, he said he did not recollect ever having given
such an order. Perceiving his embarrassment, I spoke of other
things till he had regained his usual confidence. Then his Holiness began to discuss the medals, and asked me how I had
managed to stamp them so admirably, considering their size,
for he had never seen antique medals so large. About this we
talked for a bit, and then, afraid I might read him another
lecture worse than the last, he told me the medals were most
beautiful, that he was much pleased with them, but that he
should like to have another reverse according to his own fancy,
if it were possible for a medal to have alternative reverses.
I said yes. Then his Holiness ordered from me the story of
Moses when he struck the rock and the water came out, along
with these words, *Ut bibat populus*. And he added, "Go now,
Benvenuto, and before you have finished it, I shall have made
provision for you." As soon as I was gone, the Pope declared
before them all that he would endow me, so that I could live
in riches without ever working for any one else. And I went
home and gave all my mind to the execution of the reverse
with the Moses design.

lxxii. But now the Pope took ill, and the doctors judged him
to be in danger. Then my enemy, who was afraid of me, bribed
some Neapolitan soldiers to do to me what he feared I might
do to him. So I found it no easy matter to defend my poor life.
Yet I persevered, and completed the reverse. When I took it
to the Pope, I found him in bed in a very serious condition.

Nevertheless he received me most affectionately, and wished to see the medal and the dies. He had his spectacles and candles brought him, but could see nothing at all. Then he began to feel them all over with his fingers, and having done this for some little time, he heaved a great sigh, and said to those who were standing near that he had me much on his mind; but if God gave him back his health, he would put everything to rights. Three days after the Pope died, and I found that all my pains had been for nothing. Yet I was of good courage, telling myself that through these medals I had become so well known that I should be employed by any Pope, and perhaps with greater profit than heretofore. So did I put heart into myself, and thrust behind me altogether the gross insults which Pompeo had cast on me. Then, in my armour and with my sword at my side, I set off to St. Peter's, and kissed the dead Pope's feet, not without tears.

Afterwards I came back to the Banks, to watch the great confusion which reigns at such a time. While I was sitting there with many friends around me, up came Pompeo with ten men about him, all fully armed. When he was just opposite, he stopped as if to pick a quarrel with me. The brave and adventurous young spirits who were with me signed to me to draw on him. But then quick came the thought, that if I drew, there might follow some dreadful consequence to those who had nothing to do with the thing at all. So I judged it better that I alone should put my life to the hazard. You could barely have said two Ave Marias before Pompeo, with a sneering laugh in my direction, made off again. His men, too, laughed, and there were many tossings of heads and other insulting gestures. My comrades would have begun to fight there and then, but I told them hotly that I was man enough to fight my own battles, that I needed no greater champion than myself, and that they were to mind their own business. This angered my friends, and, grumbling, they left me. Among them was my dearest comrade, Albertaccio del Bene, own brother to Alessandro and Albizzo, and to-day a very rich man in Lyons. This Albertaccio was the most splendid young fellow I have ever known, and the most courageous; he loved me as himself. Now he knew well that my patience was not for poor-spiritedness, but that it meant the most reckless bravery—for he had a perfect understanding of me—and taking up my words, he begged me to do him the favour of calling on him in any business I had a mind for. To which I answered, "Albertaccio mine, dear above all the others, be sure a time will come when you can help me; but in this affair, if you love me, give no heed to me; go about your own business, and be off speedily like the rest, for there is no time to be lost." In my haste I could say no more.

lxxiii. Meanwhile my enemies of the Banks had gone off slowly towards the place called the Chiavica, and had reached a point where cross-roads meet. But the street where my enemy Pompeo's house stood was that which goes straight to the Campo di Fiore. Now being in need of something, he had gone into the apothecary's at the corner of the Chiavica, and had stopped there awhile on his business. It had come to my ears that he had been bragging of his having braved me—for so he thought he had done; but in any case, it was the worse for him. For just when I had reached the corner, he came out of the apothecary's; his bravos made place for him, and closed about him. But with a little keen-edged dagger I forced their ranks, and had my hands upon his breast so quickly, and with such coolness, that not one of them could hinder me. I was aiming at his face, but in his terror he turned his head, so that I plunged the poniard in just below the ear. It only needed two strokes, for at the second he fell dead, which had not been at all my intention. But, as the saying is, there's no bargaining about blows. With my left hand I drew out the dagger, and in the right I took my sword for the defence of my life. But all his bravos ran to the dead body, and made no show of attacking me. So I withdrew by myself through the Strada Giulia, thinking where I could best hide. I had gone about three hundred paces when I was joined by Piloto the goldsmith, a very good friend of mine. "Brother," said he, "now that the ill is done, let's think of your safety." To which I answered, "Let's go to Albertaccio del Bene's house, for only a little ago I told him the time would soon come when I should have need of him." So we reached Albertaccio's house, and we embraced with boundless affection; and very soon there appeared the best of the young men about the Banks, of every nation save the Milanese; and each one of them offered his life to save mine. Messer Luigi Rucellai, too, sent with exquisite courtesy to say that what he had was at my service, as did many other substantial men of his condition; and there was not one of them but called down blessings on my hands; for they held my enemy had insulted me deeply, and it was a wonder I could have borne with him so long.

lxxiv. Meanwhile Cardinal Cornaro heard of the affair, and of his own accord sent thirty soldiers, with as many halberds, pikes, and arquebuses, to bring me with all due honour to his place. I accepted the offer and went off with them, while a still larger number of the young fellows swelled my guard. But by this time Messer Traiano, the dead man's relative, and chief chamberlain to the Pope, sent to the Cardinal de' Medici, a great Milanese nobleman, who informed him of the grave crime I had committed, and protested his lordship was bound to punish me. The Cardinal retorted, "Great wrong would he, indeed, have done, leaving this lesser wrong undone! Thank Messer Traiano from me for his having told me what I did not know." Then suddenly turning, in the presence of the nobleman, to the Bishop of Forli, a gentleman of his court and his familiar friend, he said, "Search diligently for my Benvenuto, and bring him to me, for I have a good will to help and defend him. And who harms him, harms me." Thereupon the nobleman flushed angrily and took his leave; and the Bishop of Forli came to seek me at Cardinal Cornaro's. Having found my host, he told him how the Cardinal de' Medici had sent for Benvenuto, and wished to be his protector. Now Cornaro, who was as irritable as a bear, answered the bishop hotly, telling him that he was just as well able to protect me as the Cardinal de' Medici. Whereupon the bishop asked as a favour to speak to me a word, outside this affair, on the Cardinal's business; but Cornaro told him that for that day he might pretend he had talked with me. The Cardinal de' Medici was highly indignant; but next night, with a good escort, I paid him a visit, unknown to my host. Then I begged him of his kindness to let me stay in Cornaro's house, telling him how kindly he had treated me. If only his most reverend lordship would permit this, I should have one more friend in my hour of need. For the rest, his lordship might dispose of me as he pleased. He replied that I was to do as I liked; and I returned to Cornaro's house. A few days later Cardinal Farnese was made Pope.

When he had put his greater affairs in order, the new Pope called for me, and let me know he wished no one but me to make his money. Whereupon one of his most intimate friends, Latino Juvinale by name, spoke to his Holiness, and said I was in hiding for a homicide committed on the person of one Pompeo, a Milanese; and then he added all that could be said in my favour. To which the Pope replied, "I did not know of Pompeo's death; but well I know of Benvenuto's excuse. So make out a safe-conduct for him, that he may rest perfectly secure." Now there stood by a great friend of Pompeo, a man very intimate with the Pope, Messer Ambrogio of Milan, and he spoke thus, "In the first days of your reign it is not wise to grant favours of this sort." But his Holiness replied, "I know better about such things than you. Learn that men like Benvenuto, unique in this profession, are not subject to the laws. And especially is this the case with him, for I know how greatly he has been provoked." So my safe-conduct was made out, and without delay I began to work in the Pope's service, with the utmost favour from him.

lxxv. One day Messer Latino Juvinale came to see me, and gave me the commission to make the Pope's money. This stirred up the wrath of my enemies, who began to put all sorts of hindrances in my way. Whereupon his Holiness, aware of their evil intentions, rebuked them all, and determined that I should do the work. So I began to make the dies for the crowns. In the middle I put Saint Paul, with the legend, *Vas electionis*. This coin gave much more satisfaction than did those of my rivals, so that the Pope told them nobody was to mention money to him again; for he had made up his mind I was to make his, and nobody else. So I set about the work with an easy mind; and Messer Latino Juvinale used to procure me audiences of the Pope, for his Holiness had given him orders to that effect. I was most eager to be reappointed stamper to the Mint; but on this point the Pope took counsel of others, and then told me that first of all I must receive pardon for the homicide. This I should have at the Holy Maries in August, by order of the aldermen of Rome. For it is the custom each year, on this solemn feast, to free twelve outlaws to these magistrates. In the meanwhile he would grant me another safe-conduct, so that I might rest secure till that time.

Then my enemies, seeing they could in no way prevent me having the Mint, bethought themselves of another expedient. The dead man Pompeo had left three thousand ducats as a dowry to a young bastard daughter of his. So they plotted that a favourite of Signor Pier Luigi, the Pope's son, should ask her in marriage, this lord himself to be the mediator. The thing was done. But the favourite was a wretched little peasant, brought up by Signor Pier Luigi; and, according to rumour, he touched little of the money, his lord seizing it for his own use. Well, several times the husband of this girl, to please his wife, asked his patron to have me arrested; and my lord had given a promise this should be done as soon as he saw my favour waning with the Pope. So things remained for about two months. The servant was trying all the time to get hold of the dowry, while his master would give him no straight answer, but kept assuring the wife he would certainly revenge her father. Though I knew something of what was going on, I presented myself several times before his lordship, who made a show of great benevolence to me. Yet all the time he was plotting either to have me murdered, or arrested by the Bargello. He had given the job into the hands of one of his men, a little devil of a Corsican soldier, ordering him to use all his wits in the business; and some other enemies of mine, especially Messer Traiano, proposed to give a hundred crowns to the assassin, who said he would do the thing as easily as he would suck a new-laid egg. Aware of all this, I walked with wary eyes, and in good company, excellently protected with under-coat of mail and with armlets, for which I had got leave. The little Corsican, in his avarice, thought he would have all the money for himself, without peril, fancying he could carry the thing through with no one to help him. So one day after dinner he sent for me in Signor Pier Luigi's name. I went at once, for my lord had spoken of having some large silver vessels made. I left home in a hurry, but armed myself as usual, and walked quickly along the Strada Giulia, thinking to find no one about at that hour. Well, I was at the top of the street, and was making for the Farnese palace, when, turning the corner wide, as is my habit, I saw the little Corsican get up from where he was sitting, and post himself in the middle of the road. Thus I was in no way taken by surprise. Ready to defend myself, I slowed up a little, and walked closer to the wall to put a wider space between us. But he followed my example; and when we were near each other, I could see plainly he was bent on doing me a mischief. And as I was alone, he thought he was going to succeed. Then I addressed him, saying, "Valorous soldier, if it were night, you might say you had mistaken me, but since it is day, you must know quite well who I am, and that I have never had anything to do with you, and never have done you any harm, but am quite capable of doing you a service." Thereupon, with a bullying gesture, and still standing in my path, he said he did not know what I was talking about. I replied, "I know very well what you want, and what you are saying; but this business you have in hand is more difficult and dangerous than you think; and perhaps it may turn out to your hurt. Remember you have to do with a man who would defend himself against a hundred; and the affair is not one for brave men like you to be concerned in." Meanwhile I, too, had been looking at him threateningly, and both of us changed colour. People had collected about us, for it was clear that our words meant bloodshed. So not daring to lay a hand on me, he cried, "We shall meet again." To which I answered, "I am always glad to see men of worth and those who prove themselves such."

Leaving him I repaired to my lord's house, to find he had never sent for me. When I was back in my shop, the Corsican sent me word by a great friend of his and mine that I need not be on the watch for him any more, for he was fain to be my good brother; but that I should keep a sharp look-out for others; that I was in the greatest peril, men of high rank having vowed my death. I sent him my thanks, and looked after my safety as well as I could. Not many days after, I was told by a great friend of mine that Signor Pier Luigi had expressly ordered I should be seized that evening. Word of this reached me in the late afternoon. I spoke of the matter to some of my friends, who urged me to escape. The order had been given for one hour after sundown; and two hours before that I was off with the post bound for Florence. The fact was, that when the Corsican had proved he had not pluck enough to fulfil his promise, Signor Pier Luigi, of his own authority, had given orders for me to be arrested, only to appease that daughter of Pompeo somewhat, who insisted on knowing what had come of her dowry. When he found it impossible to satisfy her by revenging her father in either of the two ways he had planned, he bethought him of another, which shall be told in its own place.

lxxvi. Reaching Florence, I presented myself to the Duke Alessandro, who received me with the greatest affection, and insisted I should stay with him. Now in Florence there was a sculptor called Il Tribolino, a great crony of mine, for I was god father to one of his sons. As we were talking together one day, he told me that Jacopo del Sansovino, who had been his master, had sent for him. Now as he had never been to Venice, and as he thought, besides, of the earnings to be looked for, he was most keen to go. Then he asked me if I had ever seen Venice, and I said no. Thereupon he begged me to accompany him, and I consented. So I told Duke Alessandro I should like to go to Venice first; and after that I should come back to his service. He demanded a promise from me to this effect, and ordered me to come to see him before I left. So next day, after having made my preparations, I went to take leave of the Duke, whom I found in the Pazzi palace, which at the time was inhabited by the wife and daughters of Signor Lorenzo Cibo. I sent a message to his Excellency that I wished to set off to Venice, by his kind permission; and an answer was brought back by Signor Cosimino de' Medici, to-day Duke of Florence, to the effect that I was to go and find Niccolò da Monte Aguto, who would give me fifty gold crowns; and that his Excellency gave me this money for my enjoyment, because he loved me. Afterwards I was to come back and serve him.

I got the money from Niccolò; went to fetch Tribolino at his house, and found him ready to start. He asked me if I had bound up my sword. I said a man riding forth on a journey should do no such thing; but he told me that such was the custom in Florence; and that there was a certain Ser Maurizio in power, who for the veriest trifle would have strung up St. John the Baptist himself. So you had to carry your sword bound till you were outside the gates. At this I laughed, and away we went. Soon we were joined by the Venice courier, who was nicknamed Lamentone; and we travelled in his company past Bologna, and arrived one evening at Ferrara. There we put up at the inn on the Piazza, and Lamentone went off to seek out some exiles, to bring them letters and messages from their wives, and this with the consent of the Duke. But only the courier might speak to them—no one else, under pain of the same sentence. Meanwhile, it being a little less than two hours from sundown, Tribolo and I went to see the Duke of Ferrara return from Belfiore, where he had been to watch the jousting. On the road we met a number of exiles, who looked at us hard, as though they would force us to speak with them. Tribolo, who was the biggest coward I have ever known, never stopped saying, "Don't look at them; don't speak to them, if you would ever go back to Florence." So we stayed to see the Duke's entry; then returning to our inn, we found Lamentone. About an hour after dark Niccolò Benintendi came in with his brother Piero, and an old man, who, I think, was Jacopo Nardi. With these were some other young men. They stormed the courier with questions about their own folk in Florence. Tribolo and I stood apart, so as not to talk with them. When they had spoken awhile with Lamentone, Niccolò Benintendi said, "I know those two quite well. Why are they too proud to speak to us?" Then Tribolo made me keep quiet, while Lamentone told them that the leave he had was not granted to us, which Benintendi said was ridiculous. "Plague take them!" cried he, with other pretty things of the kind. Thereupon I raised my head, and, with all the meekness I was capable of, addressed them thus, "Dear gentlemen, you can harm us a great deal, while we can in no way help you; and though you have said some things to us that had been better unsaid, yet we will not be wroth against you for that." Old Nardi declared I had spoken like the honest young fellow I was; but Niccolò Benintendi struck in with, "A fig for them and the Duke!" I answered that he was wronging us, for we had nothing to do with his affairs. Then old Nardi took up the cudgels for us, telling Benintendi he was unjust; but he went on insulting us all the same. So I warned him that I would say and do what would be most unpleasant to him, unless he minded his own business and left us in peace. But again he cried, "A fig for the Duke and you!" and told us we were a pack of asses. At these words I hurled back the lie in his face, and drew my sword. Then the old man, in his haste to be first at the stairs, tumbled down some steps, and the rest fell after him, one on the top of the other. I rushed forward, rattling my sword furiously along the wall, and shouting, "I will kill the last man of you!" But all the same I took the utmost care to do them no harm, though it would have been only too easy. Hearing the noise, the host called out; and Lamentone cried, "Keep back!" Some of them shouted, "Oh, my head!" others, "Let me out of this!" and so great was the confusion that they looked like a herd of swine. Then mine host brought a light. I retired upstairs, and sheathed my sword. Lamentone protested to Niccolò Benintendi he had done ill; and the host said to him, "It's a hanging matter to draw your sword here; and if the Duke knew of your insolence, he would string you up. I will let you off with less than you deserve; but never show your face in this inn again, else you'll repent it." Then the host came upstairs to me. I would have excused myself; but he did not let me say a word, telling me he knew I had had a thousand provocations, and advising me to be on the look-out for these men on my journey.

lxxvii. When we had supped, a boatman came to take us to Venice. I asked him if he would give us the boat to ourselves. He said yes, and the bargain was struck. In the morning betimes we rode to the port, which is some miles, I don't know how many, from Ferrara. As soon as we had got there, we found Niccolò Benintendi's brother, with three others, waiting my arrival. Among them they had two lances, and I had bought a good pike in Ferrara. Being otherwise well armed, I was not at all scared like Tribolo, who called out, "God save us! They have come to murder us!" Then Lamentone turned to me and said, "The best thing you can do is to go back to Ferrara, for I see this is a serious business. Benvenuto, my friend, I beg you, get out of the way of the fury of those mad beasts!" But I rejoined, "Rather let us go forward, for God helps the right, and you shall see how I can help myself. Have we not secured this bark for ourselves?" "Yes," said Lamentone. "Well, we shall hold it against them for all my valour is worth." I spurred on my horse, and when I was about fifty paces off, strode boldly forward with my pike. Tribolo lingered behind, hunched up on his horse, as if he had been frozen; and the courier Lamentone was puffing and blowing like the wind. It was a habit of his; but now he did it more than ever, as he stood waiting what would be the end of this devilry. When I had reached the boat, the boatman came up to me and said that some Florentine gentlemen wished to share it, if I would permit. To which I answered, "The boat is engaged for us and for no one else; and I am deeply grieved not to have the pleasure of their company." At these words a brave young fellow, one of the Magalotti, spoke up, "Benvenuto, we shall manage to procure you that pleasure." Whereupon I answered, "If God and the right which is on my side, as well as the force within me, manifest their full will and power, you shall manage nothing of the sort." And saying this, I jumped into the boat. Pointing my pike at them, I added, "With this I will show you that I am unable to avail myself of your company." Wishing to make a little show of fight, the Magalotti youth seized his weapon and came towards me. But I sprang upon the boat, and dealt him a blow that, had he not fallen backwards, I should have run him through. His friends, instead of coming to his aid, drew back. I saw I could have slain him, but instead of doing so, I said, "Get up, brother, take your weapons, and be off. You have seen that what I will not that I cannot, and what I could that I would not." Then I called in Tribolo and the boatman and Lamentone; and so we set off on our way to Venice. When we had gone ten miles along the Po, the young fellows, who had got into a little bark, came up with us, and when we were abreast of each other, that fool Pier Benintendi shouted, "Go on your way, Benvenuto, we shall meet again in Venice." "Make haste then," I said, "for I'll be there, and I'm ready to face any of you." So we arrived at Venice. There I took counsel with a brother of Cardinal Cornaro, and begged him to get me the permission to wear arms. He told me that I might certainly do so, for I ran no greater risk than of losing my sword.

lxxviii. So with my sword by my side, we went off to visit Jacopo del Sansovino, who had sent for Tribolo. He received us very kindly, and would have us dine with him, and so we stayed. But in his conversation with Tribolo, he said he had nothing for him to do just then, and bade him come back another time. At this I burst out laughing, and said jestingly to Sansovino, "Your home is rather too far away for him to come back again." And poor Tribolo, all woebegone, cried, "I have your letter here, in which you wrote to me to come." But Sansovino answered that men of his standing—men of repute and talent —could do a thing like that, and more too. Whereupon Tribolo shrugged his shoulders, and muttered "Patience!" over and over again. Then, in spite of the good dinner which Sansovino had given me, I took the part of my friend Tribolo, who had right on his side. But at table Sansovino never stopped chattering about the great things he had done, speaking ill of Michel Agnolo and of all who practised his art, and praising himself to the skies the while. I got so irritated that each mouthful of food nearly choked me. But all I said was, "O Messer Jacopo, men of worth behave like men of worth, and men of talent, who create things of beauty and excellence, are more easily recognised in the praises of others than in their own complacent boasting." At these words we all rose from the table fuming. That same day, near the Rialto of Venice, I came across Piero Benintendi, who had some others with him. Well aware that they were seeking to do me a mischief, I retired into an apothecary's shop till their excitement should pass. Afterwards I heard that young Magalotti, to whom I had spoken civilly, had cried out upon them; and so the thing passed off.

lxxix. A few days after we made our way back to Florence. When we disembarked at a place beyond Chioggia, on the left hand going to Ferrara, our host would have us pay, according to his custom, before we went to sleep. I said in other places one paid in the morning, but he declared, "I wish to be paid the night before, and in my own way." Whereupon I replied that those who wanted things done in their own way should make a world for themselves; and his customs were not ours; but he bade me not weary him with talking, because he had made up his mind to have his own way. Tribolo, who was shaking with fright, nudged me to keep still, lest we should come off worse. So we paid the people in their way, and then went off to sleep. We had indeed excellent beds, everything in them new and scrupulously clean. Yet all the same I never closed an eye all night for thinking how I could have my revenge. Once I thought of setting fire to the house; again of cutting the throats of the four fine horses he had in his stables. I saw how easy it would be for me to do either, but I did not quite see how my companion and I should escape. I finally made up my mind. First, I resolved to put my own baggage and my friend's in the boat; and this I did. Then, when the horses were attached to the towing-rope, I said no one was to move till I came back, as I had left a pair of slippers in the room where I had slept. So I went back to the inn and asked for the host, who called out that he had nothing to do with us, and that we could go to the devil. Standing by was a miserable little bit of a stable boy, gaping with sleep, who said to me, "He wouldn't move for the Pope, for he has a slut with him whom he has been after for a long time." Then the boy asked me for some drink-money, and I gave him a few little Venetian coins, and told him to go and talk to the man with the towing-rope till I looked for my slippers and came back. So upstairs I went. I took a little razor-edged knife, and cut the four beds that were there all into shreds; and I knew I had done damage to the tune of more than fifty crowns. Then I returned to the bark with bits of the bed-hangings in my pocket. Hastily I ordered the boatman to be off and away; but when we had gone a little distance from the inn, my crony Tribolo said he had left some little straps which bound up his valise, and that he really must return for them. To this I replied he need not mind about two little straps, for I would make him as many big ones as he wanted. He said that I was always jesting, but that he absolutely must go back for them. He insisted the boatman should stop, and I that he should go on. Meanwhile I told him the bad turn I had done to the host, and showed him a sample of the bed-hangings and other things, at which such a fear came over him that he kept calling to the boatman, "On, on with you quickly!" And he did not feel out of danger till he was back at the gates of Florence. When we had reached there, Tribolo said, "Let us bind up our swords, for God's sake! And no more pranks, for I have felt all the time I have been with you as if the knife were at my throat." On which I said, "Dear old Tribolo, you don't need to bind your sword up, for you have never drawn it." And this I said without looking, only because I had never once seen him play the man upon the journey. Whereupon, examining his sword, he cried out, "By God! it is the truth you tell, for here it is tied up just as it was before I left home!" To my comrade I had seemed a bad companion for having resented insults, and defended us both against those who would have harmed us. But I thought his conduct much worse, since not once did he come to my aid in times of need. Let him be the judge who looks on dispassionately.

lxxx. As soon as I dismounted I made haste to seek Duke Alessandro. I thanked him heartily for his present of fifty crowns, and told his Excellency I was most ready to serve him in whatever I was good for. Thereupon he ordered me on the spot to make the dies for his money. The first coin I made was one of forty soldi, with the head of his Excellency on one side, and on the other a San Cosimo and a San Damiano. These were silver coins, and they gave so much satisfaction that the Duke maintained they were the finest pieces in all Christendom. So said all Florence, and everybody who saw them. I therefore asked his Excellency to settle a salary on me, and give me apartments in the Mint. Thereupon he told me to give my mind to serving him, and he would allow me much more than I asked. Meanwhile he said he had given orders to the Master of the Mint, who was a certain Carlo Acciaiuoli, that I was to go to him for all the money I wanted. And this I found to be the case. But I touched my money so thriftily that there was always a balance, according to my account.

Afterwards I made the dies for the giulio. On this coin was a San Giovanni in profile, seated, with a book in his hand; and I thought I had never done anything so fine. On the other side were Duke Alessandro's arms. After that I made the dies for the half-giulios, on which I designed a head, full face, of San Giovannino. This was the first coin ever made with a full face on so thin a plate of silver. But the difficulty of the thing is not at all apparent except to the eyes of skilled masters in the art. Then I made stamps for the gold crowns. On one side was a cross, with some little cherubs, and on the other the arms of his Excellency. As soon as I had made those four sorts of money, I begged him to settle my salary, and also to grant me the apartments I had asked for, if he was pleased with what I had done. His Excellency, with much graciousness, said he was entirely satisfied, and that he would give due orders. We were in the Wardrobe during this conversation, my lord examining a wonderful little gun which he had just got from Germany. Seeing me look at the pretty tool with the utmost attention, he put it into my hand, saying he knew what delight such things gave me; and as an earnest of what he had promised me, I might take any arquebuse from his armoury I liked, save this one, though, he added, there were many more beautiful and just as good in the place. This offer I accepted with thanks. Seeing my eyes wandering round in search, he ordered his Master of the Wardrobe, a certain Pretino of Lucca, to let me take whatever I pleased. Then with a pleasant salutation he went off, and I stayed to choose the most beautiful and the best arquebuse that I ever had in my life; and I took it home with me. Two days later I showed him a few drawings, which he had asked me to make for some works in gold, intended as a gift to his wife, who was then in Naples. Once more I made the same request about the settlement of my affairs. But his Excellency replied that first of all he wished me to make a die for as fine a head of himself as I had made of Pope Clement. So I began this head in wax, and my lord ordered that at whatever hour I came to work on his portrait, I should be shown in to him. Seeing that this was to be a long affair, I called in a certain Pietro Pagolo of Monte Ritondo, near Rome, who had been with me as a very young boy there. I found him living with one Bernardonaccio, a goldsmith, who did not treat him very well. So I took him away, and taught him thoroughly how to stamp the money from the dies I had made. In the meanwhile I was engaged on the Duke's portrait. And many a time did I find him snoozing after dinner, alone with his Lorenzino, who afterwards murdered him; and it was always a great wonder to me that a Duke like him was so blindly trustful.

lxxxi. Now it came about that Ottaviano de' Medici, who to all intents governed everything in Florence, took the part of the old Master of the Mint. This fellow, Bastiano Cennini, was out of date, and had little knowledge. But his patron had mixed up his clumsy dies with mine in making the crowns. I complained about it to the Duke, who, finding it to be so, was much grieved, and said, "Go and tell this to Ottaviano de' Medici, and show him what has happened." So off I went and pointed out the injury done to my beautiful coins. But he answered me like a fool, "We like it so"; whereupon I replied that it was all wrong, and I would not have it. Said he, "And if the Duke is pleased?" But I answered, "Even then it would not satisfy me, for the thing is neither just nor reasonable." He bade me be off, and said I must swallow it so if I burst. Returning to the Duke, I related the whole of the disagreeable conversation between Ottaviano de' Medici and myself, and begged his Excellency not to let this injury be done to the beautiful coins I had made; also to give me leave to take my departure. Then he answered, "Ottaviano goes too far. You shall have your own way, for this is an insult to me."

The same day—it was a Thursday—there came to me from Rome an ample safe-conduct from the Pope, telling me to repair to him at once for the pardon of the Saint Maries in the middle of August, so that I might free myself from the charge of homicide. I went to seek the Duke, whom I found in bed, after an excess, as I was told. In little more than two hours I finished what was wanting to his wax medal, and when he saw the thing complete he was much pleased. Then I drew out the safe-conduct, and told him how the Pope had begged me to come back and do certain work for him. Thus I should regain a place in that fair city of Rome; yet, nevertheless, I should go on with his Excellency's medal. At this the Duke said, half in anger, "Benvenuto, do as I wish. Stop where you are, for I will settle your salary and give you the apartments in the Mint, and a great deal more than you would ever think of asking me, for you only ask what is just and reasonable. And whom would you leave to strike the fine dies you have made me?" Then I answered, "My lord, everything has been thought of, for I have here a pupil of mine, a young Roman, whom I have taught; and he will serve your Excellency admirably till I come back, with your medal finished, never to leave you any more. In Rome I have a shop with workmen and a deal of business; but as soon as I have got my pardon, I shall leave all the favour I enjoy there to an apprentice of mine, and then, with your Excellency's gracious leave, return to you." While we were talking, the only one present was Lorenzino de' Medici. Several times the Duke signed to him to urge me to stay, but Lorenzino would say nothing save, "Benvenuto, you would do best to stop here." I replied that I had the greatest desire to regain my old standing in Rome; whereupon he answered nothing, but stood looking at the Duke with the most evil eye. When the medal was finished as I wished, and I had shut it up in its little case, I said to the Duke, "My lord, be my good friend in this matter, for I shall make you a far finer medal than I made for Pope Clement. This is but natural, since that was the first that ever I tried my hand on; and Messer Lorenzino here will provide some beautiful design for the reverse, being a person of learning and the greatest talent." Thereat Lorenzino answered, "I have no other thought in my mind but to give you a reverse worthy of his Excellency." The Duke laughed, and, looking at Lorenzo, said, "You shall give him the reverse, and he shall do it here and not go away." And Lorenzo cried out, "I will do it as speedily as may be, and hope it may be what shall make the world wonder." The Duke, who now looked on him as something of a fool, and now as a coward, only turned over in bed and laughed at his words. I then went off without formal leave-taking, and left them alone together. The Duke, who did not believe that I was quitting Florence, said nothing more to me. But when he learned afterwards that I had really set off, he sent a servant after me, who overtook me at Siena, and gave me fifty gold ducats from his Excellency, also a message that I should spend them and remember him; likewise that I was to come back as soon as I could. "And," said the man, "Messer Lorenzo bids me say he is preparing a marvellous reverse for the medal you are going to make." I had left full instructions with Pietro Pagolo, the Roman of whom I have spoken, as to how he was to stamp the coins; but the thing was very difficult, and he never did the work very well. I remained the creditor of the Mint for making the dies, to the amount of more than seventy crowns.

lxxxii. On my way to Rome, I carried the splendid arquebuse which the Duke had given me, and many a time did I use it on the journey, to my great enjoyment, while the feats I performed with it were extraordinary. At last I reached the City. Now I had a little house in the Strada Giulia, but as it was not ready, I dismounted at the house of Messer Giovanni Gaddi, clerk of the Camera, to whom, on my departure from Rome, I had confided a number of fine weapons and many other things I valued. I did not wish to get down at my shop, but sent for my partner, Felice, and told him to have my little house put into proper order without delay. The next day I went to sleep there, having made a good provision of clothes and other necessary things, as on the morrow I intended to go and see the Pope and thank him. In my employment were two serving-lads, and on the floor beneath was a laundress, who cooked for me excellently. I had several friends to supper, and the evening having passed most pleasantly, I went to bed. The night was hardly over; it was more than an hour to dawn, when I heard a tremendous hammering at the door of my house, each knock hurrying on the top of the other. So I called for the elder of my two servants, who was called Cencio (the one whom I took with me to the wizard's circle), and told him to go and see what madman was making this devilish noise at such an hour. While Cencio went down, I lighted another lamp—I kept one burning always during the night—hastily slipped over my shirt a magnificent coat of mail, and above that whatever garments came to hand. Cencio came back crying, "Alas! my master, it is the Bargello with all his guard; and he says if you don't make haste, he will beat the door down. And they have torches and all kinds of things with them." To which I answered, "Tell him I am putting on a rag or two of clothes, and I am coming down in my shirt." Thinking it was an attempt at murder, such as Signor Pier Luigi had plotted, I took in my right hand a first-rate dagger, and in my left the safe-conduct. Then I ran to the back windows, which gave on some gardens, and there I saw more than thirty of the guards. So I knew that I could not escape by that side. Putting the two lads in front of me, I told them to open the door the very instant I should tell them. Then, quite ready, my dagger in my right hand, the safe-conduct in my left, and in a proper attitude of defence, I said to my lads, "Have no fear. Open the door!" At once Vittorio, the Bargello, with two of the guards, burst in, thinking to seize me without difficulty; but finding me prepared, they retired, saying, "This is no jesting matter." On which I called out, throwing them the safe-conduct, "Read that, and since you may not arrest me, I will not let you touch me." Then the Bargello ordered some of his men to lay hands on me, saying the safe-conduct would be seen to later. At this I flashed out my weapon furiously. "God for the right!" I cried. "Alive, I'm not for you. You can only take me dead." The room was crowded. They looked as if they would come at me with force; but I stood grimly on the defensive, and the Bargello saw he could not have me otherwise than I had said. So he called the notary, and while he was having the safe-conduct read, two or three times he made as if he were about to set his guard on me. Yet I stood firm in my resolution. Then, giving up the attempt, they threw the safe-conduct on the ground and made off without me.

lxxxiii. I went back to my rest, but I was so disturbed that I could not fall asleep again. I meant to be bled as soon as it should be daylight, so I asked advice of Messer Giovanni Gaddi, by whom I was sent to a quack of his acquaintance, who asked me if I had had a fright! Now think what a wise doctor he was, who, after hearing of such a serious matter, asked me a question like that! He was a feather-brained fool, who was always laughing, and about nothing at all. So now, sniggering as usual, he told me to take a good beaker of Greek wine, and to be merry, and to keep my mind at rest. Then Messer Giovanni said, "A thing of bronze or marble might tremble in a case like this. How much more a mere man?" Whereupon the quack replied, "Monsignor, we are not all made the same way. This man is neither of bronze nor marble, but of pure iron itself"; and, feeling my pulse, laughing idiotically the while, he said to Messer Giovanni, "Feel here now; this is no man's pulse! it is a lion's or a dragon's." Then as my pulse was beating furiously, perhaps much faster than in any case which that imbecile doctor had read of either in Hippocrates or Galen, I knew how ill I was. But that I might not make myself more agitated or worse than I was already, I pretended to be in good heart. Meanwhile Messer Giovanni had ordered dinner, and the whole company sat down to eat. Among us, besides our host, were Messer Lodovico of Fano, Messer Antonio Allegretti, Messer Giovanni Greco, all men of great learning, and Messer Annibal Caro, who was then quite a youth; and nothing else was talked about at dinner except this brave deed of mine. Moreover, they had the whole story again from my young servant Cencio, who was extraordinarily intelligent, spirited, and handsome. Every time he recounted my fierce daring—taking on my attitude in the encounter, and repeating the very words I had used—he called up circumstances I had forgotten. Then they went on to ask if he had been afraid; to which he answered they should ask me, for he had felt just as I had done.

This parrot-talk wearied me in the end; and, since I felt much shaken, I rose from table, saying I wished to go and get new suits of cloth and azure silk for Cencio and myself, for I was going to walk in the procession, four days hence, at the Saint Maries, when I intended him to carry a white lighted torch. So I departed and went to have the blue cloth cut, with a fine vest of sarcenet, also blue, and a doublet of the same. For the lad I ordered a doublet and vest of blue taffeta. When the things were cut, I went off to the Pope, who bade me speak with Messer Ambrogio, as he had given orders I was to make a large gold vessel. So I went to find Messer Ambrogio. He knew all about the Bargello affair, and had, indeed, been in alliance with my enemies to bring me back from Florence, and had rated the Bargello well for not having arrested me. That officer excused himself, saying he could not openly defy a safe-conduct. But when I went to him, Messer Ambrogio talked over the business which the Pope had given him orders about. He bade me make the designs, and everything would be arranged for the work.

Meanwhile came on the day of the Saint Maries. Now it is the custom that those about to obtain their pardon should surrender themselves prisoners. But I returned to the Pope and said to his Holiness I did not wish to be put in prison, and begged him to let me off. He said that such was the custom, and so it must be. Thereupon I knelt down once more, and thanked him for the safe-conduct he had given me, with which I should return to the service of my Duke of Florence, who waited me in all eagerness. Hearing this, he turned to one of his attendants and said, "Let Benvenuto have his pardon without the prison. Make out his papers to this effect." The document being drawn up, the Pope signed it, and it was registered at the Capitol. Then, on the appointed day, I walked in the procession, in an honourable place between two gentlemen, and received my full pardon.

lxxxiv. Four days after I was seized with a very high fever and with a shaking fit. I went to bed, and thought I was about to die. The first physicians in Rome were called in, among whom was one Maestro Francesco da Norcia, the oldest doctor in the city, and one of most reputation. I explained to the doctors what I believed to be the cause of my grave illness; that I had wished to be bled, but was advised against it; and I begged them, if it were not too late, to bleed me now. Maestro Francesco answered that to draw blood now would do me no good, but if it had been done at the right time, I should not have been ill at all. Now he must cure me in some other way. So they enlisted all their zeal and skill for my cure, and every day I got violently worse. At the end of eight days the malady had increased so much that the doctors, despairing of the case, ordered that I should be indulged and given anything I asked for. Maestro Francesco said, "While he still breathes call on me at any hour, for one never knows what Nature will do for a young man of this sort; but if he should become unconscious, give him these five remedies, one on top of the other, and send for me. I will come at any hour of the night. For I should be better pleased to save him than any Cardinal in Rome." Two or three times a day Messer Giovanni Gaddi came to visit me, and every time he would handle my fine gun, or my armour, or my sword, always saying, "This is a fine thing," or "This other is still finer." And the same did he with my models, and with all my other little possessions, till he made me furious. And with him came a certain Mattio Franzesi, who looked as if he were wearying for my death, not because he would come in for anything of mine; but, as it appeared, he merely wished for what Messer Giovanni had such a longing for.

I had with me Felice, my partner, who gave me the best aid which one man could possibly give to another in this world. My strength was ebbing all away. I had not force enough to draw a breath, but my brain was as sound as when I was in health. Yet though I was not delirious, a terrible old man used to come to my bedside, and try to haul me by force into a great boat. Then I would call for my Felice to come to me and chase the old scoundrel away. Felice, who loved me tenderly, would come running, in tears, crying, "Off with you, you old traitor, who would rob me of my all!" Messer Giovanni Gaddi, who was standing by, said, "The poor fellow raves. Ah! he'll not last long"; while the other man, Mattio Franzesi, added, "He has read Dante, and in his utter weakness his mind wanders"; then with a laugh, "Be off, you old rascal! don't vex our Benvenuto!" I saw they were laughing at me; so I turned to Messer Giovanni Gaddi and said to him, "My dear master, I would have you know that I am not raving, and that it is the truth, this old man annoys me very much. But you would do well to take that villain Mattio out of my sight, for he laughs at my misfortunes; and the next time your lordship is good enough to come and see me, let it be with Messer Antonio Allegretti, or Messer Annibal Caro, or any other of your distinguished acquaintances, men of taste and intelligence, and of quite another stamp from this brute here." Then Messer Giovanni said in joke to Mattio to be off and never come back again; but as Mattio still laughed, the joke became serious, for Messer Giovanni refused to see him again, and sent for Messer Antonio Allegretti and Messer Lodovico and Messer Annibal Caro. As soon as these worthy men had come, I was much comforted, and talked with them quite sensibly, yet every now and then entreating Felice to drive away the old man. Messer Lodovico asked me who it was I saw, and what he was like. While I was drawing his picture exactly in words, the old man took hold of my arm and hauled me forcibly towards him, so that I called out to them to help me, for he was going to throw me down to the bottom of his fearsome boat. At these last words I fell into a deep swoon, and it seemed to me that I was being thrown into the boat. They said that while I lay unconscious, I tossed about and cast evil words at Messer Giovanni, telling him he came to rob me, and not for love of me at all, and a great many other accusations which put him greatly to the blush. Then, they said, I stopped as if I were dead; and when more than an hour had come and gone, and I seemed to be growing cold, they left me for dead. Then they went home and told Mattio Franzesi, who wrote to my dearest friend, Messer Benedetto Varchi, at Florence, that at such and such an hour of the night they had seen me die. That man of great talent, and my most dear friend, hearing this false report of my death, made an admirable sonnet, which shall be set down in its own place.

More than three hours passed ere I came to myself; and having applied all the physician's remedies, and seeing that I still did not revive, my beloved Felice set off running to Maestro Francesco of Norcia's house. He knocked so loud that he awoke him and made him rise. Weeping, he begged him to come to my house, for he thought I was dead. Whereupon Maestro Francesco, who was a very hot-tempered man, called down, "My son, what do you think I should do if I came? If he is dead, I am sorrier than you. Do you think that by coming with my medicine I could blow life into his body?" But seeing that the poor lad went off crying, he called him back, and gave him a certain oil wherewith to anoint my pulses and my heart, and told him to squeeze my little toes and little fingers very hard; adding that if I came to, he was to be sent for at once. Felice left Maestro Francesco and did his bidding. When it was almost daylight, and hope was given up by the watchers, orders were given to make my shroud and to wash my body. All of a sudden I came to myself, and called out to Felice to drive off the old man who was plaguing me, and, quick, quick, I said. Whereupon Felice wanted to send for Maestro Francesco; but I said no; he was to come to me and drive away the old man, who was afraid of him. When Felice came to my bedside, and I touched him, the furious old wretch seemed to make off; so I begged him to stay by me all the time. But Maestro Francesco came at last, and he said he was determined to save me in spite of everything, and that he had never seen greater force in any young man than in me. Then, sitting down to write, he ordered perfumes, lotions, unguents, plasters, and all sorts of wonderful things. In the meanwhile, having had more than twenty leeches applied to my posteriors, I came to, but I felt as if I had been pierced, bound, and pulverised. Many of my friends came to see the miracle of the revived corpse, and among them men of the greatest importance. In their presence I said that the little gold I had—which might amount to eight hundred crowns, between gold, silver, jewels, and loose money—I wished to be given to my poor sister in Florence, who was called Mona Liperata. All the rest of my belongings, including my armour, I bequeathed to my beloved Felice, and fifty gold ducats besides, so that he might buy himself clothing. Hearing this, Felice fell on my neck, saying he wished for nothing but that I should live. Then I said, "If you wish me to live, put your hand on me as before, and cry to that old man to be off, for he is afraid of you." At these words some of them were terrified, for they said I was not raving, but spoke reasonably and with a clear head.

So my illness lingered on, and I got little better. The most excellent Maestro Francesco came four or five times a day, but Messer Giovanni Gaddi, who had been shamed, never came to see me any more. My brother-in-law, however, the husband of my sister Liperata, turned up from Florence to claim the inheritance; but he was a very good fellow and was delighted to find me alive. I was comforted more than I can tell by the sight of him, and he showed me the utmost affection, saying he had only come to nurse me with his own hands. And he did so for several days. After that I sent him away, the hope of my recovery being by that time almost sure. It was then he left the sonnet of Messer Benedetto Varchi. Here it is:

ON THE SUPPOSED DEATH OF BENVENUTO CELLINI, WHO WAS YET ALIVE

Who shall console us, Mattio? Who shall tell
  Our eyes to cease their weeping o'er his bier?
  Ah, the hard truth, that leaving us down here,
In youthful haste, he has gone up to dwell!
Clear, friendly soul, in art thou didst excel
  All that did come before thee. Much I fear
  The world shall never see again thy peer,
The world, of which the best take first farewell.
O gentle spirit, if beyond our haze
  Still thou mayst love, look on me from the sky.
  'Tis not thy bliss I weep, but mine own ill.
Now from thy place in Heaven thou dost gaze
  On the High Father; seest Him face to face
  Whom thou didst shadow with thy mortal skill.

lxxxv. My malady had been so terrible that it seemed as if it would never end; and that good man Francesco da Norcia gave himself more trouble than ever, and every day he kept bringing me new remedies, striving to repair that poor disordered instrument, my body. Yet with all these extraordinary efforts, it seemed impossible to weaken the malady's persistent hold on me; so that the doctors were almost in despair, and did not know what further they could do. I had an insatiable thirst, yet I had refrained from drinking for many days, in obedience to orders. Felice, who was very proud of having saved my life, never left me; and the old man troubled me less, though he still came to me sometimes in my dreams. But one day Felice had gone out, and an apprentice was left as nurse, with a servant called Beatrice. I asked the apprentice what had become of my lad Cencio, and why I had never seen him waiting on me. The lad told me that Cencio had been much more ill than I, and that now he lay at the point of death. Felice had ordered them not to tell me this. I was greatly grieved at the news, and I called Beatrice, the servant, a girl from Pistoja, and begged her to fill a great crystal wine-cooler, that stood near, with clear fresh water, and to bring it to me. The girl ran at once and brought it to me full. I asked her to hold it to my mouth, and promised, if she would let me drink as long a draught as I wished, I'd give her a gown. Now this servant had stolen a few little things of some importance, and in her terror lest the theft should be found out, she would have been glad for me to die. Therefore she let me drink twice of the water, and as much as I could each time, so that in truth I drank more than a flask. Then I lay down under the bedclothes, began to perspire, and fell asleep. Felice came back after I had slept about an hour, and asked the lad how I was. "I don't know," said the boy; "Beatrice brought him that wine-cooler full of water, and he has nearly drunk it all. I don't know now if he be dead or alive." They say the poor young fellow almost fell down in a swoon from the vexation he felt. Then taking a thick stick he beat the servant furiously, crying, "Alas, traitress! you have killed him." But while Felice was belabouring her, and she was howling, I dreamt. It seemed to me that I saw the old man again with ropes in his hand, and he was preparing to bind me with them. Felice now came on the scene, and was attacking him with a hatchet, so that the old wretch ran away, crying "Let me go, and I shan't come back again in a hurry!" Meanwhile Beatrice ran into my room, screaming at the top of her voice. This woke me up, and I said, "Let her alone, for perhaps in meaning me harm, she has done me more good than you ever have been able to, with all your devotion. But come now and help me, for I am all of a sweat. Quick!" Felice took heart again, dried me, and made me comfortable; and feeling greatly better, I became assured of my recovery.

When Maestro Francesco came, he saw the great improvement in me, also the servant weeping, the prentice running hither and thither, and Felice laughing. This confusion made the doctor think some extraordinary thing had happened, which had worked this change in me for the better. Meanwhile, the other doctor, Maestro Bernardino, had come in, the one who, in the beginning, had not wished me to be bled. Maestro Francesco, that splendid fellow, cried out, "Oh, power of Nature! she knows her own needs. We doctors know nothing." Whereupon that fool of a Maestro Bernardino answered, "If only he had drunk another flask, he would have been cured at once." But Maestro Francesco, a venerable man, and of great authority, replied, "Please God that such a misfortune fall on your own head!" Then turning to me, he asked me if I could have drunk more. "No," I answered, "for I had quenched my thirst." Then to Maestro Bernardino he said, "See you, Nature had just satisfied her needs, neither more nor less. So was she craving what she needed, when the poor young man requested to be bled. If you knew that the saving of him depended on his drinking two flasks of water, why did you not say so before? Then you would have got the credit." At these words the quack went off in a surly temper, and he never turned up any more.

Then Maestro Francesco said I must be taken out of the room where I lay; and he had me carried up to one of the hills of Rome. Cardinal Cornaro, hearing of my recovery, had me brought to a place of his on Monte Cavallo. That very night I was carried with the utmost care in a chair, well covered, and not jostled. As soon as I arrived, I began to vomit, and in the vomit which I brought up was a hairy worm, a quarter of a cubit in length. The hairs were long, and the worm was most hideous, and covered with different-coloured spots, green, black, and red. They kept it for the doctor, who declared he had never seen such a thing. Then he said to Felice, "Now take good care of your Benvenuto, for he is cured. Don't allow him any excesses. For though he has escaped this time, yet another disorder would kill him. You see his sickness has been so serious, that had we been bringing him the holy oil, we might have come too late. Now I am sure that with a little patience and time he will still do fine work." Then turning to me, he said, "Benvenuto, my friend, be wise, and lead a regular life; and when you are cured,

I want you to make me a Madonna with your own hand, and I will say my prayers to her always for love of you." Afterwards I asked him whether I might prudently move to Florence. He told me that I should get a little stronger first, and wait to see what Nature did for me.

lxxxvi. After eight days had passed, the improvement was so little that I was aweary of myself; for I had been more than fifty days in this great trouble. But making up my mind, I prepared to set off; and in a double basket-litter my dear Felice and I departed for Florence. Now as I had not written beforehand, when I got to my sister's house, she wept and laughed over me at the same time. That day many of my friends came to see me, among them Pier Landi, the best and the dearest I ever had in the world. Next day came a certain Niccolò da Monte Aguto, also a very great friend of mine. Now he had heard the Duke say, "Benvenuto would have done much better if he had died, for he has come here to run his head into a halter; and I shall never pardon him." So Niccolò came to me in despair, and said, "Alas, dear Benvenuto, what are you doing here? Do you not know how you have offended the Duke? I have heard him swear that you were running your head into a halter, for a certainty." Then I answered, "Niccolò, recall to his Excellency that Pope Clement wanted to hang me before now, and with as little justice. Let him keep a look-out on me, and leave me until I am better. Then I can prove to his lordship that I have been the most faithful servant he will ever have in the whole course of his life; and since some enemy must have done me this ill turn out of jealousy, let him wait till I get my health, and I can render such an account of myself as will astonish him."

Now this ill turn I owed to the painter Giorgetto Vassellario of Arezzo, perhaps in return for many good turns I had done him. For I had given him hospitality in Rome and paid his expenses, though he had been a most troublesome guest; for he suffered from a dry skin disease, and his hands were all wasted from continual scratching. Now he had slept with a good young fellow in my employment, called Manno; and when he thought he was scratching himself, he had taken the skin off one of Manno's legs with his dirty hands, the nails of which he never cut. Manno left me, and, indeed, was determined to have his life; but I reconciled them. Afterwards I got an opening for Giorgio with the Cardinal de' Medici, and continued to help him. It was for this I had deserved his slanderous report to the

Duke Alessandro that I had spoken ill of his Excellency, and had boasted I should be the first to scale the walls of Florence, in company with his exiled enemies. These words, according to what I heard later, had been put into his mouth by that gallant gentleman Ottaviano de' Medici, who wanted to revenge himself for the Duke's rating him in the matter of the coins, and my consequent departure from Florence. But I, who was innocent of this treason unjustly put to my count, had no fear in the world. And meanwhile the clever doctor, Francesco da Montevarchi, treated me with the greatest skill. He had been introduced by my friend Luca Martini, who stayed the greater part of every day with me.

lxxxvii. In the meantime I had sent my devoted Felice to Rome to look after my business there. As soon as I could just raise my head from the pillow, which was at the end of fifteen days, though I could not yet put my feet to the ground, I had myself carried to the little upper terrace of the Medici palace. There I was seated to wait till the Duke should go by. Many of my friends of the Court came to speak to me, and they were greatly astonished I had given myself the pain of being carried in this fashion, while still in such a weak condition. I might have waited, they said, till I was quite better, and then have gone to see the Duke. There was a crowd of people about me, all looking at me as if I were a miracle, and this not so much because they had heard I was dead; still stranger to them was it that now I looked like a corpse. Then I said before them all, how my lord the Duke had been told by some foul-tongued rascal that I had boasted I should be the first to scale his Excellency's walls, and that, moreover, I had spoken ill of him. Thus I had not the heart to live or die till I should purge myself of this infamous accusation, and know who was the bold slanderer that had spread the false report. As I spoke, a large number of the gentlemen gathered round me. They manifested great sympathy for me, and while one said one thing and one another, I declared that I would never go away from here till I knew who was my accuser. At these words Maestro Agustino, the Duke's tailor, made his way through the crowd of nobles, and said, "If that's all you want to know, you can learn it now." At the very moment Giorgio, the painter, of whom I have spoken, was passing, and Maestro Agustino said, "There's the man who accused you. Now you know best if it be true or not." I could not move from the spot, but I hotly demanded of Giorgio if this was the case. Giorgio said No; it was not true, and he had never said any such thing. To this Maestro Agustino replied, "O you gallows bird! don't you know that I know it perfectly?" Thereupon Giorgio made off in haste, still protesting he was not the man. In a little the Duke came along. I had myself propped up in front of his Excellency, and he stopped. I told him I had come here like this only to justify myself. The Duke looked at me, and wondered I was alive. Then he told me to give my mind to being an honest man, and to getting well. When I returned home, Niccolò da Monte Aguto came to see me, and told me I had passed through one of the most perilous storms in the world, and he never could have believed I should escape; for he had seen my evil fate written with unfading ink. But now I was to think of getting well speedily; and then I must be out of this, for danger threatened me from a powerful quarter, and at the hands of a man who had the means of doing me hurt. Then, "Look out!" he said, adding, "What harm have you done to that scoundrel Ottaviano de' Medici?" I replied, I had never done him any harm, but that he had done me many an ill turn; and I told him all about the Mint affair. Then said he again, "Be off as speedily as you can; but be of good heart, for sooner than you think, you will see yourself revenged." So I did my best to get well, and advised Pietro Pagolo in the matter of the stamping of the coins. Then I set off for Rome, without notice to the Duke or any one else.

lxxxviii. When I got back to Rome, I amused myself among my friends, and then began the Duke's medal. In a few days I had completed the head in steel, and it was the finest thing of the kind I had ever done. Now there came to see me, at least once a day, a certain Messer Francesco Soderini, a fool of a man. Seeing what I was working at, he kept on saying to me over and over again, "Ah! you heartless creature! You are bent then on immortalising that mad tyrant! And since you have never done anything so beautiful before, it is plain you are as much our determined enemy as you are their warm friend, though the Pope and the Duke have twice tried to hang you without cause. So much for the Father and the Son; look out for the Holy Ghost!" It was fully believed, I should say, that Duke Alessandro was Pope Clement's son. Moreover, Messer Francesco used to say, and firmly swear, that if he could, he would have stolen the dies for the medal. I answered that he had done well to tell me, and that I should take care he should never get a sight of them again.

I sent word to Florence to ask Lorenzino to send me the

reverse of the medal. Niccolò da Monte Aguto, to whom I had written, answered me to the effect that he had asked that mad, melancholy philosopher Lorenzino for it, who had replied, that night or day he thought of nothing else, and that he would do it as soon as ever he could. Yet, said he, I was not to depend upon his reverse, but to invent one for myself; and as soon as I had finished it, bring it boldly to the Duke, and it would be a good thing for me. So I drew what seemed a fitting design, and put my best energy into the work; but as I was not yet set up after my terrible illness, I often amused myself out shooting with my dear Felice. He, by the way, knew nothing of my craft, but as we were always together, night and day, every one supposed him to be a most skilled artist. So as he was a pleasant-tempered fellow, many a time we laughed about the great reputation he had won. Now his name was Felice Guadagni [Gain]; so he used to joke with me, saying, "I should be called Felice Guadagni-poco [Gain-little], if you hadn't got me such credit that I can call myself Guadagni-assai [Gain-much]." But I told him there were two ways of earning: by the first, one gains for one's self; by the second, for others; and then I praised the second method much more than the first—seeing he had won back for me my life.

We had many and many a talk together, but there was one day in particular—in Epiphany it was—when we were near La Magliana, and evening was coming on. That day a good many wild ducks and geese had fallen to my gun. When I had made up my mind to shoot no more, we turned our faces towards Rome. I called my dog Barucco, but not seeing him in front of me, I turned and spied the well-trained creature watching certain geese that were huddled in a ditch. So I got down at once, loaded my little gun, and at a long range brought down two with one ball. I never used to shoot with more; and even when I shot at two hundred cubits, I mostly hit my mark —and this can't be done in any other way. Of my two geese, one was almost dead, and the other was wounded and struggling to fly. My dog went for the first and fetched it back to me; while, seeing the other plunge right into the ditch, I jumped down after it. Trusting to my boots, which were very high, I thrust out one foot and it stuck in the mud. Thus, though I caught the goose, my right boot was full of water. Lifting it up, I emptied the water, and then mounting, we hurried on to Rome. But the cold was extreme, and I felt my leg freezing; so I said to Felice, "Something must be done for my leg; I cannot bear it any longer." Without another word, the good Felice got down from his horse, and gathered thistles and twigs to light a fire. But while I waited, I had thrust my hands among the breast-feathers of the geese, and it was very warm there. So I did not let him kindle the fire, but stuffed my boot with goose's feathers, and all at once I felt such comfort that my life came back to me.

lxxxix. Mounting again, we rode in hot haste towards Rome. It was night by the time we reached a certain rising ground. There, looking towards Florence, we both of us with one accord cried out in wonder, "O God of Heaven! what marvel is this that we see above Florence?" It looked like a great beam of fire, which radiated a glorious light. I said to Felice, "For certain, we shall hear to-morrow that some great event has come to pass in Florence." When we got back to Rome it was pitch dark, and as we reached the neighbourhood of the Banks, near our own house, my little horse was ambling on at a great pace. Now that very day they had piled up a heap of plaster and broken tiles in the middle of the street, and neither my horse nor I saw it. He rushed upon it furiously, and coming down on the other side, he fell, his head between his legs; and if I got no hurt, it was truly by God's help. Out came all the neighbours' lights at the great noise; but I rose quickly to my feet, and without mounting again I ran home, laughing heartily at having so barely escaped breaking my neck. On reaching my house, I found some friends of mine, and while we were having supper, I told them of all the accidents of the chase, and of that devilry in the sky—the beam of fire we had seen. Some of them said, "What meaning shall to-morrow give to this?" And I answered, "This marvel means some great event that has taken place in Florence." And so supper passed by pleasantly. Next day, late, came the news of the death of Duke Alessandro. So, many of my acquaintances came to me and said, "You spoke the truth, that in Florence some great event had happened." And then came Messer Francesco Soderini, jogging along on his old mule, laughing all the way like a fool, and saying, "This is the reverse of that rascally tyrant's medal, which your Lorenzino de' Medici promised you," adding, "You would immortalise dukes for us, would you? We'll have no more dukes"; and then he mocked at me, as if I had been head of the faction that makes the dukes. Then in came a certain Baccio Bettini, whose ugly head was as big as a corbel, and he, too, railed at me about dukes, saying, "We've unduked them. We'll have no more dukes! And you who would make them immortal for us!" and other wearisome jokes of the kind. This was too much for me in the end, and I burst out, "O you fools! I am a poor goldsmith, and I serve him who pays me; yet you rail at me as if I were the head of a party. Nevertheless, I won't cast up to you the greed, the folly, the cowardice of men like you in the past. But in answer to your foolish laughter, I tell you plainly that, before two or three days have gone by, you shall have another duke, and may be a much worse one than the last." Next day Bettini came to my shop and said, "What is the good of spending money on couriers, for you know things before they come to pass? What spirit tells them to you?" And he told me that Cosimo de' Medici, son of Lord Giovanni, was made Duke; but he was bound by certain conditions, so that he could not cut capers just as he liked. Then I began to laugh at this, saying, "Those Florentines have mounted a young man on a splendid horse; they have given him spurs, put the reins freely in his hand, set him out in a magnificent field full of flowers and fruits and all kinds of delicious things; then they tell him he must not pass certain prescribed boundaries. Now, tell me, who is he that can hold him in, once he has a mind to pass them? Laws cannot be enforced on the law's master." So they left me alone, and didn't trouble me any more.

xc. Then I gave my attention to my shop, and went on with my business, which was not, however, of great importance at the time, for I was taking good care of my health, as it did not seem quite assured after the serious illness through which I had passed.

Meanwhile the Emperor had come back victorious after his Tunis expedition; and the Pope sent for me to ask my advice concerning a suitable gift for his Majesty. Whereupon I said that, in my opinion, the most fitting gift would be a golden crucifix, for which I had almost completed an ornament: this would be just the right thing, and would do infinite credit to his Holiness and to me. I had already made three little golden figures in the round, of the length of a palm. Indeed, these were the Faith, Hope, and Charity I had designed for Pope Clement's chalice. Then I added in wax what was still needed for the foot of the cross, and when I took it to the Pope, with the Christ in wax, and a great many beautiful accessories, he was greatly pleased. Before I parted from his Holiness, we had come to an understanding on all that was to be done, and estimated the cost of the work.

This was one evening at four hours after sun-down, and the Pope ordered Messer Latino Juvenale to provide me with the money next morning. It pleased this Messer Latino, who had a great vein of foolishness in him, to suggest a new design to the Pope, which he made out of his own head. This upset all our arrangements; and in the morning, when I went for the money, he said with his brutal impudence, "It is for us to invent; for you to execute. Before I left the Pope last evening, we thought of something far better." But I cut into his words with, "Neither you nor the Pope could think of anything better than a design where Christ comes in. So out with all your courtier's tom-fooleries. I don't care a hang!" Without another word he left me in a rage, and did his best to have the work given to another goldsmith. But the Pope would not have this; and sending for me in haste, he told me that I had given him good advice, but that they wished to make use of a little book of the Hours of the Virgin, in which there were wonderful miniatures. It had cost the Cardinal de' Medici more than two thousand crowns. This would be a very suitable gift to the Empress; and for the Emperor they would afterwards make what I had designed, which in truth would be a present worthy of him. He only proposed this arrangement because there was little time; for the Emperor was expected in Rome in a month and half or so. For this book he wanted a cover made of solid gold, richly worked, and studded thickly with jewels, worth about six thousand crowns. So when I had received the materials, I set about the work, giving all my mind to it, and in a few days its beauty was so manifest, that the Pope marvelled, and heaped compliments on me. It was understood that the brute Juvenale should not come near me.

When the work was nearly finished, the Emperor arrived. Many triumphal arches of wonderful splendour were raised in his honour; and he entered Rome with extraordinary pomp. But that I'll leave to others to describe, for I have no mind to speak save of what concerns myself. Immediately on his arrival, he presented the Pope with a diamond which he had bought for twelve thousand crowns. His Holiness sent for me, and giving me this diamond, said I was to make a ring to his measure. But first he wished me to bring the book just as it was. This I did, and he was greatly pleased. Then he consulted me as to what excuse he could make to the Emperor for the work being incomplete. I suggested that a plausible excuse would be my illness, which his Majesty would be ready to believe, seeing me so worn and wan. To this the Pope answered that that would do very well; but that I was to add, from him, when I presented the book, that I made him a present of myself as well. Then he told me how I was to comport myself, and what words I should say. I repeated these words to him, asking him if he would be satisfied, did I say them so. "You could not do better," he replied, "if you have the courage to speak to the Emperor as you do to me." Then I answered that I should have far greater courage in speaking to the Emperor, seeing that he was clad like me, and that it would seem as if I were addressing a man made like myself; which was not the case when I spoke to his Holiness, in whom I saw a far greater divinity, partly because of his ecclesiastical trappings, which were as a kind of halo about him, and partly because of the fine venerable appearance of his Holiness. Both these things bred greater awe in me than did any Emperor. To this the Pope replied, "Go, Benvenuto mine, you are a very clever man. Do us credit, and it will be well for you."

xci. The Pope had two Turkish horses, which had belonged to Pope Clement, the finest that ever were seen in Christendom. He ordered Messer Durante, his chamberlain, to lead them through the corridors of the palace, and then present them to the Emperor, with a little speech which he had composed for him. Down we went together, and came into the presence. The two horses entered, and made their way through the apartments so spiritedly and with such majesty, that the Emperor and every one marvelled. Then Messer Durante stepped out most awkwardly, and knotting up his tongue in his mouth, muttered something in his Brescian dialect; and never was anything clumsier seen or heard. Even the Emperor could not quite keep from laughing. Meanwhile, I had already uncovered my work, and noticing that his Majesty had turned his eyes graciously on me, I stepped forward at once, and said: "Sacred Majesty, our most holy Pope Paul sends this book of the Madonna as a gift to you. The writing and the miniatures are the work of a master most famous in his art, and this rich cover of gold and jewels is thus incomplete, as you see, by reason of my indisposition. Therefore, his Holiness presents me to you along with the book, that I may finish it near your Majesty's person. Moreover, whatever your Majesty has a mind to have done, in that will I serve you while I live." To this the Emperor answered: "The book is pleasing to me, and so are you. But I wish you to finish it for me in Rome. And when it is finished, and you are recovered, bring it to me yourself." Afterwards in talking with me, he called me by my name, at which I wondered, for my name had come into nothing that had been said. But he told me he had seen the button of Pope Clement's cope, on which I had fashioned such wonderful designs. And so our conversation stretched out to a whole half-hour; and we talked agreeably on many different things concerning art. Then when I thought I had gone through the affair with much greater honour than I had looked for, a pause in the conversation gave me a chance to take my leave. The Emperor was heard to say, "Give five hundred crowns to Benvenuto." The man who fetched them asked on his return who was the Pope's man who had spoken to the Emperor. Then out stepped Messer Durante, and stole away my five hundred crowns. I went and complained to the Pope, who told me not to fear, for he knew everything, and how well I had conducted myself and spoken in the presence of the Emperor; and that assuredly I should have my share of the money.

xcii. Returning to my shop, I gave all my mind to finishing the diamond ring. About this business there came to me four of the first jewellers in Rome. The Pope had heard that the diamond had been set by the hand of the most famous jeweller in the world, a Venetian called Miliano Targhetta. Now as the stone was somewhat thin, it was too difficult a matter to set about without much consultation. I had a high opinion of those jewellers, though among them was a Milanese called Gaio, the most conceited beast in the world, who knew less than any of the others, and thought he knew most of all. The rest were very modest and capable men. Messer Gaio before them all began to speak thus: "Preserve Miliano's tint; and take off your hat to it, Benvenuto; for as tinting a diamond is the most beautiful and most difficult process in the jeweller's art, so Miliano is the greatest jeweller that ever lived, and this is the most difficult of diamonds." Then I answered that it would be all the more honour for me to compete with so first-rate a master; and turning to the others, I said, "Look, I am preserving Miliano's tint; and I am going to try if I cannot better it by my own invention. If not, we shall tint it again with this same. Then that fool Gaio said if I did it like that, he would gladly take off his hat to it; and I replied, "Then if I do it better, two reverences are its due." "That's so," he answered; and I began to make up my tints.

With the greatest diligence I set about the work, the method of which I shall explain in its own place. Without a doubt, this diamond was more difficult to treat than any other I have met with before or after; and that tint of Miliano's was made with very great art. However, I had no fear, and giving my very best brains to it, I produced what not merely equalled, but was far better than the other. Then seeing I had surpassed my rival, I now strove to surpass myself, and made a tint by new methods, which was ever so much finer than my first attempts. So I sent for the jewellers, and first tinted the diamond with Miliano's tint; then after cleaning it, I retinted it with my own. When I had shown it to the jewellers, one of the principal of them, whose name was Raffaello del Moro, took the diamond in his hand, and said to Gaio, "Benvenuto has surpassed the tint of Miliano." Gaio, who was unwilling to believe this, also took up the stone and said, "Benvenuto, this diamond is worth two thousand ducats more than it was with Miliano's tint." Then I answered, "Since I have beaten Miliano, let us now see if I can beat myself"; and I begged them to wait a little. So I went up to a little cupboard, where, out of their sight, I retinted the diamond, and then brought it back to them. Gaio cried out, "This is the most wonderful thing I have ever seen in all the days of my life, for now this diamond is worth eighteen thousand crowns, while we estimated it at hardly twelve!" The other jewellers, turning to Gaio, said, "Benvenuto is the glory of our art, and before his tints we must duly bare our heads." Then Gaio went on, "I want to go and tell the Pope; and I am determined he shall have a thousand golden crowns for setting the diamond." So he ran to his Holiness and told him all; and the Pope sent three times that day to ask if the ring was finished. An hour before nightfall I took it to him; and as the door was never closed to me, I lifted the portière discreetly, and saw the Pope with the Marquis of Guasto, who was trying to force him to do something he didn't want to do, for I heard his Holiness answer, "I say no. My part is to be neutral, and nothing else." As I was quickly withdrawing, his Holiness called me, whereupon I returned at once with the fine diamond in my hand. He took me aside, and the Marquis drew back. While the Pope was looking at the diamond he said to me, "Benvenuto, start a conversation with me as if it were something important, and don't stop while the Marquis stays in the room." Then he began walking about. I was quite pleased, for the thing was all to my good, and I described how I had contrived to tint the diamond. Meanwhile, as I have said, the

Marquis stood apart from us, leaning against a tapestry hanging on the wall, now twisting about on one foot and now on the other. The subject of our conversation was so important, and needed so much explanation, that we might have talked of it for three whole hours; and the Pope was so much interested that he never thought how weary the Marquis must be standing there. In my conversation I had mingled such philosophy as belongs to my profession, so that my dissertation went on for nearly an hour. Then the Marquis, tired to death, got in a rage and went out. The Pope was more affectionate than you can imagine, and said, "Wait, my Benvenuto, for I have a better reward in store for your merit than the thousand crowns which Gaio told me your labour was worth." Then I departed, and the Pope sang my praises before his courtiers, among whom was Latino Juvenale, of whom I have already spoken. Now he, who had become my enemy, tried zealously to do me a mischief; but seeing that his Holiness spoke of me with so much affection and so forcibly, he said, "Benvenuto is a man of wonderful talents; not a doubt of it. But every man is naturally bound to love his own country more than that of others. Still we should consider carefully how it behoves us to speak of a Pope. He has been heard to say that Pope Clement had the finest person of any prince that ever lived, and was extraordinarily gifted, but that he had no luck; while he says of your Holiness just the opposite, and that you're a sad sight with the tiara on your head; that you look like a dressed-up bundle of straw, and that your good luck is really all you can boast of." These words were of such weight, out of the mouth of him who knew exactly how to say them with effect, that the Pope believed them. Not only had I never said them, but I had never thought of saying them. If the Pope could have found any pretext, he would have done me a very ill turn; but, like the clever man he was, he pretended to laugh at the thing. Nevertheless, he nursed such a deep hatred for me as cannot be told, and I began to be aware of it when I had no longer the same free entrance to him as before, and indeed could only see him with the greatest difficulty. As I had a long acquaintance with the papal court, I guessed some one had done me an ill turn, and, searching prudently into the thing, I learned all that had been said, but not the name of him who slandered me. Nor could I think who he might be. Had I only known, I shouldn't have measured my revenge too nicely.

xciii. Meanwhile I was finishing my little book, and when it was done I took it to the Pope, who, in truth, couldn't keep from praising it highly. So I asked him to send me with it as he had promised. He answered that he would do his duty in the matter, and that my part was completed. Then he ordered that I should be well paid. For these works, which had taken me rather more than two months, I got five hundred crowns. For the diamond I got one hundred and fifty crowns—no more; all the rest was for the work on the little book, which yet was worth more than a thousand, for it was richly ornamented with figures and foliage, with enamelling and jewels. I took what I could get, and made up my mind to leave Rome there and then. Meanwhile the Pope sent my little book to the Emperor by one of his nephews called Signor Sforza. When he had presented the gift, the Emperor was much pleased, and immediately asked for me. Young Signor Sforza, who knew his lesson, said I had not come because I was ill. Everything was reported to me.

In the meantime I was making preparations for going to France, and I meant to go alone; but a young fellow who lived with me, called Ascanio, prevented that. This youth was of very tender years, and was the most admirable servant in the world. I took him from a former master of his, called Francesco, a Spanish goldsmith. I did not wish to take the boy, being anxious to avoid a quarrel with the Spaniard, so I said to Ascanio, "You had better not come to me, lest I anger your master." But he managed to persuade Francesco to write me a letter saying I was at liberty to engage him. Now he had been with me a good many months. When he left his former service he was thin and wan, and we called him, therefore, Il Vecchino (the little old man); and indeed I thought he was such, partly because he served me so well, and partly because he was so knowing that it did not seem natural he should be as clever as that at thirteen years old, as he said he was. But now to return to my story. In a few months his health was restored; he put on flesh, and became the handsomest boy in Rome. And since he was an excellent servant, as I have said, and wonderfully quick at learning our art, I felt like a father to him, and clothed him as if he had been my own child. When he saw himself in such good condition, he thought he had been lucky in having fallen into my hands; and he would often go and thank his master, who had been the means of it. Now this man had a beautiful young wife, and she said to the lad, "Surgetto" (so they called him when he stayed with them), "what have you done to grow so beautiful?" And Ascanio replied, "Madonna Francesca, it is my master who has made me so handsome, and so much better, too." The little spiteful thing took it very ill that Ascanio said this; and as she had the name of not being a modest lady, she managed to show the lad more attention than was honest. So I noticed that he used to go to see his mistress much oftener than he had been wont. Now one day he gave a cruel beating to one of the little shop-boys. As soon as I came back from an outing, the child complained to me with many tears that Ascanio had beaten him for no reason at all. Whereupon I said to Ascanio, "With reason, or without, never lay your hand on any of my household again, or you'll feel the weight of mine." He spoke back to me; whereupon I set on him, and with hands and feet gave him the soundest thrashing he ever had in his life. As soon as he escaped from my hands he ran out, without cloak or cap, and for two days I did not know in the least where he was—nor did I take any steps to find him. At the end of that time a Spanish gentleman, called Don Diego, came to speak to me. He was the most liberal man I have ever known in the world. I had done, and was now doing some work for him, so that he was a great friend of mine. He told me Ascanio had gone back to his old master, and if I thought good, he begged me to send him the cap and cloak which I had given him. To this I answered that Francesco had done ill, and that he had behaved like a boor; for if he had told me, as soon as Ascanio had gone to him, that the boy was in his house, I should very willingly have allowed him to stop there. But he had kept him two days before letting me know it, and I therefore refused to let the boy remain. So let him look out I did not catch the lad in his house, I said. Don Diego handed on this message, and Francesco only made fun of it. Next morning I saw Ascanio working at some trashy things in wire by his master's side. On my passing, Ascanio did me reverence, but Francesco all but laughed in my face. Yet through Don Diego he sent once more to beg me to be good enough to send Ascanio the clothes I had given him. If not, it did not matter, for Ascanio should not want for clothes. When I had listened to his message, I turned to Don Diego and said, "Signor Don Diego, in all your dealings with me you have proved yourself the most liberal and the honestest man of my acquaintance; but this Francesco is just the opposite; he is a faithless scoundrel. Tell him from me, that if before vespers he has not brought back Ascanio to my shop himself, I will certainly be the death of him; and tell Ascanio that if he does not get out of the place

by that time, I will do little less to him." Don Diego made me
no answer, but went and put such a terror on Francesco that he
did not know what to do. Meanwhile Ascanio had gone in
search of his father, who had come to Rome from Tagliacozzo,
of which place he was a native. When he heard of the trouble,
he also advised Francesco to bring back Ascanio to me. So
Francesco said to the lad, "Go without me; your father shall
accompany you." But Don Diego answered, "Francesco, I see
some great trouble in front of us. You know what Benvenuto
is better than I. Take the boy back without fail, and I will
come with you." I had made my preparations, and was pacing
up and down the shop, waiting for vespers to ring, and all
ready to perpetrate one of the most terrible deeds of my life.
Just then in came Don Diego, Francesco, Ascanio, and his
father, whom I did not know. When Ascanio entered, I looked
at them with a wrathful eye, while Francesco, pale as death,
said, "See, I have brought Ascanio back to you. In keeping him
I did not mean to offend you." And Ascanio said respectfully,
"My master, forgive me. I am here to do whatever you bid
me." Then I said, "Have you come to complete the time for
which you bound yourself?" He said, "Yes," and that he never
wished to go away again. Then I told the little shop-boy whom
he had beaten to bring the bundle of clothes, and I said to him,
"There are all the clothes I gave you. Take them and your
liberty too, and go whithersoever you will." Don Diego was
astonished, for he expected anything but this. But Ascanio
and his father, too, begged me to pardon him and take him
back. When I asked who it was who spoke for him, he told me
it was his father; to whom I said, after many entreaties, "Because you are his father, I will take him back for your sake."

xciv. Now I had made up my mind, as I said a little time
ago, to set out for France. For I saw that the Pope had not so
great a conceit of me as before evil tongues had fouled the fame
of my good service; and I feared lest they who could do this,
might do me a worse turn. So I was determined to seek another
country and better luck; and I was desirous of setting out without any one's leave, and alone. The evening before my start
I told my faithful Felice to make use of my property till I
came back, and, if I never returned, everything was to be his.
I had a Perugian apprentice who had helped me to finish the
Pope's commissions, and him I now paid off. But he begged me
to let him come along with me, and said he would pay his own
way; also if I should stop to work for the King of France, it

would be better for me to have my own Italians about me, and especially such as I knew could be of service to me. He knew how to use such persuasion that I consented to take him with me on the terms he had suggested. Then Ascanio, who was by during this discussion, said to me almost in tears, "When you took me back, I said I should stay with you for life, and I would fain do so." But I told him I would not have him with me for anything in the world. Thereupon the poor lad made his preparations to come after me on foot; and seeing his determination, I hired an extra horse for him, put one of my small valises on the crupper, and burdened myself with much more superfluous stuff than I had intended.

Leaving Rome, I travelled on to Florence, from Florence to Bologna, from Bologna to Venice, and from Venice to Padua, where I left my inn for the house of my dear friend, Alessandro del Bene. Next day I went to kiss the hand of Messer Pietro Bembo, who was not yet cardinal. Messer Pietro gave me as warm a welcome as ever man received. Then, turning to Alessandro, he said, "I want Benvenuto to stay here with all his company, though they be a hundred. So make up your mind, if you want Benvenuto, to be also my guest, for I will not give him up to you." And so I remained, and was well entertained by that most distinguished gentleman. He had prepared a room for me which would have done too much honour to a cardinal, and he would always have me sit at his table. Gradually he began to insinuate, with great modesty, that I might do his portrait. I desired nothing better in the world. So I mixed some clean fine white plaster of Paris in a box, and began. The first day I worked two hours on end, and sketched his fine head with such grace that his lordship was astounded. It must be said that though he was eminent in letters, and in the highest rank of poets, yet of my art he understood nothing at all. So he thought I had finished when I had hardly begun, and I could not make him see that it wanted a great deal of time to do the thing well. However, I made up my mind to do my best and give it all the time it deserved; but as he wore a short beard, in the Venetian fashion, I had a deal of trouble to model the head so that it satisfied me. Still I did finish it, and I thought I had never done so fine a thing, judged from the point of view of my art. But he was dismayed, for he had thought, as I had done the first rough model in two hours, I should cast it in ten; and now he saw that I had not completed the wax in two hundred hours, and I was asking leave to go off to France. This distressed him greatly; and he entreated me first to do him a reverse for the medal at least, the design to be a Pegasus within a myrtle wreath. I did it in about three hours, and put my most elegant work into it. He was much pleased, but he said, "This horse seems to me ten times more difficult to do than the little head over which you slaved so long. I do not understand why it was so hard to do." But he kept on begging me to carry it out in steel, saying, "I entreat you as a great favour. You can do it quickly, if you have a mind to." I said I was not willing to do it at the moment; but in whatever place I stopped to work I should finish it without fail.

Before this discussion was settled, I went to bargain for three horses to take me into France, and Messer Bembo kept a private watch on me, for his word was law in Padua. So when I wished to pay for the horses, having agreed to give fifty ducats for them, the owner said, "Illustrious master, I make you a present of the three horses." To this I answered, "This gift is not from you, and from the giver I will not accept it, for I have not been able to give him any of my work." The good man told me that if I did not take these horses, I should find no others in Padua, and should therefore be obliged to go on foot. Hearing this, I went back to the magnificent Messer Pietro, who pretended to know nothing of the matter. He only heaped kindness upon me, and begged me to stop in Padua. I was unwilling to consent, having fully made up my mind to go; so I was forced to accept the three horses, and with them I set off on my travels.

xcv. I took the road through the Grisons, for none of the others were safe on account of the war, and crossed the Albula and Bernina mountains. It was the 8th of May, but a great deal of snow lay on them still, and it was at the greatest peril of our lives we traversed these two mountain passes. On the other side we stopped at a place which, if I remember rightly, is called Wallenstadt, and here we put up. That night there arrived a Florentine courier called Busbacca. I had heard him spoken of as a man of credit, and capable in his profession, and did not know he had fallen into disrepute by his rascally deeds. When he saw me at the inn, he called me by my name, told me he was going on important business to Lyons, and begged me to be kind enough to lend him money for the journey. I told him I had no money to lend him, but if he liked to come with me, I would pay his way to Lyons. The rascal shed tears and cajoled me very cleverly, saying, "When it is a question of public importance, and a poor courier is in want of money, a man like you is bound to help him." Besides, he said, he was carrying things of the utmost consequence from Messer Filippo Strozzi. Now he had with him a leather case, and he whispered in my ear that in it was a silver beaker containing jewels to the value of many thousand ducats, besides the important letters from Messer Filippo Strozzi. Whereupon I said to him to let me hide the jewels on his person, which would be less dangerous than carrying them in that beaker, which he might hand over to me. It might be worth about ten crowns, I thought; but I would give him five-and-twenty on it. At this the courier said he would come along with me, since he could not do better. To give up the cup would be to his discredit.

So it was arranged; and setting off next morning, we came to a lake between Wallenstadt and Wesen. This lake is fifteen miles long, with Wesen at one end of it. When I saw the boats on the water, I was frightened, for they were made of pine trunks, not very large, and by no means solid, and neither nailed together nor tarred. And I had never ventured to embark on one, if I had not seen four German gentlemen with their four horses get into just such another. Indeed I would sooner have turned back; but I thought to myself, seeing their stupid indifference, these German waters do not drown you as do ours in Italy. But my two young lads said to me, "Benvenuto, it is a perilous thing for us to get into this boat with four horses." "Don't you see," I replied, "you cowards, that those four gentlemen have done the like before us, and that they are going off laughing? If it were wine, I should say it was for the pleasure of boozing; but since it is water, I know they do not want to be swallowed up in it any more than we do." The lake was fifteen miles long and about three wide. On one side was a very high mountain seamed with cavernous precipices, on the other a green plain. When we had gone about four miles a storm came up, and the rowers asked us to help with the oars. I signed to them to put us out on the farther bank, but they said it was not possible, for there was not water enough, and there were sand-banks which would wreck the boat and drown us all. Then again they begged us to assist them, and each man called to the other for help. Seeing them in this desperate condition, I put the bridle on the neck of my horse, a very clever animal, and took hold of the halter with my left hand. The creature, which had the intelligence of his kind, understood my meaning when I turned its face towards the fresh grass, namely, that he should swim and drag me along with him. Just then so huge

F 5¹

a wave came up that our boat was under water. "Have mercy, my father!" called Ascanio; "help me!" He was just throwing himself upon me, when I put my hand to my dagger, and told them all they were to do as I had taught them, for the horses would save their lives, and I hoped to escape, too, by the same means. Then I told Ascanio that if he threw himself upon me again I should kill him. So we went on for several miles through this mortal peril.

xcvi. When we had reached the middle of the lake, we found a bit of flat land where we could rest. And there I saw the four German gentlemen had landed. When we wished to do the same, the boatmen insisted we should do nothing of the kind. So I said to my lads, "Now is the time to show what we are made of. Out with your swords, and force them to land us!" This we did with great difficulty, for they resisted all they could. When we were on land we had to climb for two miles up that mountain, which was harder than scaling a ladder. I was clad in mail, with big boots; I had a gun in my hand, and God was raining down on us all the rain in heaven. Those devils of Germans, leading their little horses by the bridle, did wonders, while our beasts were useless at the thing, and we nearly died of the effort to make them climb the stiff mountain side. When we had got up some way, Ascanio's horse, a capital Hungarian mount, slipped in one of the bad places. Ascanio was a little in front of Busbacca, the courier, and he had given him his lance to carry. The horse went staggering back, unable to keep his feet, so that he fell on the lance which that rascal of a courier was carrying, and who had not the sense to keep it out of the creature's way. It went right through its neck. Another young fellow was coming to his help, but his horse also, a black one, slid down towards the lake. It got a hold for a moment on a bush, which, however, was but too yielding. Now the creature was laden with a pair of saddle-bags, in which was all my money and everything I had of value. I shouted to the lad to look out for himself and let the horse go to the devil. There was a fall of a mile down to where the mountain ran steep into the lake. Just under this place our boatmen were stationed, so that if the horse fell, it would be right on the top of them. I, in front, and the rest behind me, stood waiting the fall, for it seemed as if it were going to certain perdition. But as we stood there, I cried to the lads, "Don't trouble about anything! Let us save ourselves, and thank God for all! For me, I am only sorry for that poor Busbacca, who tied his cup and his jewels, to the value of several thousand ducats, to that horse's saddle-bow, thinking it would be safer so. I had but a few hundred crowns, and I fear nothing in the world, so I be in the care of God." Here Busbacca said, "I am not troubling about my loss, but a great deal about yours." So I asked him, "Why are you concerned about my little, and not about all your own property?" Then Busbacca answered, "In God's name I will tell you, for in such circumstances and straits as ours we must tell the truth. I know that yours are crowns, and real crowns, but my goblet case, in which I said there were all those jewels, is filled with caviare." Hearing this, I could not help laughing, and my young fellows laughed also. But he wept. Meanwhile the horse righted itself when we thought it was all over with it. So, laughing, we pulled ourselves together again, and set forward up the mountain path. The four German gentlemen, who had got to the top of this steep mountain before us, sent back some men to help us, so that we reached the camping-place in the outer wild. We arrived there wet, weary, and dying of hunger; but we were most kindly received, and we dried ourselves, rested, and satisfied our hunger, while our horse's wounds were dressed with certain herbs. They showed us what kind of herb to use. The hedges were full of it, and they told us that if we kept it continually on the sore, the creature would not only get better, but would serve us as if no harm had ever come to it. And we did this. Having thanked the gentlemen, and being much restored, we left the place and continued our journey, thanking God, who had saved us from such great dangers.

xcvii. We reached a place beyond Wesen, where we rested for the night. Here at every hour the whole night through we heard a watchman singing most pleasantly. As all the houses of the town are built of pine wood, the watchman's only words were a warning against fire. Every time the watchman sang, Busbacca, whom the past day's happenings had somewhat unnerved, cried out in his sleep, "Alas, my God, I am drowning!" This was partly due to yesterday's fright, and partly because he had got drunk in the evening; for he would sit drinking with all the Germans there. So sometimes he called out "I am on fire," and sometimes "I am drowning"; and again he thought he was enduring the agonies of hell, with the caviare round his neck.

We spent the evening so agreeably that all our hardships were turned to food for jests. In the morning we rose to a most lovely day, and went to dine at a gay little township called Lachen.

There we were splendidly entertained, and afterwards hired guides who were on their way back to the town of Zurich. Our guide walked along a dyke by the side of the lake, for it was the only road; and even the dyke was covered with water, so that the fool slipped, and his horse and he both went under water. I, who was just behind, stopped my horse and waited to see the brute get up. Then, as if nothing had happened, he began singing again, and signed to me to come on. I dashed off to the right, breaking through some hedges, and leading my lads and Busbacca after me. The guide shouted out in German that if the people about were to see me, they would murder me. But we pressed on and escaped that other storm, and arrived at Zurich, a marvellous city, which shines like a little jewel. Here we rested a whole day and night, and next morning betimes we were off, and came to another fine city called Solothurn. From this we went on to Lausanne, from Lausanne to Geneva, and from Geneva to Lyons, singing and laughing all the way. At Lyons I rested four days, and enjoyed myself very much with some friends of mine. Here also I was paid for what Busbacca had cost me. Then at the end of the time I took the road to Paris. It was a pleasant journey, save that when we reached La Palice, a band of brigands did their best to murder us, and it was not without some courage on our part that we got out of their hands. Thence we went forward to Paris without the least trouble in the world. Singing and laughing all the way, we reached our goal in safety.

xcviii. Having rested for some time in Paris, I went to seek Rosso, the painter, who was in the service of the King. Now I looked on Rosso as the best friend I had in the world, for in Rome I had shown him the greatest kindness one man can show to another. These acts of kindness can be told in a few words; and I will not fail to tell them, just to show his brazen-faced ingratitude. When he was in Rome, he had let loose his evil tongue about the works of Raffael of Urbino, so that the pupils of that great man determined to murder him. From this I saved him by guarding him night and day at the greatest trouble to myself. Again, he had slandered Maestro Antonio da San Gallo, a most excellent architect, and who was thus the cause of his losing a commission which he himself had got for Rosso from Messer Agnolo da Cesi. Afterwards Antonio became so set against him that he would have brought him to the point of starvation, if I had not lent him many a little sum of ten crowns to keep him alive. I had not seen a penny of it since, and knowing he was in the service of the King, I went, as I have said, to visit him, not so much because I thought of his returning my money, but that I might be helped by his favours into the King's service.

When he saw me he got uneasy at once, and said, "Benvenuto, you have spent too much on such a long journey, especially at a time when everybody's mind is full of war, and nobody has a thought for the trifling things of our profession." I told him I had brought as much money as would take me back again to Rome, in the same way I had now come to Paris; that this was not what I expected to get in exchange for all the trouble I had taken for him, and that now I began to believe what Maestro Antonio da San Gallo had told me about him. He wanted to turn the thing off with a joke, when his villainy was brought home to him; but I showed him a letter of change for five and twenty crowns on Ricciardo del Bene. The rascal then was ashamed, and was for keeping me almost by force. But I laughed at him, and went off in the company of a painter who had been present at the interview. He was one Sguazzella, a Florentine, and I went to lodge in his house, with three horses and three servants, at so much a week. He entertained me very well, and I paid him still better.

Afterwards I sought an audience of the King, and was introduced to him by a certain Messer Giuliano Buonaccorti, his treasurer. But this was after much delay; for though I did not know it, Rosso was working most zealously against my getting word with the King. When Messer Giuliano became aware of this, he took me at once to Fontainebleau, and brought me right into the presence of his Majesty, with whom I had a whole hour of most gracious audience. As he was then preparing to set out for Lyons, he told Messer Giuliano to take me with him, and that by the way we should talk together of some fine pieces of work which he was thinking of having carried out. So off I set with the court; and on the road became very intimate with the Cardinal of Ferrara, who, however, had not then the hat. Every evening I had long talks with him, and his lordship advised me to remain in Lyons, at an abbey of his in that city; and there I might enjoy my leisure till the King, who was going on to Grenoble, should come back from the war. At this abbey I should have everything put at my disposal.

As soon as we reached Lyons, I fell ill, and my young Ascanio had taken the quartan fever. By that time I was sick of the French and their court, and I longed to be back again in Rome.

The Cardinal, seeing me so strongly inclined to return, gave me money to make him a silver basin and ewer. So we set our faces homewards, mounted on excellent horses, and crossed the Simplon, in the company of certain Frenchmen for some part of the way. The quartan fever still hung about Ascanio; and I had a low fever, which seemed as if it was never going to leave me. My stomach was so disordered, that for four months I don't believe I ate a whole loaf in the week. I was full of longing to go back to Italy; for there I was fain to die rather than in France.

xcix. When we had crossed the Simplon, we came to a river near a place called Valdivedro. This river was very wide and deep, and across it ran a long narrow bridge without a railing. That morning a thick white frost lay on the ground; and when I came to the bridge in front of the others, I saw the place was very dangerous for riders, and so I ordered my apprentices and servants to get down and lead their horses by the bridle. Thus I crossed the bridge quite safely. By the way I fell into conversation with one of the Frenchmen, who was of gentle birth. The other, who was a notary, had remained behind, and was making fun of the French gentleman and myself, who, he declared, were frightened at nothing at all, since we had been at the pains of crossing on foot. At this I turned, and seeing him in the middle of the bridge, I begged him to come very cautiously, for he was in a very dangerous place. The man, like the true Frenchman that he was, cried out to me in his own tongue, that I was a poor-spirited fellow, and that there was no danger at all. Just as he said this, he pricked his spurs, and his horse slipped over the bridge, and fell feet uppermost, near a huge rock in the water. But God has oftentimes pity of fools; and both beasts, rider and horse, plunged into a great deep hole, where they disappeared. As soon as I saw this, I began running with the utmost speed, and with great difficulty climbed on the rock. Dangling myself over it, I caught the skirt of the man's garment, and thus dragged him up from below the water. He had swallowed a great quantity, and in another moment would have been drowned. So seeing him out of danger, I congratulated him on my having saved his life. Whereupon he answered me in French, saying that I had done nothing at all; that the things worth saving were his documents, which he valued at ever so many crowns; and angry enough did he seem as he stood there dripping and grumbling and muttering. I turned to the guides, and ordered them to help the beast, promising that they should be paid. One of them set to the task very cleverly; and with great trouble to himself, fished up the manuscripts so that not one was lost. But the other guide would not take the least trouble in the matter.

We had made up a purse, and I was the bursar: so as soon as we came to the place I have spoken of, and had dined, I gave some coins from the joint-purse to the guide who had helped to drag the man's property from the water. But the notary said that I might pay him with my own money; for he did not mean to give him anything save what we had agreed on for his services. I retorted with vigorous abuse. Then came up the other guide, and demanded also to be paid. And when I said, "He who bears the cross deserves the prize," he answered that soon he would show me a cross which would be a weeping matter for me. And I replied that I would light a candle at that cross; and perhaps he would carry it, when he went to do penance in a white sheet.

Now the place where we were is on the confines of Venetian and German lands; and the rascal ran about among the people and brought them back, he at the head of them, with a great boar-spear in his hand. I mounted on my good horse, and lowering my gun, I cried to my company, "At my first shot he is a dead man; and you others do your duty; for these are highwaymen, and they are only making use of this little incident as a pretext to massacre us." The host of the inn where we had dined called one of the head men, who was an old fellow, and begged him to put an end to the disturbance. "For," said he, "this is a most brave young man, and though you cut him in pieces, yet would he kill a great number of you; and, indeed, he is more likely to slip through your fingers after doing you a deal of mischief." So the thing was calmed down, and the old chief said to me, "Go in peace. You would be all too few for us, even if you had a hundred men with you." I knew he spoke the truth, and already I had given myself up for dead. But hearing no more insults cast at us, I shook my head, and said, "I would have done my uttermost to show I am alive and a man."

Then we went on our way. That evening at the first quarters we came to, we settled our accounts; and I took willing leave of the beastly French notary, parting on very friendly terms, however, with the other, who was a gentleman. Then, with only my own men and our horses, I came to Ferrara.

As soon as I had dismounted, I went to the Duke's court to

pay my respects to his Excellency, so that I might set out next morning towards Santa Maria da Loreto. I had waited till two hours after sundown, when at last the Duke appeared. I kissed his hands; he gave me a kind reception, and ordered water to be brought for my hands, as I was to sup with him. But I answered pleasantly, "Most Excellent Signor, it is now more than four months since I have eaten as much as you would think enough to keep body and soul together. Therefore, as I cannot enjoy the royal fare at your table, I shall remain and talk with you while your Excellency sups; and thus we shall have more pleasure than if I supped with you." So we fell to talking, and at that we spent three hours; after which I took my leave. On returning to my inn, I found splendid entertainment ready; for the Duke had sent me food from his own table, with plenty of good wine. And as it was more than two hours beyond my supper hour, I ate with the greatest appetite; and it was the first time for more than four months I had been able to do so.

c. Setting off in the morning, I went to Santa Maria da Loreto. Then, having said my prayers, I made my way on to Rome, where I found my dear faithful Felice. I left him the shop with all the furniture and other belongings, and opened another, much larger and more spacious, next door to Sugherello the perfumer. I felt sure the great King Francis would have no more remembrance of me; so I undertook many commissions for various noblemen, and at the same time I worked at the jug and basin which I had in hand for the Cardinal of Ferrara. I employed a great many workmen, and did a good business in gold and silver plate. Now I had bargained with my Perugian workman that he should write down all the moneys spent on his account, for clothes and various other things. With the expenses of the journey, it came to about seventy crowns. We had agreed that he should pay three crowns a month; for he earned more than eight with me. At the end of two months the rascal ran off from my shop, leaving me burdened with business, and said that he would not pay me any more. So I was advised to get my rights by the way of the law. Now I had had it in my mind to chop off one of his arms; and assuredly I should have done it; but my friends thought it was not wise for me to do such a thing, seeing that I should lose my money, and perhaps Rome, too, once more; for blows are not dealt by rule. Besides, they said, by means of the written agreement I had in his hand, I could soon have him imprisoned. So I gave heed to their advice —though I should have liked to have treated the business with a freer hand. When the case actually came on before the auditor of the Camera, I won it; and as a result of the judgment, which, however, was not given for several months, I had him put in prison. Meanwhile I was overburdened in the shop with my big orders, amongst others all the gold ornaments and jewels belonging to the wife of Signor Gierolimo Orsino, father of Signor Paolo, and son-in-law of our Duke Cosimo. When these things were nearly completed, other very important ones rained in. I had eight workmen, and I worked alongside them day and night, for honour and for profit.

ci. While I was thus conducting my business, a letter reached me, sent post haste from the Cardinal of Ferrara, which was to this effect:

"*Benvenuto, our dear friend, in these past days the great and most Christian King remembered you, and said he would fain have you in his service. To this I answered, that you had given me your promise that any time I sent for you on the King's service you would come at once. Thereupon his Majesty said, 'I desire that he should be provided with money to travel in a way befitting a man of his distinction.' And on the spot he ordered his Admiral to advance me a thousand golden crowns out of the royal Treasury. The Cardinal de' Gaddi, who was present during the conversation, at once stepped forward, and said to his Majesty that he need give no such order, for he had sent you money enough, and that you were indeed upon the road. Now if by chance the truth, as I believe, be just the contrary of what the Cardinal de' Gaddi told us, reply at once on receipt of my letter. Then I will pick up the thread of this business, and will see that you have the money promised you by this generous King.*"

Now let the world and every living man therein bear witness how evil stars and adverse fortune work against us mortals! Not twice in all my life had I spoken to that wretched little imbecile of a Cardinal de' Gaddi; and yet this arrogance of his was not meant to do me any harm in the world; it was merely a piece of feather-brained conceit on his part, meant to show how he, too, had an eye on the affairs of the artists whom the King desired to have in his service, just as much as the Cardinal of Ferrara. But he was foolish enough not to say anything to me about it; else certainly, so as to shield a silly puppet from blame—who was, after all, my countryman—I should have found some excuse to cover his blundering arrogance.

As soon as I received the letter of the most reverend Cardinal of Ferrara, I answered that, for the Cardinal de' Gaddi, I knew nothing about him at all; that, indeed, if he had suggested such a thing, I should not have moved from Italy without the knowledge of his most reverend lordship, especially as in Rome I had a larger business than ever before. But, I added, at a sign from his most Christian Majesty, handed on by so high a personage as the Cardinal of Ferrara, I should leave at once, throwing everything else to the winds. When I had sent my letter, that faithless workman of mine bethought himself of an evil trick, which had an immediate success owing to the avarice of Pope Paul Farnese, though it owed still more to his bastard son, then called the Duke of Castro. This man told one of Signor Pier Luigi's secretaries that he had been in my service for several years, and assured him that he knew all about my affairs. So he swore I was worth more than eighty thousand ducats, the greater part of which was in jewels; that these jewels were the property of the Church; and that I had stolen them in the Castle of St. Angelo during the sack of Rome. They should see, said he, about having me caught at once before I got wind of their intention.

One morning I had been working more than three hours before dawn on those things for the bride I have spoken of. While my servants were opening my shop and cleaning it, I put on my cloak and went to take a little walk. Going along the Strada Giulia, I came out at the Chiavica corner; and there Crespino the Bargello, with all his men, came upon me. "You are the Pope's prisoner," said he; to which I replied, "Crespino, you take me for some one else." "No," said Crespino, "you are Benvenuto the artist. I know you quite well, and I have to take you to the Castle of St. Angelo; for that's the place where lords and distinguished men like you are sent." Thereupon four of his corporals threw themselves on me, and would have taken my dagger from me by force, and some rings I wore on my finger; but Crespino cried out, "Not one of you touch him! Only do your duty, and see he does not escape." Then approaching me, in courteous terms he asked for my weapons. While I was giving them up, the thought came over me that just in this place I had killed Pompeo. Thence they took me to the castle, and locked me into the top chamber in the donjon. This was the first time I ever had a taste of prison, and I was then thirty-seven years old.

cii. The Pope's son, Signor Pier Luigi, having brooded over

the great quantity of money which I was accused of stealing, asked his father, as a favour, to give it to him when it should have been recovered. The Pope conceded this willingly; and, moreover, promised to help him to recover it. So I was kept in prison eight whole days; and at the end of that time, to bring the thing to an issue, they sent me to be questioned. For this purpose, I was called into a hall of the Pope's castle, a place destined for great ceremonies. One of the examiners was the Governor of Rome, who was called Messer Benedetto Conversini, a Pistojan, afterwards Bishop of Jesi; another was the Procurator-fiscal, whose name I don't remember; and the third was the Judge of the Criminal Court, Messer Benedetto da Cagli. First, these three men began their examination mildly; but their language grew most harsh and threatening after I had said to them, "My lords, for the last half-hour you have been doing nothing but question me about cock-and-bull stories and such-like nonsense; so that in truth your talk might not unjustly be called chatter or babble. For chattering is talking nonsense, isn't it? And babbling is uttering empty words. Therefore I entreat you to tell me what you want of me, that I may hear reasonable words from your mouths, and not idle fables and rubbish of that kind." At this the Governor, who was a Pistojan, no longer able to hold in his violent temper, broke out, "You speak very confidently; indeed, much too haughtily; but I will make that haughtiness of yours cringe lower than a shivering puppy, when you hear what I have to say—which will neither be chattering nor babbling, as you call it, but an ordered argument, to the consideration and the answering of which it will behove you to give your whole mind." And then he began:

"We know for a certainty that you were in Rome during the sack of this unhappy city; and at that time you were in the Castle of St. Angelo, and were employed as bombardier. And since your profession is that of goldsmith and jeweller, Pope Clement, because he had known you before, and because there were no others of your trade in the place, called you to a secret audience, and bade you take out all the jewels of his tiaras, mitres, and rings from their settings. Then, as he had confidence in you, he also ordered you to sew them into his garments. While about this business, unknown to his Holiness, you made away with property to the value of eighty thousand crowns. This has been reported to us by a workman of yours, to whom you confided it, boasting of the same. Now we say to you frankly: find the jewels, or the value of them. After that you may go free."

ciii. When I heard these words I could not help breaking out into an explosion of laughter, which lasted for some little time. "I thank God heartily," I said, "that this first time it has pleased His High Majesty to imprison me, by good fortune I am not confined for some little trifle, as generally happens to young men. Even if what you say were true, there is no danger at all of my being punished in my person; for at the time you speak of, the law did not run. Or, if the facts were as you declare, I might excuse myself by saying that, in my capacity of dutiful servant, I had guarded this treasure for the sacred, holy Apostolic Church, waiting till I could give it back to a good pope, or, indeed, to whoever should request its return, as, for instance, you." Here that ferocious Pistojan refused to listen to another word, but broke in furiously, "Put what meaning on your villainy you please, Benvenuto; enough for us to have found our own. And now out with it, if you don't want something else from us besides words." As they were getting up to go away, I said, "I have not yet been fully examined. Finish that, and then go whenever you please." So they sat down again, much enraged, and in a humour to listen to nothing I should say. Yet much of their anxiety was gone; for they thought, perhaps, they had found out all they wished to know. So I began to speak to them after this fashion: "You must know, my lords, that I have lived in Rome nearly twenty years, and have never been imprisoned, neither here nor elsewhere." At this the jack-in-office governor called out, "Yet you have murdered men of our city." To which I answered, "You say so. I make no such admission; for if a man was to try to kill you, priest though you are, you would defend yourself; and having killed him, the holy laws would hold you innocent. So let me say what I have to say, if you would refer the matter to the Pope, and judge me aright. I tell you once more, that for nearly twenty years I have been living in this marvellous city of Rome, and here I have carried out most important work in my profession. I know that this is the seat of Christ, and I had sure confidence that, if ever a temporal prince were to wrong me, I should have recourse to this holy chair and the Vicar of Christ, and he would defend my rights. Alas! what refuge have I now? And who is the prince who will defend me from such infamous wrong? Before arresting me, should you not have found out how I disposed of those eighty thousand ducats? Also, should you not have looked at the record of the jewels which the Apostolic Camera has carefully kept for five hundred years to this day? If you had found a gap in it, then you should have seized all my books as well as myself. I assure you that the books in which are recorded all the jewels of the Pope and the regalia are quite in order, and there is not a single gem belonging to Pope Clement which has not been carefully entered. Only one thing I can think of which might give colour to your proceedings. When Pope Clement was making terms with those Imperial thieves, who had pillaged Rome and outraged the Church, a man came to negotiate the terms of peace, whose name, if I rightly remember, was Cesare Iscatinaro. When he had almost concluded the treaty, the poor Pope, in desperation, and desiring to show him a little kindness, let fall from his finger a diamond ring worth about four thousand crowns. Iscatinaro stooped to pick it up, and the Pope bade him keep it for his sake. I was present at the time; and if the diamond be missing, I am now telling you where it has gone; but I have a sure conviction that this also will be found recorded. Therefore, you should be ashamed to persecute a man like me, who have served this apostolic seat so honourably. Do you not know, that had it not been for me, when the Imperial troops entered the Borgo, they would have made their way into the castle without the least hindrance? But I, who never got anything for my valorous conduct, betook myself vigorously to the guns, which the bombardiers and soldiers had abandoned, and put heart into a comrade of mine, Raffaello da Montelupo, the sculptor, who had also given up, and was hiding frightened and useless in a corner. I shook life into him; and he and I by ourselves slew so many of the enemy that the soldiers went by another way. It was I who gave Iscatinaro a taste of my powder, when I saw him speaking with Pope Clement without doing reverence, displaying, indeed, the most boorish insolence, like the Lutheran and infidel he was. Pope Clement, hearing of the affair, had the castle searched to find who had fired the shot, meaning to hang him. Then it was I who wounded the Prince of Orange, hitting him on the head below here in the trenches of the castle. Then think of all I have done for Holy Church; consider the great number of ornaments of silver and gold and jewels I have made, and all the beautiful coins, too, which have received such praise. And priests like you dare give this reward to a man who has served you with such skill, and loved with such good faith! Now go and tell all I have said to the Pope; that, as to his jewels, he has them all; that I never had anything from the Church save the wounds from the enemy's guns during the sack; and that I never counted on anything, save some small recompense from Pope Paul, which he had promised me. Now am I clear in my mind about his Holiness, and about you, his ministers."

While I was speaking these words, they remained listening in astonishment. They looked in each other's faces, and then in much wonderment they left me. All three went away together to report to the Pope what I had said. Somewhat ashamed, his Holiness ordered all the records of the jewels to be examined with the utmost care. But after it was seen that nothing was missing, they left me still in the castle without saying anything more. And Signor Pier Luigi, too, had a bad conscience. Therefore they sought to compass my death.

civ. While these agitated days were passing, King Francis heard all about the Pope's keeping me in prison so unjustly. He had sent as ambassador to Rome one of his gentlemen called Monseigneur de Montluc. Now he wrote to him to ask me from the Pope as one of his Majesty's men. The Pope was a very able and accomplished man, but in this affair of mine he behaved like a poor weak fool; and he now replied to the King's messenger that his Majesty should not trouble about me, for I was a very quarrelsome fellow. He warned him to let me alone; for he was keeping me in prison for homicide and other devilries I had committed. Again the King wrote, that in his kingdom strict justice reigned; and as he rewarded distinguished men, heaping on them extraordinary favours, so, on the other hand, did he punish disturbers of the peace. Likewise, his Holiness had once let Benvenuto go away, not caring for his service; and when he (King Francis) found him in his kingdom, he had gladly taken him into his employment. Now he asked for him as his man. These words brought only endless vexation and harm to me, although no higher compliment could have been paid to a man of my condition. But the Pope got into such a fury, fearing lest I should go and disclose his villainous treatment of me, that he kept thinking of all the possible ways whereby he could bring about my death, without injuring his own repute. The keeper of the Castle of St. Angelo was one of our Florentines, Messer Giorgio, a knight, and one of the Ugolini. This worthy man showed me the greatest courtesy possible, leaving me free to wander about the castle on parole. He was very sensible of the great wrong that was being done to me; and when I wished to give security for this freedom, he said he could not accept it. The Pope was exaggerating this affair of mine, he declared; but he would fully trust my word, for he heard from every one that I was an honest man. I gave him my word of honour, and he allowed me the means of working a little at my own craft. Meanwhile, thinking that the Pope's anger must blow over, having regard to my innocence, and also to the favour of the King, I kept my shop open, and Ascanio, my apprentice, came to the castle and brought me things to work at. And though I could work but little—hindered as I was by the thought of being thus unjustly shut up—still I made a virtue of necessity, and, as cheerfully as I could, bore with my perverse fortune. I had made friends with all the guards and many of the soldiers of the castle. Now the Pope used sometimes to come to sup within the walls; and at such times there were no guards at the doors, which stood open like those of an ordinary palace. For that reason, while his Holiness was within, the prisoners used to be locked up with the greatest care. But nothing of the kind was done to me, and I used freely to walk about the castle. Often some of the soldiers would advise me to escape, promising to help me, for they knew the great wrong done to me. To such suggestions I always replied that I had given my word to the castellan, who was a very good fellow, and had shown me great kindness. One of them, a very brave and intelligent man, would then say to me, "Benvenuto, my friend, you must know that a man in prison is not obliged, nor can be obliged, to keep faith or anything else. Do as I tell you; flee from this scoundrel of a Pope and his bastard son, who will come at your life by some means or another." But I was determined rather to lose my life than break my word to the honest castellan. So I put up with this indescribable annoyance. The companion of my misfortune was, I should say, a friar of the Pallavicini house, who was a very great preacher.

cv. This man had been seized as a Lutheran. He was an excellent comrade; but regarded as a friar, the greatest rascal in the world, one who indulged in all kinds of vices. I admired his fine talents, but greatly abhorred his ugly vices, and frankly reproved him for them. He was always telling me I was not obliged to keep faith with the castellan, since I was in prison. I answered him that as a friar he spoke the truth, but not as a man; and that whoever was a man, and no friar, had to keep faith in whatever circumstances he might find himself. So I, who was a man and no friar, would never be false to my bare word given in honour. Finding he could not corrupt me by his shrewd and sophisticated arguments, and his wonderful art in stating them, he thought to tempt me by other means. So he let several days pass, during which he read to me the sermons of Girolamo Savonarola, his admirable commentary on these being finer than the sermons themselves. I was so fascinated by this, that there was nothing in the world I would not have done for him, save break my word, as I have said. When he saw my great admiration for his talents, he thought of another way. Insinuatingly he began to ask me, what would have been my method of opening my doors and escaping, in the case of their having locked me up, and always supposing, of course, I had been willing for the attempt. So wishing to show this clever friar that I, too, was rather keen-witted, I told him I could easily open the most difficult lock, and more especially those of this prison. It would be no harder than eating a bit of fresh cheese. Then, to force my secret out of me, he threw doubt on this, saying, "Men who have the name of being clever make many a boast, which if they had to prove, would lose them credit, and be much to their disadvantage." And he had heard me say things so far from the truth, he went on, that if I were tested, he thought I should come badly out of the affair. Then, stung by this devil of a friar, I told him that my habit was to promise less in words than what I could actually perform; and for this matter of the keys I had spoken of, it was the easiest thing in the world; and in a few words I could make him see perfectly that it was as I said. Then, thoughtlessly, I proved with what ease all I had told him could be carried into effect. The friar pretended to pay no attention, but he soon learnt all with perfect intelligence. As I have already said, the honest castellan let me wander through all the castle, not even locking me up during the night, as was done with the others. Also he let me work in gold, or silver, or wax, at whatever I wished. Thus for several weeks I employed myself on a basin I was making for the Cardinal of Ferrara. But I grew so weary of my prison that this began to be burdensome; and so after that, as it was less trouble, I took to modelling little figures in wax. The friar stole a piece of this wax from me; and with it he set about having the keys made according to the method I had thoughtlessly taught him. As an accomplice in this he had taken a notary of the castellan's household, a Paduan called Luigi. But the friar ordered the keys to be made by a locksmith, who told all. Now the castellan came sometimes to see me in my room, and when he saw me working with wax, he recognised it as the same, and said, "Though this poor Benvenuto has been most deeply wronged, he should not have done such a thing to me, for I have shown him more kindness than my duty allowed me. Now I shall keep him most strictly locked up, and shall never do him kindness any more." So he had me shut up with the utmost severity; but the worst I had to endure were the words thrown at me by some of his affectionate servants. Before they had been very much attached to me, but now they cast up all the kind deeds done me by their master, and, indeed, called me an ungrateful, light-minded, and faithless fellow. Now one of these servants launched this abuse at me with more boldness than was seemly; and assured as I was of my innocence, I answered with heat that I had never broken my word, and this I should maintain with my life's blood; and if he or any one else ever did me such injustice again, I should fling the lie back in his throat. Beside himself at this reprimand, he ran to the castellan's apartment, and brought me the wax and the model of the key. As soon as I saw the wax, I told him that both of us were right, but he was to bring me to speech with the lord castellan, and I should tell him frankly how the case stood; for the matter was of much greater importance than they thought. The castellan sent for me at once, and I told him the whole story. So he seized the friar, who informed against his accomplice, and the notary was nearly being hanged. The castellan tried to hush up the thing, but already it had come to the ears of the Pope. The notary escaped the gallows; and I was given the same liberty as at the beginning.

cvi. When I saw with what vigour they followed the thing up, I began to think of my own interests, and said, "If a hurricane like this should arise another time, and if this man again distrusted me, I should no longer think myself under any obligation, but should set my wits a-working; for I am certain I could succeed better than that rascal of a friar." Then I ordered new coarse sheets to be brought me from outside; and I did not send away the soiled ones. When my servants asked me for them, I told them to be quiet about it, for I had given them to some needy soldiers; but that if the thing were known, the poor fellows ran the risk of the galleys. So my young apprentices and servants—but especially Felice—kept the affair of the sheets absolutely secret. Then I set about emptying a straw mattress, burning the straw, which, luckily, I could do, for in my prison was a chimney, and I could light a fire. The sheets I tore into strips, the third of a cubit in width. When I had torn up enough, as I thought, to enable me to descend from the high keep of the Castle of St. Angelo, I said to my servants that I had given away all I wished; that now they must bring me finer sheets, and I should always return to them the soiled ones. This thing was soon forgotten.

Now Cardinals Santiquattro and Cornaro forced my servants to shut up the shop. They told me frankly that the Pope would not hear a word of my release, and that the great favours of the King had done me more harm than good. The last message that Monsignor de Montluc sent to his Holiness on the part of the King had been to the effect that I should be handed over to the ordinary judges of the court. Then, if I had sinned, he could punish me; but if I had not, justice demanded that he should let me go free. These words had so annoyed the Pope that it was in his mind not to release me any more. But the castellan most certainly helped me all he could. Now when my enemies saw my shop shut up, they used to sneer at and insult such servants and friends of mine as came to visit me in prison. It happened one day that Ascanio, who came twice every day to see me, asked me to have a little coat made for him out of a blue satin vest of mine, which I never wore. I had only used it the day I walked in procession. But I told him this was not a time, nor was I in a place, to wear such garments. The boy was so offended I did not give him this miserable little vest, that he said he wanted to go away home to Tagliacozzo. In a great rage, I retorted that I should be much pleased to be rid of him; and he swore with the greatest heat never to come back any more. During our altercation we were walking round the donjon of the castle. It happened that the castellan was also taking a walk, and just as we came up against his lordship, Ascanio was saying, "I go then, and adieu for evermore!" To which I answered, "For ever is the word—so let it be! I shall tell the guards never to let you pass again." Then turning to the castellan, I begged him most earnestly to order the guards never to let Ascanio come through any more. "For," I said, "this little rustic only comes to fill up my cup of sorrow to overflowing. So I entreat you, my lord, let him never enter more." The castellan was much distressed, for he knew the boy to be wonderfully talented, and, besides, he was of so fair a shape that no one could see him without falling deeply in love with him. The lad went away weeping. He was carrying, I must tell you, a little scimitar, which sometimes he wore secretly under his garments. When he left the castle, his face all tear-stained, he met with two of my worst enemies. One of them was Jeronimo the Perugian, and the other was called Michele; and they were both goldsmiths. Michele, who was a friend of that rascally Perugian, and none to Ascanio, said, "What is the meaning of Ascanio weeping? Perhaps his father is dead. I mean that father of his in the castle." Whereupon the boy replied, "He is alive, but you're a dead man!" and lifting his hand, he struck twice at the man's head with his scimitar. At the first blow he knocked him down; with the second he cut off three fingers of his right hand, though he had aimed at his head; and the fellow lay there for dead. The affair was reported at once to the Pope, who cried in great wrath, "Since the King wishes Benvenuto to be judged, go and tell him he has three days to prepare his case." They made haste to fulfil his order; whereupon that worthy man the castellan went off at once to his Holiness, and made it clear to him that I was not cognisant of the thing; that, in fact, I had just chased the boy away. So admirably did he defend me that he saved my life in the great storm that raged about me. Ascanio fled home to Tagliacozzo; and from there he wrote asking my pardon a thousand times, saying he knew he had been wrong to add to my vexations and my great trouble. But, he went on, if by God's grace I got out of prison, he would never leave me any more. I sent him word that he was to go on learning his trade; and I promised, if God ever gave me my liberty, I should certainly call him back to me.

cvii. The castellan was every year the victim of a certain infirmity which bereft him of his wits. When it was coming on, he would speak, or rather he would chatter without stopping. These humours of his varied every year. One time he thought he was an oil jar; another time a frog, and then he jumped just like one. Again he thought he was dead, and he had to be buried. Thus each year he had a different delusion. Now this time he began to imagine that he was a bat; and when he went for a walk, he would every now and then give a low scream as bats do, and flutter his hands and his body as if he were going to fly. When his doctors and his old servants saw the malady upon him, they indulged him in every possible way; and since it seemed to them he took great pleasure in hearing me talk, they were always fetching me to keep him company. And the poor man sometimes kept me four or five hours talking to him the whole time. He had me sit opposite him at table, and he never stopped talking and making me talk. In spite of all this conversation I ate well; but he, poor man, neither ate nor slept. Now all this tired me out, so that I was at the end of my forces, and sometimes when I looked at him, his eyes were terrible to see, one turning one way and one the other. One day he asked me if I had ever had a fancy to fly. I answered that I had always been most eager to do, and had done, such things as come hardest to men; and as for flying, the God of Nature had given me a body more than usually agile and fit for running and leaping; and so by the aid of what little wits I possessed, I could manage some kind of mechanical contrivance; and certainly I did not want courage for the attempt. Then he began to ask me what methods I should use; to which I answered, that if we observed the flying creatures, the one whose natural powers could best be imitated by art was the bat. When the poor man heard that name of bat, the mimicry of which was the form his mania took that year, he cried with a loud voice, saying, "He speaks the truth, he speaks the truth! That's the thing—the very thing!" Then turning to me, he said, "Benvenuto, if you had the chance, would you have the courage to fly?" Thereupon I said that, if he would give me my liberty, I had pluck enough to fly as far as Prati, and would make myself a pair of wings out of waxed linen for the purpose. Then he answered, "And I, too, should not be behindhand; but the Pope has commanded me to look after you as the apple of his eye; and I know you are a clever enough devil to make your escape. Therefore I am going to lock you up with a hundred keys, so that you don't make off." I entreated him, reminding him how I had had opportunities of escape, but that, for the sake of the word I had given him, I had never broken faith. Then I begged him, for the love of God, not to add a greater misery to what I was now suffering. But even while I was speaking, he gave strict orders for me to be bound and taken to my prison, and there securely locked up. Seeing there was no help for it, I said to him, in the presence of his household, "Make fast your locks and watch me well, for I shall get out of here one way or another." Then they led me off, and shut me up with the greatest care.

cviii. From that moment I set to thinking about the best means of escape. As soon as they had shut the door on me, I went about examining the prison where I lay. When I believed I had certainly found a way of getting out, I began to devise a means of climbing down from the high castle keep. Then I took those new sheets of mine, which, as I have already said, I had torn into strips and well sewn together, and calculated what length would serve me to climb down by. When I had made up my mind about this, and prepared everything, I laid my hands on a pair of pincers, which I had stolen from a Savoyard warder of the castle. This man looked after the barrels and the cisterns; and he also worked at carpentering for his pleasure. Now he had several pincers, and amongst them some huge solid ones. Just my affair, I thought; and I stole them, and hid them in the mattress. Then the time came for me to use the tool, and I began to try the nails of the hinges. As the door was a double one, the riveting of the nails could not be seen, so that when I tried to draw one out, it gave me the greatest trouble; but in the end I succeeded. When I had drawn out the first nail, I bethought me how I should contrive that this should not be seen. I managed it by mixing some little rusty iron filings with a little wax, getting just the very colour of those long nails I had taken out. With this I began carefully imitating the nails in the supports of the hinges; and by degrees made a waxen counterfeit for every one I drew out. I left the hinges still attached at top and bottom with some of the old nails, which, however, I only put back after they had been cut, and then only lightly, so that they just held the hinge-plates and no more. This business gave me a deal of trouble; for the castellan dreamt each night that I had escaped, and every now and then he sent to have my prison examined. The man who came to investigate had a bum-bailiff's name, Bozza, and behaved as such. He always brought with him another fellow called Giovanni, surnamed Pedignone. He was a soldier, and Bozza was a menial. This Giovanni never once came to my prison without insulting me. He was from Prato, where he had been an apothecary. Every evening he examined the hinges and the whole prison very carefully; and I would say to him, "Keep a good look-out on me, for I am going to slip through your hands for a certainty." These words stirred up a furious hatred between him and me. So with the utmost care I hid up my implements, that is, the pincers, a large dagger, and other things pertaining to my plan, in my mattress, along with the strips I had made. As soon as daylight came, I used to sweep my room; and though by nature I like cleanliness, I kept my place in specially good order then. When I had done my sweeping, I arranged my bed beautifully, and laid flowers on it, which I had a certain Savoyard bring me almost every morning. This was the Savoyard who had charge of the cisterns and barrels, and who worked at carpentering for his pleasure. It was from him I stole the pincers with which I picked out the nails from the hinge-plates.

cix. Now to return to what I was saying about my bed. When Bozza and Pedignone came in, I told them they were to keep at a due distance from it, that they might not foul and spoil it. When sometimes, just to annoy me, they would touch it lightly, I would cry to them, "Oh, you dirty cowards! I'll get hold of those swords of yours, and serve you a turn that will astonish you! Do you think yourselves good enough to touch the bed of a man of my sort? No care for my own life shall hold me back, for I am sure to take yours. So leave me alone with my troubles and my tribulations, and don't add to them; otherwise, I'll let you see what a desperate man can do." All this they told to the castellan. But he expressly ordered them not to go near my bed, and to come to me without their swords; for the rest, they were to keep a sharp look-out on me.

When I was thus sure about the bed, I thought I had done everything, for therein lay what I needed most for the business. One feast-night, when the castellan was feeling very ill, and his humours were at their height, he kept on saying that he was a bat; and if they heard that Benvenuto had flown away, they were to let him go, for he would overtake me, since at night-time he could certainly fly better than I. "Benvenuto," said he, "is only a sham bat, but I'm a real one. And since he's been given into my keeping, leave the business to me, for I'll come up with him." He had been in this condition for several nights, and had tired out all his servants. And I heard about it through different channels, but especially from the Savoyard, who was a friend of mine. This feast-day evening I had made up my mind to escape at all hazards. First I prayed most devoutly to God, entreating His Divine Majesty to defend me, and aid me in my perilous enterprise. Then I prepared everything I needed for the business, working all through that night. When day was but two hours off, I removed the hinges with the greatest trouble. But the wooden frame and the bolt also resisted, so that I could not open the door, and had, therefore, to cut the wood. At last I succeeded; and then carrying the strips of linen, which I had rolled round two pieces of wood like flax on a spindle, I made my way out towards the privies of the keep. From inside I perceived two tiles on the roof, and thus I could climb up at once with the greatest ease. I was wearing at the time a white jerkin, white hosen, and a pair of buskins, into which I thrust my dagger. Taking one end of my linen rope, I tied it in the form of a stirrup round a piece of antique tile which was built into the wall, and which stuck out hardly the length of four fingers. This done, I turned my face to God, and said, "O Lord my God, defend my cause! for Thou knowest it is good; and that I help myself." Then I let myself go gently, and supporting myself by the strength of my arms, I reached the bottom. The moon was not shining, but the sky was fair and clear. When my feet were on the ground, I regarded the great descent I had made so bravely, and went off much heartened, for I thought I was free. But it was not so; for on that side the castellan had had two very high walls built enclosing a poultry-run. This place was barred with great bolts on the other side. When I saw my way thus stopped, I was much vexed; but while walking to and fro, thinking what I should best do, I fell up against a large beam which had been covered up with straw. With great difficulty I set it up against the wall. Then by force of arm I climbed up on it to the top. But as the wall was pointed, I was not solidly enough placed there to draw the pole up after me. So I determined to use a piece of the second rope of linen, as the other I had left hanging from the keep. Well, binding it fast to the beam, I climbed down by it on the other side. This was very far from easy. I was quite worn out at the end; and, besides, I had galled the palms of my hands, so that they bled. I therefore stayed to rest a while, and bathed my hands in my own urine. When I felt sufficiently recovered, I made my way to the last wall, which looks towards Prati. There I laid down my linen rope intending to fix it to a battlement, and get down from the lesser height as I had done from the greater. But just at that moment I discovered that behind me was one of the sentinels on duty. Seeing here a hindrance to my plans, and knowing my life in danger, I made up my mind boldly to face the guard, who, perceiving my resolute demeanour, and that I was coming towards him with a weapon in my hand, quickened his step, and made as if to keep out of my way. I had left my ropes some way off; now I quickly turned back for them, and though I saw another sentinel, yet he appeared unwilling to see me. When I had picked up my linen ropes, I tied them to the battlement and let myself go. But either I thought that I had almost reached the ground, while I was still some distance off, and let go my hands and jumped; or else my hands were too feeble to keep up the effort. At all events I fell, and in falling I struck the back of my head, and lay there unconscious more than an hour and a half, so far as I could judge. The day was about to break, and the fresh, cool air that comes before the rising of the sun brought me to my senses; but yet my wits were not quite clear, for I thought my head was cut off, and that I was in purgatory. Little by little my powers came back to me, and I saw that I was outside the castle, and had a sudden remembrance of all I had done. Now I felt the hurt to my head before I perceived that my leg was broken; for putting up my hands, I found them all covered with blood. But examining the place thoroughly, I came to the conclusion that the wound was not serious. When, however, I wanted to get up from the ground, I found my right leg broken three inches above the knee. But even this did not discourage me. I drew out my dagger in its sheath, at the end of which was a large ball. This it was which had broken my leg; for the bone had been jammed against the ball, and unable to bend, had snapped just there. So I threw away the sheath; and with the dagger I cut off a piece of the remainder of the linen strip, and as well as I could bound up my leg. Then, my weapon in my hand, I crept on all-fours towards the gate. I reached it only to find it shut; but I saw a stone just under the door, and as I thought it was probably not stuck very fast, I tried to move it. Putting my hands to it, I felt it move; it yielded at once, and I drew it out. Then I crawled through the hole it had stopped up.

cx. There had been more than five hundred paces from the place where I fell, to the gate by which I entered the city. When I got inside Rome, some mastiffs threw themselves on me and bit me viciously. They set on me several times and worried me, till at last I drew my dagger and dealt one of them such a blow that he yelped loudly. Then the other dogs, as their habit is, gathered about him, while I made haste, on hands and knees, towards the church of the Traspontina. When I reached the mouth of the street which turns towards Sant' Agnolo, I took the road to St. Peter's; for day was breaking above me, and I knew I was in danger. So meeting a water-carrier with his ass laden with full pitchers, I called him to me, and begged him to lift me up and carry me to the terrace by St. Peter's steps; explaining that I was a poor young man who, in getting down from the window of my lady, had fallen and broken my leg. The house I came out of was of great importance, I told him, and I was in danger of being cut in pieces. So I begged him to carry me off quickly, promising him a golden crown for his pains. And at the word I gave him a sight of my purse, which was by no means empty. He took hold of me at once, hoisted me on his back with a good will, and carried me to the open space above the steps of St. Peter's. There he put me down, and I told him to run back to his ass. At once I took the road again, crawling on all-fours towards the house of the Duchess, the wife of Duke Ottavio. She was the natural daughter of the Emperor, and had been the wife of Duke Alessandro of Florence. Now I knew that with this great princess I should find many of my friends, who had come with her from Florence. Besides, I was in her favour, for the castellan had spoken well of me in her presence. Wishing to help me, he had said to the Pope one day, that when the Duchess made her entry into Rome, I had saved them more than a thousand crowns. The heavy rain had threatened great damage to the city, and he had been in despair. But I had put heart into him; for, as he told, I had pointed several heavy pieces of artillery towards that part of the sky where the clouds were thickest, and from whence torrents of water had already begun to pour. When the artillery was discharged, the rain stopped, and at the fourth round the sun came out. Thus, said he, I had been the sole cause of the festa passing off so happily. When the Duchess heard it, she said, "This Benvenuto is one of the artists who were in the good graces of my husband, Duke Alessandro; and I shall always keep them in mind when an opportunity comes to do them a good turn." She had also spoken of me to her present husband, Duke Ottavio.

So now I made straight for the house of her Excellency, a very fine palace in Borgo Vecchio. And there I should have been quite safe, and the Pope could not have touched me. But as the thing I had done was beyond the powers of an ordinary human creature, God wished to check my vainglory through a still harder discipline than I had known in the past. And this was how it came about. While I was creeping on all-fours up the steps, a servant of Cardinal Cornaro's household recognised me. Now, as it happened, the Cardinal was lodging in the palace, and the servant ran to his master's room, and waking him, said, "Most reverend monsignor, your Benvenuto is below. He has escaped from the castle, and is crawling along on hands and knees, and covered with blood. It looks as if he had broken his leg, and we do not know where he is going." The Cardinal said at once, "Run and carry him into my room here." When I was brought to him, he told me to have no fear. Then he sent at once for the best doctors in Rome, and by them I was treated. One of them was Maestro Jacomo of Perugia, a most excellent surgeon. He set my leg very skilfully, then bandaged it, and with his own hand bled me. My veins were unusually swollen, and, besides, he wished to make a rather large incision; so the blood sputtered furiously out in his face, and bespattered him so abundantly that he had to stop his operations. This he took to be a very bad augury; and it was with great reluctance that he went on treating me. Several times, in truth, he would fain have left me, remembering that he was risking no slight penalty in doctoring me, or at least in continuing his attendance. The Cardinal had me put in a secret chamber, and went off at once to the palace to beg me from the Pope.

cxi. Meanwhile Rome was in the greatest excitement; for already the linen strips hanging from the great tower of the castle had been discovered, and every one ran to see the marvel. The castellan was overcome by one of his maddest humours; and was determined, in defiance of all his servants, to fly down, too, from the keep; for, said he, the only way of catching me was for himself to fly after me. Messer Ruberto Pucci, the father of Messer Pandolfo, having heard of the wonder, went to see for himself. Afterwards he repaired to the palace, where he met Cardinal Cornaro, who told him the whole story, and how I was in one of his apartments, and already under treatment. Together these two worthy men went and knelt before the Pope. Before they could utter a word, he cut in with, "I know all you want of me." Then answered Messer Ruberto Pucci, "Most Holy Father, we entreat of your mercy to give up that poor man to us, who for his great talents merits some considerate treatment, and who, besides, has proved a more than human courage and resource. We do not know for what sins your Holiness has kept him so long in prison. If they be too heinous, your Holiness is holy and wise; and in everything and everywhere may your will be done. But if his offences are such as can be pardoned, we beg that you will forgive him for our pleading." The Pope, who was somewhat confused, replied, "We have kept him in prison at the request of some of his friends, because he was too hot-headed; but," he added, "fully aware of his talents, and desiring to keep him near us, we had arranged to confer such benefits on him that he should have had no pretext for returning to France. I am grieved that he is so much hurt. Tell him to think of getting well; and as soon as he is cured we shall compensate him for all his troubles."

Then these two good men returned to me with this welcome message from the Pope. In the meantime the nobility of Rome came to visit me, both young men and old of every degree. The castellan, mad as he was, had himself carried to the Pope; and there he began to protest that if his Holiness did not send me back to prison, it would be doing him a great wrong. "For," he added, "Benvenuto escaped in defiance of his word of honour. Alas! alas! he has flown away, and he promised me he would not." Then the Pope, laughing, said, "Go now, go! for of a truth I will give him back to you." But the castellan entreated, "Send the governor to him, to learn who helped him to escape; for if it be one of my men, I will hang him by the neck to that very battlement from which Benvenuto got down." When the castellan had gone, the Pope called for the governor, and said to him, smiling, "This is a brave man, and it's a wonderful thing he has done; though, when I was young, I also got down from that very place." And here he spoke the truth; for once he had been shut up in the castle for forging a papal brief, when he was abbreviator in the College of Parco Majori. Pope Alexander had kept him in prison for a considerable time; and later, as his crime was of a shocking description, he even determined to cut off his head. But as his Holiness wanted to have the Corpus Domini over first, Farnese learnt all, sent for Pietro Chiavelluzzi with several horses, and bribed the warders of the castle with money. So that on the feast-day, when the Pope was in the procession, Farnese was placed in a basket and lowered to the ground by a rope. There was no outer wall of the castle in those days; there was only the great tower; so that he had not such difficulty in getting off as I had. Moreover, he was rightly imprisoned, and I unjustly. He only wanted to boast to the governor that he, too, in his time had been a youth of spirit and high courage, and did not see how he was but disclosing his own great villainy. "Go," said he, "and ask him to tell frankly who helped him. No matter who it be, it is enough for Benvenuto that I have pardoned him; and that you can promise him freely."

cxii. And so the governor came to me. Two days before, he had been appointed Bishop of Jesi. Entering, he said, "Benvenuto, my friend, though my office is terrifying to men, I am here to set your mind at ease; and for this I have the express order of his Holiness. He told me that he also had made a like escapade, but with good help and plenty of company; otherwise he would have failed. I swear to you by the sacraments which I carry upon me—for only two days ago I was made a bishop —that the Pope has liberated and pardoned you, and that he grieves over your hurt. But see to getting well; keep a cheerful mind; and the confinement, which in very truth you endured in all innocence, will prove a lasting good. You will trample poverty under your feet, and need never think of returning to France, tormenting your life out in this part or in that. Therefore tell me frankly the whole story, and who was your helper. After that, be at ease, rest, and get well." So from the very beginning I told him exactly how it had all happened, giving him the minutest details, not forgetting even to speak of the water-carrier who had carried me on his back. When the governor had heard all, he said, "Truly these are prodigious things for one man to have done by himself! No other in the world could have carried the thing through." Then, seizing my hand, he said, "Be of good cheer, and comfort you; for by this hand which you now grasp, you are free; and I promise you that, if you live, you shall be happy." Then he left me. Meanwhile he had been hindering a heap of nobles and gentlemen from seeing me. They had come to pay me a visit, having said amongst themselves, "Let us go and see this miracle-worker." They now stayed on with me for a while, and some of them offered me services, and some brought me gifts.

In the meantime the governor returned to the Pope, and repeated to him my story. And all who were there expressed their wonderment. Said the Pope, "This is certainly a prodigious thing!" Then spoke Signor Pier Luigi, who happened to be present, "Most Holy Father, if you liberate him, he will do greater prodigies still, for he is by nature a deal too audacious. I will tell you another exploit of his you do not know of. This Benvenuto of yours, before he was in prison, had some words with a gentleman of the Cardinal Santa Fiore's household. The difference arose from a mere trifling remark; but Benvenuto answered so arrogantly, and with such heat, that it was as good as a challenge. The gentleman placed the matter before the Cardinal, who said that if he could put his hands on the fellow, he would soon shake the nonsense out of him. Benvenuto, hearing this, got ready a gun, with which he used to practise shooting at a farthing; and one day, when the Cardinal was looking out at his window, Benvenuto, whose shop is under the Cardinal's palace, took his gun and aimed at Santa Fiore, who, however, being warned, got quickly out of the way. Then, that he might not appear to have meant any such thing, the fellow aimed at a wood-pigeon which was brooding in a hole at the top of the palace, and shot it through the head—a thing almost impossible to believe. So now let your Holiness do what you will with him. I should have failed in my duty had I kept silence about this. For the idea might even come into his head one day—since he thinks he was unjustly imprisoned—to shoot at your Holiness. His is a spirit too untamed and too sure of itself. When he killed Pompeo, he struck him twice in the throat with his dagger, though ten men were about him; and then made off—to their disgrace: yet were they men of worth and standing."

cxiii. While these words were being spoken, the gentleman of Santa Fiore's household, with whom I had had words, was present, and he confirmed to the Pope all his son had said. The Pope, swelling with rage, said not a word. Now I shall not be behindhand in speaking up for myself justly and truly concerning the affair in question. This gentleman of Santa Fiore came to me one day, and brought me a little gold ring, which was all stained with quicksilver, saying, "Brighten up this ring for me, and make haste about it." Now I had in hand a great many important works in gold and jewels. Besides, I was ruffled at hearing myself ordered about so arrogantly by one to whom I had never spoken before, nor even seen. So I told him I had no burnisher by me just then, and advised him to take the thing elsewhere. Then, for no reason in the world, he told me I was an ass. To which I answered that he did not speak the truth; and that on every count I was a better man than he; but that if he roused me, I would kick him harder than any donkey. He went and told tales of me to the Cardinal, painting me like the very devil. Two days after this, I was shooting behind the palace at a wood-pigeon brooding in a hole in the wall very high up. I had seen a goldsmith, Giovan Francesco della Tacca, a Milanese, shooting several times at the same bird; but he never brought it down. On this particular day the pigeon showed just its head; for it was suspicious after being shot at so often. Now Giovan Francesco and I were rivals in shooting wild birds; and certain friends of mine, who were in my shop at the time, called to me, saying, "Look, up there is Giovan Francesco della Tacca's pigeon, at which he has shot so often. Now see how suspicious the poor creature is; it will hardly show its head." Raising my eyes, I answered, "That little bit of head is mark enough for me, if the bird waits till I get aim at it." The gentlemen declared that the inventor of the gun himself could not do it; but I insisted. "Go and fetch a flask of mine host Palombo's good Greek wine," said I; "and I wager if the bird but waits till I cover it with my wonderful Broccardo (so was my gun called), I'll hit that little bit of head it shows." Then taking aim, without any rest for my arms, I did what I had promised, and without a thought in my mind of the Cardinal or any one else. Indeed I looked on the Cardinal as a great friend of mine. Thus let the world observe, when Fortune is resolved to wreck a man's career, how various are the ways she takes!

The Pope swelled and muttered in his rage, and stayed there turning over his son's story in his mind.

cxiv. Two days after this, Cardinal Cornaro went to ask the Pope for a bishopric for one of his gentlemen, called Messer Andrea Centano. It is true the Pope had promised him a bishopric, and one was now vacant. And when the Cardinal reminded him, his Holiness said that such was the truth, and he was quite willing; but that he also desired a favour, namely, that his lordship should give Benvenuto into his hands. Then the Cardinal replied, "Oh, since you have pardoned him, and given him up to me as a free man, what will the world say of your Holiness and of me?" The Pope answered, "I want Benvenuto; you want the bishopric. Let them say what they like." The good Cardinal still begged for the bishopric; but, for the rest, bade his Holiness reflect, and then do whatever was in his mind and power to do. The Pope, somewhat ashamed of betraying his word, said, "I will send for Benvenuto, and, just for my own satisfaction, I will put him down there in the rooms of my secret garden, where he can do his best to get well, and no hindrance shall be put in the way of his friends coming to see him. Also I will pay his expenses till this whim passes out of my head." The Cardinal returned home, and at once sent me a message by his friend who was looking for the bishopric; how the Pope wished to have me back again in his hands, but that I should be lodged in one of the lower chambers of the secret garden, and be free to see whomsoever I liked, just as in his house. I entreated Messer Andrea to have the goodness to beg the Cardinal not to surrender me to the Pope, but to let me manage the affair. I should have myself wrapped in my bedding and taken to a sure place outside Rome. For if he gave me up, he was sending me to certain death. They say the Cardinal

when he heard what I asked, would willingly have consented.
But Messer Andrea, to whom the bishopric was a matter of
much concern, made known our plan. His Holiness sent for me
immediately, and had me housed, as he had said, in one of the
lower rooms in his secret garden. The Cardinal warned me to
eat nothing provided by the Pope, promising to supply me with
food; and adding that what he had done he had been driven to.
I was to keep a good heart, he said; and he would help me to
regain my freedom. While matters stood thus, I had visits
every day, and fine offers were made to me by many great
gentlemen. Food was sent by the Pope, but I never touched it,
eating only what came from the Cardinal Cornaro's table. And
so I stayed like this for a space.

Now among my friends was a young Greek of five-and-twenty,
a very vigorous young fellow, and the finest swordsman in
Rome; rather lacking in courage, perhaps, but a most faithful-
hearted, honest creature, and very credulous. He had heard of
the Pope's saying he would make up to me for all my troubles.
Now it was indeed the truth that his Holiness had said so in
the beginning; but afterwards he spoke very differently. So
I took this young Greek into my confidence, and said to him,
"Dearest brother, those people have the wickedest designs on
me, so that now is the time to help me. Do they think that I
am unaware of their intentions, that I do not know their
extraordinary favours to be a mere blind?" The good young
fellow replied, "Benvenuto, my friend, in Rome the rumour
runs that the Pope has given you an office worth five hundred
crowns. Therefore I entreat you not to let this suspicion of yours
lose you such a good thing." Nevertheless I begged him, and
with my arms I made a cross to strengthen my entreaty, to get
me out of this place. Well I knew that it was in the power of
such a Pope to do me much good; yet I also knew for a certainty
he was planning secretly to do me an ill turn, without risk to his
good name. Therefore I begged my friend to act quickly, and
do his best to save me from my enemies. If only he got me out
of this in the way I could tell him, ever after I should consider
I owed my life to him, and should spend it for him in his need.
This poor young man wept and said, "O my dear brother, you
are bent on your own ruin; yet I cannot but do your bidding.
Therefore tell me your plan, and I will do all you say, though
against my own will." Thus it was arranged; and I explained
to him the whole scheme, which might very easily have been
successful. But when I was expecting him to carry it out, he

came to say that, for my own safety, he was going to disobey me, believing fully what he had heard from men who were in the Pope's confidence, and who, he said, knew the real state of my case. He had been my only stand-by; and now I remained wretched and despairing. This was the day of the Corpus Domini of the year 1539.

cxv. After this discussion the whole day passed away; and at night there came from the Pope's kitchen an abundant supply of food, as well as excellent provision from the Cardinal Cornaro's table. And some friends of mine happening to come in, I made them stay to supper. I was in bed with my leg in splints, yet I made good cheer with them, so that they stayed on. About an hour after sundown they left me; and two of my servants settled me for the night, and then lay down in the antechamber. Now I had a hairy dog as black as a mulberry. He was of the greatest use to me when I went shooting; and now he kept close to me all the time. That night he lay under my bed, and during the hours that followed I called my servant three times to take him out, for he was howling terribly. When the servants came, the dog threw himself on them, and would have bitten them. They were terrified, and feared he was mad, for he never stopped howling. So the night went on till the fourth hour. Just on the stroke of four, the Bargello with his band came into my room. The dog rushed out, flew at them with such fury, tearing their clothes and their hosen, and terrifying them so that they thought he was mad. But the Bargello, a man of experience, said, "Good dogs by instinct always divine and predict any harm threatening their masters. Here, two of you drive off the creature with sticks. You others, meanwhile, bind Benvenuto to this chair, and bring him you know where." As I have said, this happened on the night after the Corpus Domini, about the fourth hour. All muffled about with wraps, I was carried off, four of the guards walking in front, to scatter the few persons who were still about the streets. Thus they brought me to the Torre di Nona—so it is called—and put me into the condemned cell. Laying me down on a bit of a mattress, they gave me in charge to one of the warders, who all night long condoled with me on my evil fortune, saying, "Alas, poor Benvenuto! what have you done to set those people against you?" By this I was left in little doubt as to my fate, the place being what it was, and this man having warned me. I spent a portion of that night in agonised conjecture as to why it had pleased God so to punish me; and because I could think of no reason, I was much disturbed. The guard set to comforting me as well as he knew. But I entreated him, for the love of God, to be silent, and to leave me alone, so that I might the more speedily and the better possess my soul. He promised to do so. Then turning my whole heart towards God, I besought Him most devoutly to receive me into His kingdom. I had, indeed, murmured; but it was at the thought of leaving this world in such a fashion, while I was quite innocent, so far as the ordinary laws were concerned. True, I had committed homicides; but God's Vicar had called me from my own country and pardoned me, by his own authority, and in the name of the laws; and what I had done had been done in defence of that body which His Divine Majesty had lent to me, so that I could not own that I deserved this death, having regard to the conditions under which we live in the world. It seemed to me that I was in the position of unlucky persons walking in the streets, when a stone falls from some great height on their head and kills them, which may be clearly assigned to the influence of the stars. Not that the stars in any way plot against us, to do us or good or ill; but these accidents come to pass through their conjunction, to which we are subject. Yet, I reflected, I know I have free will; and if my faith were active and devout, I am very certain that the angels of heaven would bear me out of this prison, and would bring me to a sure refuge from all my troubles. But since God thinks me unworthy of such a favour, it is clear that celestial influences work out their malignity on me. This struggle lasted for a time. Then I became calm, and ere long I fell asleep.

cxvi. When the dawn broke, the warder woke me and said, "O unlucky man, yet undeserving of your fate! There is no more time for sleep. One has come with ill news for you." Then I answered, "The sooner I am out of this prison of the world, the happier for me, the more that I am sure my soul has found salvation, and that I die innocent. Christ, glorious and divine, makes me companion of His disciples and His friends, who like Him were wrongly put to death. I, too, unjustly am sent to my death; and I thank God devoutly for the same. Why does he not appear who brings me my sentence?" Then answered the warder, "He is too sorry for you, and he weeps." So I called him by his own name, which was Benedetto da Cagli, saying, "Come forward, Messer Benedetto, my friend, for now I am most well disposed and resigned. I glory much more, dying thus unjustly, than if I had been deserving of such a fate.

Come hither, I beg you; and grant me a priest, that I may speak a word or two with him—although I have no need of this, for I have already made holy confession to my Lord God. Yet fain would I observe what Holy Mother Church has commanded us; for though she has done me this hideous wrong, I freely pardon her. So come, friend Benedetto; hasten to tell me your message, while I am still in this devout mood."

When I had said these words, the worthy man told the guard to lock the door on me in the meanwhile; for without him the business could not be done. Then he went off to the house of Signor Pier Luigi's wife, who had with her the Duchess I have already spoken of. And presenting himself to them, he said, "My most illustrious mistress, be pleased, I beg you, for the love of God, to ask the Pope to send another man to speak the sentence on Benvenuto, and carry out my office; for I renounce it, and never will I fulfil it." Then sighing, and in greatest grief of heart, he went away. The Duchess knitted her brows, as she said, "This is the fine justice administered in Rome by the Vicar of God! The Duke, my former husband, had the highest opinion of this man, for his worth and his talents. He never wished him to return to Rome, but holding him very dear, he desired to keep him near his person." Then she went off with angry mutterings on her lips. The wife of Signor Pier Luigi, who was called the Signora Jérolima, then repaired to the Pope; and throwing herself on her knees before him, in the presence of several cardinals, spoke so impressively that she brought a blush to his cheek. "For your sake," he replied, "we will let him be—though we never wished him harm." But he only said so because the cardinals had heard the appeal of this wonderful and spirited lady.

In the meantime I remained in the greatest anxiety, my heart beating violently all the while. Hardly less anxious were the men on whom the horrid duty would have fallen. But when dinner time had passed, they all went about their other business, and food was brought to me likewise. In my astonishment I said, "Now has truth been stronger than the malignity of the celestial influences. And I pray God that it may please Him to save me from the fury of this tempest." Then I began to eat; and just as resolutely as I had made up my mind to the worst, so now did I bravely hope for good fortune. I dined heartily; and not a soul came near me till one hour of the night, when the Bargello arrived with a good part of his men, and had me put back in the chair in which, the night before, he had brought me to this place. On the way he spoke most kindly to me, telling me to fear nothing; and ordering his men to avoid jostling my broken leg, and to take care of me as of their own eyes. So they did; and brought me to the castle whence I had escaped; and when we were at the top of the keep, they locked me into a cell opening on a little court there for a while.

cxvii. Meantime the castellan had himself brought to the place where I was; and the poor afflicted man said to me, "See, I have got you again." "Yes," said I, "but you must own that I did escape as I told you. And if I had not been sold—on the Pope's word, too—for a bishopric, by a Venetian Cardinal and a Roman Farnese, who both spat in the face of the most sacred laws, you would never have caught me again. But now, since they have set out on this evil road, do your worst. Everything in the world is the same to me." Then the poor man began to cry aloud, "Alas, alas! he does not care whether he lives or dies; and he is more audacious than when he was well. Put him down there below the garden, and never speak of him again; for he will be the death of me!"

I was then taken to a dark cell under the garden. Water covered the floor, and it was full of tarantulas and venomous worms. A wretched mattress of hemp was thrown down on the ground for me. I was given no supper that night; and there was I left behind four locked doors. So I remained till the nineteenth hour of the next day. When at last they brought me something to eat, I asked the warders to let me have some of my books to read. Not a word did they answer; but they handed on my request to the poor castellan, who asked what I had said. Next morning I was given my Bible in the vulgar tongue, and another book which contained the Chronicles of Giovanni Villani. When I asked for certain others, I was told I should have no more, and that I had too many already.

And so in this unhappy state I continued, lying on the wretched damp mattress, which in three days' time was soaked through and through. I could barely move because of my broken leg; and when I wished to get out of bed for my natural needs, I crawled on hands and knees with the greatest difficulty in order not to befoul the place where I slept. For an hour and a half each day a faint reflection of light entered my miserable dungeon by a tiny hole; and only during that little time could I read. The rest of the day and night I waited patiently in the darkness; nor were thoughts of God and of our human frailty ever far from me. I was certain that in a few brief days I should here, and in these conditions, end my unhappy life. Yet as best I could I comforted myself, thinking how much worse it would have been to have met my death by a blow of the executioner's horrid knife: whereas now I should pass away as if drugged to sleep, which made death seem much easier. Little by little I felt the flame of my life dying down, till my fine constitution accommodated itself to the purgatory. After I felt that it had become adapted and inured to circumstances, I made up my mind calmly to bear my terrible sufferings while strength enough remained.

cxviii. I began the Bible from the beginning, reading and pondering it devoutly; and so fascinated was I by its study that, if I had been able, I should never have done anything else save pore over it. But as light failed me, then the burden of all my troubles came upon me, and tore so at my heart, that many a time I resolved to do away with myself in one way or another. Only, as they gave me no knife, it was not easy to find the means. Once, however, I took a great beam of wood I found lying in my cell, and poised it like a trap, intending it should fall on my head, which would certainly have crushed me to death on the spot. But when I had got the whole thing ready, and was making a movement to shake it down, just as I was about to put my hand to it, I was seized by some invisible thing and thrown four cubits' length from the place; and so terrified was I that I lay half dead; and there I stopped till the nineteenth hour, when they brought me my dinner. They must have come several times without my hearing them; for when I became conscious, I heard Sandrino Monaldi, who had entered, saying, "O unhappy man! See the end of such rare talent!" When these words reached me, I opened my eyes, and saw priests with their robes on, who said, "Oh, you told us he was dead!" And Bozza answered, "Dead I found him; and so I told you." Then they raised me up, lifted the mattress which was pulpy, just like a mess of macaroni, and threw it out of the room. When they described my condition to the castellan, he ordered me another mattress. Afterwards, when I pondered what it might have been that turned me back from such a deed, I felt I had been visited by some power divine, my guardian angel.

cxix. Next night there appeared to me in a dream a wonderful being, in the shape of a beautiful youth, who reproached me, saying, "Dost thou know who lent thee that body which thou wouldst have destroyed before its time?" I seemed to make answer that I recognised everything as coming from the God of Nature. Then said he, "Dost thou despise His works, seeking thus to spoil them? Let Him be thy guide, and never lose hope in His great power." And much other excellent counsel he gave me, of which I do not remember the thousandth part. So I began to reflect that this angel had, indeed, told me the truth. Casting my eyes round the prison, I saw some bits of crumbling brick, and by rubbing one piece against another, I contrived to make a little paste. Then I crawled to the door of my prison, and bit off a little splinter from the sharp edge. I waited until the light came into my cell, which was from twenty and a half to twenty-one and a half of the day. Then I began to write, as well as I could, on some blank pages of my Bible a reproof to the revolting spirits that rule my intellect, which had refused any longer to bear this life. They, on their part, replied to my body, setting forward their suffering as excuse; and then the body gave them hope of good to come. So, in dialogue form, I wrote—

The Body.
> Afflicted spirits mine! Ah, lend
> An ear. How cruel your hate of life!

The Spirits.
> If Heaven and you contend,
> Who is our champion in the strife?
> Then stay us not: we seek a better life.

The Body.
> Ah, go not yet, I pray!
> Heaven holds before your face
> Such joys as in the past you ne'er did know.

The Spirits.
> Still a few hours we stay,
> If the great God concede to you such grace
> As brings us not a heavier load of woe.

My vigour came back once again, now that I had thus comforted myself; and I went on reading my Bible. My eyes had become so accustomed to the darkness that, whereas at first I could only read an hour and a half, now I read three whole hours. Marvelling greatly, I pondered the force of God's strength in those so simple men, who believed with utmost fervour that God would grant them the desire of their hearts. I, too, looked forward to the help of God, depending on His divine strength and mercy, and likewise on my own innocence. Thus all the time these high thoughts stayed by me; and now I talked with

Him. And such delight did I begin to feel in this communion, that I did not remember any more my sufferings in the past; but all day long I sang psalms and many other verses I had made in His praise.

One thing, however, gave me great trouble, and that was the growth of my nails; for whenever I touched myself I made a wound, and I could not dress without their either turning inwards or outwards, and causing me much suffering. Also my teeth were decaying in my mouth. I became aware of this when the dead teeth were shoved up by the living ones, and little by little the gums were pierced, and the sharp points of the roots came through their cases. When I saw this, I drew them out one after the other, like knives from their scabbards, without pain or blood. However, I got used to these fresh troubles and annoyances. Sometimes I sang, sometimes I prayed, and sometimes I wrote with the brick paste I have mentioned. It was then I began a Capitolo in praise of my prison, telling all the accidents that had happened to me. This Capitolo shall be written down in its own place.

cxx. The good castellan sent often privately to know what I was doing. Now on the last day of July I was in very good heart, there all by myself, remembering the great feast that is wont to be held in Rome on the 1st of August. "In past years," I said, "I kept this pleasant feast amidst the vanities of the world. This year I shall hold it contemplating the divinity of God. Oh, how much happier am I now than then!" These words of mine were reported to the castellan, who was vexed beyond measure, and said, "O God, he thrives and triumphs in the midst of all his sufferings; while I am wretched in the midst of plenty! I die, and his is the fault. Go at once and put him in the lowest dungeon of all, where the Preacher Foiano was starved to death. Perhaps when he sees himself in such evil case, he will be less merry!"

So there came to my prison Captain Sandrino Monaldi, with about twenty of the castellan's servants. They found me on my knees, and I did not move at their entrance; for I was praying before a God-the-Father with angels around, and a Christ rising victorious, which I had drawn on the wall with a piece of charcoal I had found amongst a heap of earth in my cell. Now I had lain four months on my back on account of my broken leg, and had dreamt so often that the angels came to cure me, that by this time it had grown as strong as if it had never been broken. Well, now these men came towards me, all armed, and as much afraid as if I had been a venomous dragon. Then the Captain spoke: "You know we are here, and in our numbers, for we came in with noise enough; and yet you do not turn round to greet us." When I heard these words, my mind ran at once to the greater evil which might happen to me; but misfortune and I being old and constant friends, I said to them, "To the God Who bears me up, to the Heavenly One I have turned my soul, my contemplation, and all my vital forces. To you I turn just what belongs to you; for what is good in me you are not worthy to look on, nor can you touch it. But do to that which is yours whatever you may." The Captain was in a fright; and not knowing what I might do, he cried to four of the stoutest, "Lay down all your weapons." As soon as they had done so, he said, "Now throw yourselves on him—quick —quick—and seize him! Is he the devil that so many of us should tremble before him? Hold him fast that he may not escape!" Then I was seized with brutal violence; and looking for something much worse than what actually happened, I lifted my eyes to Christ, and said, "O God of Justice, on that high cross of Thine, didst Thou not pay all our debts? Why then has my innocence to pay the debts of some unknown sinner? Nevertheless, Thy will be done."

In the meantime they were carrying me away with a huge lighted torch; and I felt sure they were going to throw me down the Sammalò oubliette. Such is the name of a place which has engulfed many a living man; and they fall down, down, into a deep hole in the foundations of the castle. But this did not happen. So I thought I was exceedingly lucky when they put me in that horrid dungeon of which I have spoken, the one where Foiano died of hunger. There they left me without doing me any further hurt.

When I was alone, I began to sing a *De profundis clamavi*, a *Miserere*, and *In te Domine speravi*. And thus it was I kept that 1st of August feast with God, my heart rejoicing all the time in hope and faith. On the second day they drew me out of that hole, and brought me back again to the cell where I had drawn God's image on the wall. When I got back there, I was overcome with weeping for the sweetness of my joy. After that the castellan would have news every day of what I did and said.

Now the doctors had already given up all hope of saving his life; and the Pope, who had heard the whole story, said, "Before my castellan dies, I am willing to let him get rid of Benvenuto in whatever way he likes; for he is the cause of his death, and he shall not die unavenged." These words being reported to him by Duke Pier Luigi, the castellan cried, "So now the Pope gives me Benvenuto, and would have me take my revenge on him? Think no more about the matter; leave it to me." If the Pope in his heart harboured malice against me, revenge and bitterness raged in that of the castellan at that moment. Just then the invisible guardian, who had kept me from taking my own life, came to me. I could not see him, but he stood by me, lifted me up from the depths, and said in a clear voice, "Ah, me! Benvenuto, my friend, make haste. Assail God with thy wonted prayers, and cry aloud to Him!" Seized with sudden fright, I sank on my knees, and recited prayer after prayer in a loud voice, adding at the end the *Qui habitat in adjutorio*. Then I talked with God for a space. And all at once the firm, clear voice said, "Go now and rest, and have no fear."

Now this is what had happened. After the castellan had given a most brutal order for my death, all at once he withdrew it, saying, "Is he not Benvenuto whom I have defended so stoutly, and of whose innocence I am quite certain, knowing as I do all this cruelty is wrought on him unjustly? Oh, how can God ever have pity on me and on my sins, if I do not pardon those who have done me the greatest wrongs? Oh, why should I hurt a good innocent man, who has done me service and honour? Go to! instead of killing him, I will give him life and liberty; and I shall leave it written in my testament that no one is to ask him a single farthing of the great expenses I have undergone for him, which otherwise he would have to pay." Now this came to the ears of the Pope, and he was very angry.

cxxi. Meanwhile I continued to pray, and went on writing my Capitolo. And every night I dreamt the most gladsome and pleasant dreams imaginable. I always seemed to be in the company of that spirit, who had been invisible, but whom I now saw, and whose voice I continued to hear. I asked but one sole grace of him; and that I begged with all my heart, that he would bring me where I could see the sun. This, I said, was the only desire I had, and if I could but see it, then I should die content. By this time all the annoyances I had to endure in my prison had become even as my friends and companions; none of them disturbed me any more. Yet there were minions of the castellan who were looking for him to hang me from the battlement from whence I had climbed down, as I have told you; and when they saw how their master had resolved on just the opposite, they could not bear it; and all the time they kept inventing new terrors for me, so that I might never cease trembling, and ever feel that death was at hand. But, as I say, I had grown so accustomed to all these things, that I feared none of them; and the one desire that stirred within me was to see the sphere of the sun in my dreams. So did I pray without ceasing; and my heart went out to Christ, crying continually, "O true Son of God, I pray Thee by Thy birth, by Thy death upon the Cross, and Thy glorious resurrection, grant me to see the sun, if not otherwise, at least in dreams. But if Thou renderest me worthy to see it with these mortal eyes, I promise to go a pilgrimage to Thy Holy Sepulchre." This vow and these my most earnest prayers, I made to God on the 2nd day of October 1539. Next morning, which was the 3rd of October, I awoke at dawn, almost an hour before the rising of the sun; and getting up from my wretched lair, I put on a covering, for it had begun to be cold, and then prayed more devoutly than ever I had done before, beseeching Christ to grant me at least such grace as should reveal to me the sin of mine for which I was undergoing this sore penance; and since His Divine Majesty had not thought me worthy to see the sun even in my dreams, I begged Him, in the name of His great power and virtue, to make known to me the reason of my punishment.

cxxii. When I had said these words, I was taken up and carried away by that invisible power, like a wind, and brought into a place where the unknown being manifested himself visibly in human form, in the shape of a youth scarce bearded, wondrous fair of face, but austere, and no wanton. And in that place he pointed some out to me, saying, "This great company of men you see are those who from the beginning of time have been born into the world, and then have died." Whereat I asked him why he brought me here; and he made answer, "Come with me, and soon you shall know." Now in my hand I carried a dagger, and I wore a coat of mail. He led me through the spacious place, and showed me folk in their infinite thousands, walking some this way and some the other. Still he led me on, and then stepped in front of me through a little doorway into what seemed a narrow street. I found myself disarmed, and I was in a white shirt with nothing on my head, and walking on my companion's right hand. Seeing myself like this, I was full of wonder, for I did not know the street. Lifting my eyes, I saw that the light of the sun was beating on a wall, like a house front, above my head. Then I exclaimed, "Oh, friend, what must I do to rise high enough to see the very sphere of the sun?" And he pointed out to me some great stairs upon my right hand, and said, "Go that way, and alone." So I went on by myself. I mounted the stairs backwards, and little by little became aware of the nearness of the sun. I hastened my steps, and went on still in this fashion, till I perceived the whole sphere of the sun. Now the force of its rays made me instinctively close my eyes. Perceiving my error, however, I opened them and looked straight at the light, and said, "O sun, my friend, whom I have so longed for! Never again would I see aught else, though thy rays blind me." Thus I stood for a space with my eyes firmly fixed on it, till suddenly the full force of the great rays were cast upon the left of the orb, which then remained clear and rayless; and with infinite gladness did I behold it, for it seemed to me a most marvellous thing that the rays were thus removed. I stayed to ponder on the Grace Divine I had received that morning from God; and I cried aloud, "O wonderful power of Thine! O glorious virtue! How much more grace Thou grantest me than e'er I looked for!" This rayless sun appeared to me not more nor less than a bath of purest liquid gold. While I was considering this marvel, I saw something grow from the middle of the sphere; and gradually the growth took shape, and in an instant it was a Christ upon the Cross, made of the stuff of the sun itself. Such grace was in His benign aspect, that the mind of man could not imagine a myriadth part of it. And while I was contemplating the wonder, I cried aloud, "A miracle! A miracle! O God! O clemency of Thine, O Virtue infinite! What wonders hast Thou granted me to see this day!" While I stood in this ecstasy, Christ moved towards that part whither had travelled the rays; and the centre of the sun swelled out anew; and as it grew, it took shape in a Madonna of marvellous beauty. She was sitting on a high throne with her Son in her arms, in sweetest attitude, and with a smile upon her face. On this side and on that was an angel of such marvellous beauty that imagination does not reach thereto. I saw also within the sun, on the right, a figure clad like a priest. He kept his back to me, and turned his face towards the Madonna and the Christ. All these things I saw true, clear, and living; and all the time I kept crying aloud my praise to the glory of God. This wonderful thing had been before my eyes but a few minutes when it vanished; and I was thrust back to my wretched lair. Then did I exclaim, "By the virtue of God I have been deemed worthy to see His glory, which maybe no mortal eye hath ever seen before. Wherefore by this I know that I am free and happy and protected by God's grace; and you villains shall villains still remain, unhappy and under the ban of the Almighty. Hearken to what I say now; for I have assurance that at four of the night following on All Saints' Day, which was the day I came into the world (namely, the first of November of the year 1500), you will be compelled to take me out of this dark dungeon; nor will you be able to help yourselves. For I have seen it with mine own eyes writ plain upon the throne of God. That priest with his face towards God, and his back to me, was the Blessed Peter, who was pleading my cause; for he was shamed that in his house Christians should suffer such cruel wrongs. So tell whoever you will, that no one has the power to do me further hurt; and tell the lord who keeps me here that, if he will send me either wax or paper, by which I can show forth the Glory of God revealed unto me, then of a surety I shall make clear to him what mayhap he now holds in doubt."

cxxiii. Although the doctors had no hope of saving the castellan's life, yet he remained sane in mind; for those mad humours which were wont to afflict him every year, were utterly departed. His one thought was now the saving of his soul; and his conscience gnawed him, for it was much on his mind that I had suffered, and was still suffering, a very great wrong. He let the Pope know the great things of which I spoke; but his Holiness sent back the answer of one who believes neither in God nor in anything else: that I was mad, and that he should give all his mind to the care of his own health. When the castellan heard the Pope's reply, he sent me words of comfort, and supplied me with writing materials, with wax also, and some little wooden modelling tools, and sent kind messages besides, which were delivered by one of his servants who was a good friend of mine; just the opposite, in fact, of that other band of rascals, who would have liked to see me dead. With the paper and the wax I began to employ myself, and while I worked, I wrote this sonnet to the castellan—

My lord, if I to you the truth could show
  Of light eternal unto me reveal'd,
  In this low life, such faith to me you'd yield
As scarce on a high emperor you'd bestow.

If the great Pastor of the Church could know
  Mine eyes have seen God's glory without shield,
  Glory from every other soul conceal'd
Till it has left this realm of bitter woe,

The gates of holy Justice you would see
    Roll back, and impious Fury sudden fall
Helpless and bound, protesting to the skies.

Had I but light—but light! Ah me!
    To carve my vision on the heavenly wall,
Then should I all my other griefs despise.

cxxiv. When next day the castellan's servant, who was fond of me, brought me my food, I gave him this sonnet written out; and, without telling those other evil-minded servants who had an ill will to me, he handed it to his master. The castellan would willingly have let me go free, for he had the notion that the wrong done to me was the chief cause of his dying. Taking the sonnet, he read it more than once, and said, "These are neither the words nor the conceits of a madman, but of a good honest man"; and at once he ordered one of his secretaries to take it to the Pope, to give it into his own hands, and beg him to let me go free. While the secretary was carrying the sonnet to the Pope, the castellan sent me lights both for the day and for the night, and every comfort which could be looked for in that place. So I began to recover from my weakness, which had become very serious. The Pope read the sonnet several times. Then he sent word to the castellan that ere long he would do what would please him. And, indeed, his Holiness would have willingly let me go then; but Signor Pier Luigi, his son, almost in defiance of his father, kept me there by force.

The death of the castellan was drawing near. While I was designing and sculpting the marvellous miracle I have related, on the morning of All Saints' Day, he sent Piero Ugolini his nephew to show me some jewels. As soon as I saw them, I cried out: "This is the countersign of my deliverance." Whereupon the young man, who was somewhat slow-witted, said, "Don't be counting on that, Benvenuto." Then I answered, "Take away your jewels; for I am so ill-treated here that I have not light enough in this black cell; and without light it is impossible to discern the quality of the stones. But as to getting out of prison, before this day is done you will come to take me out of it. And this is fated; you cannot help yourself." Then he went away, and the key was turned on me again. But after he had been gone more than two hours by the clock, he came back for me without an armed guard, with only two lads who helped me to walk. Thus I was brought into the spacious apartment which I had in the beginning (that is in 1538), and was given all the comforts I could wish for.

cxxv. A few days after, the castellan—who thought I was out of prison and free—pressed hard by his mortal malady, passed from this present life. His place was taken by his brother Messer Antonio Ugolini, who had given the castellan to understand that he had let me go. This Messer Antonio, so far as I understood, had the authority of the Pope to let me remain in this spacious prison till he should tell him what was to be done with me. Now Messer Durante of Brescia, whom I have already spoken of, arranged with the soldier, who had been an apothecary in Prato, to give me some liquid poison in my food. It was not meant to work suddenly, but to take effect in four or five months. But in the end they made up their minds to mix diamond dust with my meat. In itself it is not poisonous at all; but being extraordinarily hard, its sharply-pointed angles do not become rounded when it is reduced to powder, as would be the case with other stones. Only the diamond keeps its sharp edge, so that, if it enters the stomach along with food, during the process of digestion it sticks to the coats of the stomach and the bowels, and as the new food comes ever pushing forward, it is not long before it pierces them, and death is the result; whereas no other kind of stone or glass sticks to the organs, but goes on its way with the food. So now this Messer Durante gave a diamond of small value to one of the warders; and it is said that a certain Lione, a goldsmith of Arezzo, and a great enemy of mine, was given the pounding of it. Now Lione was very poor, and the diamond might have been worth some dozens of crowns. Well, he gave the warder to understand that the dust he returned to him was really this diamond pounded and ready to be administered to me. So that morning—it happened to be a Friday—they put it into all my victuals. I was given it in salad, in sauce, and in soup. I set to with a hearty appetite, for the night before I had fasted, and this was a feast day. It is quite true that I felt my teeth crunching the food, but the thought of such a piece of rascality never entered my head. When I had finished dinner, a little salad was left on the plate, and my eyes happened to fall on some very fine splinters among the remains. I took them at once to the light of the window; and while I was looking at them, I remembered that my food had crunched under my teeth that morning more than usual. After examining them well, I came to the conclusion that, as far as my eyes could judge, they were particles of diamond dust. I gave myself up at once for dead. Sorrow and devotion mingled in my heart as I hastened to my prayers.

Thus facing my certain death, for a whole hour I entreated God in prayer, and thanked Him for a death so mild. Since my stars had thus ruled my fate, I thought I was fortunate to get out of life by this easy road. I felt a deep contentment, and blessed the world and the time I had lived in it. Now I was returning to a better land, by the grace of God, which I felt quite sure I had won.

While these thoughts were running in my mind, I held in my hand some tiny grains of the supposed diamond; for, indeed, I thought it to be such. But hope never dies, and even now a faint vain glimmer of it led me on. So I took a small knife and some of the grains, and placed them on one of my prison bars. Then with great care I pressed the point of the knife heavily on the grains, and felt them crumbling. Looking closer, I knew it was so. At once I wrapped myself about with new hope, and said, "This won't do me much harm, Messer Durante; it's only a soft and worthless and quite harmless stone." True, I had made up my mind to be calm and to die in peace; but I now changed my mind. First of all, however, I thanked God, and blessed poverty, which, though many times it brings about men's death, was now the real cause of my escape. For, as I have told you, Messer Durante, my enemy, or whoever it was, gave a diamond worth more than a hundred crowns to be pounded. But Lione, tempted by his poverty, kept it himself, and ground for me a citron-coloured beryl worth two carlins, thinking, probably, that any stone would have the same effect as a diamond.

cxxvi. About this time the Bishop of Pavia, brother of the Count of San Secondo, who was called Monsignor de' Rossi of Parma, was imprisoned in the castle on account of some disputes that had taken place at Pavia. Now, as he was a great friend of mine, I put my head out of a hole in my prison, and called to him loud, telling him the rascals had given me a pounded diamond, meaning to kill me; and I sent him by one of his servants some of the dust which was left. But I did not tell him that I knew it was not diamond dust. I said that they had certainly poisoned me because my good friend the castellan was dead. So for the little time I still had to live, I begged him to give me one of his loaves every day; for I did not wish to eat anything more that came from them. He promised to send me food from his table.

Messer Antonio, who was certainly not aware of the plot, made a great noise about it, and requested to be shown the powdered stone, thinking, like the rest, that it was really diamond dust. But afterwards, fearing that the Pope was the instigator of the plot, he let it pass as a mere trifle, when he had thought over the matter. After that I ate the food sent me by the Bishop; and continued writing my Capitolo on the prison, setting down each day, point by point, every new thing that happened to me. Now Messer Antonio sent me food as well, by the hand of Giovanni, the Prato apothecary I have mentioned, who was here as a soldier. This man had a great ill will to me; indeed it was he who brought me the powdered diamond. So I told him I would eat nothing he brought me, unless he first ate some himself. He answered me that it was for Popes to have their food tasted. Whereupon I answered that, as noblemen are obliged to do this service to the Pope, he, a soldier, an apothecary, a mean Prato fellow, must not refuse to do it for a Florentine like me. He threw insolent words at me in reply; but I was a match for him in that. Messer Antonio, who was somewhat ashamed of the affair, especially as he intended making me pay the expenses of my keep—which the poor dead castellan had let me off—employed another servant to bring my victuals. This man, who was friendly to me, willingly tasted my food without arguing the point. He told me how the Pope was worried every day by Monsignor de Montluc, who was continually asking for me for his King; but that the Pope had little fancy to give me up; and that the Cardinal Farnese, formerly my patron and friend, had been heard to say that I need not count on getting out of prison yet a while. Thereupon I said I'd be out in despite of them all. Then the worthy fellow begged me to be quiet, and not let any one hear me saying such a thing, for it would be against me. He counselled me, since I had put my faith in God, to await His mercy in quietness. I answered him that the power of God had no need to tremble before the malice of the unjust.

cxxvii. A few days passed, and the Cardinal of Ferrara appeared in Rome. He went to do reverence to the Pope, who kept him so long that supper time came on; for his Holiness, who was a very able man, wished to talk over French affairs at leisure with him. Now at table people say things which otherwise they would leave unsaid. So was it now. The great King Francis was always most liberal in his dealings; and the Cardinal, who knew his character well, made promises on his behalf far beyond the Pope's expectations. So his Holiness was in high spirits about this. Besides, once a week, it was his habit to indulge in a great debauch, after which he vomited. So when the Cardinal saw the Pope was in a humour to confer favours, he asked for me in the name of his master with great insistence, bringing proof that King Francis had a strong feeling in the matter. Then the Pope, knowing the moment for vomiting was at hand—and besides, his deep potations were also having their effect—said to the Cardinal with a great laugh, "You shall take him home with you this instant"; and having given express orders to this effect, he rose from the table. So the Cardinal sent for me at once, before Signor Pier Luigi should hear of it; for he certainly would have put a stop to my coming out. The Pope's messenger arrived along with two great noblemen belonging to the suite of the Cardinal of Ferrara; and at past four of the night, they took me out of prison and brought me to their patron, who gave me the warmest welcome. There I was well lodged, and I stayed in comfort.

Messer Antonio, the castellan's brother and substitute, forced me to pay all my expenses, and also the gratuities which the police officials and such-like persons are used to expect in cases like mine; nor would he pay any heed to the directions left by the castellan on this head. The business cost me many scores of crowns; but the Cardinal said I must be prudent if I valued my life; and he told me that if he had not dug me out of prison that very evening, I should not have been released. Already he had heard that the Pope much lamented having let me go.

cxxviii. I must now turn back a step to tell of certain circumstances which will be found in my Capitolo. While I was staying those few days in the apartments of the Cardinal, and afterwards in the private garden of the Pope, among other dear friends who came to see me was a cashier of Messer Bindo Altoviti, Bernardo Galluzzi by name. Now I had entrusted several hundreds of crowns to him; so he came to me in the Pope's garden and wanted to return the whole sum. But I told him that I did not know any better friend to whom to entrust my property, nor any safer place. Yet he appeared to be unwilling to the last degree; and I had almost to use force to make him keep it. Now when I was out of the castle for good, I found that this poor young Bernardo Galluzzi was ruined; and so I lost my money. While I was in prison I dreamt a terrible dream, in which some one seemed to write words of the utmost meaning on my forehead with a pen; and the writer commanded me thrice to keep silence, and to tell the matter to no man. When I awoke I found my forehead marked. In my

Capitolo on the prison I have told a great many things of the kind. For instance, I heard (though I did not know the meaning of the message) all that afterwards happened to Signor Pier Luigi, and this so clearly, and so precisely, that, for myself, I believe it was, indeed, an angel from Heaven who told it to me. Nor must I leave out one thing, the greatest surely that ever happened to any man; for I would justify the divinity of God and of His secrets, Who deemed me worthy. From the time when I saw the great vision till now, there has remained a splendour (O wondrous thing!) about my head; and this is plain to all to whom I have thought well to point it out—but these are very few. It is visible above my shadow in the morning, at sunrise, and for two hours after, and still clearer when there is dew upon the grass. In the evening, too, at sunset, it can be seen. I became aware of it first in France, when I was in Paris; for the air in those parts is much freer from haze than in Italy, where we have many more mists. Nevertheless, in every circumstance I can see it, and show it to others, too, though less clearly than when I was in France.

I will now set down my Capitolo made in prison, and in praise of the prison; after which I will go on to relate the good and evil which I have experienced from time to time; and I hope one day to add things which have still to happen in my life.

THIS CAPITOLO I INSCRIBE TO LUCA MARTINI, AND IT IS TO HIM I SPEAK THEREIN

Whoe'er would know the measure of God's strength,
  And how far man can borrow from that source,
  He must in prison lie, I firmly hold,
Harrow'd by thinking of his kindred dear,
  Wearied and sick with his own body's pain;
  And far must be his exile from his home.
Now if you fain would prove yourself of worth,
  Be dragg'd to prison guiltless; and there lie
  Month after month, while no man lends you aid.
And let them rob you of your little all,
  While you face death and outrage every day,
  Hopeless of any bettering of your fate.
Be hurl'd perforce upon a desperate deed—
  Break prison—leap from the high castle wall.
  Be then led back to a more hideous cell.
Listen, my Luca; now I tell the best:
  Your leg is broken; you've been trick'd;
  You shiver in the damp without a cloak.
No kindly word; but an there be ill news,
  The warder brings it with your meat. (The boor
  Not long ago in Prato mix'd his drugs.)

But fame's not yours without a further test.
 The stool's your only chair; there may you sit
 And waste your quick invention in this void.
The warder has his rules. No word of yours
 He hears; will give you naught; scarce dares the door
 To ope enough to let his body through.
'Tis fine diversion! Paper, pens, and ink,
 And tools and fire you'll ask in vain,
 Although a whole life's thoughts seek outlet free.
Ah, pity 'tis, my words so little tell!
 Count as an hundred every ill I've named;
 And each I could discourse on with good cause.
But to return to my first plan, and sing
 What praises to the prison house are due—
 Ah, here an angel's tongue doth scarce suffice!
No honest men are here, save those confin'd
 By tyrant rulers or their creatures vile,
 Malign'd by envy, hate, and cursèd spite.
To tell the truth as I discern it now—
 Here God is known, and every wretch doth cry
 Aloud to Him to ease the pains of Hell.
Whate'er ill fame he's gotten in the world,
 Let a man lie in prison two sad years,
 He'll come out holy, wise, belov'd by all.
Here soul and flesh and garments are refin'd;
 Here is the grossest sight etherealised,
 Till mortal man can see the thrones of Heaven.
Listen, a wonder now I tell to you—
 One day it came into my head to write;
 But I had to invent a strange device.
I walk about my cell with puzzled mien;
 Then turning towards the door see there a slit.
 I bite a splinter off—and there's my pen.
By luck, a piece of brick lies on the floor.
 A portion of it, ground to powder fine
 And mixed with water, makes my ink.
Then, then, the fire of Poesy divine
 Enters my frame—by the same way, methinks,
 Whence bread goes out. What other way was there?
But to return to my first fantasy—
 'Tis certain truth that ere he knows the good,
 A man must learn the ill ordain'd for him.
Prison's the home and school of every art.
 Would you fain know the leech's craft?
 Your very life-blood here you'll sweat away.
There is about it a strong natural power
 To lend your speech audacious eloquence,
 Laden with thoughts sublime for good and ill.
Happy the man who in a gloomy cell
 Doth linger long! When he at last comes out,
 Fine can he talk of war, of truce, of peace.
And all things then must needs go well with him.
 Ripe in the prison has his talent grown;
 Thenceforth no trifler, feather-brained, is he.
It may be said, Thou hast those years the less:
 'Tis not in dungeons thou shalt learn the way
 To make thee a full man in mind and soul.
For me, I'll praise it heartily, and yet
 Protest: the law that prisons innocence
 Should not allow the guilty man go free.

Who hath the poor and lowly in his power
Should learn his business in the prison school.
There are the lessons of good ruling taught.
Reason would shape his acts for evermore,
And in the path of justice he'd walk straight,
Nor would he breed confusion and dispeace.
And while I have been lodging here, I've seen
A crew of friars, priests, and men-at-arms;
But plenteous lack of those deserving jail.
Oh, the sore grief to see the prison door
Open for one of them, keep shut for you!
Then you lament that ever you were born.
I say no more. I am become fine gold
That may not spend itself too recklessly,
But must be sav'd and shap'd to perfect work.
And now another thing has cross'd my mind
That I've not told you, Luca mine,—The book
I wrote this in, one of our kindred lent.
There in the margins I set down the tale
Of the long pain that has my body maim'd;—
Too slow therefor, my brick-dust ink did run.
Only to make an O, three times I dipp'd
The splinter. Say, can they be vexéd more,
The wretched spirits chain'd in Hell below?
Before me have the guiltless been condemn'd;
Therefore I stop my plaint, and sing once more
The cell where grief gnaws at my heart and brain,
I sing its praises louder than the rest;
And let the untried learn from me, who've prov'd
That prison is the very school of worth.
Yet would He come, of Whom of late I've read,
To say, as once He said beside the pool,
"Rise, Benvenuto, take thy cloak and go!"
Salve reginas, credos I would sing,
And *pater nosters*. Every day the poor,
The blind, the lame, should be my pensioners.
How often have the lilies blanch'd my cheek
To death-like hue! They bar to me the sight
Of Florence and of France for evermore.
Should e'er I find upon the hospital wall
The Annunciation limn'd, then must I fly
Lest Gabriel's lily rouse the brute in me.
I do not speak of her, holy and wise,
Nor of her lilies glorious and pure,
Shining to light our earth and Heaven above.
But wheresoe'er I turn, there meet my eyes
Those with the hook-like petals. Much I fear
There are too many for the common health.
Crowds of companions have I in my woe,
Spirits born free, high-hearted, and divine,
Yet from their birth the slaves of this device.
I saw these deathly arms like thunderbolt
Fall swift from Heaven among a people vain;
Then in the wall a great new light did shine.
Broken the castle bell must be before
I am releas'd; and this I know from Him
Who all things doth make plain in Heaven and earth.
And then a dark bier I beheld bestrewn
With shattered lilies; all the signs of woe
Were there, and stricken folk that lay upon their beds.

And her I saw who wounds and frets the souls;
    Terror she struck, now here, now there, and said,
    "See me deal death to such as work thee harm."
Then 'twas the angel on my forehead wrote
    With Peter's pen those words that thrice
    He bade me secret keep in mine own heart.
And him who guides the chariot of the sun,
    Clothed in its glory, standing 'mid his court,
    I saw as mortal eyes ne'er saw before.
Then chirped a solitary sparrow loud
    Upon the keep; and I took heart and cried,
    "Life he foretells to me—and to you death."
The story of my woes I sang and wrote,
    Asking of God His pardon and His aid,
    For now in death my eyes seemed fading fast.
Was never lion, tiger, wolf, or bear
    Had such a thirst of human blood as he;
    Nor ever viper had such venomous sting.
Merciless captain of a robber band!
    Where all were bad, the greatest rascal he!
    But hush! I may not speak his name aloud.
Have you seen greedy bailiffs fall upon
    A poor man's house, his chattels to distrain,
    And hurl the holy pictures from the walls?
So on the first of August did they come
    To drag me to a yet more noisome tomb.
    Wait, for November all your spite defies!
A trumpet sounded in my ears, and I
    Declared to them the truth that was reveal'd,
    Nought recking save my grievous pain to ease.
Then, desperate to attain their end, they took
    A diamond from its setting, pounded it,
    And mixed it with my food that I might die.
I forced the low-bred villain who did bring
    My meat, to taste it first, then said,
    "Not this my enemy Durante meant."
But first I rais'd my thoughts to God on high,
    Asking His pardon for my every sin,
    And, weeping, "Miserere!" cried to Him.
Then, somewhat quieted my pain, my soul
    I gave into God's keeping, willingly
    Content to seek a better land, another state.
I saw an angel coming down from Heaven,
    Bearing a glorious palm; with joyful face,
    "Thou'lt bear thy body's burden yet awhile,"
He said; "for God shall scatter every foe
    Of thine, waging with them a bitter war,
    But thou, happy and free, art bless'd by Him,
Father in Heaven above, and Earth beneath."

END OF BOOK I.

BOOK II

i. I stayed on in the palace of the Cardinal of Ferrara, regarded by every one with the friendliest eye, and much more sought after than I had been before; for I was a greater wonder than ever now that I had lived through such unspeakable trials. While I was getting back my strength, and striving to bring my mind once more to my art, I took the greatest pleasure in writing out the Capitolo fairly. Then, that I might the sooner recover my health, I resolved to go for a few days' jaunt in the open air. So, with the leave of my good Cardinal, who also provided me with horses, I set off with two young Romans. One was a worker in my own craft; the other was not in the trade, but only came to bear me company. We left Rome, and went off in the direction of Tagliacozzo, to pay a visit to my pupil Ascanio. There I found him, together with his father, brothers, sisters, and stepmother. For two days I was entertained by them with the utmost hospitality; and then I departed on my return journey, taking Ascanio along with me. On the road we began to talk about art, which set me longing to be back in Rome and at my work again.

As soon as we arrived, I set to without delay, and managed to lay my hands on a silver basin which I had begun for the Cardinal before I was in prison. Along with the basin, I had been working on a very beautiful little pitcher; but this had been stolen along with a great number of other valuable things. I set Pagolo to work on the basin, while I took up the jug again. The ornament on it consisted of figures in the round and low reliefs. The basin was in like style, having figures in high, and fishes in low relief; and so rich was it, and so exquisitely contrived, that all who saw it were astounded both by the vigour and fancy of the design, and by the precision of the young men's work. The Cardinal used to come at least twice a day to see me; and with him came Messer Luigi Alamanni and Messer Gabriel Cesano; and many a pleasant hour did we spend thus together. Notwithstanding that I had a deal of work in hand, he thrust new commissions upon me, one of these being an order for the pontifical seal, which was to be as large as a twelve-year-old boy's hand. On it I traced in intaglio two designs. One represented St. John preaching in the wilderness, the other St. Ambrogio pursuing the Arians. The saint was on horseback, and had a whip in his hand. So vigorously was it designed, and so precisely was it carried out, that everybody said I had surpassed the great Lautizio, who stood alone in this branch of art. The Cardinal took great pride in it, and was always comparing it with the other Cardinals' seals in Rome, which were mostly from the hand of this Lautizio.

ii. Then, besides these, the Cardinal ordered me to make the model of a salt-cellar; but it was not to be after the usual pattern of such things. Concerning the design for this, Messer Luigi spoke admirably; and on the same subject Messer Gabriello Cesano made some excellent remarks. The Cardinal, a most kind listener, was very much impressed with the plans which these two distinguished men described in words. So he turned to me and said, "Benvenuto, my friend, Messer Luigi's design, and Messer Gabriello's too, please me so much that I do not know which of them to choose. So I leave the decision to you, since you have to carry out the work." Whereupon I replied, "Reflect, my lord, of what great importance are the sons of kings and emperors, and what marvellous splendour and divinity appear in them! Nevertheless, if you ask a poor lowly shepherd which he loves and cherishes most, those kings' sons or his own, he will certainly tell you he loves his own children best. So I, too, cherish the children born of my own art. Therefore, the first design which I will show you, monsignor, my most reverend patron, shall be my own work, and of my own imagining; for many things are fine in words which, were they carried out, would produce but a poor effect." Then I turned to the two men of letters and said, "Yours the words; mine the work." Messer Luigi Alamanni smiled, and with the greatest good-humour paid me many apt compliments; and it became him so to do, for he was a fine-looking man in face and figure, and had the pleasantest voice. Messer Gabriello Cesano was just the reverse, being as ugly and disagreeable as possible; and he spoke as he looked. Messer Luigi had proposed I should make a Venus and Cupid, together with diverse symbols of gallantry befitting the subject. Messer Gabriello's idea was an Amphitrite, Neptune's wife, with the sea-god's Tritons, and a great deal else very pretty to talk about, but useless for an actual design. Well, first I made an oval, a good deal more than half a cubit long, about two-thirds; and on this oval, with the idea of showing the embrace of the Sea and the Land, I made two figures, somewhat more than a palm in height, sitting with their legs intertwined, just as you can observe long arms of the sea running up into the land. The Sea was figured by a man with a richly carved ship in his hand, which was conveniently arranged to hold a quantity of salt. Under him I had placed the four seahorses; and in his right hand I had put his trident. The Earth I had represented as a woman, the most beautiful and graceful I could fashion or even conceive of. Near her I had placed a richly adorned temple, on which she rested her hand. This I intended for holding the pepper. In her other hand was a cornucopia decorated with every lovely ornament imaginable. Beneath this goddess, in the part which was meant to represent land, I had grouped all the fairest animals which the earth brings forth; while on the sea side I had designed every sort of beautiful fish and shell which I could get into the small space. The rest of the oval I decorated elaborately. Then I awaited the Cardinal; and when he came with his two distinguished friends, I displayed my work in wax. Messer Gabriel Cesano was the first to lift up his voice. "This is something that would never be finished in the lifetime of ten men," he cried. "And as for you, most reverend monsignor, you may desire it, but you'll never have it. For Benvenuto has thought well to show you the mere shadow of his children, not to give them to you in their actual shape, which was our idea. We spoke of practicable things; but his design suggests what could not possibly be carried out." Messer Luigi Alamanni took my part; but the Cardinal said the undertaking was too elaborate for him. Then I turned to them and said, "Most reverend monsignor, and you gentlemen, so full of learning as you are, I declare to you that I have every hope of carrying out this work for its destined possessor; and each man of you shall one day see it finished a hundred times more richly than the model. Indeed, I hope time may be left me to do much greater things than this." The Cardinal answered impatiently, "If it is not for the King, to whom I am going to take you, I don't think you are likely to make it for any one else." Then he showed me letters from King Francis, wherein he was bid return immediately and bring Benvenuto with him. Lifting my hands to heaven, I cried, "Oh, when will that 'immediately' come?" The Cardinal told me to make my arrangements and hasten the settlement of my affairs in Rome during the next ten days.

iii. When the time of departure was at hand, he gave me an excellent horse, called Tornon, after Cardinal Tornon, who had given it to him. Pagolo, too, and Ascanio, my pupils, were provided with mounts. The Cardinal divided his train, which was very numerous. One part, consisting of those of higher rank, went with him; and they took the road through Romagna, that he might make a pilgrimage to the Madonna of Loreto, and from there travel to his own home at Ferrara. The other part took the Florence road. This was the larger section, comprising a great number of men and the best of his horsemen. He advised me that, if I would go in safety, I had best go with him, for otherwise I should be in danger of my life; and I told his lordship that I most willingly accepted. But what Heaven ordains must needs come to pass; and it pleased God to recall to my mind my poor sister in the flesh, who had sorrowed much over my misfortunes. I remembered, too, my cousins who were nuns in Viterbo, the one abbess and the other treasurer, so that between them they had all the governing of that rich convent. They had been heavily afflicted on my account, and had offered up many prayers for me; so that I held the firm belief I had obtained of God the grace of my release through the petitions of those poor virgins. And so, all these things coming back to my mind, I set my face towards Florence; and though I should have gone free of expense, either with the Cardinal, or in his second train, I determined rather to go by myself. I travelled in the company of a celebrated clockmaker called Maestro Cherubino, a great friend of mine. Meeting by chance, we made the journey very pleasantly together.

Setting out from Rome the Monday in Passion week, we—that is Pagolo, Ascanio, and myself—travelled by ourselves till we fell in with this companion at Monte Ruosi. Now as I had declared my intention of going with the Cardinal, I never thought of any of my enemies lying in wait for me. Nevertheless it was nearly going very ill with me at Monte Ruosi; for a band of well-armed men had been sent on in front of us to do me a hurt. As God willed, having heard I was on the road, and not in the Cardinal's train, they planned to attack me while we were at dinner. Just then the Cardinal's train came up, and very glad I was to go on in safety with them to Viterbo. From there onward I had no further thought of danger, especially as I travelled several miles in front, and the best men in the retinue kept a good look-out on me. So by God's grace I reached Viterbo safe and sound; and there my cousins made much of me, as did the whole convent.

iv. I left Viterbo with the aforenamed persons, and we went on our way on horseback, now in front of, and now behind the Cardinal's train; so that on Maundy Thursday at twenty-two o'clock we found ourselves at one stage from Siena. There we fell in with some return horses, and the post folk were waiting to hire them out for a trifling sum to any one who would take them back to the post at Siena. When I learnt this, I got down from my own Tornon, put my saddle-cushion and stirrups on one of these horses, and gave a giulio to the stable-boy. I left my own horse to my young men to bring on, and set off in front of them in order to reach Siena half an hour sooner, as I had some friends to see and some business to attend to. Yet though I went at a fair pace, I did not ride the horse too hard. As soon as I came to the town, I hired good rooms at the inn for five persons, bidding the ostler take the horse to the post, which was outside the Camollià gate, but forgetting to remove my stirrups and saddle-cushion.

We passed the evening of Maundy Thursday very pleasantly. Then next morning, which was Good Friday, I bethought me of my stirrups and cushion. When I sent for them, the post-master said that he would not return them, for I had over-heated his horse. Several times messages were sent to and fro; and always the man refused to give the things back to me, using, besides, very insulting and insupportable language. The host of my inn said to me, "You'll come off well, if all he does is to keep your property"; and he added, "You must know that he is the greatest brute that ever lived in this city; and he has two sons, very daring soldier fellows, still more violent than himself. So buy what you want, and go on your way without another word on this matter." Well, I bought a pair of stirrups, thinking that by means of soft words I should have my good cushion again. Now I had an excellent mount, and was well armed with under-coat and sleeves of mail, and I carried a magnificent arquebuse at my saddle-bow. So I was not afraid of the violence of the mad beast whom my host had described to me. I had also accustomed my young fellows to wear mail under-coats and sleeves; and I had the fullest trust in the young Roman, who, I believed, had never left his off while we were in Rome. And Ascanio, too, though he was but a boy, wore mail. Besides, as it was Good Friday, I thought that madmen might be released from their folly on such a day. So we reached the Camollià gate, and there I saw the postmaster, recognising him by certain signs which had been given me. For one thing, he was blind of the left eye. I rode forward to meet him, leaving my young men and my other companions some way off, and accosted him civilly. "Postmaster, since I swear to you that I have not over-ridden your horse, why will you not return me my cushion and my stirrups?" Whereupon he answered just in the mad fashion I had been told to expect; so I demanded, "How now! are you no Christian? Will you on Good Friday bring scandal both on yourself and me?" He said he did not care a hang for Good Friday or Devil's Friday; and he swore that if I did not get out of this, he'd knock me down with a halbert he had seized, yes, me and my gun too, which I had in my hand. At these violent words up came an old gentleman of Siena. He was clad as a citizen, and was on his way back from performing the customary devotions of the day. While he was still some way from us, he had heard all my arguments perfectly; and so he began to reprove the master of the post with heat, taking my part, and crying shame on the man's two sons for failing in their duty to passing strangers. Such conduct as theirs was in defiance of God, he said, and to the discredit of the city of Siena. The two sons shook their heads, and without saying anything disappeared into the house. Their father, in a fury of exasperation at the words of the worthy gentleman, uttered the most shameless blasphemies, pointed his halbert at me, and swore he would have my life. Seeing his murderous intention, in order to keep him off me a little, I made as if to aim my gun at him. This roused him to still greater fury, and he threw himself upon me. Now though I held the gun in my hand ready for my defence, I had not lowered it quite on his level; its muzzle was too high. But it went off of itself; the ball struck the arch of the door, and, ricochetting, struck him in the windpipe, so that he fell down dead. Out ran the two sons on the instant; and one armed himself from the stand of weapons, the other seized his father's halbert; and both threw themselves on my young fellows. The son with the halbert first attacked Pagolo the Roman, striking him above the left breast. The other ran against a Milan man who was in our company, a very foolish-looking person. In vain he pleaded that he had no connection with me, and defended himself from the point of a partisan with a little stick he had in his hand; he could not escape a slight wound in the mouth. Messer Cherubino was dressed as a priest; for though, as I have said, he was a past-master in the clockmaker's art, he held benefices from the Pope, which brought him in a good income. Ascanio, who was well armed, made no attempt at flight, as the Milanese had done. But neither he nor Cherubino were hurt. I had put spurs to my horse; and while galloping I had made haste to load my gun once more. Then I turned madly back; for it seemed to me I had been treating the matter too lightly, and now I meant to go through with it in earnest. I thought that my two young companions had been killed, and I was determined to die with them. But my horse had not made many paces backwards, when I met them coming towards me. I asked them if they were hurt. Ascanio replied that Pagolo was mortally wounded by a halbert. Then I said, "O Pagolo, my son, did the halbert pierce your coat of mail?" "No," he said, "for I put the mail in my baggage this morning." "So," said I, "mail coats are for wearing in Rome, when you make yourselves fine for the ladies; but in dangerous places where they'd be of some use, you keep them in your baggage! You have got no more than you deserve, and it's you who are sending me back to my death." Even while speaking these words, I was dashing forward. Ascanio and the others begged me, for the love of God, to save my own life and theirs; for of a surety I was going to my death. Just then I met with Messer Cherubino and the wounded Milanese. The clockmaker called out to me at once that nobody was much hurt, that Pagolo's was only a surface wound. But he said the old man of the post lay dead on the ground; his two sons and other persons were preparing for revenge; and we were all doomed to be cut to pieces. "So then, Benvenuto, since Fortune has saved us from this first fury, do not tempt her again; else she will have no mercy on us." And I answered, "If you are content, so am I"; and, turning to Pagolo and Ascanio, I said to them, "Spur on your horses, and let us gallop to Staggia without stopping. There we shall be safe." Then the wounded Milan man burst out, "Devil take our sins! For this wound of mine is all on account of that trifle of meat broth I took yesterday, when I had nothing else to eat." In spite of the great tribulations we had come through, we could not but laugh somewhat at this fool and at the foolish things he said. Then, setting spurs to our horses, we left Messer Cherubino and the Milanese to come on at their leisure.

v. Meanwhile the dead man's sons ran to the Duke of Amalfi, and asked for some light cavalry, that they might overtake us and seize our persons. But the Duke, having learnt we were the Cardinal of Ferrara's men, would give neither horses nor leave. And we in the meantime reached Staggia, where we were safe. On our arrival there we sought out a doctor, the best to be had in the place, and when he examined Pagolo, it was found that his wound was only skin deep, and that there was no danger. As soon as we had ordered dinner, in came Messer Cherubino with that fool of a Milan man, who kept saying, "Deuce take your quarrels!" and moaning that he was excommunicated because he had not been able to say a single Paternoster that holy morning. Now he had a very ugly face; and his mouth, naturally large, had been slit up three inches more by his wound; so that between his antic Milanese speech and his silly utterances, instead of lamenting our misfortunes, we couldn't help laughing at every word he said. When the doctor wanted to sew up his wound, and had already made three stitches, he cried out to him to stop a bit, since he didn't want him to play the trick on him of sewing his mouth up altogether. Then, seizing a spoon, he told him he must leave a big enough opening for it to get in; so that he might return alive to his own people. Now he said all this with such funny shakings of the head, that we forgot our ill luck, and laughed without stopping. And in this merry humour we went on our way to Florence. There we got down at the house of my poor sister, and were most affectionately received by her and by my brother-in-law.

Messer Cherubino and the Milanese went about their own affairs. We stayed in Florence four days, during which time Pagolo got better. It was a curious thing, that every time we talked of that Milanese fool, we laughed just as much as we lamented over our ill luck; so that we kept on laughing and crying at the same time. Pagolo quickly got well, as I have said; and then we set our faces towards Ferrara, where we found our Cardinal had not yet arrived. But when he heard of all our misfortunes, and was condoling with us, he said, "God grant that I may bring you alive to the King, as I have promised!" In Ferrara the Cardinal assigned to me one of his palaces, a very fine place, called Belfiore, close to the city walls; and there he gave me everything I needed for my work. But afterwards he prepared to depart without me; and, perceiving I was very ill content, he said to me, "Benvenuto, all I do is for your good. For before I take you away from Italy, I wish you to be quite clear what you are meant to do in France. So in the meanwhile hurry on as fast as you can with my basin and ewer. I shall leave orders with my steward to give you all you may have need of."

Then he set off, and I remained behind very ill pleased. Indeed many a time I was on the point of taking French leave. The only thing that hindered me was the recollection that he had freed me from the clutches of Pope Paul. As for the rest, I remained much dissatisfied, and very much a loser. However, I clung to the thought of the gratitude due to the benefit I had received; and disposed myself to be patient, and see what would be the end of the business. So setting to work with my two young men, I got on wonderfully with the jug and basin. In the place where we were lodged the air was bad; and as summer came on we were all out of sorts. During our indisposition we wandered about examining the demesne, which was very large and left wild for nearly a mile of open country; and there a great number of tame peacocks bred like wild birds. When I saw this, I loaded my gun with a certain noiseless powder, and lay in wait for the young ones. Every other day I killed one, which not only provided us with abundance of food, but was of such fine quality that all our sickness left us. And so we stayed on for several months, working cheerfully, and making progress with the jug and the basin, which were elaborate works that took a great deal of time.

vi. Just then the Duke of Ferrara and Pope Paul of Rome made up some of their old differences concerning Modena and certain other cities. In these disputes the Church had so much right on its side that the Duke had to make peace by paying up a mint of money, more than three hundred thousand ducats of the Camera, I believe. Now at this time the Duke had an old treasurer called Messer Girolamo Giliolo, who had been brought up by his father, Duke Alfonso. The old fellow could not bear the thought of all this money going to the Pope; and used to go crying about the streets that Duke Alfonso, the present Duke's father, would sooner have taken Rome with the money than have let the Pope get a sight of it; and that there was no way of making him pay it out. In the end, when the Duke forced him to pay, the old man fell so ill with dysentery, that he was brought nigh unto death. While he was lying ill, the Duke called me, and ordered me to make a likeness of himself. This I did on a round black stone, about the size of a small trencher. He took so much pleasure in my work, as well as in the many pleasant conversations we had together, that often he would sit for his portrait for four or five hours on end; and sometimes he made me sup at his own table. In eight days I had finished the head; and then he ordered me to do the reverse, on which was a figure of Peace, represented by a woman, with a torch in her hand, burning a trophy of arms. She stood in a joyful attitude, full of exquisite grace, and clad in thinnest raiment. Under her feet was desperate Fury bound with many chains. I gave much pains to this work, and it brought me the greatest honour. The Duke could not tell me often enough how pleased he was; and he provided me with the legends for both sides. The one for the reverse was *Pretiosa in conspectu Domini*, which was as much as to say that the peace had been bought with a deal of money!

vii. Just when I had the reverse in hand, the Cardinal wrote to me, telling me to be in readiness, for the King had asked for me, and that his next letters would explain everything he had promised. So I had my basin and my jug well packed up; for I had already shown them to the Duke. The Cardinal's business man was a Ferrarese gentleman, Messer Alberto Bendedio by name, who had been a prisoner in his house for twelve years on account of some infirmity. One day he sent for me in the greatest hurry, and bade me take the post immediately and go to the King, who had asked for me most pressingly, thinking I was already in France. The Cardinal, to excuse himself, had said I was staying behind in an abbey of his at Lyons, somewhat indisposed; but that he would contrive that I should come speedily to his Majesty. That was the reason he urged me to come on by the post at once. This Messer Alberto was a most worthy man; but he was proud, and through his malady his arrogance had grown intolerable. And so, as I say, he ordered me to get ready at once and travel with the post. To this I replied that my art was not carried on in the post; and if I had to go, I would go at my leisure, taking with me Ascanio and Pagolo, my workmen, whom I had brought from Rome. Besides, I should need a serving-man on horseback to attend me, and as much money as would take me to my journey's end. Then the infirm old man answered me in the haughtiest accents, that just in the manner I had described, the sons of the Duke were wont to travel. Thereupon I answered that the sons of my craft were used to go as I had said; that not being the son of a duke, I did not know the customs of such; also that if he used such language in my hearing, I would not go at all. The Cardinal having broken faith, and now this insolence being cast at me, I made up my mind not to trouble myself any more with the Ferrarese. So I turned my back on him; and I muttering, and he threatening, I took my leave. Then I went to see the Duke, taking him his medal, now finished; and received more compliments in return than were ever paid to any man whatsoever. Now he had ordered Girolamo Giliolo to find a diamond ring worth two hundred crowns for my trouble, and to give it to his chamberlain Fiaschino, who should hand it to me. And Messer Girolamo obeyed. Well, Fiaschino, on the evening of the day when I had handed over the medal, about an hour after sunset, brought me a ring, set with a very showy diamond, and also the following message from the Duke: "Let the unique hand of the artist which wrought with such skill, be adorned with this diamond in remembrance of his Excellency." When daylight came, I looked at the ring; and found it was a poor, thin diamond worth maybe ten crowns. Now I did not wish those fine words which the Duke had used to be associated with so poor a reward; for I was certain he had meant to treat me well, and I felt sure the ring came from his rascally treasurer. So I gave it to one of my friends to return to Fiaschino, the chamberlain, as best as he could. My friend, who was Bernardo Saliti, did the business perfectly. Then Fiaschino came to see me and, with loud protestations, said that, if the Duke knew I had returned like that a present which he had so kindly given me, he would take it very ill, and perhaps I should live to repent it. I answered him that the ring which his Excellency had given me was worth about ten crowns; and that the work I had done for him was worth more than two hundred. But to show the Duke that I appreciated his courtesy, he had only to send me a ring for the cramp—of the sort that came from England, and are worth about a carlin—and that I should keep all my life in remembrance of his Excellency, along with the esteemed message which he had sent to me. For I held that the honour of serving so splendid a prince had amply paid me for all my trouble; but that mean jewel was an insult. These words so annoyed the Duke, that he called for his treasurer, and gave him a sounder rating than ever he had done in his life before. Then he ordered me, under pain of his displeasure, not to leave Ferrara without telling him; and he bade his treasurer give me a diamond of the value of three hundred crowns. The miserly fellow found one worth hardly more than sixty; but gave out that it cost upwards of two hundred.

viii. Meanwhile Messer Alberto had recovered his temper, and had provided me with all I had asked for. That very day I was determined to leave Ferrara at all hazards; but the busybody of a chamberlain arranged with Messer Alberto that I should have no horses. I had piled up my baggage on a mule, packing in it the basin and jug I had made for the Cardinal. Just at that moment up came a Ferrarese gentleman, Messer Alfonso de' Trotti by name, a very old man, and full of affectation. He took the greatest delight in art; but he was one of those persons who are very difficult to satisfy; and if by chance they ever hit upon something which pleases them, it is stamped upon their minds as a thing of such excellence, that they think they shall never see the like of it again. When Messer Alfonso came in, Messer Alberto said to him, "What a pity you have come so late, for the jug and basin we are sending to the Cardinal in France are already packed up." Whereupon Messer Alfonso replied that he did not care; and, calling one of his servants, he sent him back to his house for a jug made of white Faenza earthenware, most delicately worked. While the servant was on his errand, he said to Messer Alberto, "I will tell you why I have no desire to look at any more vases. Once upon a time I saw one made of silver—an antique it was—so beautiful and so wonderful, that the human mind could never dream of such excellence. And thus I have no wish to see other things of the kind, lest they should spoil my marvellous picture of that. There was a man of rank, an artist of ability, who went to Rome on some business, where this antique vase was shown to him secretly. Then by means of a great deal of money, he bribed the man who had it, and carried it away with him back to these parts. But he keeps it very fast locked up, so that the Duke may not know; for he fears to lose it in some way." Now while Messer Alfonso was telling this long story, he did not look at me, though I was standing near, for he did not know me. Then, when that blessed clay model appeared, he showed it off so pompously, with such ridiculous ceremony, and such palaver, that as soon as I had set eyes on it, I turned to Messer Alberto and said, "What a piece of luck for me to see it again!" Messer Alfonso flew into a rage, and cried out insolently, "Who are you? You don't know what you are talking about." To which

I replied, "Now listen to me; and then you'll see which of us knows best what he is saying." So I turned to Messer Alberto, a very grave and intelligent person, and said, "This is copied from a silver jug of such and such a weight, which I made at such and such a time for that quack Jacopo, the Carpi surgeon. He came to Rome, and stayed there six months, daubing with his unguents scores and scores of lords and unlucky gentlemen, whom he fleeced of many thousand ducats. At that time I made this vase for him, and another different one; and he paid me wretchedly for my pains. And now all those poor wretches in Rome, whom he daubed, are crippled to-day, and in very bad case. It is the greatest honour for me that my works have such fame with you rich gentlemen. But I assure you that in these past years I have made every possible effort to learn more of my art; so that I think the vase I am carrying to France is a deal more worthy of the Cardinal and the King than the one belonging to your quack." Hardly were these words of mine out, when it was plain that Messer Alfonso was really choking with the desire of seeing the basin and the jug; but I persistently refused. When we had argued the matter for a bit, he said he would go to the Duke, and make him force me to show it. Then Messer Alberto Bendedio, who, as I have told you, was of a very haughty temper, said, "Before you leave here, Messer Alfonso, you shall see it, without the intervention of his Excellency." At these words I set off, leaving Ascanio and Pagolo to show my work to them. Pagolo told me afterwards that they said the finest things in my praise. And Messer Alfonso wished to make my nearer acquaintance; but it seemed to me a thousand years till I should get out of Ferrara, and out of the sight of them all. Whatever benefits I had enjoyed there had come from my intercourse with the Cardinal Salviati, and the Cardinal of Ravenna, and some able musicians. Nobody else did anything for me; for the Ferrarese are a very avaricious folk, and like to get as much out of other people as they can; and they are all the same.

At two hours before sundown Fiaschino appeared, bringing me the sixty-crown diamond. It was with a glum face and few words that he begged me to wear it for his Excellency's sake. I answered him that I would do so. Then as he stood there, I put my foot in the stirrup, and set off on my journey without any one's leave. He took good note of my manner and my words, and reported them to the Duke, who in his wrath would have dearly loved to make me turn back again.

ix. That evening I went more than ten miles, always at a trot; and when next day I was out of Ferrarese territory I felt greatly pleased; for those peacocks which I had eaten, and which had given me back my health, were the only good things I had known there. We took the Mont Cenis road, avoiding the city of Milan because of the misgiving I have mentioned, so that we reached Lyons safe and sound. With Pagolo and Ascanio and a servant we were a company of four, and we were all well mounted. At Lyons we stopped for several days, waiting for the muleteer who carried the silver basin and jug, as well as our other baggage. We had our quarters in an abbey belonging to the Cardinal. But as soon as our muleteer came up with us, we put all our things in a little wagon, and sent them off on the road to Paris. We, too, set our faces in the same direction. On the way we had a little trouble, but nothing of importance.

We found the King's court at Fontainebleau; and there we sought out the Cardinal, who at once consigned us lodgings; and that night we were comfortably installed. Next day the little wagon turned up. We took possession of our things, and let the Cardinal know of their arrival. He told the King, who sent for me at once. So I went to his Majesty with the basin and jug; and when I had come into his presence I kissed his knee, and he gave me the most gracious reception. I thanked him for having brought me out of prison, saying that it was binding on every good prince, and especially on the one great prince of the world, to wit, his Majesty, to liberate men who were good for anything, especially when they were innocent, as I was; and that such deeds were written in the books of God before any others whatsoever. The good King stayed to listen till I had finished speaking, with the utmost courtesy, putting in a word or two now and then, such as could have only come from him. When I had ended, he took the vase and the basin and said, "Verily I believe even the ancients never saw such a beautiful piece of work. For I well remember to have examined the masterpieces of the best artists in all Italy; but never did I meet with anything that so roused my admiration as this." These words the King spoke in French to the Cardinal of Ferrara, and others too still more laudatory. Then he turned to me, and speaking in Italian, he said, "Benvenuto, amuse yourself for a day or two; comfort your heart, and make good cheer. In the meanwhile we shall be planning for you to do some fine work for us."

x. The Cardinal of Ferrara perceived that the King was

highly pleased at my coming. He saw, too, that the few speci-
mens I had shown him had bred in him the desire of having
some important works, which he had in his mind, carried out
by me. But just then we were following in the train of the
court, to our great discomfort, be it said. For the royal train
always plods along with twelve thousand cavalry behind it,
never less—indeed, in times of peace the complete retinue
amounts to eighteen thousand. Well, we dragged along after
it; and sometimes we would come to places where there were
hardly two houses. Then we pitched canvas tents like gipsies;
and many a time we were far from comfortable. So I went on
begging the Cardinal to remind the King to send for me and set
me to work. The Cardinal said the best thing was to wait till
his Majesty thought of it himself; but that I might show myself
occasionally to the King while he sat at table. This I did, and
one morning he called for me while he was dining. He began
to speak to me in Italian, and said he had it on his mind to have
several works executed on a large scale; and that very soon
he would arrange workshops for me, and provide me with all
I should want. And he talked very pleasantly on other matters
besides. The Cardinal of Ferrara was present; for he nearly
always ate his morning meal at the King's table. Thus he had
heard all the conversation; and when the King rose, he said
to him in my behalf—so it was reported to me—"Sacred Majesty,
Benvenuto here is most anxious to work. Indeed, it may be
almost called a sin to waste the time of an artist like him."
Whereupon his Majesty said he had spoken well, and that he
was to arrange with me all things I needed for my maintenance.
That same evening his lordship sent for me after supper, and
gave me a message from the King, namely, that his Majesty
was quite determined to set me to work, but that first he
wished me to be clear in my mind about my salary. Concerning
this the Cardinal said, "It seems to me that if his Majesty
gives you three hundred crowns a year, you will do well. Also,
I would have you leave everything to me; for not a day passes
but I have an opportunity of being of some service in this great
kingdom; and I shall always help you to the very best of my
ability." Then I answered, "When your most reverend lordship left me behind in Ferrara, without any request from me,
you promised never to take me out of Italy till I should know
exactly on what terms I was to serve his Majesty. Instead of
sending to tell me this, you ordered me to come by the post—
as if my art could be carried on under these circumstances. If

you had told me of a provision of three hundred crowns, as you do now, I should not have stirred a foot—no, not for double that sum. But yet for all which God and your lordship have done for me I am grateful; for God used you as the means of rendering me a great service in liberating me from prison. Therefore, I assure your lordship, whatever ill turn you may do me now, is made up for a thousandfold by the great good I have received from you. With all my heart I thank you, and take my good leave; and wherever I may be, while I live I shall pray God for you." Then the Cardinal got in a rage, and said in his wrath, "Go where you like. One can't do good to a man against his will." And some of his worthless courtiers who were hanging round said, "He thinks a deal of himself, refusing a salary of three hundred ducats like that!" But among them were men of understanding in art, one of whom said, "The King will never find his equal; and our Cardinal wants to bargain as if Benvenuto were a load of wood." It was Messer Luigi Alamanni who said this—so I was told. It took place in Dauphiné, in a castle the name of which I do not recall. The day was the last of October.

xi. Leaving them, I went back to my lodgings, three miles off; and with me was a Secretary of the Cardinal, who was returning to the same place. All the way he kept on asking me what I was going to do with myself, and what my own idea would have been regarding a salary. I answered only one word —I knew all. In our quarters I found Pagolo and Ascanio, who, seeing me troubled in my mind, forced me to tell them what was the matter with me. So, as the poor fellows were anxious, I said to them, "To-morrow morning I shall give you money which will amply provide for your journey home; and I am going by myself on very important business, which for long I have had on my mind." Now there was only a wall between our room and the Secretary's, and it is quite possible that he wrote to the Cardinal what I intended to do, though I never knew rightly whether he did so or not.

The night was a sleepless one; it seemed an age till day broke, and I could follow up the resolution I had made. At dawn I ordered my two horses, hastily made my preparations, and gave my two young men all I had brought with me, and fifty gold ducats besides. I kept as much for myself, as well as the diamond which the Duke had given me. Only two shirts did I take, and a rather shabby riding-suit which I had on me. But I could hardly get away from the two lads, who wished to come with me at all hazards; so that in the end I was forced to cry shame on them, and say, "One of you has his first beard, and the other's is growing hair by hair. And you have learnt from me as much of my poor art as I could teach you, so that to-day you are the first young craftsmen in Italy. Aren't you ashamed to lack the spirit to get out of leading-strings? Shame upon you! Now, if I were to let you go without any money, what would you say? So be off. God's blessing on you a thousand times! Adieu!"

I turned about my horse, and left them weeping. Then I took a very beautiful road through a wood, my purpose being to travel about forty miles at least that day, and get to as remote a place as I could find. By the time I had gone about two miles I resolved never to be seen again in any place where I was known, nor ever again to work on anything else, after I had finished a Christ, three cubits high, reflecting, as far as I could make it, that infinite beauty which had been revealed to me by Himself. Then having firmly made up my mind, I turned my steps towards the Blessed Sepulchre. I had thought myself in so remote a place that no one could find me; but just then I heard the tread of horses behind. This made me mistrustful; for in those parts is a band of brigands called Adventurers, who are given to murdering on the high road; and though every day many of them are hanged for it, it seems as if they are quite reckless. When the riders came nearer, I recognised them for a King's messenger and my lad Ascanio. The messenger rode up to me and said, "In the King's name, I order you to come to him without delay." "You are sent by the Cardinal," I replied; "therefore I will not return." Then he said that since I would not come willingly, he had authority to command the people of the country to bring me bound as a prisoner. Ascanio, too, begged me earnestly to give in, reminding me that when the King took a man prisoner, he kept him five years at least before he made up his mind to release him. The mention of prison recalled what I had suffered in Rome; and struck such terror into me, that I turned my horse without another word in the direction indicated by the King's messenger, who chattered away all the time in French, till he had brought me back to the Court—now threatening me, now saying one thing, now another, till it was enough to make me forswear the world.

xii. When we were on our way to the royal quarters, we passed in front of those of the Cardinal of Ferrara, who was standing at his door. Calling to me, he said, "Our most Christian

King, of his own free will, has made the same provision for you that he made for the painter, Lionardo da Vinci; that is, seven hundred crowns a year. Besides that, he will pay you for all the work you will do for him. Then, also, for your expenses in coming here, he gives you five hundred gold crowns, which he orders shall be paid now before you leave." When he had made an end of speaking, I answered that such sums as he had mentioned became the great King of France. Then the messenger, who had not known who I was, and now heard these fine offers made to me on the part of his royal master, asked my pardon many times; while Pagolo and Ascanio cried, "By God's help, we are back again in leading-strings, of which we think no shame."

Then next day I went to thank the King, who ordered me to make models for twelve silver statues, which were to serve for twelve candlesticks round his table. He said they were to represent six gods and six goddesses, of the same height as his Majesty, which was something less than four cubits. When he had given me this commission, he turned to the treasurer, and asked him if he had paid me the five hundred crowns. He said he had heard nothing of the matter; at which the King was much annoyed, since he had told the Cardinal to hand on the order. Afterwards, he said I was to go to Paris, and find a suitable place for carrying on my work; and he would contrive I should have it.

I took the five hundred gold crowns and went off to Paris, putting up in an apartment belonging to the Cardinal of Ferrara. There, in God's name, I set to work, and made four little wax models, two-thirds of a cubit high—Jupiter, Juno, Apollo, and Vulcan. While I was doing this, the King came back to Paris; so I went off at once to seek him, taking the models with me, and my two young men, Ascanio and Pagolo. As soon as I saw that his Majesty was satisfied with the models, and had received orders to make the first—that is, the Jupiter—of the agreed height, I presented my two lads to him, telling him that I had brought them from Italy for his service; for since I had taught them myself, I could get much more help from them at the beginning than from any craftsmen belonging to the city of Paris. To this the King replied that I should fix a salary for them, sufficient for their maintenance. I said that one hundred gold crowns for each would be a handsome provision and that I should make them earn their money well. So it was agreed. Then I said that I had found a place which seemed to me just what I wanted for my work; that it was his Majesty's private property, and was called the Petit Nesle. The provost of Paris held it free at present, the King having lent it him. But since the provost was not using it, his Majesty might give it to me to use for his service. He answered at once, "The place is my own house; and I know quite well that he to whom I gave it does not live in it, nor use it in any way. Therefore, you can take it for your business." And on the spot he ordered his lieutenant to put me in possession of the Nesle. The man demurred; indeed, he told the King he could not do it. His Majesty answered hotly that he would give his own things to whomsoever he pleased, and to a man who was of use to him, since from the other he got no service at all. And so there were to be no more words about the matter. Then the lieutenant went on to say that it might be necessary to use a little force; and the King replied, "Well, go; and if a little force be not enough, use a great deal."

Then I was conducted at once to the place. The lieutenant had to take strong measures to put me in possession; and he told me to look out carefully lest I should be murdered. I made my entrance at once; hired servants, and bought several great pikes and weapons of that sort. But for several days I stayed there in the greatest discomfort; for the former tenant was a great nobleman of Paris, and the other gentlemen, his friends, were all hostile to me, and heaped insupportable insults on me. I must not neglect to say that at the time I entered his Majesty's service, in the year 1540, I was exactly forty years old.

xiii. These bitter insults forced me to apply to the King, begging him to instal me elsewhere. But he cried out, "Who are you, and what is your name?" I was thunderstruck, not knowing what he meant; and stood there dumb, while the King once more, and angrily, repeated the same words. I replied that I was called Benvenuto. "Then, if you are the Benvenuto I have heard of, do as you are wont to do. I give you full leave." I told his Majesty that all I wanted was to keep in his favour; for having that, I knew nothing that could hurt me. He then laughed somewhat grimly, and said, "Go, then; and my favour shall never fail you." Thereupon he ordered his chief secretary, Monseigneur de Villeroy, to see I was provided with everything I might want. Now this Villeroy was a very great friend of him who was called the provost, to whom the Nesle had been given. The castle was in the form of a triangle, and was built up against the walls of the city. It was an ancient stronghold of a goodly size, but there was no guard attached to it. This Monseigneur de Villeroy advised me to seek some other place, and to quit this without fail; for the provost was a man of the greatest influence, and he would have me killed for a certainty. I answered that I had come from Italy to France only to serve the great King; and as for dying, I knew quite well I had to die one day, and that a little earlier or later would make no difference in the world to me. Villeroy, I should say, was a man of keen wit, of exceptional distinction, and immensely rich. There was nothing in the world he would not have done to harm me; but he made no show of this. He was a grave person, very handsome, and spoke with much deliberation. He gave the task of annoying me to another gentleman, called Monseigneur de Marmagne, who was treasurer of Languedoc. The first thing this fellow did was to seek out the best rooms in the place, and to have them prepared for himself. Whereupon I said the castle had been given me by the King, because I was in his service; and that I would have no one live there save myself and my servants. He was an arrogant, audacious man, of a very hot temper, and he told me he would do just what he pleased; that I was knocking my head against a wall if I thought of fighting with him; and that everything he did was done by order of Villeroy. Then I said that my authority came from the King, and that neither he nor Villeroy could do anything of the kind. Whereupon he poured out a shower of abuse in his French tongue; and I gave him the lie in my own. Roused to a pitch of anger, he made as if to seize his little poniard. So I put my hand on the big dagger which I always carried for my defence, and cried, "If you dare to draw that weapon, you're a dead man!" He had two servants with him, and I had my two apprentices. He stopped a moment, in two minds as to the better course; but the wish to do me a mischief was uppermost, and he muttered, "I will never endure such a thing." I saw the affair was going badly; so I took a sudden resolve, and called to Pagolo and Ascanio, "When you see me draw my dagger, throw yourselves on the two menials, and kill them if you can; for I'll run this fellow through at one blow. Then we'll make off at once together." Marmagne, hearing my plan, thought he would come off well, if he got out of the place alive. All these adventures—albeit a little more modestly—I wrote to the Cardinal of Ferrara, who informed his Majesty at once. The King, in a great rage, gave me in charge to another of his guard, called Monseigneur le Vicomte d'Orbec, who looked after all my wants with every courtesy imaginable.

xiv. As soon as I had put my house and shop in order, and fitted them up with everything I needed for my work, and for the honourable maintenance of my personal establishment, I set at once to making three models of the same size as the finished works in silver were to be. These were the Jupiter, Vulcan, and Mars. I made them of clay well supported with iron. Then I went off to the King, who let me have, if I remember rightly, three hundred pounds of silver, so that I might begin my work. While I was preparing these things, I finished the little vase and the oval basin, which had taken us several months. I had them beautifully gilt; and there was not another piece of plate in France which could be compared to them. I took them at once to the Cardinal of Ferrara, who thanked me heartily, and then went by himself to the King, and made him a present of them. His Majesty was enchanted, and heaped more praises on me than ever fell to a man of my condition. In return for the gift he presented the Cardinal with an abbey worth seven thousand crowns a year; and he wanted to make me a present too. But the Cardinal put a stop to that, saying that his Majesty was too hasty, since I had as yet done nothing for him. The King, however, who was most liberal, replied, "But I want to encourage him to serve me"; whereupon the Cardinal, ashamed of himself, rejoined, "Sire, I beg you will leave the thing to me. I will allow him a pension of at least three hundred crowns as soon as I have taken possession of my abbey." I never had a farthing from him; but it would be too long were I to tell all the rascality of this Cardinal. I will reserve myself for things of greater importance.

xv. I went back to Paris; and the King's marked favour of me gained me the admiration of every one. When I got the silver, I began the statue of Jupiter, hired a great many workmen, and pushed the thing forward, never resting day or night from my work; so that when Jupiter, Vulcan, and Mars were finished in clay, and the silver Jupiter was making speedy progress, the workshop made a goodly show. Just then the King came to Paris. I went to see him; and as soon as he set eyes on me, he called me in a cheerful voice, and asked me if I had anything beautiful to show him; for if so, he would come to my house and see it. Accordingly I told him all I had been doing; and he was at once taken with the strongest desire to come. So after dinner he set out with Madame d'Etampes, the Cardinal of Lorraine, and some other of his lords. Among the company were the King of Navarre, his cousin, and the Queen of Navarre, his sister, as well as the Dauphin and Dauphiness; so that all the nobility of the French Court came to see me that day. In the meantime I had gone back home, and had set to work again. When the King appeared at the door of my castle, and heard the noise of our hammers, he ordered all his suite to be quiet. Every man in the shop was hard at work, so that his Majesty took me completely by surprise. When he entered my great hall, the first thing he saw was me with a large silver plate in my hand, which I was hammering for the body of Jupiter. Another man was making the head, and another the legs; so that the noise was tremendous. Now there was a little French boy working near me, who had been annoying me in some trifling way. I gave him a kick, and, as ill luck would have it, my foot caught him in the fork of the legs, and sent him reeling more than four cubits away; so that just as the King came in, the child fell up against him. His Majesty laughed heartily; but I was all in confusion. Then he began to ask me what I was doing, and would have me go on working. But he told me I should please him best by not wasting my strength on manual labour. I was to employ all the men I wanted, and make them do the main part of the work. He wished me to keep in good health, he said, so that I might remain in his service all the longer. I replied I should fall ill at once if I did not work; nor would the work, under these circumstances, be of that quality which I should desire for his Majesty. The King thought I said this from mere boastfulness, and not because I really thought so; and he made the Cardinal of Lorraine repeat what he had said. Then I explained my reasons so fully and frankly that the Cardinal was quite convinced, and advised the King to let me work little or much, just as I liked.

xvi. The King, well satisfied with what I was doing, went back to the palace, after taking leave of me with more compliments than I have time to write down. Next day, while he was at dinner, he sent for me. The Cardinal of Ferrara was dining with him; and when I got there, the King was at the second course. At once he began to speak to me, saying, that since he had such a beautiful basin and jug from my hand, he wished for a fine salt-cellar to keep them company. So he asked me to make him a design for one, and without delay. I answered, "Your Majesty will see such a design sooner than you expect; for while I was making the basin, I thought a salt-cellar should be made to go with it; so the thing is ready, and, if it please you, I can show it to you now." Then he turned with the greatest animation to his lords who were present—the King of Navarre, the Cardinal of Lorraine, and the Cardinal of Ferrara—and said, "Verily, this is a man to make himself loved and desired by every one who knows him!" Then to me he said he would, indeed, like to see my model. Off I went, and speedily returned; for I had but to cross the Seine. I brought back with me a wax model, which I had already made at the request of the Cardinal of Ferrara in Rome. When I uncovered it, his Majesty exclaimed in his astonishment, "This is a hundred times more divine than I could ever have imagined. The man is a wonder! He should never lay down his tools." Then turning to me with a most joyful face, he said that the model pleased him very much, and that he would like me to carry it out in gold. The Cardinal of Ferrara, who was present, gave me a look as if to say he recognised the design as the one I had made for him in Rome. So I reminded him of what I had said before—that I should make it for him who was destined to possess it. The Cardinal recalled the words; and annoyed at the thought that I was having my revenge, said, "Sire, this is a very great undertaking. I doubt I shall never see it completed; for these clever men who have such fine ideas, are all agog to begin things, without considering duly when they may be finished. Therefore, if I were to order such elaborate works, I should like to know when I was to have them." To this the King replied that he who worried so anxiously about the end of a piece of work would never begin anything. And it was plain from his tone that he meant to say, such things were not for poor-spirited creatures. Then I spoke: "Princes who put heart into their servants, as your Majesty does by act and word, make the greatest enterprises easy; and since God has given me so admirable a master, I am in hopes of bringing many great and noble works to completion for him." "So I think, too," said the King as he rose from table. Then he called me into his own room, and asked me how much gold I should want for the salt-cellar. "A thousand crowns," I answered; whereupon he ordered his treasurer, Monseigneur le Vicomte d'Orbec, to give me without delay a thousand old gold crowns of good weight.

When I left his Majesty, I sent for the two notaries through whom I had got the silver for the Jupiter, as well as many other things. Then I crossed the Seine and fetched a little basket, which one of my cousins, a nun, had given me when I passed through Florence. (And it was a piece of great good luck that I took this basket instead of a bag.) I thought I could expedite the business by day—it was still early—and I did not wish to disturb my men at their work, nor even to take a servant with me. When I reached the treasurer's house, I found he had the money lying before him; and he was selecting it as the King had told him. Nevertheless, it seemed to me that the rascal used every kind of artful delay about the counting of the money; for it was not ready till three hours after sunset. But I was not wanting in prudence; and so I sent for several of my workmen to come and bear me company, saying the matter was of much importance. When I saw they did not come, I asked the messenger if he had done my errand. The villain said he had, and that they had told him they could not come. But he would carry the money for me willingly, he said. I replied that I should carry it myself. Meanwhile the contract was signed. When the money had been counted, I put it all in my little basket; then pushed my arm through the two handles, and as this was no easy matter, the basket was shut tight, and I carried the gold more safely than I should have done in a bag. I was well armed with coat and sleeves of mail; and with my sword and dagger at my side, I set off as hard as I could.

xvii. Just then I saw some servants whispering together and making off from the house at a good pace in the opposite direction from me. I walked briskly, crossed the Pont du Change, and went along a little wall by the river, which led to my apartment in the Nesle, till I came to the Augustinians. Now this is a most perilous place; and though it was only five hundred steps from my house, yet as the inhabited part of the castle was almost as far within, my voice would never have been heard if I had called out. Well, just there I was attacked. My mind was made up in a flash when I saw four armed men upon me. Quickly I covered my basket with my cloak, drew my sword, and seeing they were hotly closing round me, I cried, "You can get nothing from soldiers but their cloak and sword, and before I give you mine, I hope you will not be much the better for them." While I was answering their attack with spirit, I opened my arms wide several times, so that, should they be in league with the servants who had seen me take the money, they might come to the conclusion that I had no such sum upon me. The fight was soon over, and little by little they retired, saying in their own tongue, "This is a brave Italian, and certainly not the fellow we were in search of. Or if it be indeed the same, he has nothing on him." I spoke in Italian; and all the time I was thrusting and digging at them, so that they barely escaped with their lives. Indeed, I wielded my arms with such skill that they took me for a soldier rather than a civilian; and keeping close together, little by little they drew farther and farther back from me, muttering all the time in their lingo; while I kept saying, but without bluster, that whoever would like my sword and my cloak would have some trouble to get them. Then I began to hasten my steps, while they crept on slowly behind me; which roused a greater anxiety in me lest I should fall into another ambuscade of like rascals, and be caught between the two bands. So when I was about a hundred steps from my house I began to run as hard as I was able, crying in a loud voice, "To arms! To arms! Come out! Come out! for they are killing me." In an instant four of my young fellows ran to me, each armed with a pike. They would have chased the villains, who were still to be seen; but I stopped them, shouting at the top of my voice, "Those cowards were four against one, and yet couldn't get hold of the thousand gold crowns, which have all but broken my arm. Now let's go and put them in a safe place; and then I'll take my two-handed sword and come with you wherever you like." So we went and deposited the gold; and my young men, while condoling with me on the great peril I had run, yet said reproachfully, "You trust too much to yourself; a day will come when you'll give us all cause to weep." We had a long talk over the matter. Meanwhile my enemies had fled; and we all sat down to supper happy and gay, and laughing over those sudden strokes of fortune, which work for good as well as ill, and which, when they miss their mark, are as if they had never been. True, one says to one's self, "You will learn better against the next time." But it is not so at all; they come each time in some different form, which we had never imagined.

xviii. Next morning I set to work on the fine salt-cellar, and threw the greatest energy into this and my other works. Already I had hired a great many workmen, both sculptors and gold-smiths, Italians, French, and Germans, according as I found them useful; for I changed them from day to day, keeping only such as were most capable. Those I drove without mercy. They saw me work, and fain would have done as much; but I was robuster, and they could not stand the excessive labour. In hopes of rivalling me, they thought to restore their strength with deep drinking and much food, especially the Germans, who were more skilled and more zealous than the rest. But their constitution could not endure such abuse, and it killed them.

While I was getting on with the Jupiter, I saw that I had a good deal of silver to spare. So, without telling the King, I began to make a large two-handled vase about a cubit and a half high. Besides, I took it into my head to cast the large model of the Jupiter in bronze, and set out without delay on this new enterprise. As I had never done such a thing before, I consulted certain old masters of the art in Paris, and told them all about our Italian methods. They said they had never worked in that fashion; but if I would leave them to do it in their own way, they would cast the bronze as clean and as good as the clay. So I struck a bargain, whereby I put the burden of the work upon them, but promised them several crowns over and above what they had asked me. Accordingly they began the thing; but as I saw they were not doing it after a right method, I set to work at once on a head of Julius Cæsar, with bust and armour more than life size, which I made after a small copy of a marvellous antique I had brought from Rome. Also I took in hand another head of the same size, the model for which was a very beautiful girl whom I kept in my house. To this I gave the name of Fontaine-bleau, from the place the King had chosen for his own delight.

A convenient little furnace had been made for founding the bronze; and our moulds were got ready and baked, the French bronze-casters seeing to the Jupiter, and I to my two heads. Then I said to them, "I don't think your Jupiter will be a success; for you have not allowed enough air-holes below for the air to circulate. So you are losing your time." They answered that if their work did not turn out well, they would return me all the money I had given them on account, and would make up to me for all I had spent; but I had better have a care, they said, for my fine heads, which I was going to cast in the Italian fashion, would be a failure. During this dispute there were present the treasurers and other courtiers who used to come and visit me by order of the King. And all that was said and done they reported to his Majesty. The two old men who were to cast the Jupiter wished to put the thing off, saying they would like to adjust the moulds of my two heads. For, they said, they could not possibly come out well in my method, and it was a great pity to spoil such fine works. When the King heard this, he sent a message to them that they had better think about learning instead of trying to teach their master.

So with a great deal of laughing, they put the Jupiter into

the furnace, while I with an unmoved face, showing neither ridicule nor vexation—which I nevertheless felt—put in my two moulds, one on each side of theirs. And when our metal was well founded, with the greatest delight we poured it in. It filled up the model of the Jupiter perfectly, and at the same time my two heads. So they were overjoyed, and I was well-content; for I was glad to have been wrong about their work, and they pretended to be glad they had been wrong about mine. Then, as the French fashion is, in great spirits they called for drinks; and right willingly I gave orders that a rich collation should be served. After that they asked me for the money which was due to them, and the sum over I had promised; whereupon I said, "You have laughed about what I much fear may prove a weeping matter. For I have noticed that a great deal too much metal has gone into your mould; so I shall give you no more money than you have had till to-morrow at least." The poor fellows began to think over what I had said to them; and without a word they went off home. When morning came, they began very quietly to take the things out of the furnace. But they could not uncover their large mould until they had taken out my two heads. These turned out excellently; and they stood them up where they could be well seen. Then they began to uncover the Jupiter. But they had not gone down two cubits when they and their four workmen set up such a cry that I heard them. Thinking they were shouting for joy, I made haste and ran; for I was in my room more than five hundred paces off. When I reached them, they were like the guardians of Christ's Sepulchre in the picture, all sorrowful and afraid. Having glanced at my two heads and seen they were all right, I felt mingled pleasure and vexation. They pleaded excuses, and cried, "How unlucky we are!" Whereupon I said, "Your luck has been excellent; but what has been bad is your want of knowledge. If I had only seen you putting the inner block into the mould, with one word I could have let you see how to cast the figure to perfection. It would have done me much credit, and would have been very helpful to you. I can do without the credit; but you'll gain neither honour nor profit from the business. So next time learn how to work, and not make fun of other people." Then they pleaded with me, owning I was in the right, but saying that if I did not help them, with all that great expense and loss to make good, they would have to go a-begging with their children. I replied that if the King's treasurer forced them to pay what they were responsible for, I would make it good out of my own pocket; for I saw quite well that they had done their work honestly, as far as their knowledge went. My conduct in this affair increased the goodwill of the treasurer and the other ministers of the King to me more than I can tell. The whole thing was told to his Majesty, who, lavishly generous as was none other in the world, gave orders that whatever I wished should be done.

xix. At this time the famous captain, Piero Strozzi, came to Paris, and recalled to the King the question of his letters of naturalisation. His Majesty gave orders they should be made out. At the same time he said, "Make out letters also for Benvenuto, *mon ami*, and take them at once to his house; and let him be at no expense in the matter." Piero Strozzi's cost him many hundred ducats. Mine were brought to me by one of the chief secretaries, called Monsieur Antoine le Maçon, who handed me the letters with the most courteous messages from his Majesty, saying, "The King presents you with these, so that you may be further encouraged to serve him. They are letters of naturalisation." And he told me how, only after a long delay, and as a great favour, they had been given to Piero Strozzi in accordance with his request. But his Majesty had sent mine of his own free will; and such a favour had never before been shown to any one in the whole kingdom. Hearing this, I thanked the King effusively; and then I begged the secretary to be good enough to tell me what these letters of naturalisation were for. He was a most intelligent and well-bred man, and spoke excellent Italian. First he began to laugh heartily; then, collecting himself, he explained to me in my own Italian tongue what they were, adding that they conferred one of the highest dignities which can be given to a foreigner. "In truth," said he, "it is a greater thing than being made a Venetian noble." Then he left me, went back to the King, and told all to his Majesty, who laughed for a bit, and then said, "Now I would have him know why I have sent him letters of naturalisation. Go and make out for him a patent of lordship of the castle of the Little Nesle, where he lives. It is a part of my own patrimony. He will understand what that is much more easily than he did the other." Then a messenger came to me with this gift, and I wished to use him courteously. But he would accept nothing, saying such were his Majesty's orders. When I returned to Italy I brought those letters of naturalisation with me, together with the deeds of the castle; and wherever I go, and wherever I end my life, I shall strive to keep them by me always.

xx. Now I shall go on with the tale of my life. I had in hand the works I have mentioned, that is, the silver Jupiter, the gold salt-cellar, the large silver vase, the two bronze heads; and I was making all the haste with them I could. I was also preparing to cast the base for the statue, which was of bronze, and richly decorated. Among the ornaments were bas-reliefs, on one side the rape of Ganymede, and on the other Leda and the Swan. I cast it in bronze with great success. Then I designed another like it for the statue of Juno, hoping to carry that out too, if the King gave me silver enough. Thus by dint of hard work, I had got well on with the silver Jupiter and the gold salt-cellar. The vase was well forward; the two bronze heads were already finished. I had also made several trifles for the Cardinal of Ferrara, and, besides, a little silver vase, richly chased, to present to Madame d'Etampes. Likewise, for several Italian noblemen, Piero Strozzi, for instance, the Count d'Anguillara, the Count di Pitigliano, the Count della Mirandola, and many others, I had done a great deal of work.

As I have said, I had got on excellently with the pieces I was making for my great King. About this time he returned to Paris; and on the third day after he came to my house, with some of the best nobility of his Court. He was greatly astonished at the amount of work I had accomplished, and at its excellence. Now Madame d'Etampes was with him, and they began to talk of Fontainebleau. She advised his Majesty to order me to design some beautiful ornament for his fountain in that place; whereupon the King exclaimed, "A very good idea! And this very instant I will make up my mind what it shall be." Then, turning to me, he began to ask me what I thought should be done for the fountain. So I set before him my ideas, and his Majesty expressed his own. Then he told me he was going for fifteen or twenty days to St. Germain-en-Laye, twelve leagues from Paris; and during that time I was to make a model for his beautiful fountain, the richest and most ingenious I could think of; for the place was to his mind the pleasantest he had in all his kingdom. It was thus he commanded and entreated me to do all I could to produce something exquisite; and I gave him my promise.

When the King saw so many works well forward, he said to Madame d'Etampes, "I have never employed a man of his profession who pleased me more, nor who better earned a reward. So we must think how best we can keep him in our service. He is open-handed, loves good company, and works hard, and we must

keep his needs in mind. And—will you believe it, Madame?—
for as often as he has come to see me, and as I have gone to
see him, he has never once asked me for anything. His heart is
evidently all set upon his work. We must think of rewarding
him without delay, lest we should lose him." Madame d'Etampes
replied, "I shall remind you." So they took their departure.
Now, besides all the works I had in hand, I began the model of
the fountain, working at it with the greatest diligence.

xxi. At the end of a month and a half the King returned to
Paris; and I, who had been working day and night, went to
see him, taking with me the model, which was so well blocked
out that its design could plainly be seen. That diabolic war
between the Emperor and the King had by this time broken
out again; so that I found him in great trouble. But I spoke to
the Cardinal of Ferrara, telling him I had with me certain models
which his Majesty had ordered, and if he saw a fitting moment
for showing them, I thought the King would be much pleased
with them. The Cardinal did as I wished; and when he spoke
of the models, his Majesty came at once to the place where they
were. The first I had made for the door of the palace of Fontainebleau. I had altered—but as little as possible—the form of the
door, which was short and stumpy, after their bad French
style. The opening was nearly square; and above it was a
flattened semicircle, like the handle of a basket, in which the
King wished me to put a figure representing the nymph of
Fontainebleau. I improved the proportions of the doorway,
and then placed above it a regular semicircle. The sides I
adorned with elegant projections, under which, and above, I
placed corresponding socles and cornices. But instead of two
columns, which this style is supposed to demand, I designed
two satyrs, one on each side. The first, which was almost in
high relief, was raising one hand to support the column, while
in the other he held a great club. His countenance was haughty
and proud, striking fear into the beholders. The other figure
was in a like attitude; but the head and some minor parts were
different. For example, in his hand he held a whip with three
balls at the end of chains. Though I call them satyrs, there was
nothing of the satyr about them save the little horns and their
goat's head. The rest of them was human in shape. In the middle
of the semicircle I had designed a woman lying in a beautiful
attitude, with her left arm on a stag's neck, the stag being one
of the emblems of the King. On one side were young fawns in
half relief, and wild boars and other wild animals in lower

relief; on the other side, hunting dogs of the various breeds which are found in that lovely wood where the fountain springs. Then I had enclosed the whole in an oblong; and in each of the upper angles had placed a Victory in low relief, with torches in her hand, as the ancients were wont to represent her. Above this oblong was the salamander, the King's own device, and many other pleasing ornaments befitting the Ionic style of the work.

xxii. Hardly had the King set eyes on the model, when his spirits rose, and his mind was diverted from the worrying discussions in which he had been engaged for more than two hours. Seeing he was in the cheerful mood that just suited me, I uncovered the second model, which he was not looking for, thinking that one was enough for me to have done. This other was more than two cubits high. It was a fountain in the form of a perfect square, with very fine steps round it, which intersected each other in a way never seen in those parts, and not at all common with us. In the middle of the fountain was a pedestal, which rose a little beyond the basin; and on this I had set a nude figure of harmonious size and graceful shape. With his right hand he held a broken lance on high, and his left rested on the handle of a beautiful scimitar. He stood on his left foot, with his right on a richly chased helmet. At each of the four corners of the fountain I had placed a seated figure, raised above the pedestal, with many fanciful emblems about each.

Then his Majesty began to ask me what I meant by all those delightful conceits. My plan for the door he had understood without asking me; but for this fountain, though it seemed to him very beautiful, he couldn't make it out at all. Yet he knew I was not one of those fools who are capable of producing something rather graceful, but entirely without significance. Here I set my thoughts in order; for since he was pleased with my work, I wished him to be no less so with my exposition. "I would have your Sacred Majesty know," said I, "that this whole work is so exactly calculated, to an inch, that when it is executed on a large scale, it will retain the same grace you see now. This figure in the middle would be fifty-four feet high." (Here the King appeared to be greatly astonished.) "It is meant to represent the god Mars. These other four figures are the arts and intellectual pursuits, which your Majesty so much delights to encourage. The one on the right hand is Science. As you will see, opposite it is Philosophy, with all that pertains to it. This other represents the complete art of design—that is, Sculpture,

Painting, and Architecture. The next is Music, fitting companion for all the rest. And this one, with so gracious and benign a face, is Liberality, without which none of the endowments which God bestows on us can ever have a chance of expression. The great statue in the middle is meant for your Majesty's self, who is a very Mars; for you are the sole brave in all the world; and your bravery you manifest in justice and well-doing, in defence of your glory." Hardly had he the patience to hear me to the end, before he burst out in a loud voice, "Verily I have found a man after my own heart!" and he called his treasurers, with whom I had already had dealings, and told them to provide me with everything I might want, at no matter what cost. Then, putting his hand on my shoulder, he said to me, "*Mon ami*" —which means "my friend"—"I do not know whose is the greater pleasure, that of the prince who has found a man after his own heart, or that of the artist who has found a prince who allows him whatever he needs to carry out his best ideas." I answered that if it was I his Majesty referred to, mine was much the greater luck. He replied with a laugh, "Let's say our luck is equal." Then I took my leave; and in the highest spirits went back to my work.

xxiii. As my ill fortune would have it, nobody suggested to me I had best play just such another comedy with Madame d'Etampes. When she heard that evening, from the King's own mouth, all that had been going on, a venomous rage was roused in her bosom, and she burst out angrily, "If Benvenuto had taken the trouble to show me his fine works, he would have given me reason for remembering him at the right moment." The King made excuses for me; but in vain. I heard of the occurrence only after they had gone on a journey through Normandy, stopping at Rouen and Dieppe. However, fifteen days after, when they had returned to Saint Germain-en-Laye, I repaired to that place, taking with me the lovely little vase I had made at the request of Madame d'Etampes. I meant to give it to her, hoping thus to regain her favour. So I presented myself at her house, and showed her nurse what I had brought for her mistress. The nurse received me most kindly; and promised she would say a word to Madame, who was not yet dressed; and that as soon as she had announced me, she would usher me in. The woman gave all my messages to Madame, who answered contemptuously, "Tell him to wait." Hearing this, I clothed myself with patience, than which nothing is harder to me. However, I kept calm till after her dinner-time.

Then, seeing it was getting late, hunger roused such a fury in me that, unable any longer to bear it, I consigned her devoutly to the devil, and took myself off to find the Cardinal of Lorraine. I made him a present of the vase, only asking in return that he would keep me in the King's favour. He said there was no need for his mediation; but that should it arise, he would willingly say a word for me. Then he called his treasurer and whispered in his ear. The treasurer waited till I had left the presence of the Cardinal, and then he said, "Benvenuto, come with me and I'll give you a beaker of good wine to drink." Thereupon I answered—not rightly understanding what he meant—"For any sake, my lord treasurer, let me have just one beaker of wine and a mouthful of bread. Truly I am in want of it; for from an early hour this morning till now I have been fasting on Madame d'Etampes's doorstep. I went merely to give her that fine vase of silver gilt, and told her as much. But, only to spite me, she sent word I was to wait. Now hunger has gripped me, and I am ready to faint. But as God has willed, I have given the labour of my hands to one who deserves it more, and all I ask is something to drink; for I am somewhat of a bilious disposition, and fasting puts me so out of sorts that I am in danger of falling now from sheer weakness." While I was struggling to get out these words, there appeared a collation of exquisite wine and other dainties, so that I was perfectly restored; and having got back my vital forces, I discovered that my rage had all passed away. The good treasurer handed to me a hundred gold crowns; but I refused obstinately to have anything to do with them. When he went to report this, the Cardinal called him names, and ordered him to force me to take them, and not to come into his presence till he had done so. So the treasurer came back to me in great trouble, saying that never before had he been so abused by the Cardinal. He still persisted in offering me the money; and I was still obstinate, till he got in a rage, and said he would force me to accept. So at last I took the money. When I proposed to go and thank his lordship, he sent a message by a secretary that whenever he could do me a good turn, he would do so willingly. I returned to Paris the same evening. The King had learned everything; and they teased Madame d'Etampes about the affair, which only embittered her the more, whereby I was placed in great peril of my life. But I shall speak of that in its own place.

xxiv. Long before this I should have told of my friendship with one of the ablest, the most affectionate and friendliest men I have ever known in all my life. This was Messer Guido Guidi, an excellent physician and doctor, and a Florentine noble. But in telling of the endless troubles with which my adverse fortune assailed me, I have neglected to speak of him earlier. The omission mattered little, I thought, since I kept him ever near my heart. But now I see that the story of my life is incomplete without him; and so I shall bring him forward here, in the midst of my greatest trials; so that as he was then my strength and aid, now I can recall the good he did to me. At the beginning of our acquaintance, when he came to Paris, I took him to my castle, and there gave him a suite of apartments for his own use; and we were the best of neighbours for several years. Now there arrived also the Bishop of Pavia, Monseigneur de' Rossi, brother of the Count of San Secondo. I took this gentleman away from his inn, and lodged him in my castle, giving him also apartments of his own, where he installed himself very comfortably with his servants and equipage for many months. At another time I put up Messer Luigi Alamanni and his sons for several months. Truly God was good to me in enabling me to be of service to great and distinguished men like these. Messer Guido and I rejoiced in our friendship all the years I remained in Paris; and often did we congratulate ourselves and each other that we were gaining skill at the cost of the great and wonderful prince, each in his own profession. I can truly say that, whatever I am, whatever of good and beauty I have produced, is all due to that admirable King. So now I pick up the thread of my story, to speak of him and of the great things I executed for him.

xxv. In my castle I had a tennis-court, which I made very profitable by hiring it out to players. There were also some small rooms in the place where lived all sorts of men, and among them a very clever printer of books. Nearly the whole of his establishment lay inside my castle; and it was he who printed Messer Guido's first fine book on medicine. As I needed the rooms myself, I turned him out; but it was no easy matter. There was also a maker of saltpetre, whose rooms I wanted for some of my German workmen; but he would not budge. Several times I had asked him courteously to oblige me by quitting my rooms, since I wished to lodge in them my workmen in the King's service. The more politely I spoke, the more insolently did the beast reply; and at last I gave him three days' notice, at which he laughed, and said that in three years' time he might begin to think about it. I did not know that he was of the household of Madame d'Etampes. And had it not been that the affair with Madame d'Etampes made me rather more prudent than I was wont to be, I should have turned him out on the spot. As it was, I made up my mind to have patience for three days. When the time was up, without another word to him, I called in the aid of my Germans, Italians, and Frenchmen, all armed, as well as many of the rougher workmen I employed; and in a short time I dismantled his whole house, and turned all his property outside my castle. The treatment was somewhat severe; but I had recourse to it because he had said to me that he knew not a single Italian strong enough or daring enough to move even a nail from his walls. So now, when the thing was done, he made his appearance, and I said to him, "I am the least Italian in all Italy; and I have done nothing to you compared to what I had it in my mind to do, and what I shall do, if you venture to speak one word." And these were not the only insults I threw at him. The man, astounded and terrified, collected his things as well as he could; and then ran to Madame d'Etampes, and described me as the very devil. And she, my great enemy, painted me in still worse colours to the King, being more eloquent and more powerful. Twice, as was told me, his Majesty was on the point of being angered, and of giving an order against me. But his son Henry, the Dauphin, to-day the King of France, who had been uncourteously treated by the proud lady, and the Queen of Navarre, too, King Francis's sister, spoke in my favour so tactfully that his Majesty turned the whole thing into a jest. So, by the help of God, I escaped a greater misfortune.

xxvi. I had to do very much the same thing with another man of the kind; but I did not ruin his house: I only threw all his things out. And on this occasion Madame d'Etampes had the face to say to the King, "I believe this devil will sack Paris one day!" The King replied with heat that I did most rightly to defend myself from the low scoundrels who wished to hinder me in my service of him. Every hour the rage of this cruel lady increased. She sent for a painter who had his residence at Fontainebleau, where the King nearly always was. He was a Bolognese, and was known as Il Bologna, though his right name was Francesco Primaticcio. Madame d'Etampes bade him ask the King to give him the commission for the fountain which his Majesty had assigned to me; and she promised to second him by every means in her power. So it was agreed between them. Bologna was happier than ever he had been in his life; and felt quite sure of the thing, though it was not the kind of work he was used to. But he was a very good designer, and he had in his employment several workmen trained under Rosso, our Florentine painter, who was, of a truth, a very able man. In fact, whatever good work Bologna did was due to his imitation of the style of Rosso, who was now dead.

Their clever arguments, along with the powerful influence of Madame d'Etampes, did the work; for night and day they kept on hammering at the King. When Madame stopped, Bologna began. But what affected him most strongly was their both saying, "How is it possible, Sacred Majesty, that Benvenuto can make you the twelve silver statues you are so eager for? See, he has not yet finished one. If you encourage him in this new and important undertaking, it is certain you will never get the other things you are so set on; for not even a hundred of the ablest men could finish such great works as this one man has already in hand. It is plain he is eager for work; but for that very reason it seems likely your Majesty will lose both him and his work at one stroke." These and other reasons were set forth just when the King was in the right temper for entertaining them; and so he agreed to all they asked him. Yet he had never been shown any designs or models for the work in question from the hand of Bologna.

xxvii. About this time the second tenant I had evicted from my castle took action against me, protesting that I had stolen a great quantity of his goods when I had turned him out. This law-suit gave me endless worry, and took up so much time that often I was in despair, and wished to leave the place for good. In France they are wont to make no end of capital out of a suit against a foreigner, or any one whom they see little disposed for litigation. As soon as they find there is something to be got out of the suit, they try to sell it; for men have been known to give suits as dowries with their daughters to such as make their living out of these contracts. Another wicked custom, which nearly all the Normans have, is their skilful concoction of false evidence. So it happens that those who buy the suits, at once instruct five or six perjurers, according to the need; and thus a man who does not know the custom, and has had no hint given him to provide just as many to swear against them, has no chance of winning his case.

These things happened to me; and the whole affair seeming most dishonest, I appeared in the great hall of Paris to defend my rights. There I saw a judge, the King's deputy in civil cases, sitting on a great raised tribunal—a tall, heavy, fat man he was, of the severest aspect. To the right and left of him were a number of procurators and advocates. Others came, one at a time, and each presented his case to the judge. I heard the pleaders at his side all speaking at once; and I stood there marvelling at that astonishing man, with the Pluto-like face, in his watchful attitude, now lending ear to one, now to the other, and answering each with ability. Now it has always delighted me to see and savour every kind of skill; and this struck me as so wonderful that I would not have missed it for anything. As the great hall was already full of people, they took care to let no one enter who had no business there. The door was kept locked, and a guardian stood to bar the way. Occasionally this guard, in preventing the entrance of some one who had no right there, interrupted the judge with the great noise he made, and the judge then got in a fury and rated the guardian soundly. This happened several times; and I noticed the thing, and likewise caught the precise words which fell from the judge's lips. It happened that two gentlemen were determined to get in to watch the proceedings, and the porter was resisting stoutly. Thereupon the judge cried in a loud voice, "Silence! Silence! Satan, hence with you! Silence!" Now in the French tongue these words sound like, *Phe phe, Satan, phe phe alè, phe !* [*Paix, paix, Satan ; allez, paix !*] I had become proficient in the French language, and, hearing these words, I recalled what Dante said when he and his master Virgil entered the doors of Hell. Now Dante and the painter Giotto were together in France, and particularly in Paris, where, for the reasons I have here set forth, the place of justice is indeed an Inferno. Thus Dante, who knew the French tongue well, made use of this saying. And it has seemed to me curious that the line has never been understood in this sense; and so I declare and believe that the commentators make him say things he never thought of.

xxviii. Now to return to my own business. When I learned what was the kind of judgment I had to expect from these men of law, and saw no other way of helping myself, I had recourse for my defence to a great dagger which I possessed—for I have ever delighted in having fine weapons. The first I assaulted was the man who had brought the unjust law-suit against me; and one evening I wounded him so seriously as to deprive him of the use of his legs, as well as injuring his arms. But I took care not to kill him. Then I found the other man who had brought the suit, and gave him what made him glad enough to stop his litigation. Thanking God for this and all His other mercies, and hoping I might now be left unmolested for a time, I entreated the young men of my house, especially the Italians, to attend each to his own business, for the love of God, and give me good help for a while, so that I might complete the works I had begun. As soon as I had finished them, I wished to return to Italy; for I could not endure any more the rascalities of these Frenchmen; and if the good King once lost patience, it would go badly with me that I had frequently defended myself in the way I have described. Of the Italians the first and the dearest was Ascanio from Tagliacozzo, in the kingdom of Naples; the next was Pagolo, the Roman, a man of very humble birth, who did not know his own father. These were the two I had brought from Rome, and who had lived there with me. Another Roman had come to seek me out, whose name was also Pagolo, the son of a poor gentleman of the Macaroni house. This young fellow did not know much about art; but he knew very well how to handle his sword. Another of them was from Ferrara, Bartolommeo Chioccia by name. And one was a Florentine called Pagolo Micceri. His brother, nicknamed "Il Gatta," was noted for his skill in book-keeping, but had ruined himself in looking after the estate of Tommaso Guadagni, a rich merchant. This Gatta put my books straight, in which I kept the accounts of the most Christian King and of my other customers. Pagolo Micceri, having learnt the method from his brother, carried on the work for me, and I paid him excellently for it. He seemed to be a very good young man. I thought him devout, hearing him humming psalms all the time, and seeing him finger his rosary, and I counted much on this feigned piety. One day I said to him, "Pagolo, dearest brother, you see how comfortable you are with me, and you know you had nothing of your own to begin with. Besides, you are a Florentine. Likewise, I trust you the more that I see you very devout in the practices of religion which pleases me very much. I entreat you, therefore, to help me, for I have not too much confidence in any of the others. Therefore I beg you to look carefully after two things of great importance, out of which might arise endless worry for me. One is to watch over my property that it be not stolen; and mind not to touch it yourself. The next thing is this: you know that poor child Caterina. I keep her in my house chiefly on account of my art—for I must have a model. But since I am a man, I have also kept her for my pleasure; and it may be she will bear me a child. Now I don't want to spend my money on other people's children; still less could I support such an insult to my honour. If any one in the house were audacious enough to do such a thing, and I were aware of it, I verily believe I should kill them both. Therefore I beg you, dear brother, to help me; and if you see anything amiss, tell me at once, and I'll send her, and her mother, and her seducer to the gallows. But keep a watch first of all on yourself." The rascal made the sign of the cross from his head to his feet, and said, "Blessed Jesus! God forbid that I should ever think of such a thing! To begin with, I am not given to these villainies. Besides, don't you believe I am aware of all I owe to you?" When I heard him say these things so simply, and with such a look of affection, I believed that things were just as he said.

xxix. Two days after was a feast day; and Messer Mattio del Nazaro, another Italian sculptor in the service of the King, had invited me and my young men to a party of pleasure in a garden. So I prepared to go, and I told Pagolo that he too might come out and enjoy himself; for it seemed to me that things had now quieted down after that troublesome law-suit. But the young man answered, "It would indeed be a great mistake to leave the house unguarded. Think of all the gold and silver and jewels you have here. Being as we are in a city of robbers, we should watch day as well as night. So I will wait at home and say my prayers, guarding the house the while. Go with an easy mind and enjoy yourself. Another time one of the rest will take my place."

It seemed to me I might go off without any anxiety; and so I took Pagolo, Ascanio, and Chioccia to the garden, and there we spent a good part of the day very pleasantly. When it was drawing towards evening, another humour took me, and I began to brood over the words the villain had said to me with such an air of simplicity. So I mounted my horse and returned to the castle with two of my servants. There I nearly caught Pagolo and that hussy Caterina. As soon as I arrived, that French bawd of a mother called out loud, "Pagolo! Caterina! here's the master." When I saw them both terror-struck, coming towards me all in disorder, not knowing what they were saying, nor in their daze where they were going, their guilt was too plainly to be seen. Reason in me was choked with anger; and, seizing my sword, I resolved to kill the two of them. But Pagolo ran away; and the woman threw herself on her knees and cried aloud to Heaven for pity. My first idea was to attack the man; but I could not catch him at once; and by the time I did so I had made up my mind that the best course was to chase them both away. For I had so many violent deeds to my account, that were I to add another, I could hardly escape with my life. So I said to Pagolo, "Rascal, had I seen with my eyes what your appearance compels me to believe, then this sword would have run you ten times through. Now be off with you! And if you ever say another Paternoster, may it be San Giuliano's!" Then I hustled out the mother and the daughter, with blow and shove and cuff and kick. They were determined to revenge themselves for this treatment; and took counsel of a Norman advocate, who told them to say I had used Caterina in the Italian fashion. "At least," said he, "when the Italian hears of this, he will bribe you with several hundreds of ducats that you may hold your tongues; for he will know the grave penalty attaching in France to such a crime." So it was agreed. They brought the accusation against me, and I was summoned.

xxx. The more I longed for rest, the more did troubles spring up. Every day assailed by Fortune in divers ways, I brooded over the best course for me to pursue, whether to make off without a word to anyone, and let France go to the devil, or to fight this thing out, and see for what end God had created me. For some time I worried over this matter. At last I made up my mind to be off, and not provoke my evil fortune over-much, lest I should run my neck into a noose. I had made all my arrangements, and taken steps to dispose of the property I could not carry with me. The lighter things my servants and I were to carry on our persons as best we could.

Still, I was taking my departure with a very heavy heart. And so one day I was sitting by myself in a little study. My young men had been counselling me to be off; but I told them that I must think over the matter a little alone, though I knew that in great part they spoke the truth. For if I could only keep out of prison, and let this fury spend itself somewhat, I could much better excuse myself to the King by letters, which should prove to him how this cruel slander was the work of men who envied me. Well, as I have said, I had made up my mind to this course, when just as I rose to prepare for my departure, some invisible one took me by the shoulder and turned me about. Then a rousing voice said in my ear, "Benvenuto, do as you are wont, and fear not!" On the spot I changed my mind entirely, and said to my Italian friends, "Arm yourselves well, and come out with me, and do just as I bid you. Not another word on the matter, for I am going to answer my summons. If I were to leave next day, you would all vanish in smoke. So do my bidding, and on with me." Then all together the lads cried, "Since we are here, and live on Benvenuto, we should go with him and help him to do what he intends so long as there is life in us. There is more truth in what he says than in what we proposed; for as soon as he is out of this, his enemies would send us packing. Let us think of all the great works which are begun, and how important they are. We could not finish them without him; and his enemies would declare he had gone because their completion was beyond him." They said many sensible things besides. Macaroni, the young Roman, was the first to put spirit into them, and he enlisted also several Germans and Frenchmen who were friends of mine.

We were ten in all. I took the road with my mind fixed fast not to be taken alive. When I came into the presence of the criminal judges, I found Caterina and her mother laughing together with their advocate. On my entrance I demanded the judge in a bold voice. He was sitting raised above the others on a tribunal, swelled and big and fat. When he saw me, he shook his head threateningly, and said in a low voice, "Though you are called Benvenuto, this time you are rather Malvenuto (ill come)." I caught his meaning, and, speaking again, I said, "Dispatch this affair of mine. Let me know what I am here for." Then the judge turned to Caterina and said, "Caterina, tell all that has taken place between you and Benvenuto." She replied I had used her in the Italian manner. Then, turning to me, the judge said, "You hear what she says." And I answered, "If I have done so, it was only because I wished to have a son like the rest of you." Whereupon the judge replied that the accusation was quite other; and I answered he must be referring to some French rather than an Italian custom, since she knew more about it than I; and I ordered her to tell just what our relations had been. Then the wicked hussy said right out the beastliness which she scandalously accused me of. I made her repeat it three times one after the other; and when she had finished I cried aloud, "My lord judge, deputy of the most Christian King, I claim justice! I know the laws condemn both parties in such a crime to be burned at the stake. Now she confesses her sin. I have had nothing to do with it. Her bawd of a mother is here, and she has done more than enough to deserve the stake. I call on you for justice!" This I cried again and again in a loud voice, demanding the stake for her mother, and declaring to the judge that if he did not commit her to prison there and then, I should run to the King and tell him the wrong done to me by his deputy in the criminal courts. Those on the other side began to speak in lower tones when they heard me storming; and then I stormed yet louder. The hussy and her mother set to weeping, and I called to the judge, "To the fire with them! To the fire!" The great coward of a judge, seeing the thing was not going as he had planned, began with insinuating words to excuse the frailty of the female sex. At that I felt I had got the best in a big fight; and, grumbling and threatening, I gladly took myself off the scene. In fact I would have paid five hundred crowns never to have appeared there. Saved from that abyss, I gave thanks to God with all my heart, and returned in good spirits with my young men to my castle.

xxxi. When perverse fortune—or if we like to call it so, our unlucky star—aims at persecuting us, it never lacks new means of attack. It seemed to me that as I had just escaped a terrible abyss, my evil star would leave me alone for a time. But before I had recovered my breath after that awful peril, it suddenly sprang fresh trials upon me. At the end of three days two things happened, each of which put my life in the balance. This was the first. I went to Fontainebleau to talk with the King, who had written me a letter, saying he wished me to make the dies for the coins of the whole kingdom. In the letter he sent me a few little designs, to indicate in some way what he wanted. But, nevertheless, he gave me leave to do them exactly as I pleased; and so I made new designs after my own ideas, and in accordance with the rules of art. Well, when I got to Fontainebleau, one of the treasurers who had been ordered by the King to supply my needs—Monsieur de la Fa was he called—made haste to say, "Benvenuto, the painter Bologna has got a commission from the King to make your great Colossus; and all the orders given us by his Majesty on your account are diverted from you in favour of him. We are all very angry, for we think that Italian fellow has behaved very insolently towards you. The work was given to you on the strength of your models and your labours. He takes it from you only because he is in favour with Madame d'Etampes. It is many months ago since he got the order; yet up till now there is no sign of his having set to work." I was astonished, and said, "How is it possible that I have never heard a word of this?" Then he told me that Bologna had kept it very secret; that he had got the work, indeed, with the greatest difficulty, for the King had been unwilling; and only the persistence of Madame d'Etampes had won it for him. I felt that a great wrong had been done me; and when I thought how a work which I had gained with great labour had been wrenched from me, I made up my mind to do something decisive. So, girding on my sword, I went in search of Bologna. I found him in his room, engaged in study. He called to me to come in; and with some Lombard palaver asked me what business had given him the pleasure of a visit; and I answered, "An excellent business, and an important one." Then he ordered his servants to bring wine, saying, "Before we discuss anything, let us drink together; for such is the custom here in France." But I replied, "Messer Francesco, I would have you know that the matters we are about to discuss together do not call for drinking in the first instance. Perhaps afterwards we may do so." And so I began the discussion. "All who have any pretensions to be men of worth act so that they may be known for such; otherwise they no longer get the name of honest men. I know that you were aware the King had given me a commission to make a great Colossus. There was talk about it for eighteen months; and neither you nor any one else came forward to say a word on the matter. It was by my own great labours I proved my capacity to the King, who was pleased with my models, and for that reason entrusted the thing to me. All these months I have not heard of any other intention he had formed, till this morning when I learnt that you had got the commission, having wrested it away from me. This work I had won by my proven deeds; and you steal it from me by mere empty words."

xxxii. To this Bologna replied, "O Benvenuto, every one tries to forward his own interests in every way possible. If the King wills this, what have you to reply? You would but waste your time; for I have it all arranged, and the thing is mine. Now say what you've got to say. I shall listen." Then I replied, "I would have you know, Messer Francesco, that I have a great deal to say, which would prove to you indisputably, and make you confess that such things as you have said and done are not customary among rational beings. But I will briefly come to the point I am aiming at. So now lend me your ears, and hear me well, for the matter is of consequence." Seeing me flushed, and my face greatly changed, he was about to move from his seat; but I told him it was not yet time to move, that he was to sit still and listen to me. Then I began again, "Messer Francesco, you know that the work was mine first, and that the time is past when any one had a right to discuss the matter.

Yet I declare that I shall be content, if you make a model, and I make one too, different from my first. Then we shall take them peaceably to our great King; and whoever can boast of having produced the best work in this way will deserve the Colossus. And if you succeed, I shall banish from my mind all the thought of the great injury you have done me, and will bless your hands as more worthy than mine of such glory. Let's agree to this, and we shall be friends. Otherwise, it's war between us. And God, who always helps the right, and I who know how to help myself, will prove to you your great mistake." Then answered Messer Francesco, "The work is mine, and since it has been given to me, I will not hazard my chances." To which I replied, "Messer Francesco, since you will not take the right way, the just and reasonable one, I will show you another quite as disagreeable as your own. So now listen to me; if ever I hear that you have spoken one word about this work of mine, I'll kill you like a dog. We are neither in Rome, nor Bologna, nor in Florence; and things are managed differently here. If ever I hear you have mentioned the subject to the King or any one else, I will most certainly have your life. So choose your course, the first I suggested, which is good, or the other I now point out to you, which is bad." The man knew not what to say or do; and I was more of a mind to do the thing at once than put it off. But he said nothing save, "If I behave like an honest man, I need fear nothing in the world"; to which I answered, "That's all right; but if you do the contrary, then you'll have good reason to fear, for this is no jesting matter."

Then I left him and went to the King. His Majesty and I argued for a long time about the making of the coins, concerning which we were not of one mind. His council were present, and persuaded him that the coins should be made in the French style, as they had been up till now. But I replied that his Majesty had sent for me from Italy to do good work. If now he ordered the contrary, it did not suit me to obey. So at this point the question was put off, to be discussed at another time, and I returned at once to Paris.

xxxiii. No sooner had I dismounted than one of those good folks who take pleasure in seeing one's misfortunes, came to tell me that Pagolo Micceri had taken a house for that little baggage Caterina and her mother, and that he was always paying her visits; also that when he spoke of me, it was with contempt, as: "Benvenuto set the cat to watch the cream, and thought it would not lap it. Now all he can do is to swagger, thinking I am afraid of him. But I have girt myself with this sword and this dagger, to let him see that mine can cut as well as his; that I am a Florentine as much as he, and of the Micceri, a much better house than the Cellini." The rascal's story had such an effect on me that I was seized with a sudden fever—fever it was: I do not speak in figures. And this mad passion might have brought me to my death, had not I given vent to it as the opportunity occurred, and according to my instinct of the moment. So I told my Ferrarese workman Chioccia to come with me, and ordered a servant to follow with my horse. Having reached the villain's house, we found the door ajar. I went in and saw him with his sword and dagger by his side, seated on a chest, with his arm round Caterina's neck. Just as I came in, I heard him and her mother joking about my affairs. Pushing the door open, I seized my sword and pointed it at his throat, giving him no time to bethink himself that he too was armed. "Base coward!" I shouted. "Recommend yourself to God, for you are a dead man!" Too terrified to move, he called out thrice, "O mother mine, help me!" I had meant to kill him on the spot; but hearing him utter these foolish words, half my anger passed away. Meanwhile I had ordered my apprentice, Chioccia, not to let either the mother or daughter out of the house; for when I had punished the man, I meant to do as much to the two worthless jades. So I kept the point of my sword at his throat, now and then giving him a little prick, and raining threats on him the while. But when I saw that he did nothing to defend himself, I did not know what more to do; and it looked as if I might go on threatening him for ever. So another idea came into my head. What better could I do than force them to marry? I could wait for my revenge. Having made up my mind, I said, "Take that ring you have on your finger, coward, and marry her, that I may pay you out as you deserve." He answered at once, "If only you do not kill me, I will do anything you please." Then I said, "Put that ring on her finger." I withdrew the sword a little from his throat, and he did as I told him. "This is not enough," I added. "I wish two notaries to be fetched, that it may be a real contract." I told Chioccia to go for the notaries; and then, turning to Caterina and her mother, and speaking in French, I said, "Notaries and witnesses have been sent for. The first of you who lets out this business I will kill; indeed, I will kill the three of you. Keep that in mind." To Pagolo I said in Italian, "If you hinder my purpose, at the least word I shall tear your guts out with my dagger."

He answered, "If you only do not kill me, I will do whatever you like." The notaries and witnesses came and drew up the contract in proper form. Then the heat of the fever passed out of me; and after I had paid the notaries' fees I took myself off.

Next day Bologna came to Paris, and sent Mattio del Nasaro for me. I went to see him; and he received me with a smile on his face, begging me to hold him as a brother. He promised he would never speak about the commission again; for he knew quite well that I was in the right.

xxxiv. If I did not own that in some of these incidents I did wrong, my account of the others, in which I know I did well, would be suspect. So I own I made a mistake in revenging myself so violently on Pagolo Micceri. Had I known him to be such a weak creature, it would never have come into my head to shame him by such a vengeance. For it was not enough for me that I had made him take to wife this wicked hussy. Over and above that, to complete my scheme of vengeance, I made her pose to me as a model, naked, for thirty soldi a day. I paid her in advance and fed her well; but I used her for my pleasure out of revenge, and then cast this insult in her husband's teeth and her own. Moreover, I forced her to pose in an uncomfortable position hour after hour, which annoyed her as much as it delighted me; for her form was very lovely, and did me much credit. When she saw that I did not treat her so discreetly as before her marriage, she grew very angry, began to grumble, and then, in her French way, to brag about her husband, who had gone to be with the Prior of Capua, Piero Strozzi's brother. When she said all this about her husband, I was seized with fury; only to hear her speak of him was too much. But I bore it, though against my will, as best I could, thinking that I should never find any more fitting model for my art than she, and saying to myself, "I am wreaking a double vengeance. For she is now a wife; and therefore I do him a more serious injury than he did me when she was a mere hussy in my house. If then I can revenge myself in so marked a manner on him, and treat her severely too, making her pose in these painful attitudes, not only have I the sweets of revenge, but I get both credit and profit out of her beauty as a model. And what more can I desire?" While I was summing the thing up in this way, the creature repeated her insults, pestering me about her husband till she tired out my patience completely. So, yielding to my wrath, I took her by the hair and dragged her about the room, kicking and mauling her till I was worn out. And nobody could come to her help. When I had beaten her well, she swore she would never come back to me again. So I thought I had made a mistake, and had lost an excellent opportunity of gaining honour in my profession. Besides, all bruised and livid and swollen as she was, I saw that, even if she were to come back, it would be necessary to have her wounds treated for a fortnight, before she could be of any use to me.

xxxv. But to return to her. I sent a servant to help her to dress, an old woman called Ruberta, a most kindly person. She brought food and drink for the hussy; then she anointed the worst wounds I had dealt her with some bacon fat; and what was over they ate together. When she was dressed, she went away blustering and cursing all the Italians, together with the King who maintained them, and weeping and muttering all the way home. I confess that on this first occasion I thought I had done very wrong; and my Ruberta scolded me, saying, "You are a brute to behave so cruelly to such a pretty girl." I excused myself to the old woman, and told her all the villainies Caterina and her mother had done to me when she was living in my house. But Ruberta still scolded me, telling me that was nothing, but only the French way; and that she was certain that there was not a husband in France who had not his horns. At this I burst out laughing, and then told Ruberta to go and see how Caterina was; for I wished very much to have her again as a model till I had finished my work. Ruberta cut me short, saying I did not know the world. "For as soon as day breaks," said she, "she will come of her own accord. But if you send to ask after her, or go to see her, she'll give herself airs, and won't come at all."

Next day Caterina came to my house and knocked so furiously at the door, that I, who was below, ran to see if it was a madman or any of my own household. When I opened the door, the little wretch laughed and threw herself on my neck, embracing and kissing me, and asking me if I was still angry with her. I said no, and she said, "Give me something to break my fast on." This I did, and I ate with her in token of peace. Afterwards she posed for me again, and I amused myself with her; and then just at the same hour as before, she exasperated me so that I had to repeat the punishment. Thus it went on for several days. Every day the same things happened, with hardly a single variation.

When I had finished my figure most creditably, I prepared to cast it in bronze. In this I experienced some difficulties, to tell of which would be most interesting, so far as my art is concerned; but as it would take too long, I will pass it over. Enough to say that my figure came out excellently, and the casting could not have been surpassed.

xxxvi. While I was getting on with this work, I set apart certain hours of the day for the salt-cellar, and others for the Jupiter. As there were more persons working on the former than I could employ on the statue, the salt-cellar was the first to be finished. The King had returned to Paris, and I went to see him, taking the completed work with me. As I have said before, it was of oval form, about two-thirds of a cubit high, and was all of gold, worked with the chisel. And as I also said, when I spoke of the model, it represented the Sea and the Land. Both figures were seated, with their legs interlaced, just as arms of the sea run into the land, or as the land juts out into the water; so that their attitude was significant. In the Sea's right hand I had placed a trident, and in his left a ship, very finely worked, to hold the salt. Under the figure were his four sea-horses, which from head to chest, and then again from the legs to the fore hoofs, were like ordinary horses; the middle and all the back parts were like fishes, the tails of which were intertwined in the prettiest way. The Sea was sitting above the group in proud and noble attitude; and all round him were different kinds of fishes and other marine creatures. The water was represented by waves exquisitely enamelled in its own colour. For the Land, I had made a lovely lady with a cornucopia in her hand, naked like the male figure. In her left hand I had placed a little Ionic temple, very finely wrought, and this was meant for the pepper. Under her I had fashioned the most beautiful animals which the earth produces; and the land-rocks I had partly enamelled, and partly left in gold. The whole stood on a base of black ebony of the proper size, which was surrounded by a shallow gorge decorated with four gold figures in something more than half-relief, representing Night, Day, Twilight, and Dawn. Four other figures of the same size were meant for the four chief winds. They were carried out partly in enamel, and with all the exquisiteness you can imagine.

When I set the piece before him, the King cried aloud in astonishment, and could not look at it long enough. But he told me to take it home with me again, and he would tell me in due time what I should do with it. I did so, and at once invited some of my good friends, and we dined together very merrily, the salt-cellar being in the centre of the table. And so we were the first to use it. Then I went on with the silver Jupiter, and worked also on the great vase I have already mentioned, which was covered with many delightful ornaments and figures.

xxxvii. About this time Bologna the painter gave the King to understand that it would be a good thing if his Majesty sent him to Rome with letters of recommendation, so that he might take casts of the principal masterpieces of antique sculpture, the Laocoon, the Cleopatra, the Venus, the Commodus, the Zingara, and the Apollo. These are, in truth, the finest things in Rome. When his Majesty had seen these marvellous works, he said, he would then be able to form an opinion on the art of design; for all he had seen from the hands of our modern artists was far below the perfection of those antiques. The King was quite willing to give him all the recommendations he asked for. So off went the beast in the devil's name. He had not had the pluck to try and rival me with the work of his own hands; but played me the very Lombard trick of depreciating my work by copying antiques. Now although he had these casts excellently made, the effect he produced was just the opposite to what he had intended. But that is a thing I shall tell later on in its own place.

I had now cut myself off entirely from that wretch Caterina, and the poor unlucky young husband of hers had disappeared from Paris. Wishing now to complete my Fontainebleau, which was already carried out in bronze, also to finish the two Victories, which were meant to fit into the angles of the semicircle above the door, I took as model a poor young girl of about fifteen. She was lovely in shape, and something of a brunette; and as she was a wild little thing, with hardly a word to say for herself, swift in her movements and sullen-eyed, I called her Scorzone; but her own name was Jeanne. With this girl as model I finished the bronze Fontainebleau very satisfactorily, as also the two Victories for the door. The young thing was pure and virginal, and I got her with child. She bore me a daughter at the thirteenth hour of the 7th of June 1544, when I was just forty-four years old. This daughter, to whom I gave the name of Costanza, was held at the font by Messer Guido Guidi, the King's physician, a great friend of mine, as I have said before. He was the only godfather; for it is the custom in France to have one godfather and two godmothers. One of these was the Signora Maddalena, wife of Luigi Alamanni, a Florentine gentleman, and an admirable poet. The other was the wife of Messer

Ricciardo del Bene, one of our Florentine citizens, and a rich merchant in Paris. She was a great French lady. This was the first child I ever had, so far as I remember. I assigned to her a dowry of the amount suggested by her aunt, into whose care I gave her. After that I never had anything more to do with her.

xxxviii. I hurried on with my work, and made great progress with it. The Jupiter was almost finished; so was the vase; and the door began to show its beauties. About this time the King came to Paris; for though I have spoken of the birth of my daughter in 1544, we were still in 1543. But it seemed the most convenient place to mention this daughter of mine; and I did so, that later I might not break into the tale of other things of more importance; and I shall say no more of her till the proper time. Well, as I have said, the King returned to Paris, and before long he came to my house, and found all those works so well in hand, that any one might have been pleased at the sight; and, in truth, the pleasure that glorious King took in them was great enough even to satisfy me, on whom all the burden of them had fallen. All at once he remembered, without suggestion from me, that the Cardinal of Ferrara had done nothing for me, neither given me a pension nor anything else he had promised. Then in a whispered conversation with his Admiral, he said the Cardinal had behaved very ill to give me nothing; but he would remedy that, for he saw I was a man who would make little complaint, but might all of a sudden take myself off without a word.

When he returned home, he said to the Cardinal, after dinner, that he was to order the treasurer of the Exchequer to pay me, as soon as possible, seven thousand gold crowns, in three or four instalments, according to his convenience, and that he was not to neglect it. He said, moreover, "I gave Benvenuto in charge to you, and you have done nothing for him." The Cardinal replied he would willingly obey his Majesty in everything; but his evil nature induced him to put off seeing to the matter till it had gone out of the King's head.

Meanwhile war and strife were on the increase; for it was the time when the Emperor with his huge army was advancing on Paris. Then the Cardinal, who saw that Francis was in great want of money, began one day to speak about me to the King. "Sacred Majesty," he said, "I have thought it best not to give any money to Benvenuto—in the first place, because at present we need it too much ourselves; and, secondly, because had I given him a great sum of money, it would rather have lost you

Benvenuto. For, feeling himself a rich man, he would have bought property in Italy, and any day the idea entered his head, he would have left you with the utmost indifference. So I think it best for your Majesty to give him something in your own kingdom, if you would keep him long in your service." The King thought well of these reasons, being, indeed, in want of money. Nevertheless, like the generous soul he was, ever worthy of his great place, he was of opinion that the Cardinal had taken this course rather with a view to gaining favour for himself, than because he had gauged beforehand the needs of the great kingdom.

xxxix. Although, as I have said, the King pretended to find the Cardinal's reasons of weight, in his secret heart he thought nothing of the kind. So the very next day after he came back to Paris, without any hint or invitation from me, he came of his own accord to my house. There I met him, and led him through different rooms, where were divers sorts of work displayed. Beginning at the least noteworthy, I showed him a great quantity of bronze pieces; for long he had not seen so many. Then I led him up to the silver Jupiter, now almost finished, with all its various exquisite ornaments. It seemed to him a much more wonderful thing than it might have appeared to another; and this was on account of an unfortunate occurrence which had happened some few years before. After the taking of Tunis, the Emperor passed through Paris, by agreement with his brother-in-law, King Francis, who on the occasion wished to make him a present worthy of so great a monarch. So he ordered a silver Hercules, of the same size as my Jupiter. Now this Hercules, the King swore, was the most hideous thing he had ever seen; and he had said so to the Paris artists. They have the pretension to be the most skilled in their profession, and they protested to him that this was the perfection of what could be done in silver, and demanded two thousand ducats for their rubbish. So now when the King saw my work, it seemed to him a thing of such exquisite skill that he could hardly believe his eyes. Therefore he made a careful estimate, valuing mine also at two thousand ducats, saying, "To those others I gave no salary. But a man who gets from me about a thousand crowns a year, may well let me have it for two thousand gold crowns, seeing he has his salary besides." Afterwards I led him up to other works in silver and gold, and a good many models for new things I had in mind to do. Then just before he left, in my castle meadows I showed him the great giant, which struck him as more wonderful than anything else. Turning to his Admiral, who was called Monseigneur d'Annebault, he said, "Since the Cardinal has given him nothing, we must needs provide for him, as he himself is slow at asking. So, in a word, I wish provision to be made for him; for men who are wont to ask for nothing think that their works speak out their demands. Therefore give him the first vacant abbey worth two thousand crowns a year; and if one does not amount to that, then let him have two, or three, for it will not matter to him." I was present and heard everything; and I thanked him on the spot, as if the property were already mine. Then I told him that, when this provision should be made for me, my only desire was to labour for his Majesty, without other reward, or salary, or payment, till by force of old age I could no longer work. Then I should rest my tired body, and live in peace and honour on that provision, never forgetting I had served so great a King as his Majesty. At these words the King turned towards me, and with a smile upon his face, said in a hearty voice, "So be it." Then he went off in great good humour.

xl. When Madame d'Etampes heard how well I was getting on, she grew still more bitter against me, saying to herself, "To-day I rule the world; yet a little man like that does not care a rap for me!" And she used every means she could think of to hurt me. Now she happened upon a certain man, a great distiller, who prepared scented waters for her, which were of marvellous power against wrinkles, and never before used in France. She sent him to show some of his distillations to the King, who was much delighted with them. Seeing he had given his Majesty pleasure, the fellow asked him to give him a tennis-court belonging to my palace, as well as a small suite of apartments, which he said I did not use. The good King, who could see to the bottom of the affair, returned no answer at all; but Madame d'Etampes used every kind of cajolery which ladies employ to conquer men, and she had no great difficulty in getting her own way. It needed only that she should find him once in an amorous temper—to which he was much inclined—and he gave in to Madame in everything. Well, the man came to my castle in the company of the treasurer Grolier, a great French noble. Grolier talked Italian excellently; so on this occasion he spoke to me in my own tongue in a jesting fashion. But after these preliminaries, just at the right moment, he said, "In the King's name I put this man in possession of the tennis-court, together with the apartments which go with it." To this

I answered, "Everything belongs to the Sacred King, and therefore you might have entered here more freely. Your coming with notaries and people of the Court has an air of trickery, and not at all of a straightforward commission from so great a King. Now I swear to you that, before I carry my complaints to his Majesty, I shall defend myself after the manner he advised me the other day; and for this man whom you have thrust upon me, I shall throw him out of the window, unless I see an express order in the King's own hand." At these words of mine the treasurer went off, threatening and muttering, and I stayed where I was doing the like. But I took no active measures then. Afterwards I went off to seek the notaries who had put the man in possession. They were well known to me; and told me that the due formalities had certainly been gone through with the King's authority, but that these were of no great importance; and that if I had made some little resistance, he would not have entered into possession as he had done, for these legal forms were acts and customs of the Court, which had nothing to do with obedience to the King; so that if I could manage to get rid of him as speedily as he had come in, I should be doing well, and not a word would be said against it.

All I needed was a hint like this; and next day I began to take violent measures, and though it was no easy matter, it gave me keen pleasure. Every day I attacked the invader with stones and pikes and arquebuses; and though I fired without balls, I struck such terror into the onlookers that not a man would go to his help. Then one day, finding his answer to my attack grown rather feeble, I entered the place by force and turned him out, throwing after him every stick of furniture he had brought with him. After that I set off to the King, and told him I had done exactly what he had ordered me to do: that is, I had defended myself against those who would hinder me in his service. His Majesty laughed heartily over the affair, and sent me new letters to guarantee me against molestation in the future.

xli. Meanwhile I was making haste to finish the fine silver Jupiter, as also the gilded base for it. This latter I had placed on a wooden plinth, which was hardly seen, fixing in the plinth four casters of hard wood, half hidden in their sockets, like the nut of a cross-bow. They were so delicately contrived that a little child could turn the statue round, or move it to and fro, without the least fatigue. Having arranged everything as I wished, I set off with it for Fontainebleau, where the King then was. Now about this time Bologna had brought back from Rome the statues I have spoken of, and had them cast in bronze with the greatest care. I knew nothing about it; first, because he had had the business done very secretly, and also because Fontainebleau is forty miles from Paris. When I asked the King where he wished me to place the Jupiter, Madame d'Etampes, who was present, said to him that there was no more suitable place for it than his fine gallery. This was what we should call a loggia in Tuscany—nay, more correctly, a corridor, for loggias should be open at one side. The place was more than a hundred paces long, and about twelve wide, and richly adorned with paintings by the hand of the admirable Rosso, our Florentine. Among the pictures were arranged a great many pieces of sculpture, some in the round, others in low relief. Now it was in this gallery also that Bologna had placed all his antique master-pieces, excellently cast in bronze; and he had arranged them beautifully, each one mounted on its pedestal; and, as I have already said, they were copied from the finest antiques in Rome. So when I brought my Jupiter into this same gallery, and saw the grand display, all arranged with such art, I said to myself, "This is being under a very hot fire. Now God be my aid!" So I set up my statue, placing it to the very best advantage possible; and then I waited till the great King came in. In his right hand my Jupiter grasped his thunderbolt, as if about to hurl it; in his left he held the world. Among the flames of the bolt I had skilfully inserted a white waxen torch. Now Madame d'Etampes kept the King away till night came on, seeking to harm me, either by preventing him from coming at all, or at least till darkness should hinder my work being seen to advantage. But God protects those who have faith in Him; and so just the contrary happened. For as soon as I saw night falling, I lit the torch in the hand of the Jupiter, and as it was somewhat raised above the head of the statue, the light fell from above and made it seem much more beautiful than it had appeared by daylight.

Well, the King appeared at last, with Madame d'Etampes, the Dauphin, his son (now the King), the Dauphiness, his brother-in-law, the King of Navarre, and Madame Marguerite, his daughter, besides several lords of the Court, who had been schooled by Madame d'Etampes to speak against me. When I saw his Majesty come in, I made my lad Ascanio push the statue gently forward; and as my contrivance was arranged with some skill, this movement gave to the striking figure an additional appearance of life. The antiques were now left standing somewhat behind; and mine was the first to catch the eyes of the spectators. The King exclaimed on the instant, "This is by far the finest thing which has ever been seen; and much as I delight in works of art and understand them, I could never have imagined the hundredth part of the wonder of this one." Even the lords, whose part it was to speak against me, seemed as if they could not praise my work enough. But Madame d'Etampes said boldly, "Surely you have no eyes! Do you not see the fine bronze antiques over there? In them is displayed the real power of the sculptor's art; not in this modern rubbish." Then the King came forward—the others following him—and glanced at the casts; but as the light was below them, they did not show up well, and he cried, "Whoever wished to harm this man has done him a great benefit; for this statue of his is now proved to surpass these wonderful figures with which it is compared. So Benvenuto cannot be made too much of; for not only do his works hold their own with the antiques, but they surpass them." Thereupon Madame d'Etampes said, if they were to see the work by day, it would not seem a thousandth part as fine as now it did by night; besides, they had to consider that I had put a veil over the figure to cover up its faults. Now this was a very thin veil, which I had gracefully hung over the Jupiter, to enhance its majesty. At her words I removed it, lifting it from below, and disclosing the fine genital members. Then, giving vent to my anger, I tore it to pieces. She thought I had uncovered these parts to shame her; but the wise King, seeing her anger, and perceiving, too, that I was overcome by passion, and was about to speak my mind, said, uttering the words deliberately in his own tongue, "Benvenuto, not a word. Keep silence, and you shall have a thousandfold more money than you can wish for." When I might not speak, I writhed in my rage, which made her mutter even more angrily; and the King went off much sooner than he would have done, saying aloud, to put heart into me, that he had brought out of Italy the greatest man that ever was born—one full of talents.

xlii. I left the Jupiter where it was, meaning to set off in the morning. Before my departure I was paid a thousand gold crowns, part being my salary, and the rest to make up for what I had spent out of my own purse. With this money in my pocket, I returned to Paris in good spirits; and as soon as I reached home I made merry in my own house. After dinner I had all my clothes brought me. Among them were garments of silk, the costliest furs, and the finest cloth. I made presents from among these to all my workmen, giving to each according to his merit, down to the maids and stable-boys, thus putting heart into them to help me with a good will.

Then being refreshed, with eagerness I set about finishing the great statue of Mars. First, I had a wooden frame made; on the top of that was spread a crust of gesso an eighth of a cubit thick, carefully modelled to represent the flesh. Then I worked on the several portions of the figure, which were to be dovetailed in afterwards, as the rules of the art demand. All this I did with the greatest ease.

I must not forget to give some indication of how large the figure was, which I can best do by telling you a very laughable occurrence. Now I had forbidden all my workmen to bring into my house, or into the precincts of the castle, any loose women; and I took good care that nothing of the kind was done. But my young Ascanio was in love with a very beautiful girl, and she was in love with him. So one night she ran away from her mother and came to see Ascanio. But she did not want to go away again; and he did not know where to hide her, till he bethought himself—being a person of resource—of putting her inside the figure of Mars. So in the head he arranged a corner for her to sleep; and there, indeed, she remained a long time; and sometimes by night he would bring her out noiselessly. Now the head was very nearly finished; and, out of sheer vanity, I used to leave it uncovered, so that it could be seen over the greater part of the city of Paris. The neighbours therefore began to climb on the roofs; and many persons came on purpose to see it. Now a story ran about that a ghost had for long haunted my castle, though I never saw anything to make me believe there was any truth in it. This ghost was called by all the people of Paris *Lei Moine Bourreau*. Now while the girl was living in the head, sometimes she could not prevent her movements being seen through the eyes. So some of the foolish people used to say that the ghost had entered into the body of the huge statue, causing the eyes and mouth and head to move, as if it were going to speak; and many of them flew away in terror; while even some shrewder folk who had come to investigate, could not deny the flashing of the eyes; and they, too, declared there was a spirit in it—never dreaming that there was not only a spirit, but good flesh and blood as well.

xliii. In the meanwhile I was hard at work putting together my fine door, with all the ornaments belonging to it. Now as

I have no mind to write down in this story of my life things that rather concern writers of chronicles, I have left untold the coming of the Emperor with his great army, and the King's marshalling all his forces. While this was going on, his Majesty sought my advice about the speediest way of fortifying Paris. He came to my house on purpose, and took me all round the city; and when he understood that I had a good plan in my head for the immediate execution of the work, he ordered me to carry it out at once; and told his Admiral to give orders to the people to obey me under pain of his displeasure. But the Admiral, who had got his appointment through the favour of Madame d'Etampes, and not for any service he had rendered, was a man of little ability. His name was Monsieur d'Annebault, which in our tongue means Monsignor Anniballe; but in theirs it sounds like Asino Bue, and so do they mostly call him. Well, this fool talked the matter over with Madame d'Etampes, who ordered him to send at once for Girolamo Bellarmato, a Sienese engineer, then at Dieppe, little more than a day's journey from Paris. He came at once, and began on the work of fortification by the very slowest method; so I retired from the business. And if the Emperor had pushed on, he could have taken Paris with the greatest ease. Indeed, it was said that in the treaty, which was signed later, Madame d'Etampes, who had more hand in it than any one else, betrayed the King. I need say no more on this matter, which does not fall within my purpose.

Well, I set to work with all my might to put my bronze door together, and to finish the large vase, as well as two others of medium size made out of my own silver. After his troubles the good King came to seek some repose in Paris. As that cursed woman was born to be the ruin of the world, I must have been of some consequence for her to have held me as her chief enemy. Now one day, talking with his Majesty about my affairs, she said such harm of me that the good man, to please her, swore henceforward to pay me no more attention than if he had never seen me. These words were reported to me at once by a page of the Cardinal of Ferrara, called il Villa, who told me he had heard them from the King's own mouth. This put me in such a rage that I threw all my tools about and everything I was working at, and made up my mind to be off for good. I went at once to see the King. After dinner I was shown into a room where his Majesty was seated with two or three others. On my entrance I made him due reverence; and he responded with a smile upon his face. So I took hope and slowly approached—for some things belonging to our art were being examined. When they had talked for a little while about them, the King asked me if I had anything fine to show him at my house, and when I should like him to come and see; whereupon I said that I was prepared to show him something on the instant, if he wished. He then bade me go home, and he would follow me.

xliv. So I went off to wait for the good King, who had gone to take leave of Madame d'Etampes. She wanted to know where he was going, and said she would bear him company; but when he told her, she declared she would not go, and begged him as a favour not to go either that day. But it was not till she had pleaded over and over again that she managed to turn the King from his purpose. So that day he did not come to me. Next day I went to him again at the same hour; and as soon as he set eyes on me he swore he would come to me without delay. But as usual he went to get leave of Madame d'Etampes, who saw that all her persuasion had not been enough to draw him from his intention. So she let loose her biting tongue to speak as much harm of me as if I had been a mortal enemy of the Crown. The good King replied that he wanted to pay me a visit, only that he might reprove me and make me tremble before him; and he gave his word to Madame d'Etampes that so he meant to do.

When he came to my house, I led him to certain large apartments on the ground floor, in which I had put together the whole of my large door. When he came upon it, the King was wonder-struck, so that he could not find utterance for the abuse he had promised Madame d'Etampes he would hurl at me. Still he did not want to fail altogether to find an opportunity of reproving me according to his promise. So he began thus: "There is a most important thing, Benvenuto, that men like you, full of talent though you are, should ever keep in mind. It is this: that with all your great abilities you can do nothing by yourselves. You can only show your greatness through the opportunities we put in your way. I counsel you, therefore, to appear more docile—less proud, less headstrong. I remember that I expressly ordered you to make me twelve silver statues; and I did not ask for anything else. You have undertaken to make a salt-cellar, and vases, and heads, and doors, and ever so many other things; so that I am quite overwhelmed, seeing all my particular wishes set aside, while you are bent on carrying out your own. So if you think you can go on like this, I'll soon let you see what I am wont to do, when I wish things done in my own way. Therefore I say to you: take care to obey the orders given you; for if you are obstinate in pursuing your own fancies, you'll be running your head against a wall." While he was saying these words, all his lords stood looking on intently; and when they saw him shake his head, and knit his brows, and gesticulate with both hands, they trembled for me. But I was resolved to be in no wise afraid.

xlv. This scolding he administered to me in accordance with his promise to his dear Madame d'Etampes; and when he brought it to an end, I knelt down and kissed his tunic above the knee, saying, "Sacred Majesty, I own all you say to be true; and can only say in reply that day and night my heart and all the forces of my soul have been ever intent on obeying and serving you; and if anything in my conduct seems to give the lie to what I say, I pray you believe that the blame lies not in Benvenuto, but that my unlucky star—or my evil fortune—has made me unworthy to serve the most magnificent prince the earth has ever seen. Therefore, I pray you, pardon me. One thing only I would urge. I thought your Majesty gave me silver for one statue only. Having no more by me, I could make no other. So with the little which was over I made that vase, to give your Majesty some idea of the fine antique style, of which perhaps you have never seen a specimen before. As for the salt-cellar, if I remember rightly, your Majesty, of your own accord, ordered it one day. You were discussing the merits of one which had been brought for your inspection. So I showed you a model which I had made in Italy; and then it was your own idea to give me at once a thousand gold ducats that I might carry out the work. You said, too, that you were grateful to me for the suggestion; but more particularly I recollect that you thanked me heartily when it was finished. As for the door, I am under the impression that once, when we chanced to be talking together, your Majesty gave an order to de Villeroy, your chief secretary, who passed it on to de Marmagne and Monsieur de la Fa. They were to see I did the work, and to make provision for it. Without such an order I should never on my own account have been able to take so great an enterprise in hand. Now for the bronze heads, the pedestal for the Jupiter, and the other things. Well, the heads I did on my own account, in order to test the French clays, which, as a foreigner, I did not know at all. Without experimenting with them I could not have taken in hand to cast those large works. The pedestals I made, because I thought that they were admirably suitable for the figures. So all I have done, I have done for the best, never dreaming I was deviating from your Majesty's command. True, I have made this great Colossus—so far as it has gone—on my own account, paying for it out of my own purse. But I thought that you being so great a king, and I but a poor artist, it became me to execute, for your glory and mine, a statue such as the ancients never possessed. Now knowing that it is not God's will to make me worthy of so honourable a service, I beg you, in lieu of the great reward which your Majesty had destined for my works, to grant me but a little goodwill, likewise, leave to take my departure. If this grace be given me, I will depart on the instant and return to Italy, ever grateful to God and your Majesty for those delightful hours spent in your service."

xlvi. He took me by the two hands, and raised me from my knees in the kindest manner possible. Then he told me that I should make up my mind to remain in his service; and all that I had done was good and altogether pleasing to him. And, turning to his lords, he said with great deliberation, "Verily I believe that Paradise could have no lovelier gate than this!" His bold words were all in compliment to me; but when he ceased speaking, I thanked him again with the utmost reverence, yet repeated my demand that he should let me go; for my anger had not all passed out of me. When the great King saw I hardly estimated at its full value his unwonted and remarkable courtesy, he commanded me in a loud and terrible voice to say not a word more; else I should repent it. Then he added that he would smother me in gold; that he gave me the leave I desired; and that after I had completed the works he had ordered from me, he would be perfectly satisfied to let me undertake anything on my own account. Never again should I have any difference with him, he declared, for now he knew me. On my part, I must strive to understand him; for such was my duty. I replied that I gave thanks to God and his Majesty for all; and then I begged him to come and see how I had got on with the great Colossus. So he came to my house. When I uncovered it, he was more wonderstruck than I can tell, and on the spot he ordered his secretary to pay me back all the money I had spent on it; whatever the sum might be, it was enough if I wrote it down in my own hand. Then he went away, saying, *Adieu, mon ami*, a great and unwonted honour from the lips of a king.

xlvii. After his return to his palace, he began thinking over the words I had used in speaking to him, which had been now extremely meek, and now so haughtily proud that they had greatly angered him. Some details of the conversation he related in the presence of Madame d'Etampes and Monseigneur de Saint Paul, a great French baron, who till now had always pretended to be a good friend of mine. Of a truth, this day he showed his friendship very cleverly, in the French fashion. For, after a deal of talk, the King complained that the Cardinal of Ferrara, to whose protection he had recommended me, had never given another thought to my affairs, and it was not his fault that I had not quitted France altogether. He must really think of giving me in charge to some one who took more interest in me; for he did not wish to run further risk of losing my services. At these words Monsieur de Saint Paul offered himself as my protector, promising he would take such steps as should prevent me ever leaving the kingdom. The King replied that he would be very pleased, if Saint Paul would tell him the means he meant to take against my escape. Madame, who was present, sat there frowning; and Saint Paul stiffly refused to tell the King what he meant. His Majesty repeated the question; whereupon Saint Paul, just to please Madame d'Etampes, said, "I would hang that Benvenuto of yours by the neck; and so you should always keep him in your kingdom." At this Madame d'Etampes burst out laughing, and declared I well deserved it. So the King laughed, too, for company's sake, and said he'd be quite satisfied for Saint Paul to hang me, if first he found him my equal; and that, though I never deserved hanging, he gave him full leave to try. Thus did the day end; and I remained safe and sound, for which all praise and thanks be to God!

xlviii. By this time the King had made peace with the Emperor; but he was still fighting with the English; and those devils were giving us a great deal of worry. So his Majesty had other things than pleasures in his head. He had ordered Piero Strozzi to lead certain galleys into the English seas. Now this as was a very great and difficult undertaking, even for that marvellous soldier, unique in his time and his profession, and unfortunate as he was distinguished. Thus several months went by without my receiving any money or any order for work, so that I sent away all my workmen save the two Italians, whom I employed upon the great vases made out of my own silver—for they did not know how to work in bronze. As soon as they were finished, I went off with them to a town belonging to the Queen of Navarre, called Argentan, a few days' journey from Paris. When I reached there, I found that the King was ill. The Cardinal of Ferrara told him I had come; but he said nothing in reply; so that I had to remain there for days, not knowing what to do with myself. To tell the truth, I never was more disgusted. But after some little time I presented myself one evening to the King, and placed before him the two fine vases, which pleased him vastly. When I saw him thus amiably disposed to me, I begged his Majesty to be good enough to give me permission to make a journey into Italy, saying that I would leave the seven months' salary due to me, and his Majesty might deign to pay this up, should I need it for my return. I begged him earnestly to grant me this favour, saying it was a time for fighting, not for making statues. Besides, he had been pleased to give such permission to his painter Bologna; and so I entreated him to grant a like favour to me. While I was speaking, the King looked intently at the two vases, but every now and then he stabbed me with his terrible eye. Nevertheless, as persuasively as I could, I kept on begging this grace, till all at once I saw him get angry. Then he rose from his chair, and, speaking to me in Italian, he said, "Benvenuto, you are a big fool. Take your vases back to Paris, for I wish them gilded." And with never another word he left me.

Going up to the Cardinal of Ferrara, who was present, I begged him, since he had done me so great a service in freeing me from the Roman prison, and had helped me in many ways besides, to do one more thing for me—get me leave to go back to Italy. The Cardinal replied that he would willingly do all he could to oblige me, and that I might leave the matter in his hands. Indeed, if I wished, I might set off now, and he would explain matters satisfactorily to the King. I answered that I knew his Majesty had given me in charge to him; and if his reverend lordship gave me leave, I should depart with an easy mind, and come back at the slightest sign from him. Then he told me to return to Paris, and stay there for eight days; by that time he should have obtained leave from the King for me to be off. Should his Majesty be unwilling, he would not fail to warn me. It was agreed that if he did not write me to the contrary, it would be a sign that I was free to depart.

xlix. So to Paris I went, as the Cardinal had told me. There I made some serviceable cases for the three silver vases. When twenty days had passed, I made my preparations, packing my vases on a mule lent me as far as Lyons by the Bishop of Pavia, whom I was again lodging in my castle.

So in an unlucky hour I set off, together with Signor Ippolito Gonzaga, who was in the King's pay and in the service of Count Galeotto della Mirandola. Several other gentlemen belonging to the Court were also with us, as well as Lionardo Tedaldi, our own countryman. I left Ascanio and Pagolo behind in charge of my castle and all my property, among which were several little vases already begun. These I left so that the two young men might have something to work at. There was a great deal of valuable furniture besides; for I had lived there in great state. In all, my property was worth more than fifteen hundred crowns. I bade Ascanio remember all the benefits he had received from me. Up till now he had been a heedless boy; but the time had come for him to think like a man. Therefore I was to leave all my property in his charge, and my honour too; and if those beasts of Frenchmen proved themselves vexatious in any way whatsoever, he was to let me know at once, and I should come post-haste from wherever I might be, both to fulfil the great obligation I was under to the good King, and also to preserve my own honour. Then Ascanio feigned to weep—rascal that he was!—and said, "You have been the best of fathers to me; and everything which becomes a good son to do for his dear father I will always do for you." So it was agreed; and I set off, attended by a servant and a little French boy.

Just after midday there came to my castle certain of the royal treasurers, who were not exactly friends of mine. Those mean scoundrels declared I had gone off with his Majesty's silver; and ordered Messer Guido and the Bishop of Pavia to send after me at once and seize the King's vases. If not, they would send a messenger themselves; and it would be the worse for me. The Bishop and Messer Guido were much more frightened than they need have been, and they sent that traitor Ascanio post-haste after me. He turned up about midnight. Now I was not sleeping but was lying lamenting my fate. "To whom am I leaving my property and my castle?" I was saying. "Oh, what a cruel destiny is mine, which forces me to take this journey! Pray God that the Cardinal be not leagued with Madame d'Etampes, who desires nothing so much in the world as that I should lose the favour of the good King."

l. While this strife was going on within me, I heard Ascanio call me, and in a moment I was out of bed and asking him if he brought me good or bad news. "Good news," answered the rascal. "Only, you must send back the three vases; for those rascally treasurers are shouting 'Stop thief!' and the Bishop and Messer Guido say you must certainly restore them. Otherwise do not worry yourself, but set off cheerfully on your journey."

I gave up the vases at once, though two of them were my own, even to the silver of which they were made and everything about them. I was taking them to the Abbey of the Cardinal of Ferrara at Lyons. For though they declared I was carrying them off into Italy, everybody knows perfectly that one can't take money, or gold, or silver out of the country without special leave. I would have you think, then, if I could get out of France with those three great vases, which, in their cases, made up the whole load of a mule. It is quite true that, as these things were very beautiful and of great value, I feared for the death of the King—for I had certainly left him very much indisposed—and had said to myself, "Should such a thing take place, if I put them into the hands of the Cardinal, I shall not then lose them!" So now to be brief; I sent back the mule with the vases and other things of importance, and next morning I set forward with my companions; but the whole way I could not keep from sighing and weeping. Yet at times I found comfort in God, saying, "Lord God, Thou to whom all truth is known, knowest that this journey of mine is only undertaken to bring succour to six poor wretched maidens and their mother, who is my sister after the flesh. Though they still have their father, he is very old, and makes nothing at his trade, so that they might easily go to ruin. Therefore in this pious work I hope for aid and counsel from Thy Majesty." No other comfort had I save this as I went upon my road.

When we were a day's journey from Lyons, about twenty-two o'clock, the thunder began to rattle in the sky, though the air was clear as possible. I was a bow-shot in front of my companions. After the thunder, so great and terrible a noise was heard in the heavens, that, for me, I thought the Day of Judgment was at hand. I stopped for a time, and hail began to fall without a drop of rain, larger than chalk-balls from an air-gun. When they fell on me they hurt me greatly. Gradually they became bigger, till they were like balls from a cross-bow. My horse was terrified; so I turned him about and galloped as furiously as I could till I found my companions, who had withdrawn into a pine wood in their fright. The hailstones were now as big as lemons. I began to sing a Miserere; and while I was thus speaking devoutly to God, there fell one of such a size that it snapped a huge branch of the pine-tree under which I had thought myself safe. Another fell on my horse's head and almost knocked it down. Then one hit me, but not directly, else I should have been a dead man. At the same time poor old Lionardo

Tedaldi, who was kneeling like me, was struck so hard that he fell on all-fours. Then I saw that the branch was no longer a shelter, and that one must do something besides singing Misereres. So I began to wrap my garments around my head, and I told Lionardi, who was crying " Jesus! Jesus!" at the top of his voice, that Jesus would help him if he helped himself. It was more trouble to save him than to save myself. The fury of the storm lasted for a considerable while; but it stopped at last; and, all bruised as we were, we got upon our horses as best we could. While we were riding towards a lodging, we showed each other our scars and our bruises. But when we had gone a mile, we found the marks of much greater damage than we had suffered; indeed, our eyes were met by a scene of ruin which is impossible to describe. All the trees were stripped and broken; the beasts that had been out in the storm were killed, and many shepherds too. And we saw hailstones so big that you could not have spanned one with your two hands. We thought we had come off well; and owned then that calling on God and repeating the Misereres had served us better than if we had only tried to save ourselves by our own strength. So, with thanks to God, we set off for Lyons, reaching it next day; and there we put up for a time. At the end of eight days, when we were well rested, we set off once more on our journey, and with great ease we crossed the mountains. On the other side I bought a little pony; for the luggage I carried had rather overstrained my horse.

li. We had been one day in Italy when we were joined by the Count Galeotto della Mirandola, who was going on by post, and who put up at our inn. He told me that I had made a mistake in leaving, and that I should go no farther; for, were I to return, my affairs would go better than ever; but if I continued my journey, I was leaving the field to my enemies, and giving them full chance to work me harm. Whereas, he said, going back at once, I should put a spoke in their wheel, and hinder their further plots against me. Those, he went on, whom I trusted most were those who were playing me false. He would say no more, save that this he knew for a certainty, and that the Cardinal was in league with those two rascals of mine whom I had left in charge of all my property. And so he went on and on, repeating that I should certainly return. Then, mounting on the post, he set out on his way; and I, acting on the advice of my companions, made up my mind to go forward also. But strife was raging in my heart. Now I was fain to make for Florence with all speed, and now to go back to France. This irresolution fevered me so that I forced myself to a decision, which was to mount on the post and arrive as quickly as possible at Florence. My plan of travelling by the first post fell through; nevertheless I was still determined to press on and meet my troubles in Florence. So I parted from Signor Ippolito Gonzaga, who took the road for Mirandola, while I turned off towards Parma and Piacenza.

When I reached Piacenza, I met Duke Pier Luigi in the street, who stared me up and down, and recognised me. He had been the sole cause of all the wrong I had suffered in the castle of St. Angelo; and now I fumed at the sight of him. But not knowing any way of avoiding him, I made up my mind to go and pay him a visit. I arrived at the palace just as the table was being cleared. With him were some men of the house of Landi, those who were afterwards his murderers. When I came in, he received me with the utmost effusiveness; and among other pleasant things which fell from his lips was his declaration to those who were present that I was the greatest man in all the world in my profession, and that I had been a long time in prison in Rome. Then, turning to me, he said, "Benvenuto, my friend, I was much distressed at what you suffered, and I knew that you were innocent, but I could do nothing to help you in any way. For my father did it to satisfy certain enemies of yours, who, besides, gave him to understand that you had spoken ill of him —though I know for a certainty that there was not a word of truth in it. I was, indeed, very sorry for you." And so he went on, repeating things like these, till it looked as if he were begging my pardon. Afterwards he asked me about all the work I had done for the most Christian King; and while I was telling him, he listened attentively, giving me the most gracious audience possible. Then he asked me if I would like to serve him, to which I answered that I could not honourably undertake to do so; but that if I had completed the important works I had begun for the great King, I would leave any other prince, whosoever he might be, to serve his Excellency. Now here may be seen how the great God of Power never leaves unpunished those who work injustice on the innocent. For this man in some sense begged my pardon, in the presence of those who afterwards wreaked their vengeance on him, on my account, and on account of many another maltreated by him. And thus no one, be he ever so great a lord, should mock at God's justice—as do some whom I know, who have done me brutal wrong too, as I shall tell all in good time. And I write these things not out of vain conceit, but solely in gratitude to God, who has saved me from so many dangers. Likewise, in those perils which menace me every day, I tell all my grief to Him, and call on Him, and entreat Him to be my defender. And it ever happens—after I have helped myself as best I can, and yet my spirit is weak, and my feeble forces do not come up to my aid—that suddenly the great power of God is made visible, and, all unforeseen, descends on the wrongdoers, and on such as give little heed to the great and honourable duties which God has laid upon them.

lii. When I returned to my inn, I found the Duke had sent me an abundant provision of food and drink of exquisite quality, and I ate with a good appetite. Then, mounting my horse, I turned my face towards Florence. When I reached there, I found my sister with her six young daughters. One of them was of marriageable age, and one was still at nurse. My brother-in-law, in consequence of various unfortunate happenings in the city, worked no longer at his trade. More than a year before I had sent stones and French jewellery to the value of more than two thousand ducats; and what I brought with me was worth about a thousand crowns. I found that, though I had given them regularly four gold crowns a month, yet they always drew on the money which came from the sale of the jewellery. My brother-in-law was such an honest man that when the allowance I sent was not enough, for fear of vexing me, he chose to pawn nearly all he had in the world, and to let himself be eaten up by usurers, in his endeavour to leave untouched the money which was not meant for him. By this I knew he was a very honest man; so I was desirous to make him a better allowance, and, before leaving Florence, to provide for all his daughters.

liii. It was now the month of August 1545; and our Duke was living at Poggio a Cajano, about ten miles from Florence. So there I went to see him, merely in the course of my duty—since I, too, was a Florentine citizen; since my ancestors were very friendly with the house of Medici, and I as much as any man loved Duke Cosimo. So, as I say, I went to Poggio only to pay my respects, and with not the least intention of stopping with him—as it pleased God, who doeth all things well, that I should do. When I came into the Duke's presence, he received me with great kindness; and then he and the Duchess asked me all about the work I had been doing for the King. With the greatest good-will I explained everything bit by bit. He listened, and then replied he had heard it was indeed so, adding, with a gesture of compassion, "A poor reward for all your great labours!

Benvenuto, my friend, if you were to undertake work for me I should pay you very differently to that King of yours, of whom, out of your good-nature, you speak so well." To this I replied by explaining the great obligations I was under to his Majesty, who had first freed me from an unjust prison, and then given me such a chance of making wonderful masterpieces as had never fallen to the lot of any of my artist peers. While I was speaking thus, the Duke writhed with impatience, and looked as if he could hardly stay to hear me out. When I had finished, he said, "If you will work for me, I will give you such rewards as may perhaps astonish you—provided the result pleases me, and of that I have no doubt at all." And so, poor unlucky wight! wishing to prove to the masters of our wonderful school, that since I left Florence I had been striving for success in other departments of art besides those which they deemed mine, I answered that I would willingly make a great statue in marble or in bronze for his fine piazza. To this he replied that, to begin with, he would like from me a Perseus. This had been long in his mind; and he begged me to make a model of it for him. So I set to the task with great goodwill, and in a few weeks I had finished it. It was made of yellow wax, about a cubit in height, and very delicately wrought; for I had given all my best skill and knowledge to the making of it. The Duke returned to Florence; but several days went by before I could show him the model. Indeed, from his indifference you might have judged he had never seen or heard of me; and this boded ill, I thought, for my dealings with his Excellency. However, one day after dinner I took my model to the Wardrobe; and he came to see it along with the Duchess and some lords of his court. As soon as he set eyes on it, he was so pleased, and praised it so extravagantly that I had good hope of having found in him a patron of some discrimination. He examined it for a long time with ever-growing delight, and then he said, "Benvenuto, my friend, if you were to carry out this little model on a large scale, it would be the finest thing in the Piazza." Thereupon I replied, "My most excellent lord, in the Piazza are works by the great Donatello and the marvellous Michael Angelo, the two greatest men since the ancients. Nevertheless, as your most illustrious Excellency is so encouraging to my model, I feel within me the power to do the complete work three times as well." These words of mine stirred up a deal of argument; for the Duke kept saying that he understood such things perfectly, and knew just what could be done. I replied that my work would decide this dispute and his doubt, though most certainly I should achieve more for his excellency than I had promised him. Then I asked him to give me the means of carrying out the undertaking, as otherwise I could do nothing. The Duke replied that I should draw up a formal demand, stating precisely my wants, and he would order these to be amply provided for. Now of a truth, if I had been shrewd enough to obtain by contract all I needed for my work, I should have escaped the great annoyances which, by my own fault, I afterwards experienced. For he seemed most determined to have the work done, and to make the necessary preparations for it. But I, who did not know that his lordship was more of a merchant than a duke, treated with him most liberally, as duke rather than merchant. I drew up the petition, and it seemed to me that his Excellency most generously responded. In it I said, "Rarest of patrons, the real petition I make and the true contract between us do not consist in these words and writings. The essential is, that I succeed according to the word I have given. And when I have succeeded, I am as sure that your most illustrious Excellency will keep in good mind all he has promised me." The Duke was delighted with my words and my demeanour; and he and the Duchess heaped more favours on me than I can describe.

liv. As I had the greatest desire to begin my operations, I told his Excellency that I needed a house where I could set up my furnaces for work in clay and bronze, also in gold and silver, which required other arrangements. "For," said I, "I know you are well aware how ready I am to serve you in all these various departments, and that I need suitable rooms for the purpose." To prove to his Excellency how eager I was for his service, I had already found the house that suited me, in a very convenient part of the town. And because I did not want to annoy the Duke with demands for money or anything else till he had seen my work, I offered him two jewels which I had brought from France, and begged him to buy the house with them, and to keep them till I had earned the amount by my labours. The jewels had been exquisitely set by my workmen under my direction. He looked at them for some time, and then said with an air of utmost frankness, which roused false hopes in me, "Take away your jewels, Benvenuto. It is you I want, not them; and you shall have your house free." After that he wrote a rescript under my petition—I have kept it to this hour —to this effect: "*Let this house be seen. Find who is the owner, and what price he asks; for we wish to oblige Benvenuto.*" I thought this written order made me sure of the house; for I felt certain that my works would give far more satisfaction than what I had promised. His Excellency then gave the matter into the hands of Pier Francesco Riccio. He was a Prato man, and had been the Duke's tutor. I spoke to the brute, and told him all the things I wanted—for instance, I mentioned that in the garden I wished to build a workshop. But he gave the business over to a paymaster, a dried-up scarecrow of a man, called Lattanzio Gorini. A curious little object he was, with spidery hands, and a tiny voice that hummed like a gnat, and he crept about like a snail. As my ill-luck would have it, he sent to my house as much sand and lime and stones as would barely have built a dove-cot. Things seemed to be going at a rather chilly pace, and I began to feel alarmed. But then I said to myself, "Little beginnings sometimes lead to great ends." And, besides, I could not but be hopeful when I thought of all the thousands of ducats the Duke had thrown away on hideous works of sculpture done by that beast Buaccio Bandinelli. So I took heart and goaded Lattanzio Gorini to make him bestir himself; but I might as well have shouted to a blind boy driving a pack of lame donkeys. In spite of all the difficulties, by dint of using my own money, I had marked out the plan of the shop, and cut down trees and vines; according to my wont, hurrying on with the work eagerly—nay, furiously would be the better word.

On the other hand, I was dependent on Tasso the carpenter, a great friend of mine, whom I had commissioned to make a wooden frame on which to set up the great Perseus. This Tasso was a very clever man, the best, I think, in his craft. He was good-humoured and cheerful, too; and every time I went to him he met me with a laugh, and trolled out a ballad in falsetto. At this time my affairs in France seemed to be going very ill; and from those at home I could look for little profit, owing to the coldness of the Duke; so that I was nearly desperate. Yet he always forced me to listen to at least half his song, and after a little I even made merry in his company; and thrust my dismal thoughts as far from me as I could.

lv. I had arranged all the things I have spoken of; and my preparations for the great undertaking were well advanced—indeed I had already used some of the lime—when one day I was sent for in haste by the major-domo. I found him, after his Excellency's dinner, in the Clock hall. When I came in, I greeted him with the greatest respect; but his reception of me was most frigid. He asked me who had installed me in that house, and with whose authority I had begun to build on the premises; and said he was much astonished that I was so daring and presumptuous. I replied that his Excellency had put me in possession of the house; and that his lordship, in the Duke's name, had given the orders concerning the business to Lattanzio Gorini. Lattanzio had sent stone and sand and lime, and supplied everything I had asked for, and had said he was doing so by his lordship's orders. At this the brute turned on me with greater sharpness than before, and told me that neither I nor any of those I had named spoke the truth. Then I flew into a rage, and said to him, "Major-domo, so long as your Excellency speaks in accordance with the rank to which you have risen, I shall treat you with respect, and address you as submissively as I do the Duke. Otherwise I shall speak to you as to one Ser Pier Francesco Riccio." The man got in such a passion that I thought he was going mad there and then—even before the time appointed by Heaven—and he told me in the most insulting terms that he wondered greatly at himself for letting me speak at all to a man like him. At this I was roused to say, "Now listen to me, Ser Pier Riccio, and I'll let you know who are my equals. As for yours, they are pedagogues, just fit for teaching babes their A B C." At this the man's face grew distorted; he lifted up his voice and repeated his words still more insolently; whereupon I, too, put on a threatening air, and assuming something of his own arrogant tone, declared that my peers were worthy to speak with Popes, and Emperors, and great Kings; and that there were perhaps not two of us in the world, while a dozen of his sort could be met going out or in at any door. At this he jumped on a window seat in the hall, and ordered me to repeat once more the words I had said, which I did more hardily than before, adding that I did not care to serve the Duke any longer, and that I should return to France, which I was free to do. The brute stood dazed and ashen-coloured; and I took myself off in a towering rage, intending to shake the dust of Florence from my feet. And would to God I had carried out my intention!

His Excellency the Duke can have known nothing of this devilry at first; for not a sign did he make for several days, while I thrust all thoughts of Florence out of my head, save what concerned my sister and my nieces. I was making arrangements to leave them as well provided for as I could with the little I had brought with me. That done, I meant to return to France, and never think of seeing Italy any more. I had made up my mind to set off as speedily as possible, without leave from the Duke or any one else. But one morning the major-domo sent very humbly for me; and began one of his pedantic rigmaroles, in which I couldn't see any method, or art, or sense, or beginning or end. All I could make out was, he professed to be a good Christian, and he did not wish to cherish hatred towards any one; so he asked me, on the part of the Duke, what salary I desired for my maintenance. I stood there cool and collected, making no answer, for I had made up my mind not to remain. Getting no reply, he was shrewd enough to say, "Oh, Benvenuto, an answer is due to Dukes; and my message comes from his Excellency." As it came from his Excellency, I said I was quite willing to reply; and so he was to tell the Duke that I did not wish to play second fiddle to any of those in my profession whom he employed. Then the major-domo answered, "Bandinelli gets two hundred crowns as a retaining fee; so if you are content with the same, your salary is arranged." I said I was satisfied; and that what I earned over and above this should be given me when my work had been proved; and that I left it all to the good sense of his most illustrious Excellency. So against my will, I picked up the thread again, and set to work, the Duke heaping every imaginable favour upon me.

lvi. I very often received letters from France from my most devoted friend Messer Guido Guidi. These letters as yet had told me nothing that was not pleasant. My Ascanio also wrote, bidding me be of good cheer, for if anything of importance happened, he would let me know. But it was reported to the King how I was employed by the Duke of Florence. He was the most good-natured man in the world, and many a time used to say, "Why does not Benvenuto come back?" Then he made particular inquiries of my young men, both of whom said that, according to my letters, things were going well with me, and that I was not thinking of coming back again to serve his Majesty. The King got angry at these bold words, which never came from me, and said, "Since he has left us without any reason, we shall not ask him again. Let him stop where he is." And so those dishonest rascals got their own way in the matter; for once I was back in France, they would have been labourers under me again, as they were before, whereas, if I did not return, they remained free and in my place. So they did their best that I should not come back.

lvii. While I was having the workshop built for making the Perseus, I worked in a basement chamber. There I made the

Perseus of gesso, the same size as the finished statue was to be, intending to cast it from this mould. But when I saw that this method was a rather lengthy one, I resorted to another plan. By this time, I must tell you, there had been built, brick by brick, a miserable kind of a workshop, so wretchedly constructed that I can't bear to think of it. There I began the figure of the Medusa. First I made a framework of iron, then covered it with clay; and when that was done, I baked it. I had only some little apprentices to help me. One of these, a very handsome lad, the son of La Gambetta the prostitute, I used as a model, since no books teach art as does the human figure. I tried to secure workmen, that I might make speed with the business; but I could find none, and I could not do everything by myself. There were some in Florence who would have willingly come; but Bandinelli put a stop to that; and then after making me waste a deal of time, he told the Duke I was trying to steal away his workmen, because I found I should never be able to put together so large a figure by myself. I complained to the Duke how the brute annoyed me, and begged him to let me have some of the workmen belonging to the Opera del Duomo. But my words only convinced him of what Bandinelli had said; and seeing this I began to do my best unaided. While I was working thus day and night, my sister's husband took ill, and died after a few days, leaving my sister, who was still young, with six daughters, big and little, to my care. This was the first great trouble I had in Florence, being left father and guide of such an unhappy family.

lviii. Anxious that nothing should go wrong, I sent for two labourers to clear the rubbish out of my garden. They came from the Ponte Vecchio, one of them an old man of sixty, the other a lad of eighteen. When they had been with me about three days, the lad told me that the old man refused to work, and that I should do better to send him away; for not only did he do nothing himself, but he kept him from working also. He said that the little there was to do, he could do by himself, without throwing money away on any one else. This young man was called Bernardino Mannellini of Mugello. Seeing him so ready for hard work, I asked him if he would agree to be my servant; and the matter was settled on the spot. He took care of my house, worked in the garden, and afterwards learned to help me in the workshop; so that, bit by bit, he began to learn my art with great cleverness, and I never had a better helper. Thus, having resolved to do the whole business with only this young man's aid, I began to prove to the Duke that Bandinelli had been telling lies, and that I could get on excellently without any of his men.

About this time I suffered somewhat from an affection of the loins; and as I could not work, I was not ill pleased to hang about the Wardrobe of the Duke with certain young goldsmiths called Gianpagolo and Domenico Poggini. Under my orders they made a little gold vase, worked in low relief with figures and other lovely ornaments. It was for the Duchess. His Excellency had ordered it for her to drink water out of. He also asked me to make her a golden belt, which was to be very richly worked with jewels, and a great many charming masks and other things. This I also did. Every now and then the Duke would come into the Wardrobe; and he took the greatest pleasure in seeing me work and talking with me. When I got a little better, I sent for clay, and while the Duke was amusing himself there, I did his portrait larger than life. He was so satisfied with this work, and grew so fond of me, that he said nothing would please him better than that arrangements should be made for me to work in the palace. So he looked out large rooms where I could set up my furnaces and all my necessary apparatus; for he took the greatest interest in everything pertaining to my art. But I told his Excellency that it was not possible; for if I did so, I should not have finished the work I had undertaken in a thousand years.

lix. From the Duchess I received extraordinary kindness; indeed, she would have liked me to have given myself up entirely to her service, throwing Perseus and everything else aside. In the midst of these vain favours I knew full well that my perverse and cruel fortune would surely deal me a blow from some new quarter ere long; for I never lost sight of the blunder I had made while striving to do the thing that was best. I am speaking now of the French business. The King found it impossible to swallow his great vexation at my departure; yet would he gladly have had me back, if it could have been contrived with due regard to his dignity. But, feeling myself altogether in the right, I would not bend the knee, being convinced that were I to demean myself by writing humbly, those French ill-wishers of mine would, after their fashion, say I had owned myself in the wrong, and that certain misdeeds of which I had been unjustly accused, were now proved up to the hilt. Therefore I stood upon my dignity, and wrote in haughty terms, like a man with right upon his side. Nothing could have better pleased those two faithless apprentices of mine. In writing to them, I had vaunted the favours heaped on me by the lord and lady who held absolute sway in Florence, the city of my birth; and when they received these letters, off they would go to the King and beseech him to give them my castle, just as he had given it to me. His Majesty, who was an excellent man and very good-natured, would never agree to the audacious demands of those bandits; for he began to be aware of their villainous designs. But to keep them on tenterhooks, and give me a chance of coming back, he ordered his treasurer, Messer Giuliano Buonaccorsi, a Florentine citizen, to write me an angry letter to this effect: if I would still keep the name of honest man which I had borne, I was bound, seeing I had taken my departure without any cause, to render account of all my expenditure and work for his Majesty.

When I got this letter I was greatly pleased; nothing else could so have tickled my palate. Sitting down to answer it, I filled nine sheets of ordinary paper, narrating minutely all the works I had done, the adventures I had had with them, and the sums of money expended on them, which had always been paid to me by two notaries and one of the royal treasurers, and formally acknowledged in detail by all the men who had had money from me, either for material they had supplied, or for work they had done. I had not put a farthing of this money in my own pocket; nor had I had a penny for my finished work. All I had brought back with me to Italy were some tokens of favour and some altogether royal promises, in very truth worthy of his Majesty. "I cannot boast of having made anything out of my labours," I continued, "save some maintenance money agreed to by your Majesty; and even of that more than seven hundred gold crowns are still due, which I had purposely refrained from touching, that they might be held in reserve for my journey back. Yet, though evilly-disposed persons, from sheer envy, do me an ill turn, as I am well aware they have done, truth ever wins in the end. I glory in your most Christian Majesty, and am not moved by avarice. Moreover, though I know I have done much more for you than I promised, and the recompense agreed on has not followed, yet I have but one care in the world—to remain, in the opinion of your Majesty, the honest, upright man I have ever been. If your Majesty has the smallest doubt about this, you have but to lift a finger and I shall come flying to render an account of myself, even at the risk of my life. But seeing in what little respect you hold me, I have been unwilling to return and offer my services, aware that I shall never lack bread wherever I go. Yet were I to be called, I should always respond." In this letter there were, besides, other particulars worthy of the great King's notice, and necessary to be stated for the maintenance of my honour. Before I sent it off I took it to my Duke, who was pleased to read it. Then I addressed it to the Cardinal of Ferrara, and sent it to France.

lx. Now about this time Bernardone Baldini, his Excellency's jewel-agent, brought from Venice a large diamond weighing more than thirty-five carats. And Antonio, son of Vittorio Landi, was also interested in the Duke's buying it. The stone had once been cut in a point; but as it did not radiate the limpid splendour which was to be expected from it, its owners had blunted it; and in truth it was not suitable for table-cutting or for point. Now our Duke, who took the greatest delight in jewels, though he knew nothing about them, led that villain Bernardaccio to expect he would buy the diamond; and as the scoundrel was keen to have all the honour to himself of cheating the Duke of Florence, he never said a word about it to his comrade, Antonio Landi. This Antonio had been a great friend of mine from boyhood; and now when he saw I was very intimate with the Duke, he called me aside one day (it was near noon, and at the corner of the New Market), and spoke to me thus: "Benvenuto, the Duke will doubtless show you a diamond which he seems to wish to buy. You will see that it is a large one. Help on the sale of it. I tell you I can give it for seventeen thousand crowns. I am sure he will want your advice; and if you see he is inclined for it, I can manage to let him have it." Antonio seemed to be quite certain of his ability to negotiate the jewel. I made reply that should it be shown to me, and my opinion of it asked, I should say exactly what I thought, without prejudice to the stone.

Well, as I have said before, the Duke came every day to our shop and stayed several hours; and more than a week after Antonio Landi had spoken to me, he showed me the very diamond, one day after dinner. I knew it from certain particulars which Landi had mentioned respecting its shape and weight. Now, as I have said above, this diamond gave out a somewhat filmy radiance—for which reason its point had been blunted; and seeing its quality, I was in a mind to disadvise so much money being spent on it. However, when it was shown me, I asked his Excellency what he wished me to say; because for jewellers to value a gem after a nobleman has bought it, and to value it when its purchase is in question, are two very different things. Then his Excellency said the purchase was concluded, and I was only to say what I thought of it. I could not but point out modestly the little I knew about the stone; but he told me to take note of the beauty of its great facets; whereupon I replied that this was no such beauty as his Excellency fancied, but was only the result of the point being blunted. At this, my lord, who was well aware I was speaking the truth, frowned in displeasure, and ordered me to give my mind to valuing the jewel and tell him what I thought it was worth. Now I counted that, since Antonio Landi had offered it to me for seventeen thousand crowns, the Duke might have had it for fifteen thousand at the most; and perceiving he would take it ill were I to tell him the truth, I resolved to back him up in his mistake. So handing him the diamond, I said, "Eighteen thousand crowns you'll perhaps have given for it." At this he bawled out, "Oh!" with a mouth as big as a well. "Now I am sure," said he, "that you know nothing about it." And I replied, "Of a truth, my lord, you are mistaken. It is for you to vaunt the qualities of your diamond; a knowledge of its value is my business. Tell me at least what you gave for it, that I may learn to understand, after your Excellency's fashion." Then the Duke got up and said angrily, "Five and twenty thousand crowns and more, Benvenuto, did it cost me." Then he went away.

While we had been speaking, Gianpagolo and Domenico Poggini, the goldsmiths, were standing by; and the embroiderer, Bachiacca, who was working in an adjoining room, ran in to us on hearing the noise. So I said, "I should never have advised him to buy it; but yet if he was bent on having it, Antonio Landi offered it to me a week ago for seventeen thousand crowns and I believe I might have had it for fifteen, or less. But the Duke insists on putting a high value on his diamond. When Antonio Landi offered it to me for the price I have named, how the devil could Bernardone have over-reached his Excellency in that shameful way?" And so, utterly disbelieving that the Duke had told the truth, we laughed at his simplicity and let the matter slide.

lxi. I was getting on with my great statue of Medusa. As I have said, I had made a framework of iron. Then I laid on the clay, according to the anatomy of the figure, about half an inch thinner than the finished figure was meant to be. Afterwards I baked it well, and spread wax on the top, modelling this with the utmost care. The Duke, who often came to see it, was so afraid I might fail with the bronze, that he would have liked me to call in some master to cast it for me. But he was ever speaking with enthusiasm of my skill, which made his major-domo be always on the look-out how he could lay a trap to make me break my neck. He had authority over the high constables and all the offices in our poor, unhappy city of Florence. He, a Prato man, our enemy, a cooper's son, an ignoramus, just because he had been the mouldy old pedagogue of Cosimo de' Medici before he was Duke—he to be given such power, forsooth! Now, as I have said, always on the outlook to do me an injury, but seeing nowhere a pretext, he invented one. He went to see the mother of my apprentice boy Cencio; and between them— that rascally pedant and that cheat of a whore, Gambetta—they plotted to give me such a scare as would force me to flee from Florence. The Bargello, too, a Bolognese—afterwards dismissed by the Duke for plots of this kind—was leagued with them. Gambetta, instigated by that rascally fool of a pedagogue, the major-domo, came one Saturday evening, three hours after nightfall, to see me, bringing her son; and told me she had kept him shut up at home for several days for my good. I replied that, so far as I was concerned, she need not keep him shut up; and laughing at her bawdish tricks, I turned to the boy and said to him before her, "You know, Cencio, if I have done you any harm." He began to cry, and said, "No." Then his mother, shaking her head at him, said, "Ah, you little rascal, perhaps I don't know anything about it, eh?" Then turning to me, she bade me hide him in my house; for the Bargello was looking for him, and would take him anywhere outside my place; but there they would not dare to lay hands on him. To this I answered that in my house my widowed sister lived, and her six virgin daughters, and I wanted nobody else. Whereupon she said that the major-domo had given orders to the Bargello, and I should surely be arrested. But since I did not want to take the boy into my house, if I were to give her a hundred crowns, I might set my mind at rest; for the major-domo was a very great friend of hers, and I might be sure she would make him do whatever she pleased—always provided I gave her the money. By this time I was in a fury of rage. "Out of my sight," I cried, "you shameful whore! Were it not for respect to the world, and for the innocence of this unhappy boy you have here, I'd have cut your throat by now with this dagger of mine. More than once I've had my fingers on it." With these words, and many a hard knock besides, I drove her and her son out of my house.

lxii. When I thought over the villainy and also the power of that wicked pedagogue, I judged it best to let this scandal spend itself. So next morning early, having given my jewels and other things, amounting to nearly two thousand crowns, into my sister's keeping, I got upon my horse and set off towards Venice, taking with me Bernardino di Mugello. As soon as I reached Ferrara, I wrote to his Excellency the Duke that, though I had gone away without being sent, I should return without being called.

On my arrival at Venice, I reflected on all the various ways my cruel fortune chose to torture me. Nevertheless, feeling lusty and gay, I resolved to face her, fighting as usual. And though my own private affairs gave me much food for thought, yet I took my diversion about that beautiful and magnificent city, and went to pay my respects to the marvellous painter Titian, also to Jacopo del Sansovino, the admirable sculptor and architect, and one of our Florentines, who was handsomely maintained by the Signory of Venice. We had known each other when young, in Rome, and, of course, in Florence too, of which he was a citizen. Both of those great artists gave me the kindest reception. Next day I fell in with Messer Lorenzo de' Medici, who thereupon took me by the hand in the heartiest fashion possible; for we had known each other in Florence when I was making Duke Alessandro's money, and later in Paris, when I was in the service of the King. He had been living then in the house of Messer Giuliano Buonaccorsi; and since he had nowhere else to go for amusement, save at the greatest danger of his life, he took to spending the most of his time with me, watching me at work on some large plate I had in hand. So, as I say, on account of our acquaintance in the past, he took me now by the hand, and brought me to his house, where I saw the Lord Prior degli Strozzi, brother of my lord Piero. We had a merry meeting, and they asked me how long I meant to stay in Venice, believing me to be on my way back to France. I made answer to these gentlemen that I had left Florence for a particular reason—which I have already explained—and that in two or three days I meant to go back to the Duke's service. When I told them this, my lord Prior and Messer Lorenzo turned on me with such severity that I felt greatly alarmed. "You would do better," they said, "to return to France, where you are rich and famous; for to go back to Florence is to lose all you have gained in

France; and you will draw nothing from your stay there save vexations." I made no answer; but set off the next day, as secretly as possible, on my way back to Florence. In the meantime that devilish scandal had blown over; for I had written to my great Duke an explanation of the circumstances that had driven me to Venice. It was with his usual distant and severe manner he received me when I went to pay him an informal visit. This humour lasted some time, and then he turned towards me pleasantly, and asked me where I had been. I replied that my heart had never travelled an inch away from his most illustrious Excellency; only some good reasons had forced my body to go a-wandering. Then, relaxing more and more, he began to ask me about Venice; and thus we talked for a while. At last he bade me stick to my work, and finish his Perseus for him. So I went back home glad and light of heart, rejoiced my family, that is, my sister and her six daughters, took up my work again, and brought it forward with all the energy I possessed.

lxiii. The first thing I ever cast in bronze was the large portrait bust of his Excellency, which I had modelled in clay in the Pogginis' workshop, while I had the pain in my back. It was a work that gave much pleasure, yet I only did it to gain experience in clays suitable for casting in bronze. I knew that the wonderful Donatello had used Florence clay for casting his bronzes; but it seemed to me that he had worked under tremendous difficulties. This I believed to be due to some defect in the clay; so before beginning to cast my Perseus, I wished first to make some experiments. These taught me that the clay was good; only the admirable Donatello had not quite understood it: for I saw that his works had been cast with endless difficulty. So, as I have mentioned, I compounded the clay by a special process, and found it most serviceable. Then, as I have said, I cast the head with it. As I had as yet made no furnace, I used that of Maestro Zanobi di Pagno, the bell-founder. When I saw that the bust came out with great precision, I began without delay to set up a small furnace in the shop which the Duke had had arranged for me, according to my own plan and design, in the house which he had given me. As soon as the furnace was ready, with all haste possible I made my preparations for casting the statue of Medusa, that woman writhing under the feet of Perseus. The casting was a matter of the utmost difficulty; and to avoid any mistake, I determined to use all the knowledge I had been at such pains to acquire. Thus the first cast I made in my little furnace was perfectly successful; and so clean was it that my friends thought there was no need for me to touch it up again. Of course, certain Germans and Frenchmen, who plume themselves on knowing wonderful secrets, declare they can cast bronze so that it needs no retouching; but this is foolish talk; for after bronze has been cast, it must be worked on with hammers and chisels in the fashion of the marvellous antique masters, and of the moderns too; at least, such moderns as have learnt anything at all about the matter. His Excellency was so much pleased that several times he came to my house to see it, thus putting heart into me to do my best. But the rabid envy of Bandinello, who was always whispering harm of me in the Duke's ears, had such influence on him, that he was persuaded to think my having cast a single statue was no proof I could put the whole together. It was a new art to me; and his Excellency should take heed lest he was throwing his money away, he said. Words like these breathed in the ears of my glorious Duke, so swayed him that certain moneys for service were disallowed me after this, so that I was forced to expostulate somewhat warmly with his Excellency. One morning, therefore, when I had waited for him in the Via de' Servi, I said to him, "My lord, as I no longer receive my necessary supplies, I fear your Excellency has lost trust in me. But I assure you once more that I have it in me to carry out this work three times as well as the model. This, indeed, I have already promised you."

lxiv. I perceived that my words had no effect on his Excellency, for he made me no answer. Then all at once rage took hold on me; and I was filled with an intolerable heat of passion, which broke forth in these words: "My lord, this city has in truth ever been the school of noble genius. But when a man has become conscious of his power, and has won some little skill in his art, if he would fain enhance the honour of his city and of his glorious prince, he had best go and work elsewhere. And that this is so, my lord, I need not insist; for your Excellency knows what manner of men were Donatello and the great Leonardo da Vinci, and what are the powers of the marvellous Michel Agnolo Buonarroti in our own day. Their great talents have given increase to the glory of your Excellency. And so I, too, hope to do my part. Therefore, my lord, give me leave to go. But let your lordship be warned; and give no such leave to Bandinello. Let him have even greater rewards than he asks of you; for were he to go abroad, such is his presumptuous ignorance, that he would of a surety bring shame on our most noble school. Now give me leave to go, my lord; nor do I ask other recompense for my labours to this hour than the good-will of your most illustrious Excellency." When he saw I was in earnest, he turned to me with something like vexation, and said, "Benvenuto, if you have a mind to finish the work, you shall want for nothing." Then I thanked him, and said my one desire was to prove to those envious persons that I was man enough to carry through the work as I had promised. So I parted from his Excellency; and after this some trifling help was given me; but I was forced to dip into my own pocket, that the work might advance at even a moderate pace.

I was in the habit of spending the evening in his lordship's Wardrobe, where the brothers Domenico and Gianpagolo Poggini were working at a golden drinking-cup and at a golden girdle for the Duchess, which I have spoken of before. Besides, his Excellency had ordered from me a little model of a pendant in which was to be set the big diamond Bernardone and Antonio Landi had forced him to buy. In vain I shirked the thing; the Duke used such amiable persuasions that he made me work at it every evening till four hours after sundown. Indeed, with his insinuating speeches he would fain have forced me to work at it by day as well; but to this I refused to consent, though I felt certain I was thus bringing down his wrath upon my head. And so one evening, when I had come rather later than my wont, he gave me for greeting, "Unwelcome! [*Malvenuto*]." To which I replied, "My lord, such is not my name, but *Benvenuto* am I called. However, I think your Excellency must be jesting with me; and so I shall leave the matter." Whereupon he answered that he meant what he said; he was not jesting, and that I had better see to my behaviour; for it had come to his ears that, trusting to his favour, I cheated now one man, now another. Then I entreated his most illustrious Excellency to do me the justice of naming one single man whom I had ever cheated. Thereat he turned on me in anger with, "Go and give back what you have of Bernardone's. There's one man for you." To this I answered, "My lord, I thank you, and I beg you to do me the honour of listening to just three or four words I have to say. The truth is this: he lent me a pair of old scales, two anvils, and three little hammers. But a fortnight ago I told his man, Giorgio da Cortona, to send for these tools; and Giorgio came for them himself. And if your most illustrious Excellency finds, on the proven evidence of such as have reported these slanders, or of any one else, that from the day I was born till now, I have ever had anything from any man in the way you indicate, either in Rome or in France, then punish me unsparingly." When the Duke saw me thus moved by wrath, he turned to me like the discreetest and most affectionate master, and said, "My reproof was not meant for the blameless. And so, if it be as you say, you shall always be welcome to me as in the past." And I replied, "Be it known to your Excellency, that Bernardone's villainy forces me to ask, nay, to entreat you to tell me the price of the great diamond with the blunted point. Then I hope to show you why the miserable scoundrel seeks to bring disgrace on me." His Excellency answered, "The diamond cost me twenty-five thousand ducats. Why do you ask?" "Because, my lord, on such a day, at such an hour, at the corner of the Mercato Nuovo, Antonio, the son of Vittorio Landi, bade me try to do a deal with your most illustrious Excellency for it; and to begin with, he asked sixteen thousand ducats for it. Now your lordship knows what you bought it for. And for the truth of this, ask Domenico Poggini and his brother Gianpagolo, who are here; I told them at the time, and since then have never spoken of it; for, as your Excellency told me I knew nothing about the matter, I thought you wanted it to be considered of great value. I would have you know, my lord, that I do understand such things; and as to the other affair, I hold myself to be as honest as any man ever born into this world, be the other who he may. I will not seek to rob you of eight or ten thousand ducats at a stroke, but endeavour rather to gain them by my labours. I engaged to serve your Excellency as sculptor, goldsmith, and die-maker; a spy on the affairs of others—never! And what I now say, I say in my own defence, and want no informer's pay therefor. I speak out now in the presence of all these honest men here, that your Excellency may put no faith in what Bernardone tells you." The Duke rose up in sudden wrath, and sent for Bernardone, who had to flee as far as Venice, along with Antonio Landi. Antonio, by the way, explained to me that he had been speaking of quite another diamond.

After their flight to Venice and their return from thence, I went to see the Duke, and said to him, "My lord, what I told you was the truth; and what Bernardone told you about the tools was a lie. You would do well to bring this to the test, and I will betake me to the Bargello." The Duke replied, "Benvenuto, think only of being an honest man as in the past, and fear nothing." So the thing passed away in smoke, and I never heard it spoken of again. Meanwhile I set to finishing the jewel; and when one day I took it to the Duchess quite complete, she told me that she valued my workmanship as much as the diamond which Bernardaccio had forced them to buy. Then she desired me to attach it to her bosom with my own hand, and gave me a large pin for the purpose, with which I fastened it; and I took my leave high in her favour. Afterwards I heard that they had it set over again by a German or some other foreigner—though, if it be true, I know not—because Bernardone said the diamond would show better if set with more simplicity.

lxv. The brothers Domenico and Gianpagolo Poggini, the goldsmiths, were working, as I believe I have already said, in his Excellency's Wardrobe on some little gold vases after my design, with little figures chiselled in low relief, as well as other ingenious devices. Now many a time I said to the Duke, "My lord, if your Excellency would only pay some workmen, I should make the coins for your mint and medals with your head on them, too. I would compete with the ancients, with hope to surpass them; for since the time when I made the medals for Pope Clement, I have learnt so much that I can do far better. I can even outdo the coins I made for Duke Alessandro, which are still considered very beautiful. Besides, I could make for you great vases of gold and silver, like the many I did for the great King Francis of France; who made the work easy for me in every way, so that I wasted no time needed for great colossal statues or other works of sculpture." The Duke's answer was, "Go on then, and I shall see." But he never gave me either men or appliances or help of any kind.

One day his most illustrious Excellency supplied me with several pounds of silver, and said, "This is from my mines. Make me a fine vase." Now as I did not wish to stop working on my Perseus, and yet desired greatly to serve him, I gave it, with my designs and little models in wax, to a rascal called Piero di Martino, a goldsmith. He began it badly, and, besides, stopped working after a while; so that I lost more time than if I had done it with my own hand. When several months had been wasted like this, and I saw that Piero would neither work on it, nor let any one else do so, I made him return it to me; but it was only after the utmost efforts that I got back the body of the vase, so ill begun as I have said, and the rest of the silver I had given him. The Duke, who heard something of our bickerings, sent for the vase and for the models, and never told me why or wherefore. Enough that he gave some designs of mine to be carried out by various persons in Venice and other places, and was very badly served by them. The Duchess would often ask me to do goldsmith's work for her, to which I was wont to answer, that I was well known to everybody throughout all Italy for a skilful goldsmith; but that Italy had never yet seen sculpture from my hand. True, in the profession there were certain sculptors, mad with envy of me, who laughed at me, and called me the new sculptor. "I hope to show these," said I, "that I am an old sculptor, if God but give me grace to complete my Perseus, and set it up in his Excellency's magnificent Piazza." Then I retired to my house, and gave my mind to work day and night, never showing myself in the palace. But nevertheless I was fain to keep in the good graces of the Duchess; and therefore I had some silver vases made for her, about the size of those little pots you buy for a farthing, chased with lovely masks after the rarest antique fashion. When I took them to her, she received me with the greatest kindness imaginable; and paid for the silver and gold I had used for them. Then I recommended myself to her, and begged her to say to his Excellency that I had had little help in my great work, also to counsel him to trust less in that evil-tongued Bandinello, who was keeping me from completing my Perseus. The tears stood in my eyes as I uttered these words. The Duchess shrugged her shoulders, and said, "Surely the Duke must know this Bandinello to be a worthless creature."

lxvi. About this time I was staying much at home, rarely appearing at the palace, and working with the utmost energy to finish my statue. I was forced to pay the workmen out of my own purse; for the Duke, who had ordered Lattanzio Gorini to pay them for about eighteen months, got weary of the business, and withdrew the order. When I asked Lattanzio why he no longer paid me, he answered, shaking his spidery hands, and in his tiny buzzing voice like a gnat's, "Why do you not finish your work? It is believed you'll never carry it through." I answered him hotly and said, "The devil take you and all who believe I shall never finish the thing!"

In despair, I went home to my unfortunate Perseus, and not without tears; for I called to mind the favourable conditions of my life in Paris when I was in the service of the great King Francis. There I had everything and to spare; and here all was lacking. More than once I was inclined to give up in desperation. One of these bad days I mounted my pretty little horse, and with a hundred crowns in my pocket, I went off to Fiesole to see my natural son, whom I had put out to nurse with a gossip of mine, the wife of one of my workmen. When I reached the place, I found the little boy in good health, and with my heart full of grief, I kissed him. When I was for going away, he would not let me, holding me fast with his little hands, and bursting into a passion of tears and cries—a wonderful thing indeed, seeing he was only about two years old. Now in my desperate condition I had made up my mind, if I came upon Bandinello—who was in the habit of going every evening to a farm he had above San Domenico—that I would be the death of him. So I tore myself from my baby, leaving him crying there bitterly, and set my face towards Florence. I had just reached the Piazza of San Domenico, when Bandinello came up from the other side. Now was the moment for my deed of blood; but when I approached him and raised my eyes, I saw he was unarmed, riding on a miserable mule, no better than an ass; and with him was a boy of ten years old. As soon as he set eyes on me, he became pale as death, and shook from head to foot. Aware how vile such a deed would be, I called out, "Don't be afraid, you low coward; for I don't think you worth my blows!" He looked at me meekly and said never a word. Then I commanded my rage; and thanked God, who by His own strength had kept me from such a deed of violence. Thus having shaken off that devilish fury, I became myself again, and spoke thus: "If God lends me His grace so that I finish my work, I hope through its excellence to kill off all my rascally enemies; and thus shall my vengeance be far greater and more glorious than had I vented it all on one single man." And with this good resolution in my heart, I went home. At the end of three days I heard that my gossip had smothered my only son; and the news gave me as great grief as ever I have felt in all my life. However, I knelt down and, weeping, thanked God, according to my wont, saying, "Lord, Thou gavest him to me, and now Thou hast taken him; and for all I thank Thee from my heart." Though this great grief had almost overpowered me, yet I made a virtue of necessity, as is my habit, and as best I could resigned myself to facts.

lxvii. At the time I am speaking of a young fellow in Bandinello's service, one Francesco, the son of Matteo the smith, left him, and asked me if I had any work for him to do. I was agreeable; and sent him to touch up the figure of Medusa, which had been cast. About a fortnight later he told me he had been speaking with his master—I mean Bandinello,—who had sent me a message, that if I wished to do a figure in marble, he could give me a fine block. I answered at once, "Tell him I accept; and may it be a stumbling-block in his path; for he is always irritating me, forgetting how he was perilously in my power in the Piazza of San Domenico. So now tell him I certainly want the marble. I never speak of him, but the brute is always vexing me; and I verily believe that you came to work for me at his suggestion, just to spy on my doings. Well, go and tell him that I will have the marble willy-nilly; and mind you come back with it."

lxviii. It was long since I had put in an appearance at the palace; so I took it into my head to go one morning. The Duke had just almost finished dinner; and from what I heard, he had been talking of me that very morning, and most favourably. Among other things he had praised my talents for setting jewels very highly. Therefore when the Duchess caught sight of me, she sent Messer Sforza to call me. When I approached her Excellency, she begged me to set a diamond in point for a ring which she said she meant to wear always on her finger. She gave me the measurements, and also the diamond, which was worth about a hundred crowns, and asked me to do the thing speedily. Thereupon the Duke raised some objections, saying, "Quite true, Benvenuto had once no rivals in this art; but now he has given it up, and I fear, to make a little ring such as you desire, will be too burdensome to him. I pray you, therefore, do not trouble him about this little thing; for it will seem a considerable one to him now that he is out of the way of such work." I thanked the Duke for what he said, and then entreated him to let me do this trifling service for the Duchess. I set to work on it at once, and finished it in a day or two. It was for the little finger; so I made for it tiny cherubs in the round and four little masks, which together made the ring. I also managed to insert some fruits and connecting scrolls in enamel, so that the jewel in this setting made a delightful whole. Then I took it without delay to the Duchess, who told me, in the most courteous words, I had done an exquisite piece of work, and that she would keep me in mind. This ring she presented to King Philip; and after that was always giving me orders; but so courteously did she make her demands that I went out of my way to serve her, though I hardly knew the colour of her money. Yet God knows I was in want of it; for I was set on finishing my Perseus, and had looked up some young fellows to help me with the job, whom I paid out of my own pocket. Now I began to let myself be more seen about than I had lately been doing.

lxix. One feast day I went to the palace after dinner; and when I had come to the Hall of the Clock I saw the door of the

Wardrobe open. As I was approaching it, the Duke called to me, greeted me pleasantly, and said, "Welcome! look at that box which Lord Stefano of Palestrina has sent to me. Open it, and see what is inside." This I did, and then called out, "My lord, it is a figure in Greek marble—a marvellous thing! I swear, among all the antiques I have seen I never remember the figure of a young boy so beautifully worked, nor in so fine a style. I would like to have the restoring of it for your Excellency—the head, arms, and feet. I will make an eagle too, so that you may name it Ganymede. And though it hardly befits me to cobble statues, which is the business of a set of bungling fools—and ill enough they do it—yet the excellence of this great master calls aloud for my aid." The Duke was in great feather on hearing the statue was so fine; and he asked me endless questions about it, saying, "Tell me precisely, Benvenuto, my friend, in what consists the great art of this master who stirs such wonder in you." Thereupon I did my best to make his Excellency understand the great beauty, the high artistic knowledge, and the rare style of the thing. On these points I discoursed at length, and the more willingly that I could see his Excellency was delighted.

lxx. Now while I was thus agreeably holding converse with the Duke, a page went out of the Wardrobe; and the door being left open, Bandinello came in. When the Duke caught sight of him a shade passed over his face, and with a cold look in his direction, he said, "What are you doing here?" Bandinello made no answer to this; but suddenly spying the box with the uncovered statue, he shook his head and said, with one of his jeering laughs, "My lord, this is the sort of thing I have so often warned your Excellency against. Let me tell you, those ancient fellows knew nothing at all about anatomy, and so their works are full of blunders." I held my tongue meanwhile, paying not the slightest attention to what he was saying; indeed, I had turned my back on him. But as soon as the beast had stopped his wearisome chattering, the Duke cried, "O Benvenuto, this is exactly the contrary of what you were only now explaining to me with such fine-sounding reasons. So let's hear what you have to say in its defence." In answer to the Duke's words, which were uttered very graciously, I said, "My lord, your most illustrious Excellency should know that Baccio Bandinello is evil through and through, and always has been so; thus whatever he looks at, were it a thing of supreme excellence, is at once converted by his ugly eyes into all that is superlatively bad. Now I, who am drawn only to the good, see the truth with clearer sight. Therefore what I told your Excellency regarding this beautiful statue is the bare truth; and what Bandinello said was spoken out of that evil of which he is made up." The Duke listened to me with the utmost delight; but all the time I was speaking Bandinello was writhing and making the ugliest faces you ever saw—as if he weren't ugly enough already. Then the Duke went off, walking through some of the lower rooms, and Bandinello after him. The chamberlains tugged at my cloak to send me at their heels; and so we all followed in the Duke's train till he came to a certain room, where he sat down. Bandinello and I stood, one on his right hand and one on his left. I held my tongue; and his Excellency's attendants who were standing about, looked hard at Bandinello, sniggering to each other over what I had said when we were upstairs. Then Bandinello began a palaver, saying, "My lord, when I uncovered my Hercules and Cacus I believe of a truth that more than a hundred wretched sonnets were made about me, and they contained all the evil which the mob could find to say against me." Here I cut in with, "My lord, when our Michel Agnolo Buonarroti opened his Sacristy, with all its fine statues, to the public, the admirable school of artists in our city, friends to truth and right, made more than a hundred sonnets on him, each man vying with the other as to who should praise him best. Thus, as Bandinello's statue merited all the abuse which he himself owns was launched at it, so to Buonarroti's was due all the praise it received." Bandinello got into such a rage at my words that he nearly burst. Turning on me, he roared, "And you—what do you know against it?" "I'll soon tell you that," I rejoined, "if you have patience enough to listen to me." "Hurry up then," said he. The Duke and the others who were standing about, were all attention. Then I began thus: "I would have you know that it is a grief to me to expose the defects of your work; I shall not, however, speak from my own book, but shall utter the judgment of our noble band of Florentine masters." Meanwhile the wretch was breaking in rudely, and agitating his hands and feet in so intolerable a fashion, that he roused my wrath to such a pitch, that I took up the word again far more harshly than I should have done if he had behaved himself. "This great school of artists," I continued, "say that if you were to shave off Hercules's hair, there wouldn't be any noddle left to hold his brains; and as for his face, one can't tell whether it's a man's, or that of some cross between a lion and an ox; that it in no way corresponds to the attitude of the figure; that it is ill set on the neck, with so little art, and such plentiful lack of grace, that a worse thing was never seen. Moreover, its great hideous shoulders are like nothing so much as two pommels of an ass's pack-saddle; and the breasts and all the muscles are not modelled from a man, but from a great sack of melons set up against a wall. Then the loins look as if they were meant to represent a bagful of calabashes; and as for the two legs, it would be hard to tell how they are fastened on to that lumbering body; nor can you see on which leg he is standing, nor which he is straining; yet he is certainly not standing on both, as may be now and then seen in the statues of masters who know their business. Again, it is evident that the Hercules is bending forward more than a third of a cubit; and that by itself is the worst, the most intolerable fault to be found in the work of the veriest low-bred impostors. As for the arms, they say that they stick out in the most graceless fashion, and show no more evidence of knowledge than if you had never seen a nude model in your life; that the right leg of Hercules and that of Cacus run into each other; and if you were to separate them, there would not be enough stuff for one calf, let alone two. They say, moreover, that one of Hercules's feet is underground, and the other looks as if it were being grizzled by fire."

lxxi. The man could not rein himself in to hear with patience what I still had to say about the grave faults of the Cacus; first, because it was the truth I was telling; and, secondly, because I was revealing clearly to the Duke and the rest who were present, the kind of man he was; and they were showing by every look and movement their great consternation, and their recognition that I was in the right. Suddenly the wretch burst out, "Ah, you foul-tongued rascal! You say nothing, then, of my design?" I answered that he who designed well could never work badly; "and so I must believe that your design is on a level with your execution." Now when he saw from his Excellency's face that he was on my side, and felt the others lacerating him with their eyes and gestures, he gave free rein to his insolence, and turning on me his most abominable face, he shot out, "Hold your tongue, you beastly evil-liver!" The Duke scowled at him, and the rest looked towards him with clenched teeth and lowering brows; and I was maddened with rage at this villainous insult. Yet in a flash I mastered myself, and cried, "You fool! you go too far! But would to God I knew how to practise the noble art to which you make allusion; for one reads that Jove did so with

Ganymede in paradise; and here, on earth, the highest emperors and the greatest kings are adepts. As for me, I am only a poor and humble man, who could not, who knows not, how to take in hand a thing so much beyond him." At this none of them could contain themselves, and the Duke and all the rest broke into a tumult of laughter, such as you never heard in your life. Now, though I spoke thus jestingly, you must know, kind readers, my heart was bursting within me at the thought that the vilest scoundrel who ever breathed should have dared— and that, too, in the presence of such a prince—to hurl at me so foul an insult. But I would have you know that it was the Duke he insulted, and not me. For if I had been elsewhere save in that noble presence, I should have killed him on the spot. When the foul scoundrel, who was a blockhead to boot, saw that the gentlemen still went on laughing, he thought to turn their minds from the jests that had been made at his expense, and began on a new tack. "This Benvenuto," said he, "goes about bragging that I have promised him a block of marble." Whereupon I broke in with, "How now! Didn't you send Francesco, the son of Matteo the smith, your apprentice, to tell me, that if I had a mind to work in marble, you would give me a block? And I said, Yes; and I'll have it too." "That you shan't," said he; "make up your mind to that." Now brimful of rage as I was at the slanderous insults that had been flung at me, my senses grew dazed and blind to the presence of the Duke. I broke out in a wild fury, "I tell you plainly that if you don't send the marble to my house, you can seek another world; for if I meet you in this one, I'll rip open your bag of wind; and that's sure!" All at once I became aware I was in the presence of the great Duke; and turning humbly towards his Excellency, I said, "My lord, one fool makes a hundred. The follies of this man blurred the glory of your Excellency, and made me forget myself." Then the Duke said to Bandinello, "Is it true you promised him the marble?" And Bandinello owned it was. Whereupon the Duke said to me, "Go to the Opera, and take a block such as you want." But I insisted that he had promised to send it to my house. The words between us were terrible to hear; for I did not want the stone save in the way I had said. Next morning a block was brought to my house; and when I asked who was the sender, they said it was Bandinello, and that it was the piece of marble he had promised me.

lxxii. I had it at once carried into my workshop, and began to chisel it. While I was working at this, I made the model; but so great was my desire to be at work on marble, that I could not wait to make a model with all the care this art exacts. Now I heard it give out a cracked sound under my chisel, so that over and over again I repented having ever begun to work on it. Nevertheless, I made what I could out of it— that is, the Apollo and Hyacinth, which can be seen unfinished in my shop. While I was working on this, the Duke came often to my house, and many a time did he say to me, "Leave your bronze alone for a bit, and let me see you working on the marble." So then I would take up my tools and chisel away briskly. The Duke made inquiries about the model I had made for the marble, to which I answered, "My lord, this block is much cracked; yet for all that I shall make something out of it. So I have not been able to decide about the model; but I shall go forward with the thing as best I can." Then with the greatest despatch he sent to Rome for a piece of Greek marble, that I might restore his antique Ganymede, which had given rise to the quarrel with Bandinello. When it had come, I thought it would be a pity to break off pieces of it for the head and arms and the other parts which were wanting in the Ganymede; so I procured some more, and kept this Greek block for a Narcissus, making a little model of it first in wax. Now this stone had two holes in it, more than a quarter of a cubit in depth, and fully two inches wide; and that accounts for the attitude, which I chose in order to avoid the defects. But for scores and scores of years the block had been rained on; and the rain standing continually in these holes, had trickled through till the stone was all decayed; and how rotten it was round the upper hole was shown afterwards during the Arno floods, when the water rose in my shop more than a cubit and a half high. At that time the Narcissus was on a wooden stand; and the force of the water upset it, so that it was broken above the breasts. I mended it, and that the joining might not be noticed I made the garland of flowers which you can see on its bosom. I used to work at it for hours before daybreak, or even, indeed, on holidays, that I might not lose time I wanted for the Perseus.

Now one morning I was sharpening some chisels before beginning my work, when the finest splinter of steel flew into my right eye, entering the pupil so far that it could not be taken out by any means. I thought for certain I should lose the sight of that eye. At the end of several days I called in Maestro Raffaello de' Pilli, the surgeon. He brought with him two live pigeons. Then laying me down on my back on a table, with a knife he cut open a great vein in the birds' wings, so that the blood spurted out into my eye. This eased me at once; by two days the splinter was out, and I was at rest, with my eyesight better than before. The feast of St. Lucy coming on in three days, I made a golden eye out of a French crown; and had it offered at the saint's shrine by one of my six nieces, the daughters of my sister Liperata. She was about ten years old; and I went with her to church to thank God and St. Lucy. For some time I gave up working on the Narcissus, but I got on with my Perseus, though under the difficulties I have already spoken of; for I had a mind to finish it, and then to be off.

lxxiii. I had cast the Medusa, and it had come out perfectly; so I had great hopes of doing as well with my Perseus. The wax had been worked over it; and I assured myself that in bronze it would be just as successful as the Medusa. In wax the thing looked so fine that the Duke was much pleased with its beauty. But either some one had made him believe that it would fail in bronze, or he imagined this of himself; at all events one day, when he had come to see me, which he did with uncommon frequency at that time, he said to me, "Benvenuto, this statue cannot be a success in bronze—for the rules of the art do not permit of it." I felt the words of his Excellency very keenly, and I replied, "My lord, I know you have little faith in me; and this I believe is due to your having too much faith in those who speak ill of me, or because you know nothing of the matter." He hardly let me finish my words ere he cut in, "I profess to know a great deal; and what is more, I do know what I am talking about." Whereupon I replied, "Yes, like a prince; not as an artist. For did your Excellency understand the matter as you think you do, you would believe me on the strength of the great bronze bust I made of you, which was sent to Elba; also of my restoration of the beautiful marble Ganymede, a task of extreme difficulty, in the completion of which I had more trouble than if I had done it all over again; likewise the casting of the Medusa, which your Excellency sees now before you—and a difficult casting it was, such as no other man had ever done before me in this devilish art. Look, my lord! I made that furnace over again on a different system from any other; for besides the new improvements and clever inventions to be seen in it, I made two issues for the bronze; otherwise this difficult, contorted figure could never have come out successfully. It is all due to my intelligence that it did not fail, and that I carried through what none of the masters of the art believed possible. Know also, my lord, that of a truth, with all the great and complicated works I did in France under that marvellous King Francis, I succeeded admirably; and this only because of the encouragement which the good King gave me by his handsome provision for my needs, and his grant of as many workmen as I asked for. Indeed, there were times when I employed more than forty, all chosen by myself. That was the reason I did so many fine things in so short a time. Now, my lord, have faith in me, and grant me the help I need; for I have good hopes of carrying through a work which will please you. On the other hand, if your Excellency breaks my spirit, and gives me none of the help I need, it is impossible for me, or any other man in the world, to do anything of worth."

lxxiv. It was all he could do to stay and listen to my arguments. Now he turned this way, and now the other; and as for me, poor miserable wight, I was in despair, recalling the great state that had been mine in France, and grieving sorely after it. Then he said, "Now tell me, Benvenuto, how is it possible that that fine head of Medusa, up there in the clutch of Perseus, should ever come out well?" Whereupon I answered, "Now, see, my lord! If you had the acquaintance with the art you profess to have, you would have no fear for the success of that fine head; but you might be anxious about this right foot, seeing it is down here, and somewhat far apart from the rest." At these words he turned, half in anger, to some gentlemen who were present, and said, "I believe Benvenuto contradicts my every word out of mere conceit." Then with a half-contemptuous smile, reflected on the faces of his courtiers, he addressed me, "I am willing to listen with patience to any convincing arguments you can possibly give me in support of your statement." To this I replied, "I will present so good an argument that your Excellency shall see with the utmost clearness how the thing is." And I began, "You must know, my lord, that it is in the nature of fire to ascend, and, therefore, I can be sure that this Medusa's head will succeed perfectly; on the other hand, as it is not in its nature to descend, and I have to force it down six cubits by an ingenious device, it must be evident to your Excellency that it is impossible for the foot to come out. But I can remodel it easily." "And why," returned the Duke, "did you not think of some contrivance by which the foot would come out as you say the head will?" "I should have had to make a much larger furnace," I answered, "with a conduit-pipe as thick as my leg;

and all that weight of molten metal might then have run down far enough. My pipe, which is six cubits long to the foot, as I have said, is no thicker than two fingers. But it was not worth while making a bigger one, for I shall touch up the defective parts later. But when the mould is more than half full, as I hope, from the middle upwards, the fire will mount according to its nature, and this head of Perseus and that of the Medusa will come out to perfection; and of this you may be assured." When I had stated all these sound arguments, and endless others besides, which it would take too long for me to write down, the Duke shook his head, and left me without a word.

lxxv. By my own efforts I regained tranquillity of mind, and chased away those thoughts which every now and then would rise up before me, bringing bitter tears of regret to my eyes that ever I had left France. True, I had come to Florence, my dear fatherland, with the sole purpose of aiding my six nieces; but I saw this good deed had been the beginning of great ill for me. Yet all the same I looked forward to the time when, my Perseus finished, all my troubles should be turned to high delight and to glorious good.

And so I took heart again, and with all the resources of my body and my purse—though I had little enough money left—I set about procuring several loads of pine from the pine woods of Serristori, near Monte Lupo. While I was waiting for these, I covered my Perseus with the clay I had got ready several months before, in order that it might be well seasoned. When I had made its "tunic" of clay—for so is it called in our art—and had most carefully armed and girt it with iron, I began to draw off the wax by a slow fire through the various vent-holes I had made. (The more of these you have, the better will your moulds fill.) When this was done, I built up round the mould of my Perseus a funnel-shaped furnace of bricks, arranged one above the other, so as to leave numerous openings for the fire to breathe through. Then very gradually I laid the wood on, and kept up the fire for two days and two nights on end. After I had drawn off all the wax, and the mould had been properly baked, I set to work at once to dig a hole to sink the thing in, attending to all the strictest rules of the great art. This done, I raised the mould with the utmost care by means of windlasses and strong ropes to an upright position; and suspended it a cubit above the level of the furnace, paying attention that it hung exactly over the middle of the pit. Then gently, gently I let it down to the bottom of the furnace, sparing no pains to settle it securely there. This difficult job over, I set about propping it up with the earth I had dug out of the hole; and as I built up the earth, I made vent-holes, that is, little pipes of terra-cotta such as are used for drains and things of that kind. Then I saw that it was quite firm, and that this way of banking it up and putting conduits in their proper places was likely to be successful. It was evident also that my workmen understood my mode of working, which was very different from that of any of the other masters in my profession. Sure, therefore, that I could trust them, I gave my attention to the furnace, which I had filled up with pigs of copper and pieces of bronze, laid one on top of the other, according to the rules of the craft—that is, not pressing closely one on the other, but arranged so that the flames could make their way freely about them; for in this manner the metal is more quickly affected by the heat and liquefied. Then in great excitement I ordered them to light the furnace. They piled on the pine logs; and between the unctuous pine resin and the well-contrived draught of the furnace, the fire burned so splendidly that I had to feed it now on one side and now on the other. The effort was almost intolerable, yet I forced myself to keep it up.

On top of all this the shop took fire, and we feared lest the roof should fall upon us. Then, too, from the garden the rain and the wind blew in with such chill gusts as to cool the furnace. All this fighting for so many hours with adverse circumstances, forcing myself to a labour such as even my robust health could not stand, ended in a one-day fever of an indescribable severity. There was nothing for it but to fling myself on my bed, and I did so very ill-content. But first I appealed to my men—there were about ten or more helping me—master-founders, hand-labourers, peasants, and the workmen of my own shop. Among the last was Bernardino Mannellini of Mugello, who had been my pupil for several years. To him I said, after begging the goodwill of all the rest, "My dear Bernardino, see that you attend to everything I have taught you; and make all the haste you can, for the metal will soon be ready. You cannot make a mistake; the good fellows here will hurry up with the channels, and with these two crooks you can surely draw back the plugs. Then I know for certain my mould will fill beautifully. I feel worse than I ever did since I came into the world; and I am sure I shall be dead in a few hours." So, most ill-content, I left them and went to bed.

lxxvi. As soon as I was in bed I ordered my servant girls to take food and drink to all the men in the shop; and then I said to them, "By to-morrow morning I shall be dead." They did their best to put heart into me, saying that my sickness would pass over, and that it only arose from over-fatigue. Thus for two hours I fought the fever; but it went on rising all the time, so that I never stopped wailing that I was about to die. Now the woman who looked after all my household was Mona Fiore da Castel del Rio; and a cleverer woman was never born, nor a more devoted. Though now she went on scolding me for losing heart, yet all the same she tended me as affectionately as possible. Nevertheless, for all her brave heart, she could not keep her tears from flowing as she saw me overcome by such terrible pain and depression. Yet she hid her weeping from me so far as she could. While I lay there in this terrible distress, I saw a man come into my room, whose body was twisted like a capital S; and he spoke in the sad and grievous tones of those who proclaim to doomed men that their last hour has tolled. "O Benvenuto!" he said, "your work is spoiled; and no power on earth can save it now." Hardly had I heard the miserable creature's words, than I set up such a terrible cry as might have been heard in the heaven of fire; and rising from my bed, I took my clothes and began to dress; and I dealt kicks and blows to the servant girls, the boy, and every one who came to help me, wailing the while, "Ah, traitors! jealous monsters! this is a malicious plot. But I swear by God that I shall come at the truth of it; and before I die I shall give such proof to the world of my strong hand as shall make more than one man stand in wonder!" When I had dressed, I hurried to the shop fuming with rage; and there I saw all the men I had left in the best of spirits standing dazed and at their wits' end. I broke into their stupor with, "Wake up! Listen to me! Since you've been either too great fools or too great knaves to do as I told you, attend to me now. I am here in front of my work. And not a word from any of you; for it's help, not advice, that will serve me now." On this up spoke Maestro Alessandro Lastricati, "Listen, Benvenuto! You are taking in hand a thing which defies the laws of art, and cannot be done, whatever means you try." At that I turned on him in such a fury, and with murder in my eye, that he and all the others too cried out, "Come on! Give your orders! We are ready for all you may command, while there is any breath left in our bodies." But I believe they uttered these soothing words only because they thought I was on the point of falling down dead. Then I hurried to the furnace, and found the metal had all coagulated, or, as we say, "caked." I ordered two labourers to go to Capretta the butcher's opposite, for a load of young oak logs, which had been dry for more than a year, and which Madonna Ginevra, Capretta's wife, had already offered me. As soon as I got the first armfuls, I set about filling the ash-pot below the furnace. Now oak of this kind makes a fiercer fire than any other sort of wood, and that is why alder or pine is used in the founding of gun-metal, for which the fire should be slow. Ah, then, you should have seen how the cake of metal began to run, and how it glowed! Meanwhile, too, I forced it to flow along the channels, while I sent the rest of the men on the roof to look after the fire, which had broken out again more fiercely now the furnace was burning with such fury; and towards the garden side I made them pile up planks and rugs and old hangings to prevent the rain from pouring in.

lxxvii. When I had mastered all this confusion and trouble, I shouted now to this man, now to that, bidding them fetch and carry for me; and the solidified metal beginning to melt just then, the whole band were so excited to obedience, that each man did the work of three. Then I had them fetch half a pig of pewter, weighing about sixty pounds, and this I threw right in the middle of the solid metal in the furnace. And what with the wood I had put in beneath, and all the stirring with iron rods and bars, in a little while the mass grew liquid. When I saw I had raised the dead, in despite of all those ignorant sceptics, such vigour came back to me, that the remembrance of my fever and the fear of death passed away from me utterly. Then suddenly we heard a great noise, and saw a brilliant flash of fire, just as if a thunderbolt had rushed into being in our very midst. Every man of us was dazed by this prodigious and terrifying event, and I still more than the rest. Only when the great rumble and the flashing flame had passed, did we dare look each other in the face. Then I saw that the lid of the furnace had blown open, so that the bronze was running over. In the same instant I had every mouth of the mould open and the plugs closed. But perceiving that the metal did not run as freely as it should, I came to the conclusion that the intense heat had consumed the alloy. So I bade them fetch every pewter dish and porringer and plate I had in the house, nearly two hundred in all; and part of them I threw, one after another, into the channels, and put the rest into the furnace. Then they saw my bronze was really melted and filling up my mould, and gave me the readiest and most cheerful help and obedience. Now I was here; now I was there, giving orders or putting my own hand to the work, while I cried, "O God, who in Thy limitless strength didst rise from the dead, and glorious didst ascend to Heaven . . . !" In an instant my mould filled up; and I knelt down and thanked God with all my heart; then turned to a plate of salad lying on a bench there, and with splendid appetite ate and drank, and all my gang of men along with me. After that, as the day was but two hours off, I betook myself to bed, sound of body and in good heart; and, as if I had never known an ache in my life, sank gently to my rest. That good serving woman of mine, without my saying a word to her about it, had cooked a fine fat capon; and when I rose from my bed near dinner-time, she met me with a cheery face, and cried, "Oh, so this is the man who thought he was dying? I do believe that the blows and the kicks you gave us last night, when you were so furious that one would have said you were possessed of the devil, so scared that terrible fever that it ran away, lest it should be belaboured too." Then all my poor family breathed once more after their fright and their formidable labours; and off they went to buy pots and pans of earthenware instead of the pewter vessels I had cast into the furnace. After which we sat down to dinner in the best of spirits; and in all my life I never remember eating with a gladder heart nor with a better appetite. After dinner all my helpers came to see me. They did nothing but congratulate each other, and thank God for the way things had turned out, and tell me they had seen things done which other masters held to be beyond any one's power. And I was proud, for I thought myself a very clever fellow—nor did I hide my opinion of myself; and putting my hand into my pocket, I paid every man to his full content.

But that scoundrel, my mortal enemy, Messer Pierfrancesco Ricci, the Duke's major-domo, ferreted out the whole story of the affair. And the two men whom I suspected of having caused the caking of my bronze, told him I was no man; that of a surety I was a great demon, for I had done what by mere art could not be achieved. And all sorts of other prodigies they related of me, which would indeed have taxed a devil's powers. As they made the thing out to be much more astounding than it had been in reality, the major-domo wrote to the Duke, who was at Pisa, adding to their tale still more fearful and marvellous inventions of his own.

lxxviii. For two days I let my work cool, and then uncovered a little bit at a time. First of all I found that, thanks to the vents, the head of Medusa had come out splendidly—had I not told the Duke that it is in the nature of fire to ascend? Then I went on uncovering the rest, and found the other head, that of Perseus, was just as perfect; at which I wondered more; for, as you can see, it is much lower than that of Medusa. I had placed the mouths of the mould above the head and on the shoulders of the Perseus, and now I found that this head had taken all the remaining bronze in my furnace. Wonderful to relate, there was nothing left in the mouth of the channel, and yet there had been enough for my purpose. This appeared to me so marvellous—indeed, nothing short of a miracle—that the whole operation seemed as if it had been guided and brought to a happy end by Almighty God. Luck still followed me as I uncovered farther; everything I found had come out successfully till I came to the right foot on which the figure rests. There I found the heel perfect, and on further examination evidently the whole foot as well. On the one hand I rejoiced; on the other I was half annoyed, but only because I had said to the Duke that it could not happen so. However, when all was disclosed, I found the toes and a little portion above them were wanting, so that about half the foot would have to be added. Though this would give me a little extra work, I was glad, nevertheless; for I could show the Duke that I understood my own business. A larger part of the foot, indeed, had come out than I looked for; but the reason was that, from various causes, the metal had been subjected to a greater heat than is ordained by the laws of the art; and then, too, I had thrown in extra alloy in the shape of my pewter household vessels, as I have told you—a thing nobody ever thought of doing before.

Now seeing the great success of my work, I set off at once for Pisa to see the Duke. He received me as kindly as possible, and so did the Duchess; and though their major-domo had told them the whole story, their Excellencies thought it still more prodigious and astounding when they heard it from my own lips. When I came to the foot of the Perseus, and related how, just as I had warned his Excellency before, it had not come out, I could see his wonder grow every moment, and he told the Duchess how, indeed, I had foretold this. Perceiving that my lord and my lady were in good humour with me, I begged the Duke to let me go to Rome. He consented with the greatest kindness, bidding me return ere long to finish his Perseus; and gave me letters of recommendation to his ambassador, Averardo Serristori. These were the first years of Pope Giulio de' Monti's reign.

lxxix. Before my departure I instucted my men to go on with the work in the way I had shown them. Now my reason for going away was this. I had made a life-size bronze bust of Bindo, the son of Antonio Altoviti, and had sent it to him at Rome. He had placed it in his study, which was very richly adorned with antiques and other fine things; but it was not a room suitable for showing sculpture or paintings, for the windows were under the level of these; so that the light coming from beneath did not show them to such advantage as if it had been better arranged. Now one day, as it happened, Bindo standing at his door, saw Michel Agnolo Buonarroti the sculptor pass by, and begged him to do him the honour of coming in to see his study; and he led the way. As soon as he was within and had looked round, Michel Agnolo asked, "Who is the master who has done so good a likeness of you, and in so fine a style? I assure you that head pleases me as much, nay, rather better than those antiques; and yet one can see there are good things amongst them. But if these windows were above instead of underneath, your works of art would show far better; and your portrait, even among these other fine works, would hold its own." As soon as Michel Agnolo had left Bindo, he wrote me the kindest of letters to this effect: *My Benvenuto, for years I have known you to be the greatest goldsmith ever heard of; and from this time I shall look on you as a sculptor of like merit. You must know that Messer Bindo Altoviti showed me a bust of him in bronze, and told me it was from your hand. It pleased me greatly; but I was vexed that it had been placed in a bad light; for if it were properly lighted, it would prove itself to be the masterpiece it really is.* The letter, besides, was full of loving words and compliments to me. Now before I left for Rome I showed it to the Duke, who read it with a friendly feeling towards the writer, and said to me, "Benvenuto, if you will write to him, and persuade him to return to Florence, I'll make him one of the Forty-eight." So I wrote to him most affectionately, promising him in the Duke's name a hundred times more than I had authority for. But that there might be no mistake in this, I showed it to the Duke before I sealed it; saying to his most illustrious Excellency, "Perhaps, my lord, I have promised him too much." But he answered, "He is worthy of more than you have named; and I will do more for him than that." To this letter Michel Agnolo never made any answer, and it was plain to me that the Duke was very angry with him.

lxxx. When I got to Rome I went to lodge in Bindo Altoviti's house. He told me at once how he had shown my bronze bust of

him to Michel Agnolo, who had greatly praised it, and about
this we talked for a long time. Now Bindo had twelve hundred
gold crowns of mine, part of a sum of five thousand he had lent
to the Duke, four thousand being his and the rest mine, but in
his name. For this loan I received such interest as fell to my
share. This was the beginning of my setting to work on his
portrait. When he saw it in wax, he sent me fifty golden crowns
by a notary of his household, Ser Giuliano Paccalli. But I did
not wish to take this money, and sent it back by the messenger,
afterwards saying to Bindo, "It is enough for me if you invest
that money of mine well for me, so that I may gain something
on it." Now I saw that he was in an ill-humour with me; for
instead of treating me with kindness, as formerly, his manner
was very cold to me; and though he kept me in his house, he
was never frank with me, but remained morose. Still, the
business was settled in a few words. I got nothing for the
making of the bust, nor for the bronze; and we agreed that he
should keep my money for me at fifteen per cent. during my
natural life.

lxxxi. I put off no time after my arrival in Rome in going to
kiss the Pope's feet. While I was speaking with him, in came
Messer Averardo Serristori, the ambassador from our Duke. I
had submitted some propositions to his Holiness; and I believe
we should have easily come to an understanding, in which case
I should have willingly returned to Rome, considering what were
the great difficulties I encountered in Florence. But I found that
the ambassador had put a spoke in my wheel. Then I went to
see Michel Agnolo Buonarroti, and repeated to him the message
from the Duke, which I had already written to him from
Florence. He answered that he was employed on the building
of St. Peter's, and that therefore he could not leave. But I argued
that since he had made up his mind on the plan of the building,
he could leave the work to be carried out by his pupil Urbino,
who would obey him exactly; and I made him various other
promises in the Duke's name. Thereupon he looked me straight
in the face, and with something of a grim smile, said, "And how
are you pleased with him yourself?" Although I protested that
I was well content, and that I was very well treated, he let me
see that he was aware of the greater part of my troubles; and
he told me decisively that it would be difficult for him to leave.
Still I persisted that the best thing he could do was to return
to his native city, which was governed by a most just Prince,
than whom a greater lover of art had never been born into the

world. As I have said, he had with him a lad from Urbino, who had been of his household for many years, more as a serving-man than anything else; as was plain enough, for he knew nothing of his master's art. Now while I was pressing all my good arguments on Michel Agnolo, so that he had no answer to them on the spot, he turned to Urbino to ask what he thought about it; whereupon Urbino cried out loud, in his countrified way, "I'll never part from my Messer Michel Agnolo till I've flayed him or he has flayed me." I couldn't help laughing at these silly words. Then, without a word of farewell, I went away crestfallen.

lxxxii. After making that wretched bargain with Bindo Altoviti, losing my bronze head and giving my money into his keeping for life, I knew what the faith of merchants was like; and it was in very low spirits I returned to Florence. Without delay I went to the Palace to see the Duke; but he was at Castello, beyond Ponte a Rifredi. I found Messer Pier-francesco Ricci, the major-domo, in the Palace; and when I went up to him to salute him, as courtesy demands, he cried out in the greatest astonishment, "Oh, you're back again, are you?" And he still looked as if he could not get over his surprise. Then he clapped his hands as he said, "The Duke is at Castello," turned his back on me, and made off. I did not know, nor could I imagine, why the brute should have behaved so strangely. But I made my way to Castello; and as soon as I entered the garden I saw the Duke in the distance. When he caught sight of me, he showed every sign of surprise, and gave me to understand I might go about my business. Now I had been relying on his Excellency showing me as much kindness as before I went away—nay, more; but when I saw him in this strange temper, I returned to Florence very ill pleased. There I set to work again; but while I was striving to complete my statue, I vainly tried to guess what the Duke's coldness could have arisen from. And I could not help noticing that Messer Sforza and some other of his Excellency's most intimate friends looked at me in a peculiar manner. So I asked Messer Sforza what it meant, and he replied, with a smile, "Benvenuto, you've only to think of being an honest man. That's all that concerns you."

A few days after I was granted an audience of the Duke, who greeted me with a kind of sulky civility, and asked me what I had been doing at Rome. As well as I could I kept up the con-versation, telling him about the bronze bust I had made for Bindo Altoviti, and all that followed. When I saw he was listening to me very attentively, I went on to tell him about Michel Agnolo Buonarroti. Thereupon he showed some signs of anger; but Urbino's words to his master made him laugh. Then he said, "Well, so much the worse for him!" And then I went away.

For sure Ser Pierfrancesco, the major-domo, had done me an ill turn with the Duke; but it did not succeed. For God, the Friend to truth, saved me, as He hath ever done to this day, from a host of dangers, and as I hope He ever may save me to the last hours of my troubled life. And so I go boldly forward, armed but with His strength, nor fear the storms of fortune, nor my perverse stars. I only entreat that He keep me in His grace.

lxxxiii. Now listen, gentle reader, to a terrible tale I have to tell. I made all haste possible to finish my statue; but I used to spend every evening in the Wardrobe of the Duke, helping the goldsmiths who were working there for his Excellency, mostly after designs which I had made. And as I saw that the Duke liked to watch me at work and to talk with me, I made up my mind to go there during the day sometimes. So on one of these occasions he came in as usual, and the more willingly that he knew I was there. He began to converse with me very pleasantly on a great many different subjects; and I answered vivaciously, and so amused him that he was in a better temper than I had ever seen him in before. Suddenly one of his secretaries entered and spoke a word in his ear, as if on a matter of great importance. Then the Duke got up, and withdrew with the secretary to another room. Meanwhile the Duchess had sent to inquire what his Excellency was doing; and her page went back to tell her, "The Duke is talking and laughing with Benvenuto, and he is in the best of humours." When she heard this, she came to the Wardrobe; but not finding the Duke, she sat down beside us, and looked on for a while as we worked. Then in the pleasantest manner she turned to me, and showed me a necklace of large pearls—very rare they were, in fact—and asked me what I thought of them. I replied that they were very beautiful. Then her Excellency said, "I want the Duke to buy them for me; therefore, my Benvenuto, say all you possibly can to him in their praise." But at these words, I spoke out my real opinion to the Duchess, saying with the utmost respect, "My lady, I thought this necklace of pearls was yours already; in which case I might have refrained from uttering what was in my mind to say, nay, what I must say, now I know that they do not belong to your Excellency. Therefore, I would have you know that my trained eye sees so many defects in these pearls, that I should never advise your buying them." To this she replied, "The merchant will take six thousand crowns; if the necklace had none of these slight flaws, it would be worth more than twelve thousand." But I went on to say that, were it perfect in quality and condition, I should never advise any one to go as high as five thousand crowns; for pearls are not jewels, they are but fishes' bones; and in time must lose their value. Whereas diamonds, rubies, emeralds, and sapphires, never grow old; all these four are real jewels, and worth buying. At this the Duchess was somewhat piqued; but she persisted, "I am determined to have these pearls; and so I beg you to take them to the Duke, and say all you can think of in their praise; and if you have to tell some little lies about them, do so to serve me, and you will have no reason to repent it." Now I have always been the greatest friend of truth and the enemy of lies; but such pressure being put upon me, and unwilling to lose the favour of so great a princess, I took those accursed pearls, and in a very ill humour went with them to the other room to which the Duke had retired. As soon as he saw me, he called out, "Well, Benvenuto, and what are you about?" So I showed him the pearls, and said, "My lord, I have come to let you see an exquisite necklace of pearls. Most rare they are, and really worthy of your Excellency; and I do not believe that eighty pearls could ever be strung together to better advantage. So buy them, my lord, for they are truly marvellous." But he answered me at once, "I will not buy them; for they are neither so rare nor so beautiful as you say. I have seen them, and I don't like them." Then I replied, "Forgive me, my lord, these pearls far surpass any which were ever strung together before for a necklace." The Duchess had got up in the meanwhile, and was standing behind a door listening to every word. So when I had gone on to say a thousand things more in their praise than I am writing here, the Duke turned an indulgent face on me, and said, "O Benvenuto, my friend, I know that you understand all about these things; and if the pearls were as fine and rare as you say, I should not be unwilling to buy them, whether to give pleasure to the Duchess, or for the sake of possessing them; for such things I am always in need of, not so much for her use, as for that of my sons and daughters." But as I had begun to lie, I now went on lying with still greater audacity, though very plausibly, trusting to the Duchess to support me at the proper time. I was to have more than two hundred crowns for doing the business—so the Duchess had signified to me; but I was quite determined not to touch a penny of it, so as to be on the safe side, and that the Duke might never think I had done it from greed. Once more he spoke in the kindliest tones to me, and said, "I know that you understand all about these things. So now on your faith as an honest man, which I have always thought you to be, tell me the truth." Then I blushed hotly, and my eyes grew wet with tears, as I said, "My lord, if I tell your most illustrious Excellency the truth, the Duchess will become my deadly enemy. I shall be forced to depart from Florence, and my enemies will immediately pour scorn on my Perseus, which I have held out to the expectations of your Excellency's most noble school. So now I recommend myself to your Excellency."

lxxxiv. When the Duke learnt that all I had said I had been forced to say, he comforted me. "If you trust in me, fear nothing." But again I answered, "Alas, my lord, how can this be kept from the Duchess?" Whereat the Duke swore with uplifted hand, "Consider all you have said as buried in a diamond casket." Since he had honoured me by such words, I told him at once the truth about the pearls, so far as I knew it; that they were not worth much more than two thousand crowns. Now the Duchess thought we had made an end of talking, for we were speaking as softly as possible; so she came forward and said, "My lord, be so good as to buy me this necklace of pearls, for I have the greatest craving for it; and your Benvenuto has told me he never saw a finer one." Then the Duke replied, "I do not wish to buy it." "Why will not my lord please me by buying it?" "Because I don't want to throw money away." But the Duchess insisted, "Oh, why should it be throwing money away, since your Benvenuto, in whom you have, and rightly, so much confidence, told me that if you paid even more than three thousand crowns, it would be a very good bargain?" The Duke replied, "My lady, my Benvenuto has told me that were I to buy it, I should be throwing money away; for the pearls are not round, neither are they all of a size, and some of them are old; and if you don't believe it, look at this one, and this other; examine them all. No, no, they are not my affair!" At this the Duchess gave me the angriest look, and shaking her head at me in a threatening fashion, she left the room; and I was much inclined to be off and out of Italy without delay. But as my Perseus was nearly finished, I was unwilling to leave without exhibiting it publicly. Yet consider, every man of you, what a cruel position I was now in! The Duke had ordered the door-keepers—for I heard him—to give me free entrance to his Excellency's apartments whenever I came to seek him; while the Duchess now gave counter-orders to them that when I presented myself at the palace, they were to chase me away. So now as soon as they saw me, they would come outside and hustle me off; but they took care the Duke should not see them; for if he caught sight of me before these rascals, either he called out to me, or made me a sign I was to come to him.

Well, now the Duchess sent for Bernardone the broker, a man of whose meanness and worthlessness I had heard her many a time complain, and took counsel of him as she had done before of me. "My lady," he replied, "leave the affair to me." So this scoundrel presented himself to the Duke with the necklace in his hands. As soon as the Duke caught sight of him, he told him to be off; whereupon the rascal raised that great voice of his, which came through his big nose for all the world like the braying of an ass, and said, "I pray you, my lord, buy this necklace for the poor lady, who is dying to have it; nor can she live without it." And he went on braying out his silly words, till the Duke lost patience, and said, "Get out of this, I say; else, come here and puff your cheeks out." Now this rascally buffoon knew quite well what was meant; for if by puffing out his cheeks, or by singing *La bella Franceschina*, he could persuade the Duke to the purchase of the pearls, he would gain the good graces of the Duchess, and his commission into the bargain, which would come to several hundreds of crowns. And so he puffed out his cheeks; and the Duke gave him several sound smacks; and to be rid of him, did it rather harder than usual. Not only did his cheeks get very red with this sound smacking, but the tears came into his eyes as well. Nevertheless, he said, "Here, my lord, behold your faithful servant, who merely tries to do his duty, and is willing to suffer any disgrace, if only that poor lady have her will." Then the Duke, tired of the rascal, either to make up for the slaps he had given him, or for love of the Duchess, whom his Excellency was ever anxious to please, called out, "Get out of this, and a murrain on you! Go and make the bargain, for I am content to do whatever the Duchess may desire." Now look you at the rage of evil fortune against a poor man, and how shamelessly she favours a gross rascal! I lost all the good-will of the Duchess, which was well-nigh reason enough for my losing the Duke's too; and he got that big commission, and their favour besides. So it is not enough to be just an honest man of talent.

lxxxv. It was now the war with Siena broke out; and the Duke, desiring to fortify Florence, distributed the different gates among his sculptors and architects. To me was given the Prato gate, as well as the little gate of the Arno, which is on the road leading to the mills. The Cavaliere Bandinello had the San Friano gate; Pasqualino d'Ancona that of San Pier Gattolini; Giulian di Baccio d'Agnolo, the worker in wood, that of San Giorgio; Particino, another carver in wood, the Santo Niccolò; Francesco da Sangallo the sculptor, called Il Margolla, the gate of Santa Croce; while to Giovan Battista, called Il Tasso, was given the Pinti gate. Certain other bastions and gates were consigned to various engineers. I don't remember whom, nor does it matter here. The Duke, who had always proved himself a man of keen intelligence, went all round the city himself; and when his Excellency had thoroughly examined everything, and made his plans, he called for Lattanzio Gorini, a paymaster of his. Now Lattanzio took a great interest in this art; and so the Duke ordered him to make various designs for the fortification of the gates, and afterwards he sent to each of us the plan for his particular one. Well, I looked at mine, and saw that it was not the thing at all; that it was, indeed, very incorrect. I went at once to find the Duke with the plan in my hand, purposing to point out to him its defects. But no sooner had I begun to speak than he turned on me in a fury, saying, "Benvenuto, I'll yield to you in the making of statues; but in this business you must give in to me. So go and carry out the plan I have given you." These overbearing words I answered as meekly as possible, saying, "My lord, even in regard to the best methods of sculpture I have learnt something from your Excellency; for we have often had discussions on the subject; so in the matter of the fortification of the city—a far more important affair than statuary I admit— I entreat your Excellency to deign to listen to me. By talking it over with you I shall best learn how I should serve you." So by these conciliatory words I persuaded him to discuss the matter with me. Then I proved to him by weighty and clear arguments that the designs given me were faulty; and his Excellency said, "Well, go and make one yourself, and I'll see what I think of it." So I drew out two plans for the fortification of the two gates, according to good methods, and took them to him. He knew the true from the false, and said to me amiably, "Go and do it in your own way then; I am quite pleased"; and I set to the task without delay.

lxxxvi. Now on guard at the Prato gate was a Lombard captain. A formidable man he was, of great size, brutal in his speech, very presumptuous, and extremely ignorant. He at once began to inquire what I was after; whereupon with the utmost courtesy I showed him my plans, and was at much pains to explain to him my method. Then the uncouth brute shook his head, writhed his body about, first standing on one foot and then on the other. Pulling his long moustaches—they were huge—and drawing his cap down over his eyes, he muttered, "The devil! I can't make out a word of this business!" In the end the brute annoyed me; so I said, "Well, leave it to me then, for I do understand it"; and I turned my back on him and was going about my business. Then he shook his head at me threateningly, and with his left hand on his sword hilt, he raised the point suggestively, and said, "Hulloa, master! you want to pick a quarrel, do you?" At that I turned on him fiercely, for he had put my blood up, and cried, "It would be a much easier matter to run you through than to make the bastion for this gate." And at the word we both put our hands to our swords; but before we had unsheathed them, a crowd of honest men came up, some of them Florentine citizens and others hangers-on of the Court. The majority of them cried out on him, saying his was the fault, and that I was a man to make him repent of it—and woe to him if the Duke got wind of the matter! So then he went about his business, and I set to work on my bastion.

When I had done my work there, I made my way to the other little Arno gate, where I found a captain from Cesena, the most courteous gentleman I have ever met with in his profession. He looked like a gentle-mannered damosel; but upon occasion he was the bravest, even the most relentless of men. This charming person took such an interest in what I was doing, that at times I was overcome with shyness. He was so eager to understand my methods, that I explained them to him with the utmost politeness. To be brief, we were rivals in courtesy; and I succeeded far better with this bastion than with the other.

My bastions were almost finished when an incursion of Pier Strozzi's mob so terrified the Prato folk that they all cleared out; and with all their belongings piled up on their carts, they made their way into the city. They came in such numbers, their carts knocking up against each other on the road, that when I saw all the confusion, I told the warders of the gates to look out that no such accident should happen as had taken place at the gates of Turin, when, there being occasion to lower the portcullis, it would not work. So ours might stick fast upon one of the carts. That great brute of a captain hearing my words, turned on me with a torrent of insolence; and I gave him back as good, so that we were like to come to a worse quarrel than before. However, we were kept apart. Then having finished my bastions, I touched a very pretty number of crowns I had not looked for; and very glad I was of them, too. But it was with great pleasure I went back to my Perseus.

lxxxvii. About this time certain antiquities were found in the neighbourhood of Arezzo, among them the Chimera, the bronze lion which can be seen in the apartment adjoining the great hall of the Palace. Besides the Chimera, there were also found a number of little bronze statuettes, covered with earth and rust, and each of them wanting something, head or hands or feet. The Duke took great pleasure in cleaning them himself with gold-smiths' chisels. Now one day I had occasion to speak to his Excellency; and while we were talking together he handed me a little hammer, with which I struck the chisel the Duke was holding; and it was so we cleared off the earth and rust from the little figures. Several evenings we spent like this, after which he ordered me to supply the missing portions of the statuettes; and so full was his head of these trifles that he made me work on them by day as well; and if I was late in putting in an appearance, he would send for me. More than once I gave him to understand that if I left my Perseus during the day, various misfortunes might happen; and the chief of these, and the one I was most afraid of was, that his Excellency might grow impatient at the long time I took over the work—a thing that did indeed come to pass. Then, besides, I had several workmen; and when I was not at hand, they were apt either to ruin my work, or to do as little as possible. So the Duke agreed that I need only go to him from twenty-four of the clock. By this time I had made myself so agreeable to his Excellency, that when I came to him in the evening he heaped more and more kindness upon me. In these days they were building the new rooms towards the Lions; and his Excellency desiring to have a more private place of his own, arranged a little cabinet for himself in the newly built apartments, and gave me orders to come there by a private way through his Wardrobe, across the stage of the great Hall, and then by various little dark holes and corners. But in a few days the Duchess stopped my passage this way, locking all the doors of access. So every evening I came to the Palace, I had to wait a great while because the Duchess was privately occupied in these ante-chambers through which I had to pass; and as she was of weak health, I never once came without inconveniencing her. On this account, as well as for other reasons, she took such an ill will to me that she could not bear the sight of me. Still in spite of being greatly hindered and subjected to annoyance, I persisted in going. The Duke had given the most precise orders that the very instant I knocked at the doors, they were to open to me, and to let me go wherever I liked without a word. Thus it came about that sometimes, when I came in softly and un-expectedly to these private rooms, I greatly inconvenienced the Duchess. Then she would burst out into a fury of rage, so that I shook in my shoes, and she would cry, "Will you ever have done cobbling these little figures? I declare your constant passing to and fro is becoming intolerable!" I answered in all meekness, "Lady, my only patron, my sole desire is to serve you faithfully and with the utmost obedience. But this work which the Duke has ordered me to do, will go on for some months still. Therefore, your Excellency, tell me if you wish me to come here no more. If so, I shall certainly not come, whoever calls me. Even were the Duke to summon me, I should say I was not well, and should never appear again." To this she replied, "I do not say you are not to come, and I am not bidding you disobey the Duke. But it seems to me as if this work of yours were never coming to an end." Now whether the Duke heard something of this, or whatever was the reason, he did just as before; that is, he sent for me as soon as it was nearing twenty-four o'clock; and the message I received was always, "Be sure not to fail, for the Duke expects you." And so for several evenings I went on coming, always meeting the same difficulty. But once, when I entered as usual, the Duke, who had perhaps been discussing private matters with the Duchess, turned on me in the greatest fury imaginable; whereupon I was all of a tremble and was for withdrawing at once. But next moment he said, "Enter, Ben-venuto, my friend, and set about your work, and I shall be with you ere long." While I was going on my way, Don Garzia, a little child at the time, took me by the cloak and played me the prettiest baby tricks imaginable. The Duke looked on the while with delight, saying, "One can see that my boys and you are excellent friends."

lxxxviii. While I was engaged on these trifles, the Prince and Don Giovanni and Don Arnando and Don Garzia were always at my elbows; and they would give me a nudge every now and then, when their father was not looking. I begged them for pity's sake to behave themselves. "We cannot," they replied. So I said, "Very well, what can't be done, won't be done. So come on"; whereupon the Duke and Duchess burst out laughing.

Another evening, when I had finished the four little bronze figures which are attached to the base of my statue—I mean the Jupiter, Mercury, Minerva, and Danaë with her little son Perseus at her feet—I had them brought into the room where I used to work, and set them up in a row, rather above the level of the eyes, so that they made a splendid effect. The Duke heard what I had done, and came in earlier than his wont. Now the person who told his Excellency had spoken of them in extravagant terms—calling them "finer than antiques," and so on. So the Duke came in with the Duchess, talking about my work in great good spirits. I rose on the instant, and went forward to meet them. He greeted me with his noble courtesy, and raising his right hand, in which he held a magnificent slip of a pear tree, he said, "Take this, my Benvenuto, and plant this pear tree in the garden of your house." Much pleased, I answered, "Oh, my lord, does your Excellency really mean me to plant it in the garden of my house?" So he repeated, "In the garden of your house—your very own house. Do you understand?" Then I thanked his Excellency and the Duchess, too, in my best manner. Afterwards they both sat down opposite the little figures; and they stayed there talking of nothing else for more than two hours. Indeed, the Duchess was so delighted that she said to me, "I am very unwilling for these charming little statues to be lost in the pedestal down in the Piazza there, where they might only too easily be injured. I would fain have you set them up in one of my rooms, where they would be housed with all the respect their peculiar merits call for." I gave many excellent reasons for objecting to this plan; but as I saw she had made up her mind I should not fix them to the pedestal—where now they are—I waited till next day; and then about twenty-two of the clock I made my way to the Palace. I found that both the Duke and the Duchess had gone riding; so I had the little statues brought down, and I soldered them to their appointed places on the pedestal, which was quite ready. Oh, what a rage the Duchess was in when she heard it! Indeed, if it had not been for the Duke, who vigorously took my part, I should have come badly out of the affair; and what with her vexation about the pearl necklace, and now this business, she determined to deprive the Duke of his little pleasure; and so I went no more to work in his apartments. I soon found the same hindrances as before put in the way of my entering the palace.

lxxxix. I returned to the Loggia, where my Perseus had already been set up, and went on completing it, but meeting always the same old difficulties—no money, and every kind of hindrance thrown in my way. Half of them might have overwhelmed a man of adamant. But I toiled on with my usual obstinacy; and one morning when I had heard mass in San Piero Scheraggio, Bernardone, the broker, that incapable goldsmith, and, by the Duke's favour, purveyor to the Mint, passed me by. Hardly was he outside the door of the church, when the foul hog let out such a sound you might have heard it at San Miniato. "Pig!" I cried, "coward, ass! Is that the language of your filthy wits?" And I ran for a stick. He withdrew into the Mint; and I stayed just inside my own door, stationing a little lad outside to sign to me when the pig should come out of hiding. But when I had waited a good while, I got weary; and as my anger cooled off, I began to reflect that there is no bargaining about blows, and I might get into trouble if I thrashed him. So I made up my mind to have my revenge in another way. Now this happened nigh upon the feast of our Saint John, a day or two before it. So I made these four verses, and stuck them up in a place of retirement outside the church. They were to this effect—

> Big Bernard, ass and hog, here lieth low,
> Broker, spy, thief. To Pandora sole heir
> For all her blackest ills. Yet doth he share
> These with the blockhead Buaccio whom we know.

The story of the incident and the verses went the round of the palace; and the Duke and Duchess laughed heartily. Before Bernardone heard of it, a great number of people had stopped to read the lines, and roared with laughter. All the time they looked towards the Mint, and fixed their eyes on Bernardone; and his son Maestro Baccio noticing this, came in a fury and tore them down from the wall, while his father gnawed at his finger, and bellowed threats through his nose. He made a great fuss about the affair.

xc. When the Duke heard that the whole of my Perseus was ready for exhibition, he came to see it one day; and it was very evident that he was much pleased. But turning to some gentlemen who were with him, he said, "Though this seems a very fine thing to us, it has still to please the people. And so, Benvenuto, my friend, before you give it the last touches, I should like you, just to please me, to uncover it towards the Piazza one mid-day, to see what they will say about it. For there is no doubt that when it is seen in the open, it will appear quite different from what it does now in this narrow space." I answered meekly, "My lord, I assure you it will look twice as well. Oh, does not your Excellency remember having seen it in the garden of my house? There, with abundant space about it, it made so fine an effect, that Bandinello came through the garden of the Innocents to see it; and for all his sour and evil nature, he could not but speak well of it, though he had never spoken well of any man's work before in his life. I see your Excellency is too willing to be influenced by him." The Duke smiled not too agreeably at my words; yet he said quite good-naturedly, "Do what I wish, my Benvenuto, just to give me some satisfaction."

Then he went off, and I gave orders to have the statue uncovered. But some gold was still wanting, likewise varnish here and there, and various other little things, before the whole could be called complete; and I began to murmur wrathfully, and lament and curse the evil day that led me back to Florence. For by this time I saw clearly the tremendous loss I had sustained by quitting France; nor did I see any prospect of benefit which would accrue to me from my lord in Florence; for from the beginning all along till now, whatever I had done for him had profited me less than nothing. So it was with a mind full of discontent that next day I uncovered my statue.

Now, as it pleased God, so soon as the people caught sight of it, there rose a great shout of applause, and this gave my heart some comfort. While I had been putting the finishing touches to the thing, people never stopped pinning up sonnets to the posts of the door, over which hung a curtain. I declare to you that one day, when it was open for several hours, more than twenty sonnets were stuck up, all of them couched in terms of the very highest praise. After I had covered it again, every day a great number of sonnets were pinned up, and Latin and Greek verses, too; for it was vacation time at the University of Pisa, and all the great distinguished doctors and scholars were each other's rivals in the matter. But what pleased me most, and gave me hope, too, of favour from the Duke, was that the artists, sculptors, and painters vied with each other as to who should say the finest thing about it. One of those whose praise I valued most was the able painter Jacopo da Pontormo. Still more did I set store on that of his pupil, the excellent painter Bronzino, who was not satisfied with sticking up several sonnets he had made, but sent them by his Sandrino to my house. So eloquently did they speak my praise, in that fine style which is a rare gift of his, that I did, indeed, draw some real consolation from them. Then I covered up the statue again, and set about completing it.

xci. My Duke was well aware of the compliments which had been heaped on me by the distinguished artists of the Florentine school during the brief exhibition of my work. Nevertheless he said, "I am much pleased that Benvenuto should have had this little satisfaction. It will urge him to the desired end with more speed and diligence. But he need not think that when the whole of the statue is uncovered, and they can see all round it, that the people will speak in this tone. For all its defects will then be pointed out to him—nay, more than there really are. So let him arm himself with patience." Now these words were but a repetition of what Bandinello had said to the Duke; and he had adduced the example of certain works by Andrea del Verrocchio, who made those fine bronzes, the Christ and the Saint Thomas, which can be seen on the façade of Orsammichele; and other statues besides, even the admirable David of the divine Michel Agnolo Buonarroti, which, he said, only looked well if seen from the front. Then he spoke of his own Hercules and Cacus, and the abusive sonnets which had been written on it; and went on to hurl insults at the people of Florence. The Duke, who was far too much influenced by him, had egged him on to say this, and felt confident that the thing would turn out as he said; for Bandinello's heart was so full of envy that he never stopped from evil-speaking. And once when that hangman Bernardone, the broker, was present, he said to the Duke, by way of giving weight to Bandinello's words, "My lord, you must know that to make great statues is a very different matter from making little figures. I don't mean to say he has not done these little trifles very cleverly; but you will see that in this larger work he will have no success." And so he went on concocting his calumnies, like the treacherous spy that he was, piling up a whole mountain of falsehood.

xcii. Now, as it pleased my glorious Lord, the immortal God, I brought the thing at last to its end; and one Thursday morning I showed it openly to the whole city. No sooner had I removed the screen, though the sun was barely risen, than a great multitude of people gathered round—it would be impossible to say how many—and all with one voice strove who should laud it highest. The Duke stood at one of the lower windows of the Palace, just above the door; and there, half hidden in the embrasure, he heard every word that was said about the statue. When he had stayed listening for several hours, he got up in the best of spirits, and turning to Messer Sforza, one of his gentlemen, he said, "Sforza, go and find Benvenuto, and tell him from me that he has satisfied me far more than I expected. Tell him also that I shall satisfy him in a way that will surprise him. And so let him be of good heart." And Messer Sforza came to me on his splendid errand, which gave me great comfort. That day was a very happy one for me, what with this good news from the Duke, and with the people pointing me out to this stranger and that, as some really marvellous and unheard-of wonder. Amongst those who were most complimentary to me were two gentlemen, ambassadors from the Viceroy of Sicily to our Duke on some affairs of state. These two most courteous men met me in the Piazza. I had been pointed out to them as I passed, and they were all eagerness to come at me. So now, cap in hand, they made me such a speech of ceremony that it would have more than satisfied a pope. I bowed as low as I could; but they so overwhelmed me with their politeness that I entreated them to be good enough to come out of the Piazza with me; for the people were stopping to look at me more than they did at my Perseus. In the midst of all their ceremonious speeches they had the face to propose I should go to Sicily, promising to make a most satisfactory bargain with me. They went on to tell me how Fra Giovan Agnolo de' Servi had made them a complete fountain, adorned with many figures; but that it had none of that excellence displayed in my Perseus, though, they added, they had made a rich man of him. They would have gone on at greater length; but I broke in, "I am very much astonished at your seeking to persuade me to leave the service of so great a lord. No prince was ever so great a lover of the arts as he. Besides, I am here in my native city, the school of all the higher arts. Oh, if I had craved for riches, I might have remained in France in the service of the great King Francis, who gave me a thousand gold crowns for my maintenance, in addition to paying for all the works I did for him, so that I made more than four thousand gold crowns a year. And I left in Paris the labours of four years." With these and other words of the kind, I made short work of their courtesies. Yet I thanked them for the great praise they had bestowed on me, than which no better reward can be given to the labours of an artist. They had, I said, so increased my desire to do well, that I hoped in a few years' time to be able to show another work, which I believed would give much more satisfaction to the noble Florentine school than the one they had seen. The two gentlemen would fain have picked up the thread of their ceremonious eloquence; but with a sweep of my cap and a low bow, I bade them adieu.

xciii. When two days had come and gone, and the praises of my work swelled louder and louder, I determined to go and pay my respects to my lord Duke. He received me very amiably, saying, "Benvenuto, my friend, you have pleased and satisfied me; but I promise to satisfy you also in a way that will astonish you, and this not later than to-morrow, I tell you." Hearing these great words of hope, I turned the full strength of my soul and body to God, giving thanks to Him in all sincerity. Then on the instant I drew near to my lord Duke, and, well-nigh weeping in my joy, I kissed the hem of his garment, and said, "O my glorious master, true and most liberal patron of the arts, and of such as labour in their pursuit, I pray your most illustrious Excellency to give me eight days' leave to go and return my thanks to God; for my efforts have indeed been tremendous; and I know that my strong faith has moved Him to be my Helper. For His wonderful aid to me, now and at other times, I would fain go on an eight days' pilgrimage, only to give thanks to the immortal God, who ever aids such as sincerely call upon Him." Then the Duke inquired where I meant to go; and I replied, "To-morrow I shall take the road for Vallambrosa; thence I shall go on to Camaldoli and the Eremo, and from there to the Bagni di Santa Maria, and perhaps even to Sestile, where I hear there are fine antiquities. Afterwards I shall return by way of San Francesco dell' Alverna; and then, my heart still full of gratitude to God, come back with a right good will to serve you." The Duke gave cheerful answer, "Go then, and come back again; for verily I am much pleased with you; but let me have a line or two to remind me of your business, and leave the rest to me." Therefore, I wrote two or three lines, in which I set down my gratitude to his Excellency, and gave them to Messer Sforza, who handed them to the Duke. He took them, and then, returning them to Messer Sforza, said, "Put this every day where I shall see it; for if Benvenuto were to come back and find I have not kept my promise, I verily believe he would murder me." So, laughing, his Excellency said he was to be reminded of the business. That evening Messer Sforza repeated to me these deliberate words, laughing also, and wondering at the marked favour shown me by the Duke. Then he said good-naturedly, "Be off then, Benvenuto, and make haste back. Of a truth I envy you."

xciv. I left Florence in God's name; and I never ceased singing psalms and saying prayers to the honour and glory of God all that journey, which I much enjoyed, for the weather was lovely. It was summer-time; and my road lay through country which was new to me and very beautiful, so that I went my way full of wonder and content. One of my young workmen had come with me as guide. He was a native of Bagno, and his name was Cesare. I had the kindest reception from his father and all his household, among whom was a very charming old man more than seventy years old. He was Cesare's uncle, a surgeon by profession; and he had some trifling knowledge of alchemy. This worthy man pointed out to me that the Bagni contained gold and silver mines, and showed me many beauties of the country-side; so that I never had a better time in my life. One day, after we had grown very intimate, he said to me, "I must not fail to tell you something which is on my mind; and if his Excellency would give ear, I believe it would be much to his profit. It is this: near Camaldoli there is a pass so unde-fended that Pier Strozzi could not only cross it with ease, but could take Poppi without the slightest risk." And it was not enough for him to show me this in words; the good old fellow took a piece of paper from his pocket, on which he had drawn a plan of the whole neighbourhood, so as to make the real danger perfectly plain. I took the chart and left Bagno. Then as speedily as I could, I went on my way back to Florence by Prato Magno and San Francesco dell' Alverna.

Without stopping to do more than take off my riding-boots, I betook myself to the palace. Just by the Badia I met the Duke, who was walking along by the palace of the Podestà. As soon as he caught sight of me, he greeted me very amiably, yet with some astonishment, and said, "Oh, why have you come back so soon? I wasn't expecting you for a week." I answered, "I have come back for the service of your Excellency. Otherwise I'd have gladly stopped a few days longer on my wanderings through that lovely country." "Well, what's the news?" said he. And I answered, "My lord, there is something of the highest importance which I must show you." Then I went off with him to the palace, and there he took me in all secrecy into a room where we were quite alone. I told him all, and showed him the little plan, and he seemed to be much pleased to have it. I said to his Excellency that precautions were very urgent; whereupon he stood thinking for a while, and then said, "I may tell you that we have come to an understanding with the Duke of Urbino that he is to look after the business. But keep our counsel." Then having received marks of special favour from him, I returned home.

xcv. Next day I presented myself at the palace; and after we had talked together for a little while, the Duke said to me graciously, "To-morrow without fail I will dispatch your business. So be easy in your mind." And I, who had the utmost faith in his word, waited the morrow with eagerness. When that much-longed-for day arrived, I set out for the palace, and as bad news has ever a way of travelling faster than good, Messer Jacopo Guidi, his Excellency's secretary, called to me out of his crooked mouth and in his haughty voice, drawing himself up the while as stiff as a stick, or as if he were a frozen icicle: "The Duke says he would like to know what you ask for your Perseus." I was struck all of a heap with astonishment; nevertheless I made haste to say I was not in the habit of putting prices on my work; and that this was not what his Excellency had led me to expect two days ago. Then the fellow in a louder tone commanded me, in the name of the Duke, to tell him what I wanted for it under pain of the grave displeasure of his most illustrious Excellency. Now, not only had I been looking forward to getting a reward from his lordship, considering all the compliments he had showered on me, but still more was I confident of having secured his entire good-will, for that was all I had ever asked from him. So now this unexpected treatment of me—but especially the way in which that venomous toad did his errand—roused me to a pitch of fury. I said that were the Duke to give ten thousand crowns, I should be ill paid; and that if I had ever dreamed there would be chaffering of this sort over my work, I should never have consented to stop with him. Then the malicious creature hurled insults at me; but I gave him as good.

Next day I went to pay my respects to his Excellency, who signed to me to come near. When I did so, he called out angrily, "I could have cities and palaces built with ten thousands of ducats"; upon which I retorted that he would find any number of men capable of building cities and palaces, but maybe not one man in all the world who could make another Perseus. And I took myself off without further parleying. After a few days the Duchess sent for me, and begged me to leave her to settle my dispute with the Duke; for she felt confident she could manage the affair satisfactorily. To her kind words I made answer that the only reward I had ever asked for my labours was the good-will of the Duke, and that his Excellency had promised should be mine. What need, I asked, to place once again in their Excellencies' hands what I had freely left there from the very beginning of my service? And I added that if the Duke were to give but a *crazia*—and that's five farthings—for my trouble, I should be pleased and satisfied, if only his Excellency did not withdraw his good-will from me. The Duchess smiled somewhat and said, "Benvenuto, you would do best to follow my advice." Then she turned and left me. I had thought it prudent to speak in this humble fashion, but I could not have done worse for myself; for although she had been a good deal vexed with me, her treatment of people was not without a certain kindliness.

xcvi. In those days I was very intimate with Girolamo degli Albizzi, commissary of his Excellency's militia. So one day he said to me, "Benvenuto, you had much better arrange that little difference of yours with the Duke; and I assure you that, if you trust the affair to me, I can settle it. I know what I am saying. He is really growing angry, and it will be a bad thing for you. Enough for the present. I can't tell you everything." Now after the Duchess had spoken to me, I had been told by some one—but perhaps he was a rascal—that he had heard the Duke say—I don't know on what occasion—"For less than two farthings I'd throw the Perseus into the gutter, and that would end the disputes!" So I was anxious enough; and I told Girolamo degli Albizzi that I would leave the matter to him, and should be content with whatever he did, if only I regained the Duke's good-will. Now the excellent fellow knew all about soldiering, especially matters concerning the militia, who are all country-men; but he cared nothing for sculpture, and therefore had not the least understanding of it. So when he went to speak to the Duke, he said, "My lord, Benvenuto has put himself into my hands, and has begged me to recommend him to your Excellency's favour." To this the Duke answered, "And I, too, put myself into your hands, and shall be satisfied with whatever you decide." So Girolamo wrote a very ingenious letter in my behalf, in which he gave it as his opinion that the Duke owed me three thousand five hundred gold crowns, to be paid in gold; that this did not suffice as payment for such a masterpiece, but was to be regarded as an instalment for maintenance; yet I should be satisfied with it. And he added a great deal else, but all to the effect that this was the price we had decided on. The

Duke agreed to this, just as pleased as I was ill content. When the Duchess heard of it, she said, "The poor man would have done better to have depended on me, for I should have secured him five thousand gold crowns"; and one day when I had gone to the palace, she said the like to me in the presence of Messer Alamanno Salviati; and she laughed at me, saying my ill luck served me right.

The Duke arranged for me to have a hundred gold crowns in gold a month, till the whole sum should be paid up; and so the thing dragged on for several months. Afterwards Messer Antonio de' Nobili, who had the affair in hand, began to give me only fifty; then sometimes it would be twenty-five; and again nothing at all. So when I saw all this delay I asked Messer Antonio very courteously why he did not pay up the sum; and just as politely did he reply. However, in this reply he seemed to me to give himself away somewhat. But judge for yourselves. For first he said that the reason why he did not go on paying me, was that the palace was in sore want of money; but when money came in he would discharge the debt to me. Then he added, "On my soul, if I were not to pay you, I should indeed be a rascal!" I wondered to hear him say such a thing; yet I hoped still that when he could he would pay up. But when I saw that quite the contrary happened, and that I was being outraged, I got angry, and with bold and fiery words I reminded him of the name he said he should deserve were he not to deal honestly with me. But the man died; and five hundred gold crowns are owing to me still to-day, and we are near the end of 1566. Besides, there was a balance due to me for salary, which I thought would never be paid up now; for nearly three years had passed. But the Duke fell ill of a serious malady, the natural functions of his body being suspended for forty-eight hours. Seeing that the doctors' remedies were of no avail, perhaps he turned to God, and for that reason ordered that all those in his employment should be paid what was due to them. And I, too, was paid; but not the balance of the money for the Perseus.

xcvii. I had all but made up my mind not to write another word about my unfortunate Perseus. But something happened so important that I am forced to tell it. So I'll turn back a little and pick up the thread I had dropped. I thought I was doing very wisely when I told the Duchess that I could not make a compromise about what had passed out of my hands; for I had told the Duke that I should be satisfied with whatever he should give me. I had said this, thinking to ingratiate myself a little with them; and not only did I take this humble tone, but I sought out every possible means of pleasing the Duke. And need was there I should do so; for some days before he came to the understanding with Albizzi, he had proved he was extremely wroth with me. And this was how it came about. I went to complain to his Excellency of certain disgraceful injuries which I had suffered at the hands of Messer Alfonso Quistello, Messer Jacopo Polverino, the procurator-fiscal, and, worst of all, Ser Giovanbattista Brandini of Volterra. Well, when I was setting my case before him with some show of heat, the Duke flew into the most furious rage you can imagine. And in his fury he cried out, "It is just as it was with your Perseus, for which you asked ten thousand crowns. You let your greed get the better of you. So I shall have the thing valued, and shall give you just what it is judged to be worth." I answered rather over-boldly and with some anger—which it ill becomes one to show to the great— "How could my work possibly be valued at its true worth, since there is not a single man in Florence to-day fit to do it?" Thereat he grew more furious than ever, and he poured out his wrath on me, saying, "There is in Florence to-day a man who is quite capable of making such another statue, and, therefore, quite fit to judge it." He meant Bandinello, Knight of Saint James. Thereupon I answered, "My lord, your most illustrious Excellency has enabled me, here in the greatest school of all the world, to produce a great masterpiece, in whose execution every difficulty had to be met; and the work has received more praise than any other ever exhibited in this divinest school. My chief boast is in the praises of those who understand and are themselves masters of the art—Bronzino the painter, to name one, who was at the pains to write four sonnets, in which he spoke of me in the choicest and most glorious terms possible. Probably it was he, indeed, who woke the city to such a pitch of fervour. And I declare that had he given himself to sculpture as he has done to painting, perhaps he might have done the thing himself. Moreover, your Excellency, my master, Michel Agnolo Buonarroti, could have done it when he was younger, though it would have been no easier task to him than it was to me. But now that he is a very old man, assuredly the task would be beyond him. And I don't believe there is any other man alive who could have carried the thing through. Now my work has received the greatest reward I could desire in this world— especially as your Excellency has not only declared yourself satisfied with it, but has praised it more highly than any one else. What greater or more splendid reward could I long for? I assure your Excellency that you could pay me in no more glorious money, nor could you add anything to it, no matter what treasure you showered upon me. I am thus overpaid; and with all my heart I thank your most illustrious Excellency." To these words of mine the Duke gave answer, "I suppose you think that I have not money enough to pay you; but I tell you that I shall give you more for the thing than it is worth." To this I replied, "I never thought of any other reward from your Excellency; but I hold myself nobly paid by the approval of our Florentine school; and having this, I desire to take my leave in all haste; nor do I even wish to enter again that house which you gave to me; for I would turn my back on Florence for evermore." We had just reached Santa Felicità, and the Duke was returning to the palace. At these hot words of mine he turned on me in a great rage and said, "You shall not go! Take good heed not to go!" And I, almost terror-stricken, went along with him to the palace.

There he called for Bartolini, the Archbishop of Pisa, and also Messer Pandolfo della Stufa, and gave them orders to tell Baccio Bandinello from him that he was to make an examination of my Perseus, and to value it; for he wished me to be paid with strict justice. So these two worthies went off to find Bandinello. When they had delivered their message, he said that he had examined the work thoroughly, and knew perfectly what it was worth; but as he had had many differences with me in the past, he did not wish to be mixed up with any affairs of mine. Then the two gentlemen went on to say, "The Duke commands you, under pain of his displeasure, to value it; and says if two days or three be necessary for the business, you are to take that time. Then you will tell us what seems to you a fair price for the labour." So Bandinello replied again that he had examined the thing well; and since he might not disobey the Duke, he would say that the work was rich and beautiful, and, in his opinion, was worth sixteen thousand gold crowns at the least. The gentlemen brought back this message to the Duke—who was extremely irritated—and to me as well. But I replied that I had no desire for the eulogies of Bandinello, who spoke ill of everybody. My words were reported to the Duke, and then it was the Duchess entreated me to leave the matter to her. All this is the pure truth. But I should have done best to let the Duchess decide the question; for I should have been promptly paid, and more handsomely too.

xcviii. The Duke sent a message to me by Messer Lelio Torello, his High Chancellor, that he wished me to make some bronze bas-reliefs for the choir of S. Maria del Fiore. But the choir was by Bandinello; and I did not want to enrich his wretched work by my labours—though he had not designed it, knowing nothing at all about architecture. The design was from the hands of Giuliano, son of Baccio d'Agnolo, the carver, the man who spoiled the cupola. In any case, there is no merit about it whatsoever. So for good reasons I was unwilling to undertake the work; still, all the same, I courteously assured the Duke that I should do what he commanded me. Then his Excellency ordered the building committee of S. Maria del Fiore to co-operate with me. He would himself give me my two hundred crowns a year as before; but the rest of my provision they were to pay out of their own treasury. Well, I appeared before these officials, who told me all the Duke had ordered. Now it seemed a much easier thing to put my arguments before them than before his Excellency; and so I began to show them that the expense of all these bronze bas-reliefs would be tremendous, and the money would all be thrown away. And I gave my reasons for saying so, which they perfectly understood. The first was, that the style of the choir was quite incorrect. There was neither harmony, nor art, nor convenience, nor grace, nor good design about it. Besides, the proposed bas-reliefs would be placed below the level of vision, where the dogs would foul them. Therefore I must refuse to carry out the work. Yet I did not wish to waste my best years by falling out of the employment of his Excellency, whom I would still fain please and serve; and so if he would make use of my talents, I would have him give me the execution of the middle door of S. Maria del Fiore. Such a work, now, would be seen, and so would bring more glory to his lordship. I should strike a bargain that, unless mine was better than the finest of the Baptistery doors, I should have nothing for my pains. On the other hand, if I executed it according to my promise, I should be content to have it estimated, and to receive a thousand crowns less than its worth as stated by the valuers. The committee were much pleased with my proposal, and went to lay it before the Duke, Piero Salviati being one of them. They felt sure he would be greatly satisfied too. But not at all. He said I was always wanting to do exactly the opposite of what he suggested. And so Piero left him, with the business still undecided. When I heard this, I went at once to the Duke myself. He appeared to be in an ill humour with me; but I begged him to have the goodness to listen to me; and thus far he agreed. So I began from the beginning, and placed such excellent reasons before him that he understood at last the real state of the case, and that his own proposal meant throwing good money away. Then I soothed him by saying that, if he was not willing to give the order for the door, at least two pulpits were wanted for the choir; that these would be important works redounding to the glory of his Excellency; I would make a large number of bronze bas-reliefs for them, narrative subjects, with rich decorations. So I coaxed him to agree; and he ordered me to make the models.

I made several of these, taking the utmost pains with them. With one of them, which had eight sides, I took especial trouble, and to my thinking it was the most convenient and suitable for its purpose. After I had taken them several times to the palace, his Excellency sent me word by Messer Cesare, his Master of the Wardrobe, to leave them for his inspection. Then, when he had examined them, I saw that he had chosen the least beautiful. One day he sent for me; and while we were talking over the models, I told him—and I proved my point with many arguments—that the octagonal would be the best for the purpose, as well as the most beautiful. But he said he wished it square; he liked it better so; and we conversed together pleasantly for a long time. I did not fail to say all I could think of in the interests of art; but whether he knew I spoke the truth, and still wished to have his own way, or whatever was the reason, I heard nothing more of the business for a long time.

xcix. It was about this time that the huge block of marble for the Neptune was brought up the Arno, and then by the Grieve to the Poggio a Caiano road, that it might be brought to Florence by that level way. I went out there to see it. Though I was well aware that the Duchess had got it for the Cavaliere Bandinello by her special favour, I felt no jealousy of him; but pity seized me for that poor unlucky block of marble. For, observe, if a thing be marked out for an evil destiny, it is useless to try to save it from a threatening ill. Something far worse only befalls it. So was it with this marble when it came into the hands of Bartolommeo Ammanato, of whom I shall speak the truth in its own place. Well, after I had looked at this magnificent block, I measured it carefully every way, and when I went back to Florence I made several little models proportionate to its dimensions. Then I set off for Poggio a Caiano, where the Duke and Duchess were with their son, the Prince. I found them at table; and as the Duke and Duchess were eating apart from the rest, I began to talk to the Prince. After a time the Duke, who was in an adjoining room, heard me, and did me the honour of calling me. When I entered the presence of their Excellencies, the Duchess began to speak very amiably to me, till at last I was able to introduce the subject of the splendid block of marble I had seen. Then I went on to tell how their fathers had bred great talents in the noble school of Florentine art only by pitting the best artists against each other in honourable rivalry. So was the wonderful cupola, and so were the exquisite doors of San Giovanni made, and many other temples and statues besides, which were now a crown of genius on their city's head, the like of which had never been seen since ancient days. All at once the Duchess broke in angrily, saying she understood my drift quite well, and she forbade me ever to speak another word about that marble in her hearing, for it displeased her. I answered, "Then I displease you in desiring to be your Excellencies' procurator, and in striving that you be better served? Think a little, my lady; if your Excellencies will consent that each of us make a model for the Neptune, though you have made up your minds to give it to Bandinello, it will come about that, for his own credit, he will take more pains with his than if there were no competitors. Thus you will be better served, and will not bring discouragement to this marvellous school of Florence. You will see which of us is in the right way—I mean, who follows the great style of our wonderful art; and will prove yourselves to be princely patrons of taste and understanding." The Duchess got in a temper and told me I wearied her to death, and that she wanted Bandinello to have the marble. "Ask the Duke," she went on, "for his Excellency is of the same mind." When the Duchess had finished, the Duke, who till now had been dumb, said, "It is twenty years since I had that fine block dug up specially for Bandinello; and so I want him to have it for his very own." Then I turned to him and said, "My lord, I beg that you will be good enough to hear me while I say three or four words in your own interest." He answered I might say what I liked; he would listen. Then I went on, "You must know, my lord, that the marble out of which Bandinello made his Hercules and Cacus was dug for the divine Michel Agnolo, who had made the model of a Samson with four figures about him. It would have been the finest thing in the world. Now your Bandinello only got two figures out of it; and a wretched bit of cobbled work it was, too; so that the noble school still cries out at the great wrong which the fine marble suffered. I believe that over a thousand sonnets were stuck up, crying shame on the miserable bit of work; and I know your Excellency remembers the circumstance quite well. And so, my valorous lord, because those who were responsible for that work were so ignorant as to take away the fine block of marble from Michel Agnolo—though it had been quarried for him—and give it to Bandinello, who spoiled it, as is plainly to be seen, will you suffer that he should spoil this still more wonderful block, though it be his, rather than give it to an abler man, who would get the best out of it for you? I entreat of you, my lord, consent that whoever has the will may make a model. Then let them all be exhibited to the school; your Excellency will hear what the artists say; and with your good judgment you will know how to choose the best. In this way you will neither be throwing away your money, nor taking the heart out of so talented a school as ours, unique to-day in all the world, and the chief glory of your Excellency." The Duke had listened very amiably; and when he got up from table, he turned to me and said, "Go, my Benvenuto; make a model, and win the fine marble; for it is the truth you tell me. That I own." But the Duchess shook her head threateningly, and muttered I know not what in her anger. I did them reverence, and went back to Florence, dying with impatience to begin upon the model.

c. The Duke returned to Florence, and came to see me at my house without a word beforehand. I showed him two different designs I had made. He praised them both, but said he liked one better than the other, and bade me finish it carefully, for it would be to my profit. He had seen Bandinello's and the others' too; but he said mine was a long way better than the rest. So was I told by many of the people of his court who had heard him. Among other notable things I remember in this regard, there is one which merits every attention. The Cardinal of Santa Fiore came to Florence on a visit, and the Duke took him to Poggio a Caiano. As he passed along the road, he saw the block of marble. He praised it greatly, and then asked his Excellency for what sculptor he intended it. The Duke answered without hesitation, "My Benvenuto, who has made me a magnificent model for it." And this was told me by trustworthy persons. So I went to pay a visit to the Duchess, and took her some pretty little trifles of my jeweller's art, which gave her great pleasure. Thereupon she asked me what I was working at; and I answered, "My lady, I have undertaken for my own pleasure one of the most difficult things in the world. It is a Christ of whitest marble on a cross of blackest marble, of the size of a well-grown man." She asked at once what I meant to do with it. "I would have you know, my lady," I answered, "that I would not give it for two thousand gold ducats paid in gold; for surely never did any man before take in hand a thing of such extreme difficulty. Neither would I have undertaken to do it for the greatest prince, lest I might be shamed by my failure. I bought the marbles with my own money; and for about two years past I have kept a lad to help me with it; so that between the marbles, and the iron framework on which it is set up, and wages, it has cost me more than three hundred crowns. And, therefore, I would not sell it for two thousand in gold. But if your most illustrious Excellency will do me a very permissible favour, I shall give it you freely with much good-will. It is only this, that you neither favour me nor take sides against me in this matter of the models of the Neptune, which his Excellency has ordered for the great block of marble." At this she was very angry, and said, "So you are quite indifferent both to my help and to my disfavour?" "Nay, my lady," I answered, "since I am now making you an offer of what I deem worth two thousand ducats. But I am so confident in the result of the hard, disciplined study I have devoted to my art, that I think to gain the palm, even were the great Michel Agnolo Buonarroti in the running, from whom alone in all the world I have learnt what I know. And I would much rather have him as rival, with all his skill, than those others with their little; for I should reap great honours in contest with the great master; but there is little credit to be had in surpassing the rest." When I had made an end of speaking, she got up as if vexed with me; and I went back to my model to work at it with all the energy that was in me.

As soon as it was completed, the Duke came to inspect it, accompanied by two ambassadors from the Duke of Ferrara and the Signory of Lucca. He was much pleased with it, and said to the gentlemen, "Without a doubt Benvenuto deserves it." Then they complimented me warmly, more especially the ambassador from Lucca, who was a man of taste and learning. I had gone apart that they might say whatever they liked; but hearing these complimentary words, I went up to the Duke and said, "My lord, your Excellency should demand still another test; you should order those of us who care to undergo it, to make a clay model of the size which the marble will allow of.

Then you will see much better who deserves the order. And I say that if your Excellency should give it to an incapable man, this will not wrong the deserving sculptor so much as it will wrong yourself; for you will lose both your money and your credit. Whereas, if you give it to the right man, you will win the greatest glory, and make an excellent investment of your money; and all persons of taste will believe you do, indeed, take delight in art and have a knowledge of it." The Duke shrugged his shoulders at my words. When he was moving away, the ambassador of Lucca said to him, "My lord, this Benvenuto of yours is a terrible man!" And the Duke replied, "He is much more terrible than you know; and it would be a good thing for him if he had been less so; for then he'd be more prosperous to-day than he is." These deliberate words were reported to me by the ambassador himself, as if he would have chid me for my conduct. I answered that I wished to do my duty to my lord as became his loving and faithful servant; but I did not know how to flatter him. A few weeks after this Bandinello died; and the rumour was, that besides his excesses, his sorrow at the prospect of losing the marble had some part in his death.

ci. Now when Bandinello heard that I was making the Crucifix I have spoken of, he got hold of a piece of marble, and made the Pietà which can be seen to-day in the Church of the Annunziata. I had intended my Crucifix for Santa Maria Novella, and had already put up the great hooks on which I meant it to hang. All I asked in return was to make a little tomb under it, where my bones might lie when I was dead. The brothers told me they could not grant such a thing without the leave of the church-wardens; whereupon I said to them, "My brothers, why did you not crave their leave before finding a place for my fine Crucifix? You never asked them whether I might fix up the hooks and make the other arrangements." So I had no more mind to give the results of all my hard labour to the Church of Santa Maria Novella, though the wardens afterwards came to beg me for it. I turned my steps at once to the Church of the Annunziata; and when I offered it on the same conditions as I had made to Santa Maria Novella, the good brothers of the Annunziata were all agreed that I should place it in their church; and allowed me to make my tomb in whatever fashion seemed good to me. Bandinello got wind of this; hurried on with his Pietà, and besought the Duchess to get him the Pazzi Chapel for it. This he got with some difficulty, and then made all haste to fix up his Pietà there. But he died before it was finished.

The Duchess declared that as she had helped him in life, so would she be his friend in death; and though he was dead, I need never make any effort to get the marble. And so Bernardone the broker told me one day when I met him out in the country, that she had settled the matter; whereupon I said, "O unhappy marble! Surely, its fate would have been evil enough had it fallen into the hands of Bandinello; but left to Ammanato, it fares a hundred times worse." The Duke had ordered me to make a clay model as large as the block would allow of; and he had supplied me with wood and clay, and let me raise a kind of screen in the Loggia where my Perseus is, paying a workman to help me. So with all haste I made the wooden framework after my excellent method. Then I finished the model with good success, though I had given up the thought of carrying it out in marble, knowing the Duchess was determined I should not have the commission. But I did not care. I was, indeed, pleased to give myself all this trouble; for I looked forward to making her very sorry, when she should have seen my finished design—she was an intelligent person, as I was afterwards aware—for doing so great a wrong to the marble and to herself. Giovanni the Fleming, too, made a model in the cloisters of Santa Croce, and Vicenzio Danti the Perugian made one in the house of Messer Ottaviano de' Medici; another was begun by the son of Moschino at Pisa; and another by Bartolommeo Ammanato in the Loggia, which we divided between us. When I had blocked mine well out, and was about to finish the head, which I had already done in the rough, the Duke came down from the palace; and Giorgetto the painter took him into Ammanato's place to see the Neptune—on which, by the way, Giorgino himself had been working for several days, along with Ammanato and all his helpers. While the Duke was looking at it, I was told that it pleased him very little; and though Giorgino would have rammed a deal of silly nonsense down his throat, his Excellency shook his head, and turning to Messer Gianstefano, said, "Go and ask Benvenuto if his giant is well enough on for him to be willing to give me a glimpse of it." Messer Gianstefano delivered the Duke's message to me in most courteous and amiable terms, adding that if my work did not seem to me in a condition to be shown, I was to say so frankly; for the Duke was well aware that I had had little aid in my great undertaking. I answered that I should esteem his coming a great favour, and that though my work was still very incomplete, his Excellency's intelligence was such that he would understand perfectly how it would appear when finished. So the worthy gentleman carried my message back to the Duke, who came eagerly to see my model. No sooner was he inside my enclosure and had glanced at my work, than he showed his full satisfaction. He walked all round, stopping to examine it from all four sides, just as if he had been the most accomplished judge of the art; and his every look and gesture proved his great delight. But all he said was, "Benvenuto, you have now only to polish it up." Then turning to those who had come with him, he expressed his high approval of my work, saying, "The little model I saw in his house pleased me very much; but this far surpasses it in excellence."

cii. It pleased God, who doeth all things for our utmost good—at least He is ever the defender of such as confess Him and believe in Him—that in those days I fell in with a rascal from Vicchio called Piermaria d'Anterigoli, commonly called Lo Sbietta, a sheep-farmer by occupation. As he was a near relative of Messer Guido Guidi, the physician, now the provost of Pescia, I gave ear to him when he offered to sell me a farm for the term of my natural life. I would not go and see the farm, being all eagerness to finish the model of my huge Neptune; and, indeed, there was no need for me to see it, since he only sold me the income of it. This he had written down for me as consisting of so many bushels of grain, so much wine, oil, growing corn, chestnuts, and whatever else the land produced; and I reckoned that, according to current prices, these were worth upwards of a hundred gold crowns in gold; while I paid him six hundred and fifty, counting the taxes. Thus, as I had a script in his own hand, promising to keep up the income of the farm at its present state of efficiency during my lifetime, I had no desire to go and see the place—although I made the most searching inquiries as to whether Sbietta and his brother Ser Filippo were substantial enough persons to render my investment safe. Many different persons who knew them, told me that the security was all that could be desired. The lawyer whom we called in was Ser Pierfrancesco Bertoldi, notary to the Mercantanzia; and without delay I put into his hands the written acknowledgment of what Sbietta bound himself to hand over to me, thinking that this would appear in the contract. But the lawyer who drew it up was so busy over the noting down of two and twenty particular conditions which Sbietta insisted on, that it seems to me he must have forgotten to include in the agreement the statement of the income which the seller had bound himself to give me. All the time the notary was writing, I kept on working; and as he plodded over his task hour after hour, I got well forward with my Neptune's head. When the contract had been duly drawn up and signed, Sbietta began to show me the most marked politeness; and I was no less courteous to him. He sent me presents of kids, cheeses, capons, curds, and different fruits, until I became not a little ashamed. In return for his kindness, I used to bring him away from his inn every time he came to Florence, and lodge him in my own house; and if any of his relatives were with him, as frequently happened, they came to me, too. Then he began to say to me in a jesting fashion how it was a shame that I had bought a farm weeks and weeks ago, yet had never made up my mind to leave my business to my men even for three days, in order to come and see it. At last he cajoled me into consenting; and, as ill luck would have it, I set off one day for the farm. Sbietta gave me the kindest and most honourable reception in his house—he could have done no more for a duke; and his wife was still more demonstrative. And so things remained between us till he had fully arranged what he and Ser Filippo his brother had planned to do.

ciii. But all this time I was hurrying on with my work on the Neptune; and already I had blocked it out, as I have said, on an excellent method, which no one had ever used or thought of before. And though I was sure the marble was not for me—I have already told you why—I had a mind to finish the model as soon as possible, and show it off on the Piazza, merely for my own satisfaction.

The season was warm and pleasant; and as I had been coaxed by the two scoundrels, I set out one Wednesday—it was a double Saints' day—from my villa at Trespiano. I stayed so long over an excellent lunch that it was more than twenty o'clock when I reached Vicchio. At the gate of the town I met with Ser Filippo, who seemed to know where I was going. He was all politeness to me, and took me to Sbietta's house, where we found that shameless wife of his, who likewise overwhelmed me with attentions. I presented her with a hat of the finest straw, and she said she had never seen a more elegant one. But Sbietta was not there. As evening drew on, we supped together very pleasantly. I was shown to a handsome chamber, where I slept between sheets as white as snow; and my two servants were also well entertained, according to their rank. When I got up in the morning, this kindness still continued. I went to look at my farm and was much pleased with it; and I was put in possession of a certain quantity of grain and standing crops.

When I got back to Vicchio, the priest Ser Filippo said to me, "Benvenuto, let your mind be at rest. You may not have found to-day the whole of what was promised you. Yet be assured; it will turn out all right, for you are dealing with honest men. But I must tell you we have sent that labourer whom you know packing, for he is a rogue." He was speaking of a man called Mariano Rosegli, who now said to me, repeating it more than once, "Look out for your own. In the end you'll know which of us is the bigger rogue." When the countryman said this to me, he sniggered in a malicious fashion, tossing his head as if to say, "Go and see for yourself."

I could not help thinking there was something wrong; but I never imagined what actually happened to me. When I returned from the farm, which is two miles from Vicchio, towards the Alpi, I found the priest, who greeted me with his wonted politeness, and we sat down to meat together. It was not dinner, but an excellent collation. Then I went for a walk about Vicchio, where the market had already begun; but I observed that everybody looked at me as if I were some very unusual kind of being, and especially a very honest man, an old inhabitant of the place, whose wife bakes bread for sale. He has some good land of his own about a mile away; but he likes to live like this; and rents a house of mine in the town, which came to me along with the farm of La Fonte I have been speaking of. Now he said to me, "I am your tenant, and I'll pay the rent when it falls due, or before then, if you like. You may be sure we shall not quarrel." While we were talking, I noticed him looking hard at me; so I could not help saying, "Tell me, dear Giovanni, I beg you, why you go on staring at me so fixedly?" And the worthy fellow answered, "I shall tell you willingly, if you promise me, on your word as an honest man, not to tell whom you heard it from." I gave him the promise; whereupon he said, "Well, I'd have you know that that rascally priest Ser Filippo, not many days ago, was going about boasting of his brother Sbietta's clever trick in selling his farm to an old man for his lifetime, who would not last the year. You have got into the hands of a pack of scoundrels; so take good care of your life. Be wide awake, for there's need of it. I will say no more."

civ. While I was going about the market, I came across Giovanbatista Santini; and the priest brought us both back to supper. And as I said before, the meal was prepared for about twenty o'clock. It was on my account we supped so early, because I wished to return that night to Trespiano. So everything was got ready, and Sbietta's wife fussed about a great deal with their menial Cecchino Buti. The salads were dressed, and we were just sitting down to table, when that wicked priest said, with an evil leer, "You must pardon me; but I cannot sup with you, for I have a bit of important business on hand for my brother Sbietta. As he is not here, I must look after it for him." We all entreated him to remain with us; but he would not be persuaded. So he went off, and we sat down to eat. We had eaten our salad off common plates; but when the boiled beef was to be served, each of us was given a bowl. Santini, who was sitting opposite me, said, "They give you quite different dishes from the rest of us. Did you ever see anything finer?" I replied that I had not observed it. Then he bade me ask Sbietta's wife to sit down at table with us; for she and Cecchino Buti were running about, fussing here and there in the strangest manner. In the end I persuaded the lady to sit down; and then she began to lament, "My food does not please you; you eat nothing at all." I praised the supper over and over again, saying I had never eaten a better, nor with more appetite. But now I was quite satisfied. I couldn't think why the woman pressed me so to eat. It was past twenty-one o'clock when we had finished supper; and I was in a hurry to get back that night to Trespiano, so that I might get on next day with my work in the Loggia. I bade farewell to them all, thanked the lady, and took my departure. I had not gone three miles before I felt a burning in my stomach; and I was in such pain that I thought I should never reach my farm at Trespiano. But, as it pleased God, I got there at last after great efforts. It was late, and I prepared at once to go to bed. All that night I could not sleep for the disorder in my bowels. As soon as it was daylight, I discovered from my motions what made me suspect I had eaten something poisonous; and I went over and over in my mind what it could possibly have been. Then I bethought me of the plates and bowls and other dishes given me by Sbietta's wife, which were different from the others; and how that rascally priest, Sbietta's brother, had been so officiously polite, and yet would not stay to sup with us. Moreover, I recalled how he had boasted of his brother's clever trick in having sold a farm to an old man for his lifetime, who would not last the year—according to the report of that honest man Giovanni Sardella. So I felt sure that they had given me a dose of sublimate in the sauce, which was very well made, and most pleasant to the taste; for sublimate produces exactly the symptoms I noticed in myself. I am not used to eat much sauce or any seasoning with my meat, except salt; and yet I had eaten two mouthfuls, because it tasted so good. Then I went on to remember how often the wife of Sbietta pressed me in all sorts of ways to take more of it; so that I was convinced that they had put a dash of sublimate in my sauce.

cv. Wretchedly ill as I was, I was determined to work on my huge statue in the Loggia. However, after a few days, my sore sickness was too much for me, and I stopped in bed. And as soon as the Duchess heard that I was ill, she had the accursed marble given over to Bartolommeo Ammanato. He sent me word by Messer . . . living in the Via . . . that I might do whatever I liked with the model I had begun, since he had got the marble. This Messer . . . was one of the lovers of Bartolommeo Ammanato's wife; and as he excelled all the others in gentleness and tact, Ammanato gave him abundant opportunities. Of this I could tell much. But I have no wish to do like Bandinello, his master, who never kept to the point in talking. Enough to say that I told Ammanato's envoy that I had known it all the time. I sent Bartolommeo the advice to strive to prove his gratitude to Fortune for this great mark of favour shown him through no merit of his own.

So I stayed in bed in wretched case, cared for by that most excellent man, Maestro Francesco da Monte Varchi, the physician. The surgeon, Maestro Raffaello de' Pilli, co-operated with him; for the sublimate had so burnt my intestines that I suffered from continuous diarrhœa. At last Messer Francesco recognised that the poison had done all the ill it could; for there had not been enough of it to overcome the vigour of my excellent constitution; so he said to me one day, "Benvenuto, give thanks to God; for you have conquered; and rest assured that I am going to cure you, just to spite the scoundrels who wished you ill." Then Maestro Raffaello said, "This will be one of the most wonderful and hardest cures ever heard of; for you must know, Benvenuto, that you swallowed a mouthful of sublimate." But Maestro Francesco cut in with, "Perhaps it was a poisonous caterpillar." And I answered that I knew quite well what poison it was, and who had given it to me. And here we all became silent. They went on tending me for more than six whole months; and a year had gone by before I regained my full strength.

cvi. About this time [October 28, 1560], the Duke made his public entry into Siena; and Ammanato had gone there several months beforehand to erect the triumphal arches. A natural son of his who had stopped behind in the Loggia workshop, had taken off the coverings from my unfinished Neptune model. I went at once to lay my complaint before Signor Don Francesco, the Duke's son, who had proved himself a good friend of mine, and told him how they had uncovered my unfinished figure. Had it been complete, I should not have cared. Thereupon the Prince replied, shaking his head in a threatening fashion, "Benvenuto, do not be vexed at its being uncovered; for they do most harm of all to themselves. However, if you prefer that I should cover it up again, I shall do so." And his most illustrious Excellency added several other words complimentary to me in the presence of several of his lords. Then I begged him to give me the means of completing it; for I would fain make a present of it, along with the little model, to his Excellency. He replied that he should be pleased to accept both; and that he would order that everything necessary for my work should be supplied to me. And so I fed on this little favour, which, indeed, was the saving of my life; for so many terrible ills and vexations coming on me all at once, I felt myself failing under them. But this little courtesy strengthened me with some hopes of life.

cvii. A year had now gone by since I had bought the La Fonte farm from Sbietta; and as if poisoning and cheating me were not enough, I found that the land did not produce half what they had promised me. Besides the contract, I had a document in Sbietta's own hand, in which he declared himself bound before witnesses to keep up the stated income. So I betook myself to the Lords in Council. Messer Alfonso Quistello was living then. He was procurator-fiscal, and sat in the Council, of which Averardo Serristori and Federigo de' Ricci were also members. I do not remember the names of all; but one of the Alessandri was among them; and at all events, they were very important persons. Now when I had put my case before these magistrates, they all with one accord decided that Sbietta should give me back my money—except Federigo de' Ricci, who was making use of Sbietta at that time himself. The rest expressed their regret that he hindered the settlement of the business. Indeed, Averardo Serristori made a great fuss about it, and so did Alessandri; but Federigo was clever enough to make the affair drag on till these magistrates' term of office was up. So some time after this I came upon Serristori one morning in the Piazza dell' Annunziata; and he called out to me, in the most reckless fashion, "Federigo de' Ricci has got the better of the whole of us; and you are wronged against our will." I will say no more about this, lest it should prove too offensive to the highest powers of the State. Let it suffice to say that I suffered gross injustice because of the arbitrary will of a rich citizen, who happened to be in need of the services of that cheat of a sheep-farmer.

cviii. I then betook myself to Leghorn, where the Duke was, to beg him to let me leave his service. For I felt my strength coming back, and yet I was left without employment; and it angered me to see such wrong done to my art. So now I made my mind up; and reaching Leghorn, found the Duke, who received me most kindly. I stayed there several days, and every day I rode out with his Excellency. Thus I had an excellent chance of saying all I wanted; for he used to ride four miles out of Leghorn, shaving the sea-coast, to a place where he was building a small fortress. He did not wish to be troubled by a train of courtiers, and so he liked to have me with him to talk to him. Well, one day seeing him very well disposed to me, I began on the subject of Sbietta, I mean Piermaria d'Anterigoli, and said, "My lord, I should like to relate to your Excellency a most curious occurrence, which will explain to you what prevented me from finishing the Neptune in clay, that I was working at in the Loggia. I must tell you that I had bought a farm from Sbietta for my lifetime." In brief, I told him the whole story in all its particulars, stating the bare truth without a stain of falsehood on it. Then when I came to the poison, I begged him, if I, his servant, had ever found favour in his sight, instead of punishing Sbietta or those who gave me the poison, rather to give them some reward. For the poison had not been enough to kill me, but just enough to cure me of a deadly viscosity, which had attacked my stomach and my intestines. So well had it done its work, and so much had it bettered my health, that, whereas in the condition in which I was, I had but three or four years to live, now I could look forward to more than twenty. "And so with better will than ever I give thanks to God. And, therefore, it is true what I have often heard folk say,

God sends us ill that good may come of it."

The Duke was an attentive listener for more than two miles of our road. The only thing he said was, "Oh, the scoundrels!" But I ended my tale by saying I was beholden to them; and started other and pleasanter topics. I waited for the right day, and then finding him in a good humour, begged his Excellency to give me leave to go away, that I might not waste the years in which I should still be good for something. What was owing to me for my Perseus he might give to me when it pleased him. Then I went on to thank his lordship, and to pay him high compliments at great length. He answered nothing at all; indeed he looked as if he had taken my words in ill part. Next day Messer Bartolommeo Concino, one of the Duke's chief secretaries, paid me a visit; and said to me, in a rather overbearing way, "The Duke says that if you want to go, you can. But if you wish to work, he'll put work in your way. May you only be able for all his Excellency gives you to do!" I replied that I desired nothing better than work, and from his most illustrious Excellency more than any other man in the world, were he pope, or emperor, or king. "I would more willingly serve him for a sou than any other for a ducat." Thereupon he said, "If you are of that way of thinking, you and he are agreed; and there is no more to be said. So take your way back to Florence; and be easy in your mind, for the Duke wishes you well." And so I returned to Florence.

cix. As soon as I had got back, I had a visit from a man called Raffaellone Scheggia, a cloth-of-gold weaver. He said to me, "Benvenuto, my friend, I should like to make up the quarrel between you and Piermaria Sbietta." I replied that no one could do that save the Lords in Council; and that on the present bench Sbietta would not have a Federigo de' Ricci, a man careless of God and his own honour, who, for the sake of two fat kids, would uphold so villainous a cause and fly in the face of holy justice. When I had said this and a great deal else, Raffaello still insisted with gentle obstinacy, that it is better to eat a thrush in peace than a fat capon got by strife. Besides, he said, it was the way of lawsuits to spin out to wearisome length; and that I would do much better to spend my time in the production of some masterpiece, which would bring me a great deal more honour and profit. I knew it was the truth he was speaking; so I began to lend an ear to his words, and in a short time we came to this agreement. Sbietta was to be my tenant on the farm at a rent of seventy gold crowns in gold a year, for all the time of my natural life. However, when the contract between us was drawn up by Ser Giovanni, Ser Matteo of Falgano's son, Sbietta declared that by our proposed arrangement we should pay a higher tax. He would stick to his word; but it would be better that he should take the farm on a five years' lease; and he promised he would renew it without provoking any further suits at law. His rascally brother, the priest, promised the same; and so the contract was drawn up for five years.

cx. I should like to speak of something else, and leave off talking for a while of all this shocking roguery; yet I must first of all tell what took place at the end of the five years. The two scoundrels then refused to keep a single one of their promises; they were for giving up my farm, and renting it no longer. I complained loudly; but they faced me boldly with the contract; and I was helpless against this breach of faith on their part. So I told them that neither the Duke nor the Prince of Florence would tolerate such abominable treatment of their citizens; and this threat put a terror on them so that they again sent to me Raffaello Scheggia, the man who had made it up between us before. They had said, you must know, that they would not pay me seventy gold crowns in gold, as they had done for the last five years; and I had answered that I would take nothing less. Well, Raffaello came to see me, and he said, " Benvenuto, my friend, you know I have your interests at heart. Now, they have left the whole affair to me"—and he showed me a declaration to this effect signed by them. I had no idea that he was a near relative of theirs; and I thought I could not be better served than by him, and put myself unconditionally into his hands. Well, my fine gentleman comes to me one evening about half an hour past sundown—it was the month of August—and after a deal of palaver, he induced me to draw up the contract right away; for he knew that were it put off till the morrow, the trick he was playing on me would fail. So the agreement was signed, whereby they bound themselves to pay me sixty-five crowns *di moneta* a year, in two instalments, for the term of my natural life. In vain did I chafe against it, and declare I would not abide it. Raffaello pointed to the agreement written in my own hand; and so induced everyone to hold me in the wrong. He had done everything for my good, he declared; he had been acting in my interest; and as neither the notary nor any one else knew how nearly related he was to the other parties, everybody told me I was at fault. So I soon gave up the fight; and now I must do my best to live as long as possible. But I blundered again a little after, in the December of next year, which was 1566; for I bought half the farm of Poggio from them, that is from Sbietta, for two hundred crowns *di moneta*. It was to revert to them at the end of three years; and I let it out to them meanwhile. The farm borders on my land at La Fonte. I did this for the best. But it would take too long to write down all their villainous conduct towards me. I give the matter into the hands of God, who has ever been my protector against such as have willed to do me harm.

cxi. When I had brought my marble Crucifix to completion, it seemed to me that by raising it several cubits it would show to much more advantage than did it rest on the ground. It looked very well as it was; but when it was raised, its beauty was enhanced, and I was well satisfied with it. Then I began to show it to all who were curious to see it. As God willed, word of it was brought to the Duke and Duchess; so that one day after they came back from Pisa, their Excellencies took me by surprise. With all the nobility of their court they came to my house, merely to see the Crucifix. It pleased them so much that neither the one nor the other could stop singing its praises; and, of course, all the lords and gentlemen who were with them followed suit. Then when I saw how much they admired it, I thanked them, saying in something of a mildly jesting humour, that their refusal of the marble for the Neptune had been my opportunity of carrying through all the labours of the present work, the like of which no man had ever undertaken before; and though it had cost me greater efforts than I ever made in all my life, I felt assured they had been well spent, more especially since their most illustrious Excellencies had heaped such praises on it. Then I added, "As I can never hope to find any one more worthy of it than are your Excellencies, I make you a present of it with right good will." All I begged of them was that before they went away, they would deign to come down to the basement of my house. Thereupon they got up at once with the greatest good humour, left the shop with me, and entering my house, saw my little model of the Neptune and the fountain, which the Duchess had never seen before. She was so struck with the sight of it, that she uttered a great cry of wonder; and, turning to the Duke, she said, "By my life, I never could have conceived the tenth part of such beauty as this!" while the Duke went on repeating, "Didn't I tell you so?" And they talked amongst themselves for a long time; and it was all in compliment to me. Then the Duchess called me to her, and praised my work to me almost as if she were excusing herself. (Indeed, from her words you might have judged she was asking my pardon.) She said she would like me to have a block of marble dug up for myself, and then to set about the work. I answered that, if their Excellencies gave me the means of doing so, I would willingly, for love of them, begin the formidable undertaking; whereupon the Duke replied, "Benvenuto, whatever you require for the work will be given you; and on my own account, I shall provide you with means far beyond what you can ask for." With these courteous words they took their leave, and I was very well content.

cxii. Week after week passed by; but there was no word of me and my commission; and seeing no preparations made for it, I was nearly desperate. About this time the Queen of France sent Messer Baccio del Bene to our Duke, to negotiate a loan of money; and the Duke granted the request most graciously, it was reported. Now Messer Baccio and I had once been very intimate; and when we met again in Florence, we were most pleased to renew our intercourse. He told me of all the great honours done him by his Excellency; and, in the course of our conversation, asked me if I had any great works on hand. So I told him the whole story of the huge Neptune statue and the fountain from the beginning, and the great injustice done me by the Duchess. On hearing this, he informed me that her Majesty was most eager to have the tomb of her late husband King Henry completed; that Daniello of Volterra had undertaken to make for it a great bronze horse, but that the time was up in which he had promised it. The most splendid ornaments would be wanted for the tomb; so if I would return to France, to my own castle, she would supply me with every convenience for carrying on my work which I might ask for, had I but the will to serve her. I told Messer Baccio to ask me from my Duke; for, were his Excellency willing, I should gladly return to France. Then Messer Baccio, in high spirits, said, "We shall go back together"; and spoke as if the thing were done. So next day, in an interview with the Duke, he spoke of me, and said that if his Excellency would graciously permit it, the Queen would employ me in her service. Thereupon the Duke made answer, "Everybody knows what a clever man Benvenuto is; but now he has no more desire to work"; and then he talked about other things. The day after I went to see Messer Baccio, who told me everything. Then I could keep myself in no longer; and I cried out, "Ah! when his Excellency gave me nothing to do, I, on my own account, completed one of the most difficult works ever man attempted. It cost me more than two hundred crowns, which I paid out of my poverty. What, then, should I not have done if his Excellency had employed me? I tell you of a truth, a great wrong has been done me." The worthy gentleman reported all my answer to the Duke; whereupon his lordship told him it was all a joke, and that he wanted to keep me for himself. This angered me so, that many a time I was on the point of making off without anybody's leave. But the Queen dropped the subject, lest she should offend the Duke; and I remained where I was, very ill pleased.

cxiii. About this time the Duke set out on a journey with all his court and all his sons, save the Prince, who was in Spain. They made their way by the Sienese marshes to Pisa. The Cardinal was the first to be affected by the poisonous air of the Maremma. In a few days he was attacked by a pestilential fever; and shortly after he died. He was as the Duke's right eye, a handsome youth, and a good; and his death was a great misfortune. I let several days pass, till I thought their tears might be dried; and then I set off for Pisa.

HERE ENDS BENVENUTO'S MANUSCRIPT.

BENVENUTO'S LAST DAYS

CELLINI wrote his *Life* at intervals, from 1558 to 1566, but he carried his story no further than 1562, and stopped there very abruptly. Old age and ill-health were on him, and the zest for life was passing—though perhaps his spirit was not quite so much bowed as the plaintive tone of his correspondence might lead us to believe; for even in his lusty days his letters were apt to be pitched in a minor key. But at least the best was over: he had few more triumphs to record, and a good many petty defeats, disappointments, and chill neglect. He took up his pen again, but it was to retell part of the old tale in the *Trattati*. These, written for a special occasion, necessarily interrupted his work on the *Memoirs*, and by the time they were finished it is possible that the domestic happiness he evidently enjoyed in his latter days may have had the effect of lulling his irritability—or shall we say diverting his self-assertion?—and these with him were the chief impulses to autobiography. In 1565 he married Piera di Salvadore Parigi. She had been his servant and his mistress; and he made her his wife out of gratitude for her good nursing during the last serious illness recorded in the *Memoirs*, the result, as he asserts, of his being poisoned by Sbietta and his rascally brother Ser Filippo. After his marriage his wife bore him two children— *dolci figliuolini*—a daughter and a son, Maddalena and Andrea Simone. But the children of the same mother, born out of wedlock, were also legitimised; and one of these, Giovanni, was for several years his chief hope and treasure. There is a ring of real sorrow in his letter to Varchi telling of the death of the child: "In all my life I have never had anything more dear."

But before the birth of Giovanni he had adopted a boy, Antonio, son of Domenico di Parigi, or Sputasenni, perhaps a relative of Piera who became his wife. The boy's mother was Dorotea, Cellini's model for the Medusa; Domenico his father was a cloth-weaver, afterwards a gate-keeper at Pisa and Florence, and always a scoundrel. While Domenico was in prison, Benvenuto lodged his wife and family, Tonino and Bita, in his own house; and though he tried, without success, to get paid for their board, or at least made a very definite memorandum of their indebtedness to him, all the credit for his charity need not be taken from him, for he did his best to be a father to the boy, called him by his own name, and adopted him in the hope of training him as a goldsmith. Benvenutino could or would learn nothing. He hardly got to know his A B C or anything else in six years, says Cellini, who sent him to school to the *frati* of the Annunziata—evidently without any decided intention of making a friar of him. Cellini may not have been an ideal trainer of youth, but it appears he did what he could to interest the boy, now called Fra Lattanzio, and employ him profitably. For instance, we hear of his arranging with Fra Maurizio to teach him the organ. When Domenico, who had been in Pisa, came to take charge of one of the Florence gates, Benvenuto was naturally afraid lest all he and the friars had done for the lad would be wasted. So, while permitting him to receive visits from his parents (who by this time were complaining loudly of his being turned into a friar), and even urging on him particular courtesy towards them—he may even "kiss the ground on which they tread"—he forbade him to go to their house, where he would see "infinite poverty and filth." The boy snapped his fingers at the prohibition; and, indeed, the friars seem to have upheld Benvenuto's authority very little. So in 1569 Cellini disinherited the scapegrace. Next year Domenico brought an action against him for breach of contract in the matter, and won. This meant that Benvenuto had not only to maintain Antonio, who had left the Annunziata, but that a claim was made on his estate. He appealed to the Duke, relating the disobedience and worthlessness of his former ward, and insisting on the fact that now he had a family of his own, very dear to him, and in need of all he could earn for them. In this appeal, by the way, he somewhat changes his tone about the condition of Antonio's parents, pleading that they are "young and make good earnings, while I am old and poor and earn nothing at all." The final judgment was that while he lived he should contribute to Antonio's support, but that after his death the Sputasenni should have no claim on his estate. The story of his relations with this family merits being related, not only because it is one of the few things told in detail in the *Ricordi*, but also because it seems to have occupied Benvenuto's mind a great deal during the last eleven years of his life.

The other records are meagre enough, and mostly refer to money matters. His appeals to the Duke and his officers for payment of arrears of salary and for work done are constant.

But that he plays so frequently the rôle of begging-letter writer is a fact not entirely personal to Benvenuto. It was partly due to the conditions under which artists were patronised and supported by the later Medici. He was often underpaid, and sometimes not paid at all. Still money-making, whether from growing avarice, or from a haunting fear of coming poverty for himself and his children, absorbed a good deal of his energies. He owned a considerable amount of property; was much interested in investments; and had now at least the will to be a good business man. Yet *ora sono poverissimo* is ever his cry. Of course, he had always an abundance of goldsmith's work to do; but in his later days no great sculpture commissions were given him. Failing powers and the jealousy of rivals partly account for this, though the main cause was, doubtless, the fact that his patrons preferred being less well served by men more docile and more easy-tempered. And his health was bad; he suffered much from gout. At the death of Michael Angelo, in 1564, he was chosen along with Ammanati to represent sculpture at the great man's funeral, but he was not well enough to join in the ceremony. Neither did his health permit him to take part with his fellow-artists in the celebration of the marriage of Don Francesco, Duke Cosimo's eldest son, with Jane of Austria in the following year. When he recovered, he had the idea of paying his homage "not in clay or wood" but with his pen. And so he wrote the *Trattati*. But when it was published in 1568, after its revision by Spini, Don Francesco was perhaps not so high in the writer's favour; for it was dedicated to his brother, the Cardinal Fernando. Yet to the end the regent employed him. Between 1568 and 1570 Cellini painted his portrait in wax, which Don Francesco sent to his beloved Bianca Cappello.

He lived for three years after the publication of the *Trattati*, dying of pleurisy, 13 February, 1571, in his house in the Via del Rosaio in Florence. He was buried "with great pomp" in the Church of the Annunziata. Many were the candles and the lamps that were lit, we are told. His fellow-artists and the *frati* did him every honour. A friar pronounced a eulogy on his life and works, and "the good disposition of his soul and body"; and the people crowded in to see the last of Benvenuto—who, in spite of his glory, had never been far removed from themselves —and to make the sign of the Cross over the body, once so restless, and now at peace.

NOTES

BOOK I

ii. *p.* 4, *l.* 9. It need hardly be said that Cellini's account of the origin of Florence is, to say the least, very fragmentary; while, of course, his story of the origin of the name is merely an exaggerated example of the bragging (*boriosità*) which he has just been declaring natural to auto-biographers.

ii. *p.* 4, *l.* 11. *Colosseum.* Supposed to have been near the modern Piazza Peruzzi.

ii. *p.* 4, *l.* 12. *Old Market.* The Mercato Vecchio was destroyed to make room for the present Piazza Vittorio Emmanuele.

ii. *p.* 4, *l.* 12. *The Rotonda.* The earlier authorities declare this—now the famous Baptistery of St. John—to be the original temple dedicated to Mars in commemoration of the Roman victory over Etruscan Fiesole. Not improbably the main part of the existing building dates from the fourth century, and was modelled on the Pantheon. But some portions of it are as late as the eleventh and twelfth centuries.

ii. p. 4, *l.* 13. *Our Saint John.* St. John the Baptist, the patron saint of Florence.

For the old legends of the origin of Florence, see Villani, li. c. 28; and for the early history of the origin of the city, see Villari, *I primi due secoli della Storia di Firenze*, I. c. i., Florence, 1895; Davidsohn, *Geschichte von Florenz*, Berlin, 1896; and Gardner's *Story of Florence*, pp. 5 et seq., Dent, 1900.

ii. *p.* 5, *l.* 30. *House in the Via Chiara.* On No. 6 Via Chiara can be read to-day the inscription—*In questa casa nacque Benvenuto Cellini il dì primo di Novembre del 1500 e vi passò i primi anni.* There is a mistake in the date. He was born on the 2nd of November.

ii. *p.* 5, *l.* 39. *The second Bartolommeo.* Bartolommeo (Baccio) Cellini was a noted carver in wood; and it is curious his nephew does not record his fame. Vasari mentions him more than once.

iii. *p.* 5, *l.* 41. *Andrea Cellini ... architecture.* The truth seems to be that Andrea was a mason, not an architect. See Bacci's edition, p. 8.

iii. *p.* 6, *l.* 40. *Cosa*, i.e. Niccolosa.

iii. *p.* 7, *l.* 4. *Half-past four.* The hour was counted from sunset to sunset; and so it is impossible to translate it into our terms of reckoning unless the season of the year be known.

iii. *p.* 7, *l.* 16. *Welcome*, i.e. Benvenuto.

v. *p.* 8, *l.* 26. *Lorenzo de' Medici*, the Magnificent, died 1492. *Piero*, his son, was drowned in 1504.

v. *p.* 9, *l.* 6. *Greater guilds of silk and wool.* The seven greater guilds and the fourteen lesser were instituted early in the thirteenth century. The former included such professions as medicine and law as well as the more important industries.

vi. *p.* 9, *l.* 14. *Piero, when he was exiled.* Nov. 9, 1494.

vi. *p.* 9, *l.* 16. *Soderini* was the only gonfalonier of Florence elected for life (1502); but he was exiled in 1512.

vi. *p.* 9, *l.* 35. *Medici came back.* Giovanni de' Medici, afterwards Pope Leo X., and Giuliano, Duke of Nemours, returned by the aid of the Spaniards in 1512.

vi. *p.* 9, *l.* 40. *Their palace.* Now the Riccardi Palace.

vi. *p.* 9, *l.* 41. *Arms and insignia of the Commune.* A red cross on a white ground.

vi. *p.* 10, *l.* 11. *Leo X.* Elected March 13, 1513; died 1521.

vi. *p.* 10, *l.* 15. *Salviati.* Son-in-law of Lorenzo the Magnificent, was gonfalonier for only two months in 1514.

vii. *p.* 10, *l.* 25. *The Cavaliere Bandinello's father.* Of the son, the eminent and most unpleasing sculptor, and Cellini's rival and enemy, much will be heard in the later part of the *Memoirs*. The father's name was Brandini; his son changed it to Bandinello. He was a goldsmith of great ability. See Vasari's life of his son the sculptor, vol. vi.

vii. *p.* 10, *l.* 28. *Coal-chandler.* Bacci says this is a mistake; that his father was a blacksmith.

viii. *p.* 11, *l.* 17. *Giovannino de' Medici.* The famous Giovanni delle Bande Nere, of the younger branch of the family, great-grand-nephew of Cosimo, *pater patriae*. His mother was the celebrated Caterina Sforza; his son was Cosimo, the first Grand Duke of Florence. After a most distinguished career he died in 1526, at the age of twenty-eight, at Governo, killed by the Imperialist troops. Cellini wrote a eulogistic sonnet to his memory. See Mabellini, *Rime*, p. 215.

viii. *p.* 11, *l.* 38. *The Eight.* The criminal magistracy of the city.

ix. *p.* 12, *l.* 13. *Pope Clement.* Clement VII. Later, one of Cellini's chief patrons. He was Giulio de' Medici, natural son of Giuliano, the brother of Lorenzo II. Magnifico. Elected Pope 1523; died 1533.

ix. *p.* 13, *l.* 5. *Had me dismissed.* Bacci, *op. cit.*, p. 12, gives a quotation from a document in the archives which puts a different complexion on this. There Giovanni is described as *senex et inhabilis ad sonandum*, but, on account of his long service, gets a small pension.

x. *p.* 14, *l.* 26. *Cecchino.* Diminutive of Francesco.

x. *p.* 15, *l.* 13. *Fish Stone.* The fish-market on the quay.

xii. *p.* 17, *l.* 5. *Torrigiani.* Popularly known as the man who broke Michael Angelo's nose, was a Florentine sculptor of eminence, whose work is well known in England from his monument to Henry VII. in Westminster Abbey. He went from England to Spain, where he felt himself to be so badly treated that, according to report, he starved himself to death. Cellini's description of him is borne out by Vasari in his life of him, vol. iv.

xii. *p.* 17, *l.* 22. *Cartoon of that most divine master.* Cellini never swerved from his loyalty to and admiration of Michael Angelo. The cartoon referred to was executed in 1504–5 for the Sala del Consiglio in the Palazzo Vecchio. Hardly anything remains of it or of Leonardo's. Michael Angelo represented an episode in the battle of Cascina in the war with Pisa; Leonardo's the battle of Anghiari.

xii. *p.* 17, *l.* 41. *Great chapel of Pope Julius.* The Sistine Chapel, Rome.

xiii. *p.* 18, *l.* 3. *Church of the Carmine . . . chapel of Masaccio.* The Brancacci Chapel in the Carmine, Florence, decorated by Masaccio (died 1428) with incidents in the life of St. Peter.

xiii. *p.* 18, *l.* 18. *Francesco . . . son of Filippo.* Filippo is Filippino Lippi, the eminent painter (died 1504), son of the still more celebrated Fra Lippo

Lippi. Cellini's friend, better known as Giovanfrancesco, gained great distinction in his own art.

xiii. *p.* 18, *l.* 35. *Il Tasso* (1500–55), was architect as well as carver in wood, and designed the Loggia of the Mercato Nuovo. See Vasari, ed. Milanesi (full reference in Index).

xiii. *p.* 19, *l.* 3. *Gate of San Pier Gattolini.* Better known as the Porta Romana.

xiv. *p.* 20, *l.* 16. *Rotonda.* The Church of Santa Maria della Rotonda in Rome, the ancient Pantheon.

xv. *p.* 22, *l.* 19. *Salvadore and Michele Guasconti.* Cellini speaks of Salvadore very amiably in his *Treatises,* p. 4.

xvi. *p.* 22, *l.* 34. *In a cloak.* Unless a man was a soldier, his wearing of a cloak instead of a citizen's mantle by day, was held to be a sign of ruffianism.

xvi. *p.* 22, *l.* 42. *Prinzivalle della Stufa.* A strong partisan of the Medici; headed a conspiracy in their favour against the gonfalonier Soderini. He was made a senator by Duke Alessandro in 1532. Died 1561.

xvi. *p.* 23, *l.* 11. *Puritan fellows, with the tails of their hoods twisted up.* This was the mark of the democratic party, republicans who clung to the principles of Savonarola.

xvi. *p.* 23, *l.* 16. *Four bushels of flour.* The fine was really twelve bushels. See Bacci, p. 32.

xvi. *p.* 23, *l.* 17. *Murate convent.* A celebrated convent of closely immured nuns in Florence. Catherine Sforza died and was buried there.

xvi. *p.* 24, *l.* 19. *Nor did I do them the very least harm.* This is not true. Benvenuto wounded Gherardo Guasconti and another man very severely; and for his violence was condemned to death by the Eight. See Bacci, p. 32.

xviii. *p.* 24, *l.* 25. *Santa Maria Novella.* The well-known Dominican church in Florence.

xviii. *p.* 24, *l.* 26. *Alesso Strozzi.* This was the friar who afterwards betrayed Frà Benedetto da Foiano. See note to *p.* 186, *l.* 31.

xviii. *p.* 25, *l.* 22. *Benedetto da Monte Varchi.* The distinguished poet, scholar, and historian commonly known as Varchi, born 1503, died 1565. He was ever a good friend to Cellini, wrote a sonnet on his supposed death (see p. 130), and, what is more creditable to him, refused to revise Cellini's manuscript. See p. 1.

xix. *p.* 25, *l.* 35. *The Paglia.* River below Orvieto.

xix. *p.* 26, *l.* 4. *Bishop of Salamanca.* Francesco de Bobadilla came to Rome in 1517 to attend the Lateran Council; was with Pope Clement VII. in the castle of St. Angelo, during the siege, in 1527.

xix. *p.* 26, *l.* 6. *Gianfrancesco.* Gian Francesco Penni, Florentine painter, a favourite pupil and part-heir of Raphael. He and Giulio Romano strove to complete some of Raphael's unfinished works. He was surnamed Il Fattore. Born 1496, died 1536. See his life by Vasari, vol. iv.

xix. *p.* 26, *l.* 11. *Chapel of Michel Agnolo,* i.e. the Sistine Chapel.

House of Agostino Chigi. Built about 1510 from designs of Peruzzi. After 1580 it became known as the Villa Farnesina.

xix. *p.* 26, *l.* 32. *Madonna Porzia.* Sigismondo Chigi's wife was called Sulpizia. She had a sister Porzia. See Bacci, p. 39.

xix. *p.* 27, *l.* 7. *Figure of Jupiter.* In Raphael's painted story of Cupid and Psyche in the Chigi palace.

xxiii. *p.* 31, *l.* 14. *Ferragosto,* i.e. Feriæ Augusti, a Roman festival on the 1st of August.

xxv. *p.* 35, *l.* 19. *Cardinal Cibo . . . ordered a vase.* Cellini refers to this vase and to Salamanca's in the *Treatises,* p. 84. Cibo was a nephew of Leo X.

xxv. *p.* 35, *l.* 21. *Cardinal Cornaro.* Marco Cornaro, nephew of the Queen of Cyprus. Died in Venice, where he had gone to escape the plague in 1524.

xxv. *p.* 35, *l.* 22. Cardinals Ridolfi and Salviati were both nephews of Leo X. For Cellini's quarrel with the latter, see p. 88.

xxv. *p.* 35, *l.* 31. *Leda with her swan.* This medal may possibly be identical with a cameo now in Vienna. See Plon, p. 140.

xxvi. *p.* 36, *l.* 1. St. John's day is the chief Florentine festival.

xxvi. *p.* 36, *l.* 3. *Rosso.* A distinguished Florentine painter, and one of the artists whom Francis I. patronised, resided for some time at the French court. After a series of misfortunes he poisoned himself in 1541. See Vasari, vol. v.

xxvi. *p.* 36, *l.* 9. *Rienzo da Ceri.* A noted captain of adventurers, at this time in the service of France.

xxvi. *p.* 37, *l.* 22. *Caradosso.* Noted medallist and goldsmith. Better known as Ambrogio Foppa. For Cellini's story of his nickname and his opinion of him, see *Treatise on Goldsmithing*, pp. 17, 45, 51.

xxvi. *p.* 37, *l.* 23. *Paxes.* Small tablets with sacred images and emblems, which are hung in Italian churches to be kissed by the faithful.

xxvii. *p.* 38, *l.* 6. *At this time,* i.e. 1523. The plague had been at its height the year before.

xxviii. *p.* 39, *l.* 29. *Giacomo Berengario da Carpi.* A very distinguished physician and surgeon, professor at Bologna. Died in Ferrara, and bequeathed his fortune to the Duke. For the later story of the vases, see p. 212.

xxix. *p.* 41, *l.* 18. *Jacocacci.* Probably Cardinal Jacobacci.

xxx. *p.* 42, *l.* 39. *Michel Agnolo.* The Sienese sculptor, must not be confused with the great Buonarroti. His most famous work was the monument of Adrian VI. in the German church, Santa Maria dell' Anima. But Peruzzi made the design for it.

xxx. *p.* 43, *l.* 3. *Giulio Romano* (1492–1546). Celebrated painter and architect; pupil and heir of Raphael. Worked for Clement VII., for the Chigi, and afterwards in the famous Palace del Tè at Mantua. See Vasari, vol. v.

xxx. *p.* 43, *l.* 17. *Bachiacca.* Either Francesco or Antonio Verdi, twin brothers, who both bore this surname. The former was a miniature painter, the latter an embroiderer.

xxxii. *p.* 48, *l.* 39. *Luigi Pulci.* Grandson of the famous author of the *Morgante.*

xxxiv. *p.* 53, *l.* 23. *The whole world was in arms.* The war between Charles V. and Francis I. had broken out in 1521. At the moment referred to by Cellini the Pope had broken with the Emperor, who was sending the Constable of Bourbon to attack Rome (1527).

xxxiv. *p.* 53, *l.* 24. *Giovanni de' Medici,* i.e. Giovanni delle Bande Nere.

xxxiv. *p.* 53, *l.* 33. *Bourbon.* Charles of Bourbon broke with his cousin, Francis I., in 1523, and joined the Emperor. Now at the head of a body of Germans and cosmopolitan bandits he was marching on Rome. He was killed by a shot from the walls. Cellini claims the credit of the deed; but no one confirms his statement.

xxxiv. *p.* 53, *l.* 36. *The Colonnesi.* Headed by Pompeo Colonna, they roused the populace, and forced Clement to take refuge in St. Angelo till he signed a treaty in favour of the Emperor, 1526.

xxxiv. *p.* 54, *l.* 28. *Orazio Baglioni.* One of the great and fierce Perugian family of that name. He was a prisoner of the Pope in St. Angelo; but Clement released him for the defence of the castle and the city. He was afterwards commander of the Bande Nere. Died fighting at Naples, 1528.

xxxv. *p.* 56, *l.* 27. *Duke of Urbino.* Francesco Maria della Rovere, general of the papal troops. Cellini's veiled taunt (*l.* 37) was well deserved by his incapacity and probable treachery.

xxxvi. *p.* 56, *l.* 41. *Cardinal de' Gaddi.* Given as a hostage to the Imperialists, and sent to Naples. When Alessandro de' Medici was murdered, he made a vain attempt to re-establish the Florentine republic. Died 1552. He appears more than once in Cellini's story.

xxxvi. *p.* 57, *l.* 24. *Cardinal Farnese.* Afterwards Pope Paul III.

xxxvi. *p.* 58, *l.* 25. *Revenged my father on . . . Salviati.* See p. 10.

xxxvi. *p.* 58, *l.* 29. *Had I killed him.* An allusion to Cellini's long imprisonment in St. Angelo by Pope Paul III.

xxxvii. *p.* 60, *l.* 6. *Gian di Urbino.* A distinguished Spanish captain serving under the Prince of Orange.

xxxviii. *p.* 60, *l.* 23. *Filippo Strozzi.* Married a daughter of Piero de' Medici, but was one of the sturdiest opponents of that family. After the unfortunate battle of Montemurlo he killed himself, or was killed by the orders of Duke Cosimo, in prison in 1539.

xxxviii. *p.* 60, *l.* 35. *Made myself a little furnace.* See *Treatises*, p. 82.

xxxviii. *p.* 61, *l.* 11. *Prince of Orange.* Philibert de Châlons deserted the service of Francis I. for that of the Emperor, and succeeded Bourbon as head of the besieging army. Died 1530 at the battle of Gavinana.

xxxix. *p.* 62, *l.* 9. *Peace was made.* The castle surrendered on the 5th of June; but Clement remained a prisoner till December 8.

Though Benvenuto certainly helped in the defence of St. Angelo, his account of the siege and his own prowess must be received with caution. For the chief authorities on the sack of Rome see Bacci, *op. cit.*, p. 71.

xl. *p.* 63, *l.* 36. *Palazzo del Te.* Outside the Porta Pusteria at Mantua, built by Giulio Romano, and decorated by him and other distinguished artists.

xl. *p.* 63, *l.* 40. *Reliquary for the Blood of Christ.* See Plon, p. 156.

xl. *p.* 64, *l.* 12. *The Cardinal his brother.* Ercole, brother of Duke (at this time Marquis) Frederico Gonzaga, was Bishop of Mantua, and Cardinal in 1527. Regent after his brother's death. Died while presiding over the Council of Trent, 1563.

xl. *p.* 64, *l.* 29. *Signor Giovanni,* i.e. Giovanni delle Bande Nere.

xl. *p.* 64, *l.* 41. *Died of the plague.* About 40,000 persons died in Florence between May and November, 1527.

xl. *p.* 65, *l.* 1. *Liperata,* i.e. Reparata.

xli. *p.* 65, *l.* 32. *Medici . . . exiled.* When Clement was shut up in St. Angelo, the Florentines took the opportunity of restoring the republic under the gonfalonier Niccolo Capponi But when the Pope made peace with the Emperor, he besieged Florence, and took it; and Alessandro de' Medici became Duke.

xli. *p.* 66, *l.* 43. *Luigi Alamanni.* Man of letters and poet, one of the most distinguished opponents of the Medicean tyranny; was exiled to France, where he lived under the protection of Francis I. Died 1556.

xliii. *p.* 69, *l.* 14. *Not money enough.* This hardly agrees with his earlier statement on p. 85.

xliii. *p.* 70, *l.* 15. *Button for my cope.* This famous piece of Cellini's workmanship was, according to Plon (p. 145), taken out of its setting, and the gold of it along with that of other precious jewels helped to pay the war tributes of Napoleon.

xlv. *p.* 73, *l.* 15. *Dies made for his money.* See *Treatises*, p. 67.

xlv. *p.* 73, *l.* 19. *Datary.* The Papal Datario was the chief secretary of the office for requests, petitions, and patents.

xlvi. *p.* 75, *l.* 14. *Giovanni Gaddi.* Florentine, a great patron of art and letters. He was the dean of the Apostolic Camera, or Exchequer.

xlvi. *p.* 75, *l.* 18. *Antonio Allegretti.* Florentine poet.

xlvi. *p.* 75, *l.* 19. *Annibal Caro* (1507–1566). Gaddi's secretary, one of the most celebrated writers of the day. He was a good friend of Cellini, though well aware of his incorrigible temper. See Plon, p. 95.

xlvi. *p.* 75, *l.* 20. *Messer Bastiano the Venetian* (1485–1547). The famous painter, better known as Sebastian del Piombo. See Vasari, vol. v.

xlvi. *p.* 75, *l.* 42. *Coin of the value of two carlins.* See *Treatises*, p. 68.

xlvii. *p.* 76, *l.* 19. *Bargello,* i.e. the chief of police.

xlvii. *p.* 76, *l.* 33. *Bertino Aldobrandi.* An account of him and of his death is given by Varchi, *Storia Fior.* l. xi.

xlix. *p.* 78, *l.* 22. *Torre di Nona.* The criminal prisons.

xlix. *p.* 79, *l.* 15. *That valiant soul passed out.* For an account of Cecchino Cellini's death see Varchi, *Storia Fior.* l. xi.

l. *p.* 79, *l.* 18. *Church of the Florentines.* The original S. Giovanni de' Fiorentini, Rome, was begun under the pontificate of Leo X. Jacopo da Sansovino, San Gallo, and Michael Angelo were the architects.

l. *p.* 79, *l.* 26. *Epigram.* This memorial inscription is no longer to be read in the church.

l. *p.* 79, *l.* 34. *Cecchino del Piffero,* i.e. Frank, the piper's son.

l. *p.* 80, *l.* 8. *Real Cellini arms.* Plon, p. 2, reproduces a drawing of the family arms from the hand of Benvenuto, which is in the National Library at Florence.

lii. *p.* 83, *l.* 27. *Francesco del Nero,* who cast suspicion on Cellini, was not too honest himself, according to report. He was suspected of appropriating to himself the public funds in Florence when he was depositario there. See Varchi, l. iii.

lii. *p.* 83, *l.* 28. *Bishop of Vaison,* near Avignon. He was Girolamo Schio, Clement's confessor.

lv. *p.* 85, *l.* 42. *Huge inundation.* October 8 and 9, 1530. According to its historian Comesio, this took place without warning, no rains having fallen for some time back.

lvi. *p.* 86, *l.* 42. *Fraternity of the Piombo.* The Piombo is the office in the Papal court where seals of lead (piombo) are attached to Bulls. Laymen were sometimes appointed to it, among the most famous being the great architect Bramante and Sebastiano Veneziano (del Piombo). When the latter got it, it was his undoing, for he did little more work.

lvi. *p.* 87, *l.* 40. *Bartolommeo Valori.* Florentine, devoted to the Medici till he experienced their ingratitude, when he joined Filippo Strozzi's conspiracy. Beheaded in 1537. See Varchi, ll. xii. and xiv.

lvi. *p.* 88, *l.* 14. *Roberto Pucci.* Florentine, also a Medici partisan, but more faithful than Valori. He tried to persuade Clement against attacking Florence.

lvii. *p.* 88, *l.* 26. *Pope went . . . to Bologna*—to meet Charles V. and discuss a league against the Turks, also a council about religious differences.

lx. *p.* 91, *l.* 36. *Tobbia.* It appears he was not a Milanese but a Camerinian.

lx. *p.* 92, *l.* 9. *King Francis.* He and Clement met at Marseilles in 1533, at the marriage of Catherine de' Medici and the Duc d'Orléans, son of the French King.

lx. *p.* 92, *l.* 32. *Wardrobe.* This apartment was armoury and general store-house in the palace.

lx. *p.* 93, *l.* 18. *Take away the Mint from me.* This was probably at the end of 1533.

lxii. *p.* 97, *l.* 7. *My chalice in my hand.* For a description of this work, which was finished by Niccolo Santini, see Plon, pp. 162 et seq.

lxiii. *p.* 98, *l.* 11. *Felice.* Felice Guadagni, one of Benvenuto's most faithful friends.

lxv. *p.* 101, *l.* 21. *Badia di Farfa.* In the Sabine hills.

lxvii. *p.* 103, *l.* 38. *Cardinal de' Medici.* Ippolito de' Medici, natural son of Julian, Duke of Nemours, was as much soldier as Churchman. He conspired against Alessandro; then offered his services to Charles V. in the expedition to Tunis; but died in Apulia in 1555, some say poisoned.

lxvii. *p.* 104, *l.* 13. *Giovanbatista Savello.* A Roman gentleman, captain of cavalry troops in the service of Clement VII. At Palombara, about twenty miles from Rome, near Mte. Gennaro, can still be seen the Savelli Castle.

lxvii. *p.* 104, *l.* 21. *Solosmeo.* Antonio da Settignano, a mediocre sculptor, pupil of Sansovino. He was only one of several artists employed on the tomb of Piero de' Medici (son of Lorenzo il Magnifico, drowned 1504). Their common hatred of Bandinelli was a bond between him and Cellini. See Vasari's "Life of Bandinelli," vol. vi.

lxviii. *p.* 104, *l.* 37. *Carlo Ginori.* Gonfalonier of Florence for two months in 1527.

lxviii. *p.* 105, *l.* 36. *Viceroy of Naples*. Pietro Alvarez de Toledo, Marquis of Villafranca. Elected 1532. Died 1553.

lxx. *p.* 108, *l.* 13. *Peace was represented*. The medal was to celebrate the peace which lasted from 1530 to 1536. For another description of it see *Treatises*, p. 73.

lxx. *p.* 108, *l.* 23. *Carnesecchi*. A Florentine, secretary of Clement VII., and a great patron of letters. He became acquainted with Valdes in Naples, and Melanchthon in France, and his opinions being much influenced by theirs, he was accused of heresy, and beheaded and burnt in Rome in 1567.

lxx. *p.* 108, *l.* 31. *Ut bivat populus*. In allusion to a great well sunk by Clement in 1528 at Orvieto, the monumental part of which was made by Antonio da San Gallo. The medal is described in *Treatises*, p. 73. The dies are preserved in the Uffizi.

lxxii. *p.* 110, *l.* 8. *The Pope died*. September 25, 1534.

lxxiv. *p.* 111, *l.* 42. *Cardinal Cornaro*. Francesco Cornaro, brother of the Marco Cornaro mentioned on p. 35.

lxxiv. *p.* 112, *l.* 33. *Cardinal Farnese was made Pope*. Alessandro Farnese, elected Pope as Paul III., October 13, 1534.

lxxiv. *p.* 112, *l.* 37. *Latino Juvinale* (or Giovenale) de' Manetti. Celebrated as poet and scholar, a friend of Bembo, of Castiglione, and of all the chief men of letters of his day.

lxxv. *p.* 113, *l.* 15. *Saint Paul*. See Plon, p. 199.

lxxv. *p.* 113, *l.* 25. *Holy Maries in August*. A Florentine name for the feast of the Assumption, 15 August. Cellini was liberated by the Confraternity of the Butchers.

lxxv. *p.* 113, *l.* 28. *Another safe-conduct*. A translation of the text of this new *motu proprio* is given by Plon, p. 33.

lxxv. *p.* 113, *l.* 34. *Pier Luigi Farnese*. Son of Pope Paul III., had honours and offices heaped on him by his father. In 1545 he was made Duke of Parmo and Piacenza. He was a worthless and dangerous scoundrel. His own courtiers rid the world of him in 1547.

lxxvi. *p.* 115, *l.* 31. *Il Tribolino* (1500-50). Niccolò de' Pericoli, Florentine sculptor and architect, pupil of Jacopo Sansovino, did some important works in Rome, Bologna, and Loreto. His chief employers were the Medici. Made a model of the city of Florence for Clement VII. during the siege. See Vasari, vol. vi.

lxxvi. *p.* 115, *l.* 33. *Jacopo del Sansovino*. Giacomo Tatti, Florentine sculptor, pupil of Andrea Contucci dal Monte a Sansovino. At the sack of Rome he went to Venice, after which he was mainly engaged in architecture. Died 1570. See Vasari (ed. Milanesi, vol. ix. Index).

lxxvi. *p.* 116, *l.* 1. *Lorenzo Cibo*. Brother of Cardinal Cibo. He was jealous of Alessandro's attentions to his wife, and conspired with the Cardinal de' Medici against the Duke.

lxxvi. *p.* 116, *l.* 13. *Ser Maurizio*. A Milanese, head of the Florentine criminal court. Segni calls him "cruel and bestial" in the execution of his office.

lxxvi. *p.* 116, *l.* 22. *The Duke*. Ercole II., Duke of Ferrara.

lxxvi. *p.* 116, *l.* 34. *Jacopo Nardi* (1476-1563). The celebrated Florentine historian, and one of the most patriotic and upright of the anti-Medicean party. Exiled to Leghorn in 1530, and afterwards to Venice, where he wrote the history of his country and translated Livy. The two Benintendis were exiled in 1530. Niccolò had been one of the Eight.

lxxvi. *p.* 121, *l.* 12. *Dies for his money*. Cellini refers to his Florentine coins in the *Treatises*, p. 68.

lxxvi. *p.* 122, *l.* 13. *His wife . . . in Naples*. Margaret of Austria, the illegitimate daughter of the Emperor, betrothed to Alessandro in 1530. The marriage took place in Naples, 1536. When she arrived in Florence, some months later, she was fourteen.

lxxvi. *p.* 122, *l.* 26. *His Lorenzino*. Of the younger branch of the Medici family, son of Pierfrancesco. He murdered his cousin Alessandro in 1537; and was himself murdered in Venice in 1548.

lxxxi. *p.* 122, *l.* 29. *Ottaviano de' Medici.* A distant connection of the Duke's, being descended from neither Cosimo *Pater-patriae* nor his brother Lorenzo. He gained great power; was even suggested as Alessandro's successor; but was exceedingly unpopular.

lxxxi. *p.* 124, *l.* 2. *Reverse worthy of his Excellency.* So Lorenzino grimly jests about his murderous project, which was long in his mind.

lxxxiv. *p.* 128, *l.* 2. *Mattio Franzesi.* Well known and very popular in the literary society of the day as a burlesque poet and a wit.

lxxxiv. *p.* 130, *l.* 39. *Whom thou didst shadow.* A reference to Cellini's representation of the Almighty on the Pope's button. See p. 70. In the original MS. the Sonnet is signed by Varchi.

lxxxvi. *p.* 133, *l.* 10. Cellini arrived in Florence, November 9, 1535.

lxxxvi. *p.* 133, *l.* 33. *Giorgetto Vassellario,* i.e. Giorgio Vasari (1512–74), the painter, and famous biographer of Italian artists. In spite of their differences, his judgment of Cellini was just and even lenient, though he did not write a separate Life of him. Vasari also speaks well of Manno the goldsmith, mentioned in this curious anecdote.

lxxxviii. *p.* 135, *l.* 29. *Francesco Soderini.* Banished to Spello in 1530 as an enemy to the Medici.

lxxxviii. *p.* 135, *l.* 38. *Duke Alessandro was Pope Clement's son.* This was the general rumour; but some said his father was Lorenzo, Duke of Urbino.

lxxxix. *p.* 137, *l.* 32. *Death of Duke Alessandro.* He was murdered by Lorenzino de' Medici on the night of the 5th January, 1537.

lxxxix. *p.* 138, *l.* 13. *Cosimo . . . was made Duke.* Cosimo was elected on January 9, 1537.

xc. *p.* 138, *l.* 30. *Tunis expedition.* Here Cellini has turned back a year or two. The Emperor reached Naples from Tunis, November 30, 1535. He entered Rome, April 5, 1536.

xc. *p.* 138, *l.* 33. Respecting the crucifix, the book of Offices, etc., see *Treatises,* pp. 32, 33.

xcii. *p.* 141, *l.* 43. For an interesting account of the tinting of the diamond, see *Treatises,* pp. 32–39.

xciii. *p.* 144, *l.* 13. *Signor Sforza.* His mother was the daughter of Paul III. He afterwards became a distinguished captain, first in the Imperial, and later in the French army.

xciii. *p.* 144, *l.* 19. *Ascanio.* This boy makes many appearances in Cellini's *Memoirs.* He accompanied him to France, and remained there after he left, as goldsmith to Henri II. He married a daughter of the famous della Robbia family of artists. It appears that he became Seigneur de Beaulieu.

xciv. *p.* 147, *l.* 17. *Bembo.* Born Venice, 1470, died 1547, elected Cardinal 1539, but better known as a man of letters and a patron of learning than as a Churchman.

xciv. *p.* 147, *l.* 26. *His portrait.* It is very doubtful whether the medal was ever finished by Cellini. See Plon on the subject, p. 328.

xcv. *p.* 148, *l.* 28. *The war,* i.e. between the Imperialists and the French in Piedmont, terminated by the Treaty of Nice, 1537.

xcv. *p.* 149, *l.* 2. *Filippo Strozzi.* Then at the head of the Florentine exiles. See note to p. 60, l. 23.

xcviii. *p.* 152, *l.* 37. *Antonio da San Gallo.* The younger, pupil of his uncles Antonio and Giuliano, worked at Loreto, Orvieto, and Rome, where he was employed on St. Peter's. See his Life by Vasari, vol. v.

xcviii. *p.* 153, *l.* 35. *Cardinal of Ferrara.* Ippolito d'Este, son of Alfonso, Duke of Ferrara. Lived some time at the court of France. A patron of art and letters.

xcix. *p.* 154, *l.* 11. *A River.* Probably the Doveria in the Val di Vedro Tyrol.

c. *p.* 157, *l.* 6. *Girolamo Orsini.* Lord of Bracciano, a famous soldier. His wife was Francesca Sforza. His son, Duke of Bracciano, married Duke

Cosimo's daughter, Isabella, killed her, and then married Vittoria Accoramboni, the heroine of Webster's *White Devil*.

c. *p.* 158, *l.* 41. *A taste of prison*. He was arrested October 16, 1538.

ciii. *p.* 161, *l.* 13. *Cesare Iscatinaro*. This should be Giovan Bartolommeo Gattinara, who discussed the arrangements (which fell through) with Clement VII. for the capitulation.

ciii. *p.* 162, *l.* 7. *Speaking these words*. The official report of the interrogating exists, and was published by Bertolotti. There Benvenuto seems to play a less hardy and less eloquent part.

civ. *p.* 162, *l.* 19. *Monseigneur de Montluc*. Afterwards Bishop of Valence. Chief agent in the election of Henri of Anjou to the throne of Poland. His brother Blaise was the celebrated Marshal.

civ. *p.* 163, *l.* 33. *Friar of the Pallavicini family*. Imprisoned in 1538 (probably not for the last time) for over seven months as a heretic. He was known as a celebrated preacher.

cvi. *p.* 167, *l.* 4. *Jeronimo the Perugian*. Cellini's former assistant, who travelled with him to France, and at whose instigation he was imprisoned.

cx. *p.* 172, *l.* 35. *Church of the Traspontina*, i.e. S. Maria della traspontina.

cx. *p.* 173, *l.* 9. *The Duchess*. Natural daughter of the Emperor, married Alessandro de' Medici, and after his murder, Ottavio Farnese, nephew of Paul III. She made her entry into Rome on November 3, 1538.

cxi. *p.* 175, *l.* 21. *College of Parco Majori*. The Collegi degli Abbreviatori di *Parco maggiore e minore*, instituted by Pope Paul II. Alessandro Farnese (Paul III.) did, indeed, break prison, but it appears it was under Innocent VIII.

cxx. *p.* 186, *l.* 31. *Preacher Foiano*. Fra Benedetto Tiezzi of Foiano, of the Dominican Order, attached to the convent of Sta. Maria Novella, an adherent of Savonarola, and a lover of liberty. During the siege of Florence he preached eloquently against the Medicean tyranny, and was imprisoned by Clement VII. in St. Angelo, and starved to death.

cxx. *p.* 187, *l.* 25. *Sammalò*. Rucsoni and Valeri say the name of this horrible oubliette was derived from San Marocco, from the image of a saint, or a chapel near its mouth.

cxxiv. *p.* 192, *l.* 42. *In* 1538. This should be 1539.

cxxv. *p.* 193, *l.* 8. *Durante*. Prefect of the Camera, afterwards Bishop of Brescia and Cardinal, learned in letters and in law. Benvenuto does not shirk charging men of the highest repute with crime. The Leone mentioned below was a celebrated sculptor and goldsmith, and somewhat Cellinesque in temperament. In 1540 he was sent to the galleys for violence. See his Life by Vasari, vol. viii.

cxxvi. *p.* 195, *l.* 25. *Cardinal Farnese*. Son of Pier Luigi Farnese, and Archbishop of Parma. He was ambitious for the papacy; but the Medici party strenuously opposed him.

cxxvii. *p.* 196, *l.* 14. *Took me out of prison*. The date, according to Bacci, was December 24, 1539. That at least is the date given in the order for his release. But letters of Caro and Alamanni would seem to prove he was let go early in the month.

cxxviii. *p.* 197, *l.* 3. *All that afterwards happened to Signor Pier Luigi*, i.e. his murder eight years later.

Capitolo. The Capitolo is written in *terza rima*, but it has seemed to me an indefensible waste of ingenuity to fit English rhymes to what in the original is turgid, slipshod, and slovenly. Its subject-matter has enough interest to justify a prose translation.

Capitolo, *p.* 199, *l.* 31. *Yet would He come*, etc. Here one is reminded of the song of another Italian prisoner of a very different stamp, Fra Jacopone da Todi:

Troppo giaccio a la piscina,

.   .   .   .   .

Pur aspetto mi sia detto,
Ch'io mi lievi, e tolla 'l letto.

. . .

La mia matre Religione
Fa gran pianto con sua scorta,
L'alta voce udir opta,
Che mi dica, Vecchio surge.

Capitolo, p. 199, *l.* 37. *The lilies.* The Farnesi arms contained seven lilies "with the hook-like petals"; those of Florence one, and those of France three.

Capitolo, p. 199, *l.* 42. The Archangel Gabriel is generally depicted with a lily in pictures of the Annunciation.

Capitolo, p. 199, *l.* 55. In his visions he says he had premonitions of the death of the castellan and of Pier Luigi.

Capitolo, p. 200, *l.* 4. *The angel.* See p. 197.

Capitolo, p. 200, *l.* 16. *Was never lion,* etc. In this and the following lines Pier Luigi is meant.

Capitolo, p. 200, *l.* 27. *November.* He had told the jailers he would be released in November.

BOOK II

i. *p.* 202, *l.* 12. *St. Ambrogio pursuing the Arians.* St. Ambrose is the patron saint of Milan. At the battle of Parabiago, 1339, he is said to have suddenly appeared on horseback in aid of his countrymen against Lodovico Visconti. Ever after he was pictorially represented as a horseman, but dressed in pontifical robes. For this medal see Plon, p. 192.

ii. *p.* 203, *l.* 40. *This work.* For its execution see p. 248.

iii. *p.* 204, *l.* 10. *Tornon.* Cardinal Tournon, a famous minister of Francis I.

iii. *p.* 204, *l.* 39. *Monte Ruosi,* i.e. Monterosi, between Rome and Viterbo, on the road to Florence.

iv. *p.* 207, *l.* 40. *Staggia.* Between Siena and Poggibonsi.

v. *p.* 208, *l.* 5. *Duke of Amalfi.* Alfonso Piccolomini, governor of Siena for Charles V.

vi. *p.* 209, *l.* 34. *More than* 300,000 *ducats.* The sum was 180,000, in return for which the investiture of the D'Estes was confirmed.

vii. *p.* 211, *l.* 35. *Ring for the cramp.* These metal rings are still in vogue for various ailments.

viii. *p.* 212, *l.* 11. *Alfonso de' Trotti.* This minister of the Duke of Ferrara was afterwards a tenant of Cellini in a house he had in the Piazza S Maria Novella, Florence. See Bianchi, p. 528.

viii. *p.* 213, *l.* 9. *Paid me wretchedly.* This hardly agrees with his earlier version of the story. See p. 40.

ix. *p.* 214, *l.* 6. *The misgiving.* He does not explain what it was he feared.

ix. *p.* 214, *l.* 16. *Fontainebleau.* Cellini probably arrived there September 1540.

x. *p.* 216, *l.* 19. *Dauphiné.* Dimier says Francis was in Paris at the time.

xi. *p.* 217, *l.* 17. *That infinite beauty.* See p. 190.

xii. *p.* 219, *l.* 2. *Petit Nesle.* Part of the famous Château or Tour de Nesle, on the left bank of the Seine. The Institute and the Mint occupy its site to-day.

xv. *p.* 221, *l.* 43. *Madame d'Etampes.* Anne de Pisseleu had been a maid of honour of Francis's mother, Louise of Savoie. Her husband, Jean de Brosse, was made Duc d'Etampes. As the King's mistress she wielded great power, but her influence was partly due to her own strong mind and will. In her later years she became a Calvinist. She died 1576.

Cardinal of Lorraine. Son of René II., Duke of Lorraine and titular King of Jerusalem.

xv. *p.* 222, *l.* 2. *King of Navarre.* Henri II. Marguerite de Valois, his wife, sister of Francis I., was one of the most justly distinguished women of her generation. She was the author of the *Heptameron*, and a staunch friend to freedom of thought.

xv. *p.* 222, *l.* 3. *Dauphin.* Afterwards Henri II. His wife was Catherine de' Medici.

xvii. *p.* 224, *l.* 25. *Pont du Change.* The Pont Neuf now takes its place.

xix. *p.* 228, *l.* 8. *Piero Strozzi.* Son of Filippo Strozzi. After the defeat of the Florentine exiles at Montemurlo he entered the service of Francis I., who made him a marshal.

xix. *p.* 228, *l.* 9. *Letters of naturalisation.* The document is given by Bianchi, p. 579. The King's letter putting him in possession of the Petit Nesle will also be found in Bianchi, p. 581.

xx. *p.* 229, *l.* 32. *Twelve leagues.* "Leagues" should be "miles."

xxi. *p.* 230, *l.* 12. *That diabolic war.* For about five years, 1537–1542, there had been peace between Charles V. and Francis I. War broke out again in May 1542, and lasted till the Treaty of Crépy, 1544.

xxi. *p.* 230, *l.* 40. The Nymph was never placed on the château door. After the death of Francis I. it was given by Henri II. to Diane de Poitiers, who placed it above her door at Anet. It is now in the Louvre.

xxi. *p.* 231, *l.* 6. *The Salamander.* The device of Francis I. It is seen on many royal buildings and coins of his time.

xxiv. *p.* 234, *l.* 1. *Guido Guidi.* Born in Florence, grandson of the painter Domenico del Ghirlandajo, was in France from 1542 to 1548 as court physician. Afterwards he was professor at Pisa. His book on medicine, or rather on surgery, mentioned here, was a translation of Hippocrates and Galen, printed at Paris, 1544. Guido's printer (and Benvenuto's evicted tenant) was Pierre Gauthier.

xxvi. *p.* 235, *l.* 39. *Primaticcio* was employed by François I., Henri II., and François II. See his Life by Vasari, vol. vii.

xxvii. *p.* 237, *l.* 30. *Dante . . . made use of this saying.* The reference is to

> *Pape Satan, pape Satan aleppe,*
> Cominciò Pluto con la voce chioccia.
>
> *Inf.* vii. 1.

Cellini's interpretation is only a little more fantastic than that of the other commentators of whom he speaks so contemptuously. It is possible that Dante was in Paris. It is doubtful if Giotto ever was; and of their journey there in company there is no evidence at all.

xxxiii. *p.* 246, *ll.* 5–9. *Bologna . . . knew . . . I was right.* But it seems Primaticcio got the commission after all. It may have been after the departure of Cellini.

xxxiv. *p.* 246, *l.* 27. *Prior of Capua.* Leone Strozzi. Like his brother Piero he was in the service of France. Was killed in the Sienese war in 1554.

xxxvi. *p.* 248, *l.* 6. *The salt-cellar.* This is one of the most famous of Cellini's existing works. It is now in Vienna. It was given to the Archduke Ferdinand of Austria, and remained for some time in his castle of Ambras in the Tyrol. After his death it was sold to the Emperor Rudolf II. See Plon, p. 168.

xxxvii. *p.* 249, *l.* 9. *The Laocoon,* etc. Primaticcio was helped in the casting of these copies by Vignola. Some of the casts are preserved in the Louvre.

xxxviii. *p.* 250, *l.* 37. *The Emperor . . . advancing on Paris.* Charles V. in 1544 occupied Luxembourg, entered Champagne, and it looked as if the siege of Paris was at hand.

xxxix. *p. 252, l. 2. Monseigneur d'Annebault.* Claude d'Annebaut, marshal and admiral of France. He had been fellow-prisoner with Francis I. at Pavia, and was deservedly high in the King's favour.

xl. *p. 252, l. 39. Grolier.* The famous Jean Grolier, the great collector of books and medals.

xli. *p. 253, l. 37. Jupiter.* For this statue see Plon, p. 181. It was the only one of the twelve ordered by Francis which Cellini finished. But no trace of it exists.

xlii. *p. 256, l. 32. Le Moine Bourreau* (the hangman monk). Other readings of Cellini's *Lemonnio Boreò* are *Le Démon Bourreau,* and *La Moine bourru,* i.e. *vêtu de bourre ou bure.*

xliii. *p. 257, l. 15. Asino Bue.* Ass and Ox.

xliii. *p. 257, l. 17. Bellarmato.* An exiled Sienese, was one of the greatest military architects of his time, in spite of Cellini's low opinion of him. Francis I. appointed him his engineer-in-chief. At this time he fortified the faubourgs of Montmartre and Saint Antoine.

xliii. *p. 257, l. 23. Madame d'Etampes . . . betrayed the King.* There seems some reason for this statement. From jealousy of Diane de Poitiers she is said to have prevented the bridge of Epernay being destroyed before the advance of the Imperial troops. Seeing them on their way to Paris, Francis had to make ruinous concessions.

xlviii. *p. 261, l. 27. Peace with the Emperor.* The peace of Crépy, September 18, 1544. But Henry VIII. was no party to it, and hostilities between the French and English lasted till 1546.

xlviii. *p. 262, l. 36.* This account of his leaving France hardly tallies with that in the *Treatises,* p. 144.

li. *p. 266, l. 14. Landi.* Whether the Landi actually did the deed is doubtful; but they were in the conspiracy, and in the palace at the time.

lii. *p. 267, l. 14. Six young daughters.* Two of them took the veil in Sant' Orsola, Florence. After the death of her husband Tassi, Liperata married one of Cellini's workmen, Paolo Paolini.

liii. *p. 267, l. 31. Poggio a Cajano.* The well-known Medicean villa on the road to Prato, a few miles from Florence.

liii. *p. 267, l. 39. Duchess.* Eleonora di Toledo, daughter of the Viceroy of Naples, married Duke Cosimo in 1539.

liii. *p. 268, l. 13. Wonderful school.* L'Accademia del Disegno of Florence.

liii. *p. 268, l. 36. Works by . . . Donatello and Michael Angelo.* The Judith of Donatello is in the Loggia dei Lanzi. Michael Angelo's David used to be also in the Piazza, but is now in the Belle Arti.

liv. *p. 269, l. 30. House that suited me.* The house is in the Via del Rosaio (or della Colonna), Florence. The entrance is in the Via della Pergola, where a tablet has been placed with the inscription, *Casa di Benvenuto Cellini nella quale formò e gettò il Perseo e poi vi morì il 14 febbraie 1570-71.* (It should be 13 Febbraie.)

liv. *p. 270, l. 4. Pier Francesco Riccio.* In spite of Cellini, this majordomo was, according to the evidence of distinguished men of his day, a very estimable person. His mind was unsound for some years, but he did not die mad, as Vasari says.

liv. *p. 270, l. 18. Buaccio Bandinello.* See note I. vii. 10. Buaccio is a wilful misspelling on the part of Cellini. Baccio is the familiar form of Bartolommeo. Buaccio means "great ox."

liv. *p. 270, l. 26. Tasso.* See note I. xiii. 18.

lv. *p. 270, l. 42. Clock hall.* In the Palazzo Vecchio. So called from the cosmographical clock made by Lorenzo della Volpaia for Lorenzo de' Medici, one of the first of its kind.

lix. *p. 275, l. 10. An angry letter.* He refers to this letter in the *Treatises,* p. 145. But there is no mention of the King's demand for accounts. Dimier has examined the whole matter, and his conclusion is much in Benvenuto's disfavour.

lx. *p.* 276, *l.* 10. *Antonio Landi.* Man of letters as well as Florentine merchant, author of a comedy, *Il Commodo*.

lx. *p.* 276, *l.* 15. *Table-cutting*, etc. For Cellini on the treatment of diamonds see *Treatises*, p. 31.

lxii. *p.* 279, *l.* 12. *Arrival at Venice.* Here ends the autograph of the boy amanuensis.

lxii. *p.* 279, *l.* 17. *Titian.* The great Venetian painter, Tiziano Vecelli, born 1477 at Pieve di Cadore, died 1576 at Venice. He was held in the highest honour by the Venetian government and people, and lived like a great noble.

lxii. *p.* 279, *l.* 18. *Jacopo del Sansovino.* See note I. lxxvi. 115.

lxii. *p.* 279, *l.* 23. *Lorenzo de' Medici.* See note I. lxxxi. 122.

lxiii. *p.* 280, *l.* 18. *Portrait bust of his Excellency.* The bust is now in the Bargello, Florence.

lxiii. *p.* 280, *l.* 38. For Benvenuto's theory and practice of bronze-casting see *Treatises*, pp. 111 et seq.

lxv. *p.* 284, *l.* 29. *Silver . . . from my mines.* These were at Pietrasanta and Campiglia. From the former the Duke drew about a hundred pounds of silver yearly, from the other less. In the seventeenth century they were abandoned.

lxvi. *p.* 286, *l.* 7. *Farm . . . above San Domenico.* "On the Fiesole hill," says Vasari in his "Life of Bandinelli," "he bought a very fine farm called lo Spinello."

lxvi. *p.* 286, *l.* 28. *My only son.* Who was the mother of this child is not known. It has been conjectured by Guasti that she was Dorotea, his model for the Medusa.

lxviii. *p.* 287, *l.* 14. *Messer Sforza.* Sforza Almeni, a Perugian, the Duke's Chamberlain. In 1566 Cosimo killed him with his own hand for revealing to his son, Don Francesco, his amours with Eleonora degli Albizzi.

lxviii. *p.* 287, *l.* 34. *King Philip.* Philip II. of Spain, son of Charles V., King of Naples and Sicily, and afterwards of England by his marriage with Queen Mary.

lxix. *p.* 288, *l.* 3. *Lord Stefano of Palestrino.* Stefano Colonna, great general and patron of arts.

lxx. *p.* 289, *l.* 17. *Hercules and Cacus.* Still in the Piazza at Florence. The Florentines were enraged because it deprived them of a great Samson by Michael Angelo, though its own defects were enough to have inspired the ridicule that was poured on it. Some of the sonneteers were imprisoned by Duke Alessandro.

lxx. *p.* 289, *l.* 21. *Sacristy*, i.e. of San Lorenzo—where are the well-known statues of Dawn, Day, Twilight, and Night, with the statues of Giuliano de' Medici, Duke of Nemours, and Lorenzo de' Medici, Duke of Urbino.

lxxi. Of this quarrel of Benvenuto and Bandinelli there is a confirmation in Vasari's Life of the latter. There Bandinelli plays a slightly more spirited rôle.

lxxii. *p.* 292, *l.* 6. *Apollo and Hyacinth.* These statues are lost. So is the Narcissus.

lxxii. *p.* 292, *l.* 29. *Arno floods.* August, 1547.

lxxiii. *p.* 293, *l.* 32. *Elba.* Duke Cosimo's bust till 1781 was on the gate of the fortress of Portoferraio. It was afterwards brought to Florence.

lxxiii. *p.* 293, *l.* 33. *Marble Ganymede.* Now in the Uffizi.

lxxvi. *p.* 297, *l.* 6. *Mona Fiore.* His good opinion of her did not last long. He dismissed her 1556, employed her again 1560, and two years later sent her away as a thief.

lxxvi. *p.* 297, *l.* 15. *Those who proclaim to doomed men.* The fraternity of the Neri, who before a prisoner's execution spent the last night with him.

lxxviii. *p.* 300, *l.* 42. *Pope Giulio de' Monti.* Julius III. (Giovanni Maria Ciocchi), elected February 1550.

lxxix. *p.* 301, *l.* 3. *Bindo Altoviti.* This bust is now in the South Kensington Museum. Till lately it was in the Palazzo Altoviti in Rome. Altoviti, a Florentine, was a rich merchant in Rome, and as an enemy of the Medici, a patron of many Florentine exiles.

lxxix. *p.* 301, *l.* 32. *The Forty-eight.* The Senate of Florence, created in 1532 by Clement VII. It was not the first time Duke Cosimo held out this bribe to Michel Agnolo.

lxxx. *p.* 302, *l.* 16. The contract between Benvenuto and Altoviti is given by Tassi, vol. iii. pp. 26–34.

lxxxi. *p.* 302, *l.* 33. *Urbino* was Francesco Amatori. Michael Angelo loved this assistant of his like a son. In a letter written after his death he calls him *un valente uomo, pieno di fede e lealtà.*

lxxxiv. *p.* 307, *l.* 25. *La Bella Franceschina.* A popular song of the day.

lxxxv. *p.* 308, *l.* 3. *War with Siena.* 1552. Siena, in the hands of the Emperor Charles V., was garrisoned by Spaniards. The Sienese made a French alliance, and elected Piero Strozzi as their captain, but were defeated in 1555. Cosimo took the side of the Spaniards. The Emperor promised him that if the city were saved from the French, it should be his.

lxxxvi. *p.* 310, *l.* 2. *Gates of Turin.* In 1543, when Turin was occupied by the French, a captain of the Imperial army sent six waggon-loads of hay to the gates of the city. The waggons contained soldiers, whose part it was to keep the portcullis raised. But the stratagem failed.

lxxxvii. *p.* 310, *l.* 12. *The Chimera.* Now in the Archæological Museum at Florence.

lxxxvii. *p.* 310, *l.* 37. *Towards the Lions,* i.e. on the side of the palace that looks towards the Via dei Leoni.

lxxxvii. *p.* 311, *l.* 4. *Weak health.* When the Duchess Eleonora died in 1562 she had been in bad health many years.

lxxxviii. *p.* 311, *l.* 42. *The Prince and Don Giovanni,* etc. These were the sons of Duke Cosimo, all young boys at the time. The Prince, Don Francesco, was twelve.

lxxxix. *p.* 313, *l.* 4. *The Loggia,* i.e. the Loggia de' Lanzi, in the Piazza of Florence.

lxxxix. *p.* 313, *l.* 9. *San Piero Scheraggio.* This church, which was the scene of many notable events in Florentine history, was pulled down in 1561, to make room for the Uffizi.

lxxxix. *p.* 313, *l.* 11. The Mint was opposite—where the Post Office now stands.

lxxxix. *p.* 313, *l.* 16. *My own door.* He means that of his workshop enclosure in the Loggia de' Lanzi.

lxxxix. *p.* 313, *l.* 28. *Buaccio.* Not his enemy Bandinelli this time, but Baccio Baldini, Bernardone's son, a distinguished physician and scholar, and first librarian to the Laurentian Library.

xc. *p.* 314, *l.* 30. *Sonnets.* Some of these have been published by Tassi, Milanesi, and Mabellini.

xc. *p.* 314, *l.* 42. *Jacopo da Pontormo* (1494–1556). A distinguished pupil of Andrea del Sarto. See Vasari, vol. vi.

xc. *p.* 315, *l.* 1. *Bronzino.* Angioli Allori, called Il Bronzino (1502–72), a pupil of Pontormo, and a distinguished Florentine painter. The Sandrino mentioned here is his nephew, also a painter of merit, and, like his uncle, a writer of occasional verse. See Vasari, ed. Milanesi (references in Index).

xcii. *p* 315, *l.* 40. *Openly to the whole city.* This was on April 27, 1554.

xcii. *p.* 316, *l.* 27. *Giovan Agnolo de' Servi* (or da Montorsoli). A celebrated sculptor of the Order of the Servi di Maria. Worked at Messina and Florence. See his Life by Vasari, vol. vi.

xciii. *p.* 317, *l.* 28. *Eremo.* The famous Eremo of Camaldoli. *Bagni di Santa Maria* (delle Grazie). Otherwise Bagno.

xciii. *p.* 317, *l.* 29. *Sestile* should probably be Sestimo.

xciv. *p.* 318, *l.* 43. *The little plan.* Cellini in his appeal to the Soprassindachi in 1570 quotes this as a proof of his services to the Duke and to Florence. See Bianchi, p. 550.

xcvi. *p.* 320, *l.* 15. *Girolamo degli Albizzi.* A cousin of Duke Cosimo's, and an enthusiastic partisan of the Medici. He was accused, probably with gross injustice, of poisoning Guicciardini, the historian.

xcvii. *p.* 322, *l.* 38. *Very old man.* Michael Angelo was then eighty years old.

xcviii. *p.* 324, *l.* 7. *Baccio d'Agnolo . . . who spoiled the cupola.* Baccio altered Brunelleschi's plan, so that Michael Angelo said he had made the cupola like a cage for crickets. See his Life by Vasari, vol. v. Giuliano and Bandinelli also spoiled Brunelleschi's design for the choir. In 1841 some of their hideous ornaments were taken away.

xcviii. *p.* 325, *l.* 26. *Heard nothing more of the business.* Benvenuto did not carry out the work. Bandinelli prevented that.

xcix. *p.* 325, *l.* 28. *This time.* There is a long gap between this and the last chapter, nearly three years, 1556-59. Benvenuto spent part of the time in prison for various offences.

xcix. *p.* 325, *l.* 29. The Grieve does not pass near Poggio a Caiano. It should be the Ombrone.

xcix. *p.* 325, *l.* 38. *Ammanato.* See Vasari's "Life of Bandinelli" for an account of the strife between Bandinelli, Cellini, and Ammanati for the Neptune. Ammanati was a pupil of Jacopo Sansovino. A better architect than sculptor, he reconstructed the Santa Trinità bridge, and was engaged on the Pitti Palace. Died 1592. See Vasari, ed. Milanesi (references in Index).

c. *p.* 329, *l.* 18. *Bandinello died.* February 7, 1560.

ci. *p.* 329, *l.* 23. *Pietà.* It is very doubtful whether Bandinelli had any thoughts of rivalling Benvenuto's Crucifix. His Pietà is said to have been begun by his son. The father continued it in imitation or rivalry of Michael Angelo. It exists still in the Pazzi Chapel in the Church of the Annunziata.

ci. *p.* 330, *l.* 20. *Giovanni the Fleming.* Celebrated sculptor, better known as Gian Bologna, born at Douai in 1524, but spent most of his life in Italy. His most celebrated works are The Rape of the Sabines, in the Loggia de' Lanzi, the Mercury, in the Bargello, and the fountain in the Piazza of Bologna. Died 1608.

ci. *p.* 330, *l.* 28. *Giorgetto*, i.e. Vasari.

ciii. *p.* 332, *l.* 29. *Trespiano.* In 1548, and again in 1566, Cellini bought property at Trespiano. See documents in *Ricordi* (Tassi, vol. iii. pp. 18 and 70).

ciii. *p.* 332, *l.* 31. *Vicchio.* Seven miles to the east of Florence, on the Arno.

cv. *p.* 335, *l.* 13. *Ammanato's wife.* This passage is so blotted in the original MS. as to be illegible. Perhaps Cellini erased the slander himself in a fit of repentance. The lady, Laura Battiferra, was a most estimable person, and a minor poetess. Cellini himself praised her in a sonnet, comparing her to Petrarch's Laura.

cvi. *p.* 336, *l.* 1. *My unfinished Neptune model.* Nothing is known of the fate of this model of Cellini.

cxi. *p.* 340, *l.* 22. *I make you a present of it.* But their Excellencies would not accept the Crucifix as a gift. In 1565 Duke Cosimo bought it for fifteen hundred gold crowns. It was in the Pitti Palace till 1576, when the Grand Duke Francesco sent it as a present to Philip II. It is now in the choir of the Church of San Lorenzo in the Escurial.

cxii. *p.* 341, *l.* 5. *Queen of France.* Catherine de' Medici, widow of Henri II., and regent of France.

cxii. *p.* 341, *l.* 17. *Daniello of Volterra.* Painter and sculptor, contemptuously called *il Braghettone* because he painted garments to cover Michel Agnolo's nude figures in his "Last Judgment." He never finished the bronze horse referred to here, but Richelieu had it adapted to fit the statue of Louis XIII.

cxiii. *p.* 342, *l.* 4. *Save the Prince.* Don Francesco left for Spain, May 23, 1562. On his return he assumed the government of Florence, as his father had abdicated in June 1563.

cxiii. *p.* 342, *l.* 5. *By the Sienese marshes.* The journey was begun in October 1562.

cxiii. *p.* 342, *l.* 5. *The Cardinal.* Giovanni de' Medici, the Duke's second son, died at Rosignano, November 21, 1562. He was nineteen years old. The younger brothers, Garzia and Fernando, also took ill, and the former died on December 6. Their mother only survived him twelve days. There were many scandalous rumours about the successive calamities, one report being that Don Garzia killed the Cardinal, and was himself killed by his father. There appears to be not a word of truth in them. The season was a very unhealthy one, and the air of the Maremma was pestilential.

BENVENUTO'S LAST DAYS

p. 343, *l.* 19. *Out of gratitude.* See Bianchi, *Documenti*, p. 538.

p. 343, *l.* 27. *Letter to Varchi.* See Bianchi, *Documenti*, p. 497.

p. 344, *l.* 2. *Memorandum.* See Bianchi, *Documenti*, pp. 593, 594.

p. 344, *l.* 23. *Disinherited.* The whole story of the adoption and disinheritance may be read in Bianchi, *Documenti*, pp. 528–531, and pp. 535–541.

p. 345, *l.* 18. *Death of Michael Angelo.* See Vasari, vol. viii.

p. 345, *l.* 25. *With his pen.* See Plon, p. 116.

p. 345, *l.* 31. *Portrait in wax.* See Plon, *Nouvel Appendice*, 1884.

p. 345, *l.* 35. *With great pomp.* See Bianchi, *Documenti*, p. 574.

INDEX

368 THE LIFE OF BENVENUTO CELLINI